Developing C# Apps for iPhone and iPad Using MonoTouch

iOS Apps Development for .NET Developers

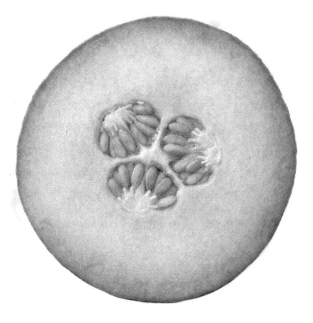

Bryan Costanich

Apress®

Developing C# Apps for iPhone and iPad Using MonoTouch: iOS Apps Development for .NET Developers

ISBN-13 (pbk): 978-1-4302-3174-5

ISBN-13 (electronic): 978-1-4302-3175-2

Trademarked names, logos, and images may appear in this book. Rather than use a trademark symbol with every occurrence of a trademarked name, logo, or image we use the names, logos, and images only in an editorial fashion and to the benefit of the trademark owner, with no intention of infringement of the trademark.

The use in this publication of trade names, trademarks, service marks, and similar terms, even if they are not identified as such, is not to be taken as an expression of opinion as to whether or not they are subject to proprietary rights.

President and Publisher: Paul Manning
Lead Editor: Steve Anglin
Development Editor: Matthew Moodie
Technical Reviewer: Geoff Norton
Editorial Board: Steve Anglin, Mark Beckner, Ewan Buckingham, Gary Cornell, Jonathan Gennick, Jonathan Hassell, Michelle Lowman, James Markham, Matthew Moodie, Jeff Olson, Jeffrey Pepper, Frank Pohlmann, Douglas Pundick, Ben Renow-Clarke, Dominic Shakeshaft, Matt Wade, Tom Welsh
Coordinating Editor: Adam Heath
Copy Editor: Tracy Brown
Compositor: MacPS, LLC
Indexer: BIM Indexing & Proofreading Services
Artist: April Milne
Cover Designer: Anna Ishchenko

Distributed to the book trade worldwide by Springer Science+Business Media, LLC., 233 Spring Street, 6th Floor, New York, NY 10013. Phone 1-800-SPRINGER, fax (201) 348-4505, e-mail orders-ny@springer-sbm.com, or visit www.springeronline.com.

For information on translations, please e-mail rights@apress.com, or visit www.apress.com.

Apress and friends of ED books may be purchased in bulk for academic, corporate, or promotional use. eBook versions and licenses are also available for most titles. For more information, reference our Special Bulk Sales–eBook Licensing web page at www.apress.com/bulk-sales.

The information in this book is distributed on an "as is" basis, without warranty. Although every precaution has been taken in the preparation of this work, neither the author(s) nor Apress shall have any liability to any person or entity with respect to any loss or damage caused or alleged to be caused directly or indirectly by the information contained in this work.

The source code for this book is available to readers at www.apress.com. You will need to answer questions pertaining to this book in order to successfully download the code.

Life is a beautiful mess. Laugh or cry; choose one.

Contents at a Glance

Contents

About the Author

 Bryan Costanich

About the Technical Reviewer

Geoff Norton is a developer for Novell, working on the Mono Project. He is the lead on the MonoTouch project and the MonoMac runtime, and is a member of the MonoDroid team. Geoff has been a Mono Project contributor since 2004, and he is also responsible for the OSX port of the Mono runtime.

Acknowledgments

This book would not have been possible if it weren't for the help of Geoff Norton, the product head of MonoTouch at Novell. He served as the technical reviewer, making sure that everything in here is as accurate as can be. My sincerest thanks to him for all his hard work.

I'd also like to thank my friends for sticking it out while I worked tirelessly on this book for nearly a year, barely seeing them. I'm free now, so let's hang.

Preface

Thanks for purchasing *Developing C# Apps for iPhone and iPad Using MonoTouch*. It's been a long time in coming, but I hope you feel it's worth the wait. The goal of this book is to not only introduce MonoTouch, but to really give you a solid, thorough understanding of iOS programming with it. If you go through this book, front to back, and learn the concepts and gain an understanding of the content, you should consider yourself a well-versed iOS developer.

Chapter 1

Getting Started with MonoTouch

When most people think about developing applications for the iPhone, iPad, or iPod Touch, they think of writing applications in a low-level language like Objective-C. But the truth is, as the iOS ecosystem has matured, a number of ways to develop apps for it has emerged.

The reason is largely developer-driven. For many developers, learning Objective-C was seen as a huge barrier to entry. For .NET developers, many of whom have never had to worry about memory management, pointers, and other C language concepts, Objective-C also forced on them many responsibilities that they were unfamiliar with.

Many also feel that the tools for developing in Objective-C are lacking. Apple's XCode Integrated Development Environment (IDE) lacks many of the features found in other modern IDEs, such as Visual Studio.

All this has changed, however, as more players have entered the iOS space. In addition to MonoTouch, Adobe has entered it with Flash CS5, and Unity for the iOS powers some of the best-selling games available on the iPhone and iPad.

The MonoTouch framework itself is part of Novell's Mono project. The Mono project is an open-source implementation of the Microsoft .NET platform published standards. It allows you to run .NET applications on nearly any platform, including Apple, FreeBSD, Linux, Unix, and others.

MonoTouch was introduced in the fall of 2009, and extends Mono by allowing you to write applications using C# and the .NET platform Base Class Library (BCL) that run on the iOS, using Cocoa Touch's UIKit API.

MonoTouch is an extremely powerful way to write applications for the iOS because it combines a number of features:

- **Ability to call Objective-C, C, and C++:** MonoTouch harnesses all the power of low-level languages such as Objective-C, C, and C++. You can use libraries written in Objective-C, et al. from your MonoTouch code.

- **Modern language constructs:** Because MonoTouch is based on the .NET Platform, you get nearly all of the modern language features available from it, such as automatic memory management, typed exceptions, etc.

- **Modern IDE:** The MonoDevelop IDE has all the features you have come to expect in modern development environments, including automatic code completion, an integrated debugger, intregrated source control, and code refactoring tools.

Developing for the iPhone and iPad

The iPhone and iPad are tremendous devices, and MonoTouch goes a long way toward making the transition between traditional .NET applications and applications for the iOS easier. However, it's important to take in consideration that developing for these devices is very different than working with traditional .NET applications. Let's look at how mobile development for the iOS differs from traditional application development.

Limited Multitasking

While the iOS v4.0 introduced multitasking to the iPhone 3GS (and newer) and the iPad, it's not true multitasking. In nearly any modern desktop operating system, multiple applications can be running at once without issue. However, in the iOS, if your app needs to keep processing when it's not the foreground application, it needs to tell the iOS what type of background tasks it wants to perform, and then it is given limited processing time. Because of this, if you wish to support background processing, you have to design your application very carefully. We'll cover this in greater depth in Chapter 11.

Limited System Resources

The iPhone has a very small amount of RAM (128MB for the 3G, 256MB for the 3GS and iPad, and 512 for the iPhone 4). Because of the complex nature of the graphics that support iPhone applications, and the fact that it's fairly normal for OS processes to take up more than half of your RAM, you can run out of memory very quickly on the iOS.

When the device is running low on memory, it will try and terminate known internal memory-hungry applications (such as Safari) to reduce memory pressure, and then it will let your application know that the system is low on useable memory and you should take steps to clean up unused objects in memory.

Small Screen Size

While the iPad sports a much larger screen (1024x768) than the iPhone (960x640 for the 4G and 320x480 for 3Gs and older models), they're both small by comparison to the standard screen size many desktop applications are built for.

While the iPad allows some flexibility in how you design screens, in the iPhone it's especially important to try to simplify screens into one task at a time in the UI. However, this limitation is actually mitigated considerably by Apple's UI Framework controls, which are designed specifically to provide a pleasant and efficient user experience, even with the small screen.

Device-specific Technology

Each device that runs the iOS may have different features specific to it. For instance, the GPS and/or Compass feature isn't available on all devices. Some devices have a camera on the front, some devices can shoot video with their camera, some can only do still photos. Some allow multitasking, some don't. The list goes on and on.

Because of this, it's important check for the presence of and ability to use a feature before actually trying to use it.

Constrained Response Time

In order to retain the responsive feel that users have come to expect from iOS applications, several operations in iOS are response-time sensitive. For instance, if your application takes longer than ten seconds to start up, the iOS will abort its launch. When a user clicks the home button to close your application, you have 5 seconds of processing time to save any settings or state information before it's terminated. The same goes for multitasking features: your application is given a certain amount of time to perform certain tasks, and if it fails, it can be terminated.

As a result, you need to design your application in such a way as to handle these transitions very quickly in order to prevent the loss of state and/or data.

Constrained Access

iOS applications run in what's called a sandbox. That is, they have limited permissions on the device. For instance, they can only write files to their own directory, and can read files from their directory and certain system directories. They can't, for instance, write to or read from any other application's sandbox. They also can't make low-level device calls, etc. Therefore, when developing iOS applications, you must take this constrained access into consideration.

MonoTouch Background

Now that we have an understanding of the basics of iOS development, let's examine some of the basics of developing MonoTouch applications.

iPhone vs. iPod Touch vs iPad?

It's important to note that developing for the iPod Touch is nearly identical to developing for the iPhone, except for the fact that it doesn't have a cellular radio. Additionally, both the iPhone and the iPad run iOS and, besides User Interface (UI) concerns, developing for them is nearly identical. We'll explore the differences between them in Chapter 2.

How Does It Work?

The MonoTouch.dll (the base library that all MonoTouch applications are built against) is equivalent to the Silverlight .NET 4.0 profile with some things added back in, such as System.Data and System.Net. This allows you to write applications using many of the .NET Framework technologies that you're already familiar with, including Windows Communication Framework (WCF), Workflow Foundation (WF), etc.

It also includes nearly all of the Base Class Library (BCL), including things like garbage collection, threading, math functions, cryptography, and parallel processing framework. For a list of available standard .NET assemblies in MonoTouch see http://monotouch.net/Documentation/Assemblies.

This is accomplished through a MonoTouch-specific set of base .NET libraries, similar to how Silverlight and Moonlight (Mono's implementation of Silverlight) work.

This means that you can compile standard .NET 4.0 code libraries using the MonoTouch core assemblies and use them in your application. So if, for example, you have a specialized library that does advanced math functions for engineering problems that you use for other applications, you can simply include the code library in your MonoTouch solution, and reference it. When you build your solution, it will compile it using the MonoTouch libraries, and it will then be available in your application.

MonoTouch also includes wrappers to the native iOS APIs, such as Location (GPS and Compass), the accelerometer, address book, etc. It also gives you the ability to bind to native Objective-C libraries that are not wrapped, so you can interop directly with existing Objective-C code.

How Do I Build a User-Interface (UI); Can I Use Silverlight?

MonoTouch application UIs are typically built using Apple's Interface Builder (IB) application that ships with the iOS SDK. Interface Builder uses Cocoa Touch (Apple's UI Framework for iOS, also known as UIKit) objects that are native to the iOS. This means that you have all the standard iOS controls available to your application, including Pickers, Sliders, and Buttons, etc.

You can also create your interface programmatically by instantiating Cocoa Touch objects and adding them to your application's Views (more on Views later).

You cannot, however, create your MonoTouch interface using traditional .NET technologies such as Silverlight, WPF, or Winforms. You can, however, build games using Microsoft's XNA Toolkit that target the Windows 7 phone and port them using the open-source XNA Touch project (we'll cover this in Chapter 21). Additionally, there are indications from the MonoTouch team that Moonlight will be supported at some point in the future. Time will tell if that bears fruit.

Cocoa Touch uses a rough amalgamation of the Model View Controller (MVC) pattern that we'll discuss in Chapter 3.

By utilizing the UIKit, developers can make iOS applications using the same familiar control set as applications written in Objective-C. However, if you wish to branch beyond that, you can. MonoTouch also exposes the underlying graphics framework so that you can create rich 2D and 3D applications that allow you to go well beyond the UIKit control framework.

How Do I Distribute My Apps?

MonoTouch applications are distributed the exact same way that traditional iOS applications are distributed, either via the Apple App Store, Enterprise, or ad-hoc deployment.

The App Store is an online repository that allows users to pay for applications (if they're not free), and download them. It is available from within iTunes, or directly from the iDevice itself. In order to get a license to distribute via the App Store, you must register with Apple, and pay $99/year. For more information, go to http://developer.apple.com and read about their development program.

Enterprise deployment is for those wishing to develop internal applications for a company and distribute them, for example, to employees, without listing them with the App Store.

Ad-hoc deployment allows you to deploy to a limited number of devices mainly for the purpose of testing and development.

What Is the Licensing Model?

Unlike Mono, MonoTouch is not open source—it is a commercial product. That means, if you want to do anything useful with it, you have to purchase a license to use it. MonoTouch comes in three flavors and prices:

- **Professional ($399):** A single personal developer license that allows you to develop applications and distribute them via the Apple App-Store

■ **Enterprise ($999):** A single corporate developer license that allows you to develop applications and distribute via the App-store, or via enterprise deployment

■ **Enterprise, 5 Seat ($3,999):** The same as the Enterprise license, but includes 5 seats

■ **Academic ($99):** A single personal developer license that only allows non-commercial distribution via ad-hoc deployment

All three options include a year of free updates.

There is also an evaluation edition that allows you deploy to the simulator only (the simulator is part of the iOS SDK, which I'll talk about later in this chapter). For the purposes of most of this book, the evaluation edition of MonoTouch is all you need. If you wish to try out any of your code on an actual device, you will have to purchase a licensed copy of MonoTouch.

Are There Any Limitations of MonoTouch?

As powerful as MonoTouch is, it has some limations that the larger .NET Framework does not. Let's examine them.

No Just-in-Time (JIT) Compilation

Per Apple's iOS policy, no application can include code that requires just-in-time (JIT) compilation. But wait a second, that's exactly how .NET works, right? This is correct; however, the MonoTouch framework gets around this limitation by compiling your application down to a native iOS assembly. This, however, introduces several limitations.

■ **Generics:** Generics are instantiated by the JIT compiler at run-time. However, Mono has an ahead-of-time (AOT) compilation mode that will generate all the methods and properties for things like List<T>. Other uses of Generics, such as Generic virtual methods, P/Invokes in Generic types, and value types that don't exist in the core library in Dictionary<TKey, TValue> are not supported (although there is a workaround for Dictionary<TKey, TValue>).

■ **Dynamic code generation:** Because dynamic code generation depends on the JIT compiler, there is no support for any dynamic language compilation. This includes System.Reflection.Emit, Remoting, runtime proxy generation for WCF, JIT'd RegEx, JIT'd serializers, and the Dynamic Language Runtime.

C# Is Currently the Only Language

Additionally, currently, the only .NET language available for writing MonoTouch applications is C#.

More Information

For a full list of limitations and more information, including workarounds, see http://monotouch.net/Documentation/Limitations.

Getting Started

In order to get started building MonoTouch applications for the iPhone we'll need a few things:

- An Intel Mac computer running 10.6 (Snow Leopard) or better
- The latest Apple iOS SDK
- The current version of Mono
- The MonoTouch SDK
- An IDE such as MonoDevelop or XCode, or a text editor program

Mac Computer Running Snow Leopard

This is an important and easily missed requirement. While theoretically you could build most of your application on other platforms, the iOS SDK (and therefore the iOS device simulator and Interface Builder) are only available for Snow Leopard. Additionally, the compiler itself uses some low-level magic specific to the Intel Mac machines, so having one is an absolute must.

MonoTouch is currently working on tools that will allow you to write in Visual Studio via their MonoTouch Tools for Visual Studio. However, it has yet to be released, and you will still need a Snow Leopard machine to run the simulator and to compile for the actual device.

Apple's iOS SDK

Available at http://developer.apple.com/devcenter/ios, the iOS SDK is a free download, but you must register with Apple to get access to it. Along the way, Apple may ask you to pay $99 to get an iOS developer account, which allows you to deploy your applications, but for the purposes of this tutorial, you just need the SDK. The iOS SDK includes Interface Builder, the iOS device simulator, Xcode, and a few other things.

After you have installed the iOS SDK, make sure you can launch the iOS Simulator. You can find the simulator by opening Spotlight and typing "iOS Simulator."

Mono for OSX

Once you've tested out the iOS simulator, install the latest version of Mono for OSX. Mono can be downloaded from http://mono-project.com/Downloads. Make sure you click on the "intel" link, and not the CSDK. Also, install Mono *before* you install the MonoTouch SDK. Mono comes in a disk image; double-click the installer package and follow the instructions.

MonoTouch SDK

Next, download and install the latest MonoTouch SDK. You can either buy it at the MonoTouch store, http://monotouch.net/Store, and you'll receive a link to download, or you can download an evaluation version from http://monotouch.net/DownloadTrial. If you purchase MonoTouch, you can deploy your applications to a properly configured device, but for most of the book, the evaluation version is fine.

Text Editor or Integrated Development Environment

If you want to create MonoTouch applications, all you need are the previous items and a text editor. You could create all your code files and manually compile using the command line (terminal window). This would be quite a pain, though, so we're going to use an integrated development environment (IDE) to develop our applications.

You have several options for this, but all of our examples in this book will be based on MonoDevelop. I've chosen MonoDevelop for two reasons, first, it's free, and secondly, it's the only IDE that completely integrates MonoTouch.

You can find the MonoDevelop install at http://monodevelop.com/Download.

You can also use Visual Studio to write libraries for use in MonoTouch, but it involves converting your standard C# class library projects to MonoTouch iOS class library projects. For more information, and a tool to help automate this, check out: http://manniat.pp-p.net/blog/post/2009/11/18/MonoTouch-in-Visual-Studio.aspx.

You can either modify/hack Xcode (installed with the iOS SDK) to use the MonoTouch libraries and compiler, or you can use MonoDevelop.

If you have installed Mono correctly, MonoDevelop should open up without error.

Documentation

One of the biggest drawbacks to developing for MonoTouch is that, while there is a wealth of documentation for developing for the iOS in general, the MonoTouch documentation itself is lacking. You can access the MonoTouch documentation directly from MonoDevelop in the Help menu, or you can view it online at http://www.go-mono.com/docs/index.aspx. You can also find the .NET documentation online at http://msdn.microsoft.com.

Xcode/iOS Documentation

Probably the single most useful source of documentation for developing MonoTouch applications is the iOS documentation. It's all based on the Objective-C API and includes Objective-C samples, but it should be considered the bible for iOS development.

You can access the iOS documentation either online at http://developer.apple.com, or in Xcode. To view it in Xcode, open Xcode and choose Developer Documentation in the Help menu.

> **NOTE:** I've included a short Objective-C primer in chapter 21, which deserves a once-over. It will significantly help to understand the examples in the iOS documentation.

MonoTouch Rosetta Stone

Additionally, Miguel de Icaza (the creator of Mono) keeps a "Rosetta stone" which maps the MonoTouch API to the underlying iOS API at http://tirania.org/tmp/rosetta.html.

Resources

As you learn and develop with MonoTouch, when you get stuck, and you probably will, there are quite a few resources online to help you work through it:

- **MonoTouch forums:** You can find forums dedicated to MonoTouch development at http://forums.MonoTouch.net

- **IRC channel:** There is a very active IRC community to be found on the #MonoTouch channel on the irc.gnome.org and irc.gimp.net servers. The MonoTouch team themselves are very active on there. You can access the channel directly from the MonoTouch website at www.MonoTouch.net/chat, if you're unfamiliar with IRC.

3rd Party Libraries

There is an active and growing number of open source 3rd party libraries for MonoTouch. Many of the most popular libraries for Objective-C have been wrapped for native use in MonoTouch. We'll cover 3rd party libraries in Chapter 21, but you can also find a current list at http://wiki.monotouch.net/.

Summary

Congratulations, you've made it through the first chapter. By now, you should have a pretty good understanding of MonoTouch's place in the world, what tools you need to use it, and where to go for help when you encounter issues. You should also understand the basic constraints of developing for the iOS. In the next chapter we'll leverage what we've learned so far to build our first MonoTouch application.

Chapter 2

Our First Application

Once you have everything installed from the first chapter, you're ready to start building iOS applications. In this chapter, we're going to build a single-screen "Hello, World" application specifically for the iPhone/iPod Touch. By the end of this chapter, you'll be familiar with:

- Creating MonoTouch projects
- Using Interface Builder to create screens
- Wiring up controls via outlets and creating actions
- Handling UI events in code
- Deploying to and running applications in the iOS Simulator

Without further ado, let's get started.

Starting the Example

First, launch MonoDevelop. Your screen should show something similar to following (Figure 2–1).

Figure 2–1. *MonoDevelop*

As a standard IDE, it should look pretty familiar. It's very similar to such environments as Visual Studio, Eclipse, Visual C# Express, and others.

We're going to create a new solution in which to put our iPhone project. Solutions are exactly the same as they are in Visual Studio and, in fact, you can open up solutions you created in Visual Studio in MonoDevelop. One thing that is different in MonoDevelop, though, is that you can actually have multiple solutions open in one instance of MonoDevelop, as illustrated in Figure 2–2.

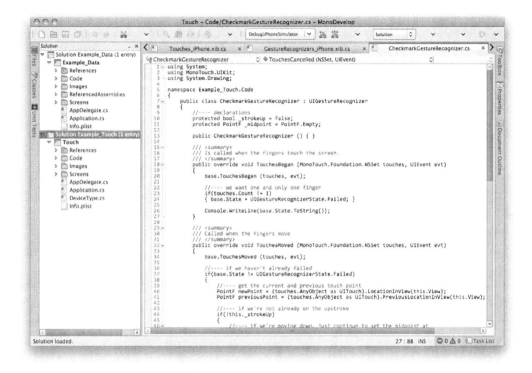

Figure 2–2. *MonoDevelop with multiple solutions open*

This is a pretty important feature since, in the Mac OS, you cannot have multiple instances of an application open without terminal or scripting trickery. So, if you need to switch between solutions (for example, if you want one open for sample code), you can simply open more than one at once.

Create a New Solution

So, with all that said, let's create a new solution. In the menu, go to **File ➤ New ➤ Solution**.

We want to create an **iPhone Window-based Project,** as shown in the following figure. Let's go ahead and call it `Example_HelloWorld_iPhone`.

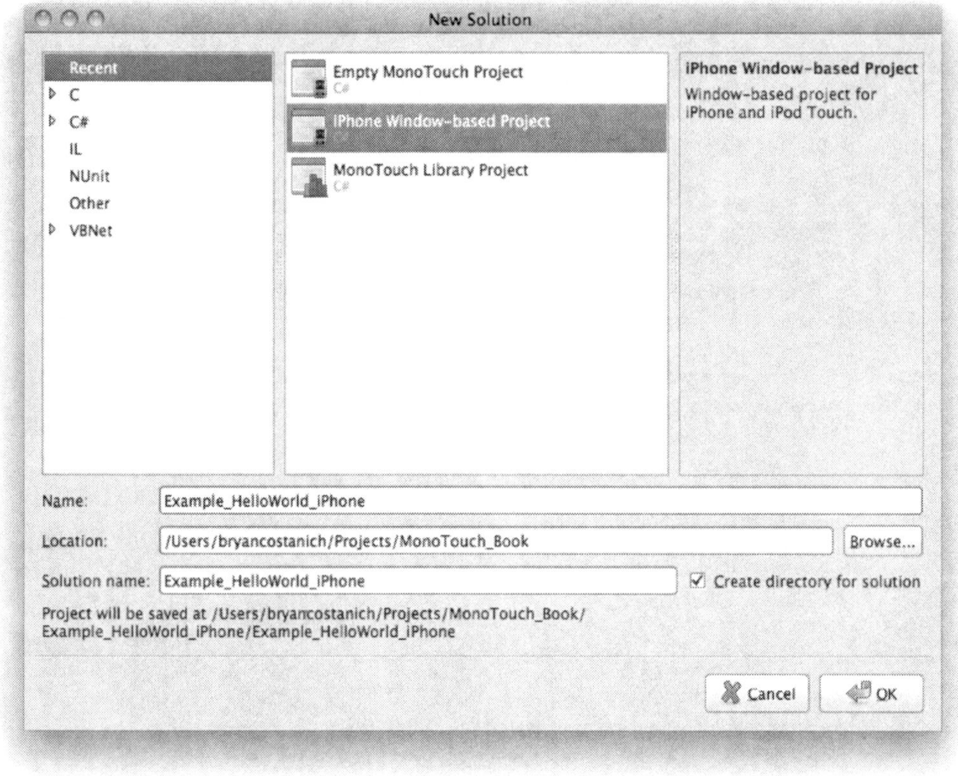

Figure 2–3. *MonoDevelop new solution dialogue window*

Again, this is very similar to Visual Studio's dialog for creating new solutions. Click OK, and you should now have a solution view that looks something like the one in Figure 2–4 (note, I've expanded the arrows in the solution view to show all the files and references).

Figure 2–4. *The solution window*

Examining the Code

Let's go through these:

- **References:** This folder contains the basic references needed for a MonoTouch application. The MonoTouch assembly includes everything needed that is specific to the iOS, including all the wrappers to the Cocoa Touch controls and the core iOS stuff such as Location, Data, etc. The System.* assemblies are the .NET Base Class Library and runtime that have been tailored to run on iOS devices.

- **Main.cs:** This is the same as it would be for a console application, a WPF application, or the like. In here is our static void Main call, which serves as an entry point for the application. We'll take a look at this in more detail in a second.

- **MainWindow.xib & MainWindow.xib.designer.cs:** This is analogous to a Winforms Window, or a WPF Window. The xib file will actually be edited in Interface Builder (which we'll examine in just a bit), and the designer.cs file will hold our properties for that form.

Let's examine the code in the Main.cs file, as shown in Listing 2–1.

Listing 2–1. *The code in the Main.cs file*

```
using System;
using System.Collections.Generic;
using System.Linq;
using MonoTouch.Foundation;
using MonoTouch.UIKit;

namespace Example_HelloWorld_iPhone
{
    public class Application
    {
        static void Main (string[] args)
        {
            UIApplication.Main (args);
        }
    }

    // The name AppDelegate is referenced in the MainWindow.xib file.
    public partial class AppDelegate : UIApplicationDelegate
    {
        // This method is invoked when the application has loaded its UI
        // and it's ready to run
        public override bool FinishedLaunching (UIApplication app, NSDictionary options)
        {
            // If you have defined a view, add it here:
            // window.AddSubview (navigationController.View);

            window.MakeKeyAndVisible ();

            return true;
        }
    }
}
```

There are two classes in here: the Application class and the AppDelegate class. This is where things start to get a little different from traditional .NET GUI development.

The way iOS applications work is that your application class contains all your Windows, Views, Controls, Resources, etc., and then you have an application delegate class (derived from UIApplicationDelegate) that handles application lifecycle and runtime events.

Lifecycle events include things like application startup and shutdown, and runtime events include things like low memory warnings and device orientation changes.

By handling these events in your application delegate class, you have an opportunity to respond to them. For instance, when your application is shutting down, the WillTerminate method is called on your application delegate, and you have an opportunity to save any user data, application state, etc.

In our Application class, we have a Main method. By calling UIApplication.Main, the Objective-C runtime will look for your MainWindow.xib file (which contains the name of your UIApplicationDelegate class), instantiate your Application class (as a Singleton) and then start calling lifecycle events on your AppDelegate class.

> **NOTE:** You don't have to name your primary window (also known as the Main Interface File) MainWindow.xib. You can name it whatever you want, but you have to tell the build system to look for whatever file you create. If you want it to look for a different file, open up the project options by right-clicking on your project file, click **Options**, and then in **Build ➤ iPhone Application ➤ Main Interface File**, set that to whatever .xib file you want to be your primary window. The Objective-C runtime will then try to load that window when your application runs, and will find your application delegate from the setting in that file.
>
> Additionally, you can name your application delegate class whatever you want. By default it is called AppDelegate. To change it, open your Main Interface File in Interface Builder, and change the name of your Application Delegate.
>
> Furthermore, you don't even need to define your window in a xib file at all. In fact, as a standard practice, I never define my window in a xib. It's easier to just do it programmatically. In Chapter 4, we'll look at how to do exactly that.

We'll come back to our Main.cs file in a bit, but first let's dig into the actual GUI of the application.

Interface Builder

So far we've seen a little bit of the code side of our iPhone application, let's dive into building the interface. Apple's application design toolset is called Interface Builder. Interface Builder is loosely coupled to your development environment. It creates xib files that define your applications user interface. MonoDevelop then examines those xib files and provides hooks in your code for you to access them.

> **NOTE:** Sometimes people refer to xib (pronounced "zib") files as Nibs, and in this book you'll see lots of references to Nibs as well. For practical purposes, they can be used interchangeably. A xib file is an XML file that defines a user interface in Cocoa Touch, and a Nib file is usually a compiled collection of xib files.
>
> This is similar to creating XAML in WPF/Silverlight. Your interface is represented by XML nodes. When your application is built, that XAML is compiled with your code into one assembly.
>
> In Mac OS, a similar thing happens. Your xib files get compiled into a Nib, which is then packaged with your application bundle into an .app file.

Whether you write Objective-C in XCode, or C# in MonoDevelop, you still use Interface Builder the same way. This is possible because MonoDevelop listens for changes to the xib files, and adds/removes the appropriate code to the designer.cs files that map to the xib files.

You can create your entire GUI programmatically, without ever having to open up Interface Builder, and in fact, some developers choose to do just that. There are many things that Interface Builder can't do, so at some point you're likely to wind up doing some things programmatically. Interface Builder hides some of that complexity, though, so in the beginning it's easier to use Interface Builder to become familiar with some of the concepts of iOS application GUIs. We'll examine this in more detail in Part 2, when we start looking at controls in more depth.

Exploring Interface Builder

So, with all that said, let's fire it up. Double-click the **MainWindow**.xib file. Interface Builder should launch and you should see something like the Figure 2–5.

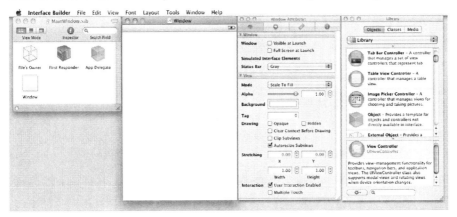

Figure 2–5. *Interface Builder*

Let's look at these windows one-by-one. From left to right, these are: the Document window, the Design window, the Inspector window , and the Library window.

Let's look at the Document window first (Figure 2–6).

Figure 2–6. *The Document window*

This window shows all of the objects that are in a xib file. This is the default view, and while pretty, you'll find it isn't very useful because your objects in your interface are actually a hierarchy, and the icon view only shows one level at a time. As we add controls to our window, they won't show up in this view like this. So, let's change it to list view by clicking the center icon in the **View Mode** toolbar. It should now look something like Figure 2–7.

Figure 2–7. *The Document window in list view*

The next window is the **Designer** (Figure 2–8). This is where we'll actually drag our Cocoa Touch controls to design our interface.

Figure 2–8. *An empty Designer showing the main window*

It is empty right now because we haven't put any controls onto it.

Our next window is the Library window, as shown in Figure 2–9. The Library window contains all of the Cocoa Touch controls that we can use on our design surface.

Figure 2–9. *The Library window*

This is the default view of the library, however, just as in the Document window, you can change its view. To change the view in your Library window, right-click in the control view and you can choose between a few different styles. You can also click the Gear button on the bottom left of the window. Figure 2–10 shows the Icons and Labels style.

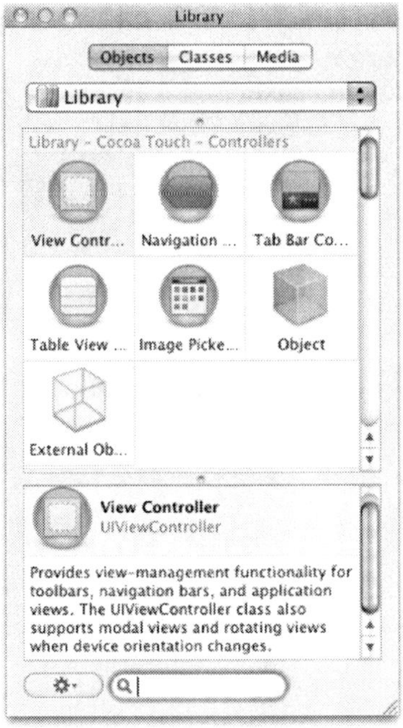

Figure 2–10. *The Library window in Icons and Labels view*

Our final window is the Inspector window, as shown in Figure 2–11.

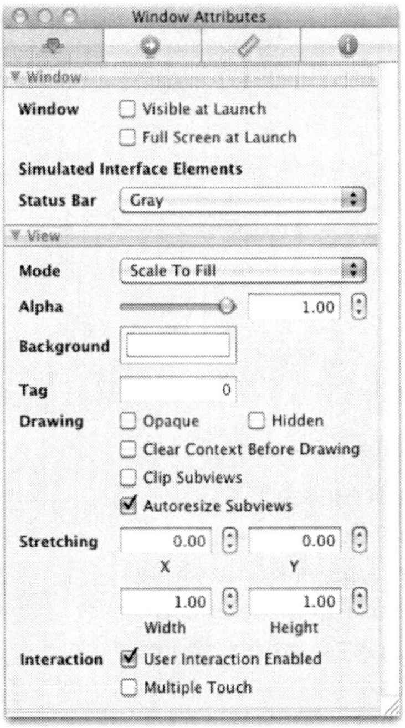

Figure 2–11. *The Inspector window*

The Inspector window has four different views, accessible via the tab bar at the top of the window. These views are called **Attribute Inspector**, **Connections Inspector**, **Size Inspector**, and **Identity Inspector**. The Inspector is roughly analogous to the Property Explorer window in Visual Studio. It shows you all the properties of the currently selected Cocoa Touch object. With it you can set visual properties, layout, and more. In the previous figure, we've selected the Window object in the Document window, so it's displaying the attributes for that object.

Building the Interface

Now that we have an overview of the Interface Builder windows, let's actually build something. Let's create an interface, as shown Figure 2–12.

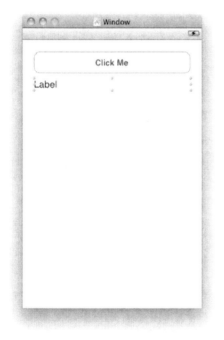

Figure 2–12. *Main window interface after controls have been added*

1. First, drag a **Round Rect Button** (UIButton) onto the window from the Library window. Then, double-click the button to set the text. You will notice that, as you do this, you'll start to get little guidelines. These guidelines are based on Apple's *Human Interface Guidelines* (you can find them in the iOS Developer Documentation in the *Human Interface Guidelines* document) and will help you to position your controls on your view with the appropriate spacing, etc.

2. Resize the button by clicking on the button and then dragging the resize controls.

3. After you've got your button on the window, drag a **Label** (UILabel) control. Resize the label so it takes up nearly the width of the window.

If you've done everything correctly, your Document window should look like Figure 2–13 (click the arrow next to **Window** to see its child controls).

Figure 2–13. *The Document window after controls have been added*

We've now created our first window interface. However, unlike in traditional .NET GUI development, you cannot access your controls programmatically yet. For example, if this were a WPF application, as soon as you drag a control onto the design surface, you could access it from your code via this.ControlName. Right now, if you view the MainWindow.designer.cs file, you'll see that it's empty, except for a property for window.

So, let's see how to access our controls.

Outlets

In order to make our objects accessible to our code-behind, we have to wire them up via outlets. An outlet is just a plumbing construct to make interface elements available to code. When you create an outlet in Interface Builder, MonoDevelop will add a matching property in the designer.cs file for that class, which then allows you to have programmatic access to the control.

Let's add outlets for our label and our button, so that we can access them from our code-behind.

1. Select your AppDelegate in the Document window, as shown in Figure 2–14.

Figure 2–14. *The Document window with the AppDelegate class selected*

2. Select the Identity Inspector tab of the Inspector window (Figure 2–15).

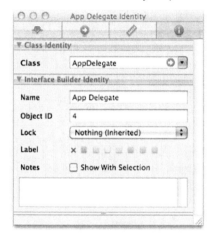

Figure 2–15. *Identity Inspector tab showing the selected class from the Document window*

3. Click the circled arrow to the right of the AppDelegate class, which will navigate to that class in the Library window (Figure 2–16).

Figure 2–16. *The Library window showing the selected class*

4. Change the drop-down that says Inheritance to Outlets, as shown in
    Figure 2–17.

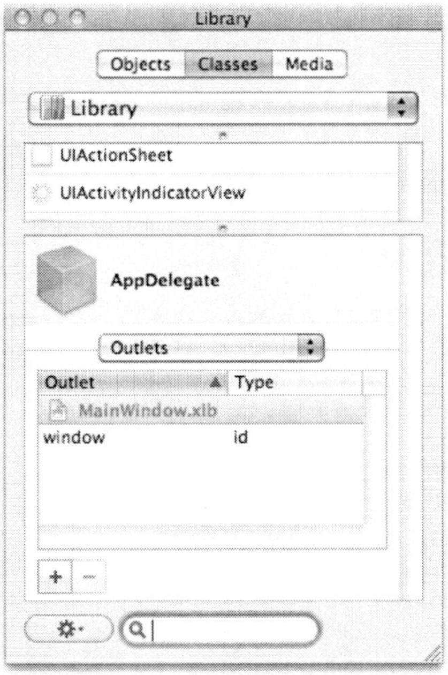

Figure 2–17. *The Library window showing the selected class*

5. Click the + button twice to create two new outlets.

6. Each outlet has a name and a type. Name represents the name of the control property, and is analogous to ID in ASP.NET, or Name in WPF. Type is the actual type of the outlet, such as a UIButton, UILabel, UITextView, etc. To name them, double-click their name and type in a name. For our outlets, we're going to create btnClickMe and lblResult.

7. Right now, both of their types are id. If you leave the type as is, you can hook the outlet up to anything, because id means the type is dynamic, and is essentially an object in the .NET world. The type of id is fine, but we're going to give one of them an actual type. We'll see what difference this makes in a second. For now, double-click the type of our btnClickMe and type in UIButton for the type. Your **Class Outlets** window should now look like Figure 2–18.

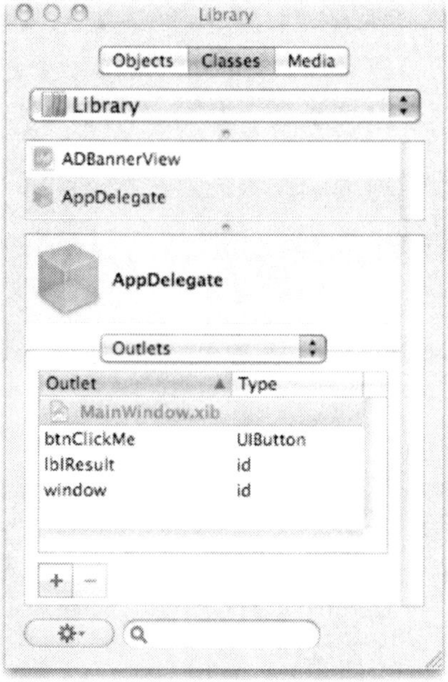

Figure 2–18. *Newly created outlets*

8. Now that we have these outlets created, we need to actually assign them to our controls. First, click the second tab in the Inspector window to bring up the **Connections** Inspector. In the **Outlets** section, we should now see the two new outlets that we created. However, they're not hooked up to anything.

9. To hook up our outlets, we need to drag from the circle next to the outlet in the **Outlets** section, over to the control we want to hook up. When we do this, we'll get something like Figure 2–19.

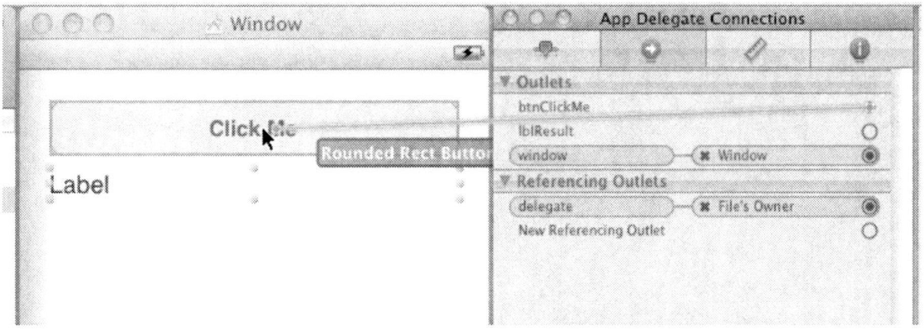

Figure 2–19. *Newly created outlets*

10. We need to do this to both outlets. You can also drag from the
Connections Inspector onto the Document window. This is especially
helpful if you have overlapping controls.

As we do this, you may notice something interesting. Because we gave btnClickMe a
type of UIButton, when we drag the outlet to the window, it will only allow a connection
to be created if the object we're dragging to is of that type—in this case, UIButton.
lblClickMe, on the other hand, can be dragged onto anything, because it has the
dynamic id type.

Many people strongly type their outlets so that it's more difficult to accidentally hook
them up to the wrong control. It's not necessary, but can be a good practice to do so.
Personally, I find it tedious and not worth the effort, since wiring up outlets is pretty
simple.

OK, now that we have our interface created and our outlets hooked up, save your work
in IB and head back over to MonoDevelop to wire everything up.

Outlets Exposed to Code

If you open up MainWindow.designer.cs, you'll now see two more properties in there, as
shown in Listing 2–2.

Listing 2–2. *MonoTouch auto-generated Designer code showing outlets*

```
[MonoTouch.Foundation.Connect("lblResult")]
private MonoTouch.UIKit.UILabel lblResult {
    get {
        this.__mt_lblResult = ((MonoTouch.UIKit.UILabel)(this.GetNativeField("lblResult")));
        return this.__mt_lblResult;
    }
    set {
        this.__mt_lblResult = value;
        this.SetNativeField("lblResult", value);
    }
}

[MonoTouch.Foundation.Connect("btnClickMe")]
```

```
private MonoTouch.UIKit.UIButton btnClickMe {
    get {
        this.__mt_btnClickMe =
        ((MonoTouch.UIKit.UIButton)(this.GetNativeField("btnClickMe")));
        return this.__mt_btnClickMe;
    }
    set {
        this.__mt_btnClickMe = value;
        this.SetNativeField("btnClickMe", value);
    }
}
```

These two properties now make our label and our button accessible via our code-behind. Notice an interesting thing here—even though we declared our lblResult as a type of id, the property that got created for it is strongly-typed as a UILabel. This is because MonoDevelop is smart enough to look at the actual underlying type of the outlet and create a property of the appropriate type. This is good for us, because it means we don't have to cast the lblResult property to a UILabel every time we want to use it as one.

Let's go back now to our Main.cs file, and look at the AppDelegate. Let's look at the FinishedLaunching method (Listing 2–3).

Listing 2–3. *FinishedLaunching method*

```
// This method is invoked when the application has loaded its UI and it's ready to run
public override bool FinishedLaunching (UIApplication app, NSDictionary options)
{
    // If you have defined a view, add it here:
    // window.AddSubview (navigationController.View);

    window.MakeKeyAndVisible ();

    return true;
}
```

As the comment suggests, this method is called by the Objective-C runtime after the application is instantiated, and is ready to run. The first call, window.AddSubview, is commented out, and we'll look into what that actually does in the next chapter when we examine the Model View Controller (MVC) pattern in Cocoa Touch.

The next call, window.MakeKeyAndVisible, sets the MainWindow to be the main window and actually makes it visible. In iOS development, only part of this is actually interesting because you only ever have one, and only one window. If you want different screens on an iOS app, you create new views, and have a view controller push them into the front. However, if you don't call this method, the iOS won't send events to your window. So really, the MakeKey part makes sense, but the AndVisible part is really just vestigial from the traditional OSX Cocoa framework, in which you might have multiple windows.

We're going to add some new code to this file. When we created our outlets, we created them on the AppDelegate. That means that they're now available in the AppDelegate class, so we're going to access them from here.

> **NOTE:** Ordinarily, when building MonoTouch applications, we would actually have different views that we would add controls to, and then expose them as outlets on the controllers that manage them, but for the sake of this simple application, we've created our outlets directly in our AppDelegate class. In Chapter 2, we'll do this a bit differently, when I introduce controllers.

Let's change our AppDelegate class to look like Listing 2–4.

Listing 2–4. *Our complete AppDelegate class that responds to button clicks and updates the screen*

```
// The name AppDelegate is referenced in the MainWindow.xib file.
public partial class AppDelegate : UIApplicationDelegate
{
    //---- number of times we've clicked
    protected int _numberOfClicks;

    // This method is invoked when the application has loaded its UI and its ready
    // to run
    public override bool FinishedLaunching (UIApplication app, NSDictionary options)
    {
        // If you have defined a view, add it here:
        // window.AddSubview (navigationController.View);

        window.MakeKeyAndVisible ();

        //---- wire up our event handler
        this.btnClickMe.TouchUpInside += BtnClickMeTouchUpInside;

        return true;
    }

    protected void BtnClickMeTouchUpInside (object sender, EventArgs e)
    {
        //---- increment our counter
        this._numberOfClicks++;
        //---- update our label
        this.lblResult.Text = "Hello World, [" + this._numberOfClicks.ToString () + "]
        times";
    }
}
```

The first thing we added is a variable to track the number of clicks, _numberOfClicks. Next, we added this line:

```
this.btnClickMe.TouchUpInside += BtnClickMeTouchUpInside;
```

This wires up the TouchUpInside event of btnClickMe to be handled by the BtnClickMeTouchUpInside method.

> **NOTE:** We use `TouchUpInside` rather than `TouchDown` because it allows a user to cancel an accidental click of a button by moving their finger off and releasing the button. In other words, we only want to register a touch if it starts and finishes inside the button. This is in conformance with Apple's *Human Interface Guidelines*, and you should follow this pattern in your applications as well.

Then, in our `BtnClickMeTouchUpInside` method we simply update our label with how many times our button has been clicked.

Running the Application

All right, now that we've done all this, let's build and run the thing. Let's build first. In the menu, select **Build ➤ Build All**. If you've done everything correctly so far, it should build without errors. Next, let's run it on the iPhone Simulator!

In the toolbar, make sure that **Debug|iPhoneSimulator** is selected, as in Figure 2–20.

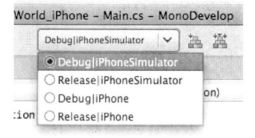

Figure 2–20. *Build mode set to Debug|iPhone Simulator*

To run this, either select **Run ➤ Run** from the menu, or press ⌘ + **enter** on the keyboard.

> **NOTE:** In the evaluation version of MonoTouch, you can only run on the simulator; if you try to run on your device, you'll get an error.

If everything goes right, the simulator should pop up (it may, in fact, hide behind your MonoDevelop window, so you might have to switch over to it), and you should see the following (Figure 2–21).

Figure 2–21. *Our Hello World application in the simulator*

Clicking the button should result in the label text getting updated, as shown in Figure 2–22.

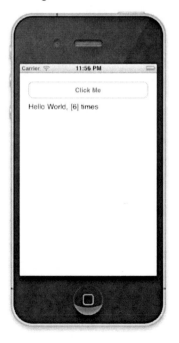

Figure 2–22. *Our Hello World application counting our clicks*

Congratulations! You've just created and run your first iPhone application. Let's look at two more things, and then we'll finish this chapter.

Actions

In the application we just created, we have outlets that are accessed via properties in our code. Just like in other .NET GUI paradigms, we can wire up event handlers to them and then respond to events. But MonoTouch offers another way to respond to user input. These are called actions. Actions are similar to commands in WPF, in that they allow multiple controls to invoke the same method, and then decide how you want to handle it, depending on who invoked it.

Adding an Action

Let's look at this in a little more detail.

1. Make sure you have your Example_HelloWorld_iPhone application open in MonoDevelop.

2. Open up MainWindow.xib in Interface Builder by double-clicking the file. Now add two buttons below our label, similar to Figure 2–23.

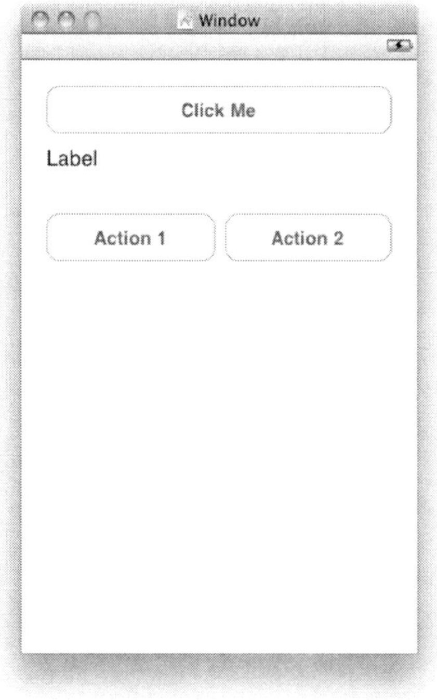

Figure 2–23. *Action buttons added to the main window*

3. Actions are added in the same place outlets are: in the Library window, make sure you have your AppDelegate selected, and down below select the **Actions** tab instead of the **Outlets** tab. Create a new action called actnButtonClick. Your Library window should look something like Figure 2–24.

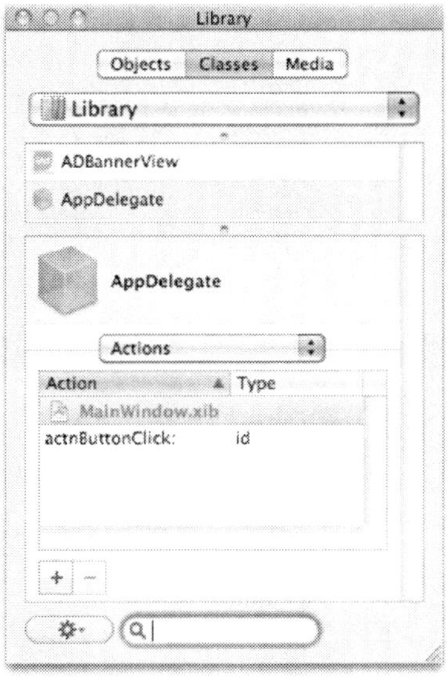

Figure 2–24. *Action actnButtonClick added*

IB automatically appends a colon to the end of your action name. You can ignore this, it's an Objective-C thing, but our action will work just the same.

What we've just done is created a generic action on our AppDelegate called actnButtonClick. Now what we need to do is associate our buttons' TouchUpInside events with it, so when they get clicked, our action is called.

Make sure AppDelegate is selected in the Document window, then drag the actnButtonClick in the **Connections Inspector** to the **Action 1** button, as shown in Figure 2–25.

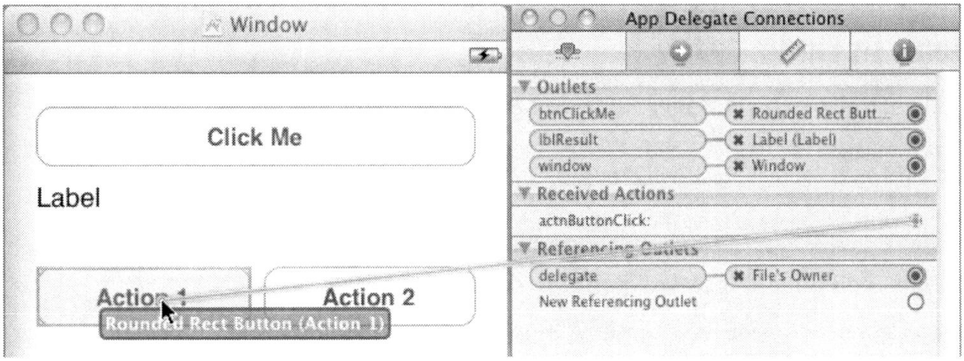

Figure 2–25. *Wiring up an action*

When we drag to the button, it gives a list of events to trigger the action. Select **Touch Up Inside**, as shown in Figure 2–26.

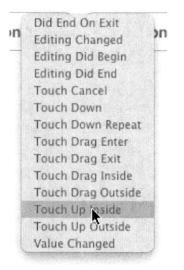

Figure 2–26. *Choosing an event to call the action*

Do this for both of the action buttons. If we view the **Connections Inspector** for our AppDelegate, it should have the action wired up to both buttons, as shown in Figure 2–27.

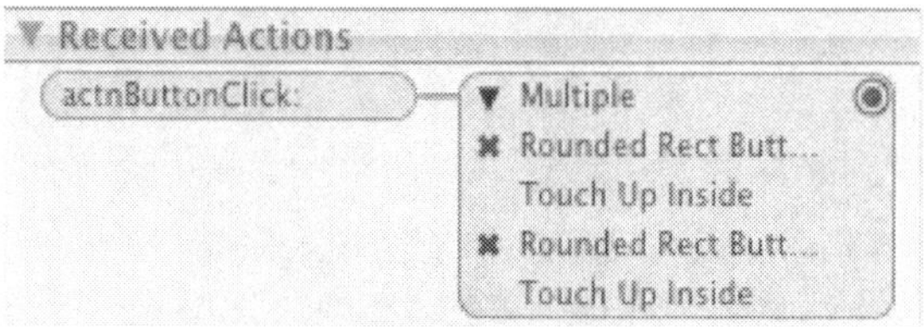

Figure 2–27. *Action wired up to multiple controls*

Save your work in Interface Builder, and then go back to MonoDevelop.

Actions in Code

If we look at MainWindow.designer.cs, we should see a new line of code:

```
[MonoTouch.Foundation.Export("actnButtonClick:")]
partial void actnButtonClick (MonoTouch.UIKit.UIButton sender);
```

This is the partial declaration of our action. Notice it's decorated with the MonoTouch.Foundation.Export attribute. This allows the Objective-C runtime to find the appropriate method that is associated with our action.

The compiler actually ignores any partial method declarations that don't have any implementation (as we see in this one), so really, this is here so that you get code completion when you go to implement the method. If we go back to Main.cs, we'll see this. In your AppDelegate class, notice that if you type partial, you'll automatically get the code completion for our actnButtonClick, as shown in Figure 2–28.

```
partial
       actnButtonClick (UIButton)
```

Figure 2–28. *Code completion for actions*

Let's put the following code in there:

```
partial void ActionButtonClick (UIButton sender)
{
    //---- show which button was clicked
    this.lblResult.Text = sender.CurrentTitle + " Clicked";
}
```

Now, if we run the application, and click the action buttons, we should see something like Figure 2–29.

Figure 2–29. *Hello World application after the Action 1 button has been clicked*

Choosing Which Device to Simulate

Thus far, we've deployed only to the standard resolution iPhone Simulator. However, we can also deploy to the iPhone 4 (with Retina Display resolution) iPhone Simulator, as well as the iPad Simulator.

To change which device you'd like to deploy to in the simulator, change Project : Active Simulator Target in the application menu. As of writing, you have three options:

- **Default:** The iPhone 3G Simulator with a resolution of 320x480

- **iPhone Simulator 4.3:** The iPhone 4G Simulator with the 640x960 Retina Display

- **iPad Simulator 4.3:** The iPad Simulator with a 1024x768 resolution

For example, if you choose iPad Simulator 4.3 and then debug it, it will launch the iPad Simulator with the application running in it (Figure 2–30).

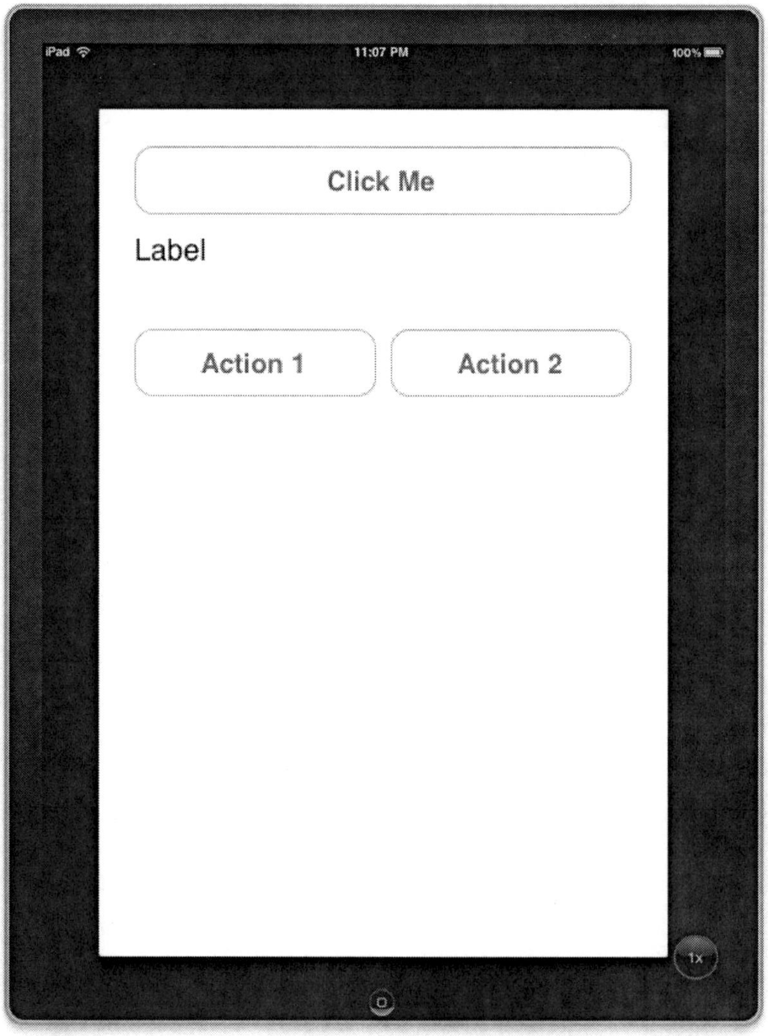

Figure 2–30. *Hello World application running on iPad simulator*

As you can see, while the application runs in the iPad, it's definitely non-optimal. In the next chapter, we're going to take a look at building applications for both the iPhone and the iPad.

> **NOTE:** If you want to debug your application in the iPhone 4G Simulator with Retina Display, you must first launch the iOS Simulator and then choose Device : iPhone (Retina) from the Hardware menu. Then, in MonoDevelop, change your iPhone Simulator Target to iPhone Simulator 4.3 and run/debug it. If you don't change the device in the iOS simulator first, it will simulate the iPhone 3G, rather than the iPhone 4G. This is an Apple strangeness and also happens if you're developing in Xcode.

Application Name and Icons

The last thing I want to cover in this chapter is how to specify your application name and icons.

If you run the application as it is, and then click the Home icon on the iOS Simulator, you'll notice that our application name is displayed as our project name and the icon is blank (Figure 2–31).

Figure 2–31. *Blank icon and truncated application name*

Application Name

To specify an application name that's different from the project, right-click the project and choose Options. Then choose iPhone Application in the left pane, and specify the name in the Display name field, as shown in Figure 2–32.

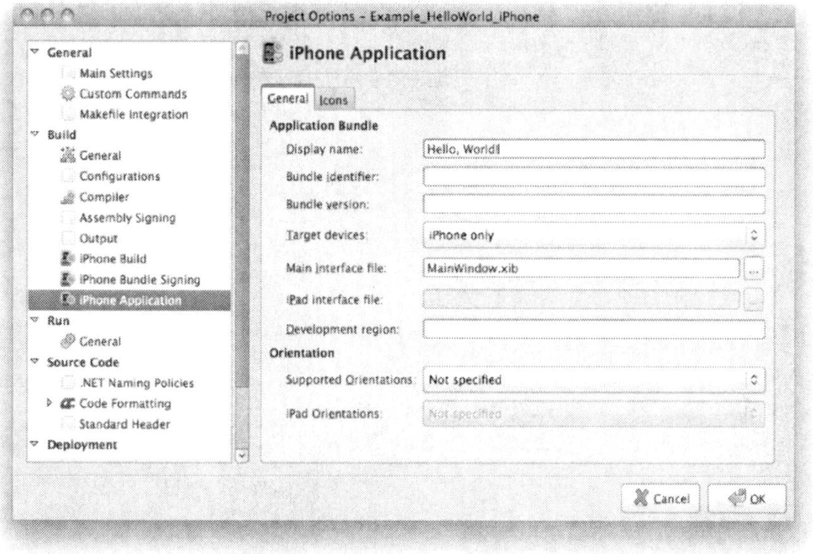

Figure 2–32. *Specifying an application display name*

Now, when you run your application, you should see the display name you set, under the icon (Figure 2–33).

Figure 2–33. *Application with a friendly display name*

Application Icons

Applications require a number of *icons*, each of a different size, depending on the device and where the icon is displayed. Icons are standard .png files, and for iOS applications, there are potentially six different icons, depending on whether your application is intended for consumption on the iPhone, iPad, or both:

- **iPhone Icon:** This icon shows up on the home screen of the iPhone 3Gs (and below). It should be 57x57 pixels in size.

- **iPhone 4 Icon:** This icon is the same as the icon, except for Retina Display devices. It should be 114x114 pixels.

- **Settings/Spotlight Icon:** This icon shows up in the iOS Settings Application as well as the Spotlight/Search on the iPhone 3Gs (and below). It should be 29x29 pixels.

- **iPhone 4 Settings/Spotlight Icon:** This icon is the same as the previous, except it's for the Retina Display devices. It should be 58x58 pixels.

- **iPad Icon:** This icon shows up on the home screen of the iPad and should be 72x72 pixels.

■ **iPad Spotlight:** This icon shows up in the iOS Settings Application as
well as the Spotlight/Search on the iPad. It should be 50x50 pixels.

The iOS will automatically mask the corners of your icons to make them round and add
the glassy effect, so you don't have to.

To add icons to your application, right-click your project and choose Add Files. Then,
navigate to your icons and select them. Finally, check Override default build action, set it
to Content, and click Open (Figure 2–34).

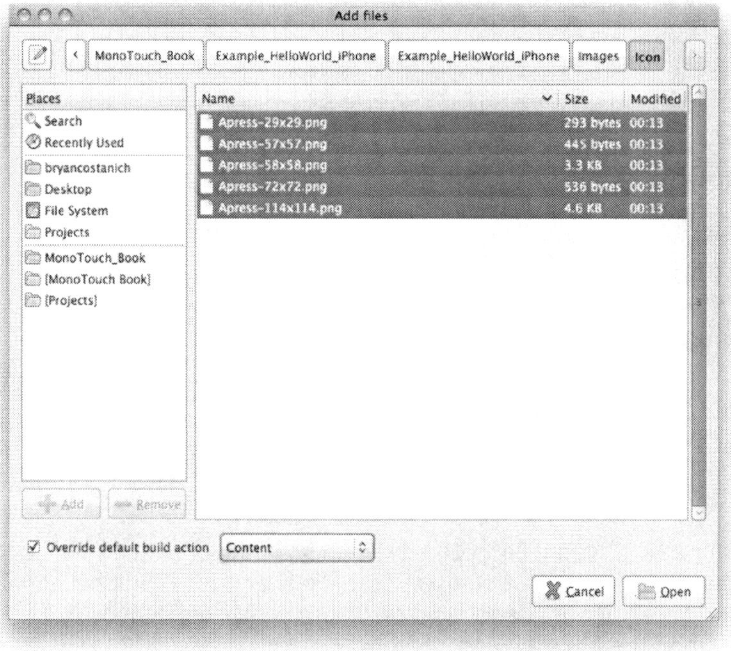

Figure 2–34. *Adding icons to your application*

Setting the build action to Content will make sure that the files are copied into the
application package and made accessible to the iOS. We'll cover including images in
more depth in Chapter 6.

After you've added your images to your project, you can set your icons by going back
into the Project Options dialog and choosing the Icons tab in the iPhone Application
section, as shown in Figure 2–35.

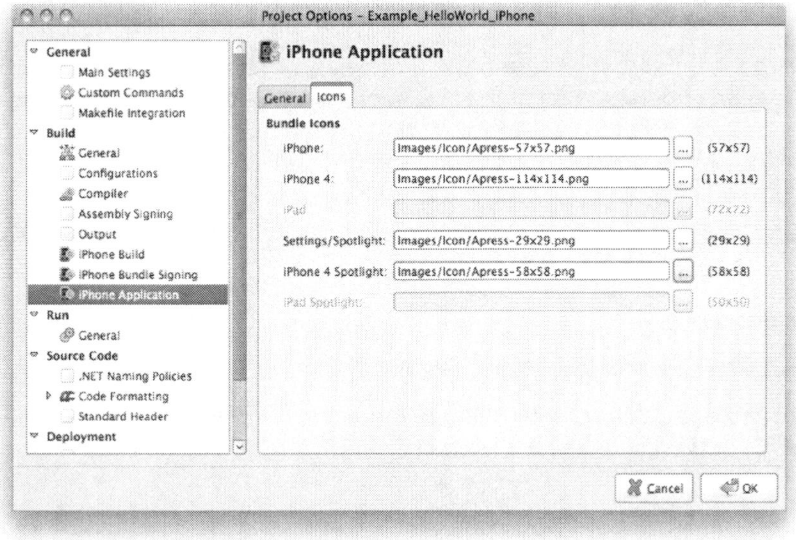

Figure 2–35. *Specifying the location of your icons*

After you specify your icons and run your application, they will show up (Figure 2–36).

Figure 2–36. *Application icons on the Home, Spotlight, and Settings screens, respectively*

Summary

At this point, we've gone through making a basic iPhone application using MonoTouch. You should now have an understanding of the iOS application fundamentals including the UIApplication, the UIApplicationDelegate, outlets, and actions. You also know how to run your application on the simulator, set your application display name, and add icons.

However, there are two things fundamentally missing from the application we built in this chapter, namely:

- It only has one screen
- It's really just designed for the iPhone, not the iPad

In Chapter 3, we're going to address both of those issues as we delve into the Model View Controller (MVC) pattern and how it's used in Cocoa Touch.

Creating Multi-Screen Applications Using the MVC Pattern

In the first chapter, we created our first application using MonoTouch for the iOS. We used outlets and actions, got to know the basic application structure, and made a simple user interface. However, it had a couple major flaws, one of which is that it only had one screen. In this chapter, we're going to look at how to create multi-screened applications in the iOS using Views and View Controllers.

Specifically, we'll use the UINavigationController to navigate to two different pages/screens in our application. Before we begin, however, we need to briefly review an important design pattern that Cocoa Touch uses, called the Model-View-Controller (MVC) pattern.

Model-View-Controller (MVC) Pattern

Cocoa Touch uses the MVC pattern to handle the display of their GUI. The MVC pattern has been around for a long time (since 1979, specifically) and is intended to separate the burden of tasks necessary to display a user interface and handle user interaction.

As the name implies, the MVC has three main parts, the Model, the View, and the Controller, as shown in Figure 3–1.

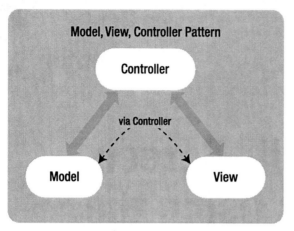

Figure 3–1. *The constituent parts of the Model, View, Controller pattern*

Model

The Model is a domain-specific representation of data. For instance, let's say we were making a task-list application. You might store these in a DB, an XML file, or even pull them from a Web service. The MVC pattern isn't specifically interested in where/how they're persisted, or even if they are. Rather, it deals specifically with how they're displayed and how users interact with them.

If we are persisting the Task items to some sort of storage, one approach might be to create a TaskManager class that handles persistence and retrieval of them for us via methods such as TaskManager.Save(Task item) or TaskManager.Get(int itemID). Or perhaps we might take a different approach and simply add the retrieval and persistence logic to the Task items themselves via Task.Save() and Task.Get(int itemID).

In the MVC pattern, it doesn't matter which approach we choose, the only thing that is important to understanding it is that we have a model representation of our data, in this case, a Task object.

View

The View is the class or item that is responsible for how our data (or Model) is actually displayed. In our hypothetical task application, we might display these tasks on a web page (in HTML), or a WPF page (in XAML), or in a UITableView in an iOS application. If a user clicks a specific task, say to delete it, typically the view raises an event, or makes a callback to our Controller.

In many frameworks, views actually contain a hierarchy of other views. For instance, the page/screen itself is often a view, and it contains a number of controls that are also views. In this instance, the top-level view is referred to the root view, and the entire set of views is referred to as the view-hierarchy.

iOS is no different in this regard, the main page view is the root view, and it can contain many different controls such as buttons, which are themselves views.

Controller

The Controller is the glue between the Model and the View. It's the Controller's job to take the data in the model and tell the View to display it. It is also the Controller's job to listen to the View when our user clicks the task to delete it, and then either delete that task from the Model, by calling some sort of manager object, or tell the Model to delete the task itself.

Benefits of the MVC Pattern

By separating the responsibilities of displaying data, persisting data, and handling user interaction, the MVC pattern tends to create code that is easily understood. Furthermore, it encourages the decoupling of the View and the Model, so that the Model can be reused. For example, if in your app you had both a web-based interface and a WPF interface, you could still use the same code for your Model for both.

Views and View Controllers in MonoTouch

In an iOS application, you only ever have one window, but you can have lots of different screens. This is accomplished by creating different views that you display when appropriate.

In Apple's Cocoa Touch UI framework (also known as the UIKIT), controllers are usually called ViewControllers, so if you see a class like UIViewController, it's actually a controller.

A single controller can manage many different root views, but typically, in order to keep controller code manageable, they only manage one root view. If the controller does manage different root views, they're typically simple derivatives of the other views it manages. For example, you might have a single view controller that manages four different views for the different orientations of the device. We'll explore that in more depth in Chapter 5 when we examine handling rotation on the device.

In MonoTouch, views are represented by the UIView class, and nearly all controls inherit from this class. Views handle user interaction and notify their controller via events. For example, a button raises a TouchDownInside event when a user puts their finger on it, and a TouchUpInside when the user releases their finger. To make a rough analogy, this relationship is slightly similar, to the ASP.NET or WPF model, in which the user interface is defined in HTML or XAML, and then a code-behind page handles events such as clicks, etc.

In this chapter's sample application, we're going to use a specialized controller called the Navigation Controller (UINavigationController) to manage our different screens.

The `UINavigationController` manages a stack of view controllers, each of which represents a screen. When you want to display a new screen, you push a view controller onto the navigation stack that the navigation controller manages. The navigation controller then renders a navigation bar control that allows users to click a button to move backwards through the hierarchy, by removing the top most (visible) controller from the navigation stack.

The `UINavigationController` is seen in many of the stock iOS applications. For example, when you're viewing a list of your text messages, if you click one, the top bar gets a left arrow tab at the top that takes you back a view to the message list, as shown in Figure 3–2.

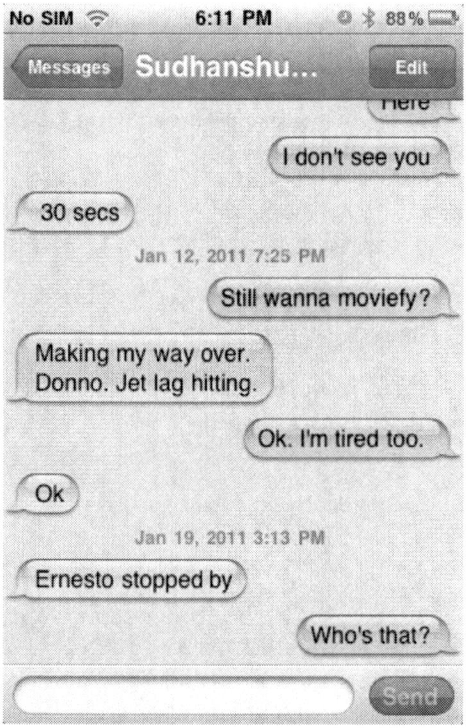

Figure 3–2. *The text message application in iOS uses a navigation controller to handle navigation*

It's worth noting that, in this application, we're only going to be dealing with views and controllers. The model portion is not strictly necessary in the MVC pattern, despite its inclusion in the pattern name. It's really only used when you want to display data, and in this case, we're going to be exploring the navigation hierarchy, and not data.

Sample Application

Now that we understand how multiple screens work in concept, let's actually create an application that utilizes them.

1. First, create a new MonoTouch iPhone solution in MonoDevelop and name it Example_HelloWorld_iPhone_MultipleScreens (refer to the first chapter if you've forgotten how to do this).

2. Next, create create three View Controllers. To do this, right-click your project and choose **Add**▶**New File**, then select **iPhone** and **View Interface Definition with Controller**, as shown in Figure 3–3.

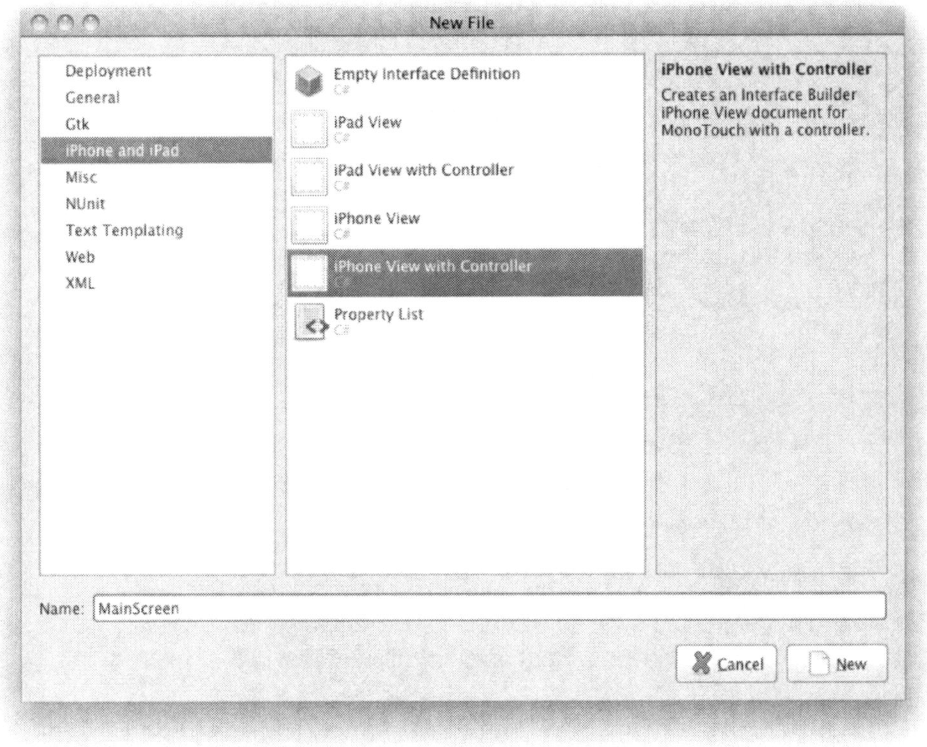

Figure 3–3. *New View with Controller*

Name your three view controllers:

- MainScreen
- HelloWorldScreen
- HelloUniverseScreen

Adding the Navigation Controller to the Main Screen

Once you have your screens created, open up the MainScreen.xib in Interface Builder. This is going to be the main screen of our application and will have our Navigation Controller on it.

1. Navigation controllers need to be the root controllers in a screen, so let's delete the view from this screen. To do this, select the view object in the **document window** and either press the delete key or select the view and choose **Edit►Delete** from the menu.

2. Next, drag a **Navigation Controller** item from the **library window** onto the document. Your **document window** should look like Figure 3–4 (I've expanded the tree to show the full hierarchy).

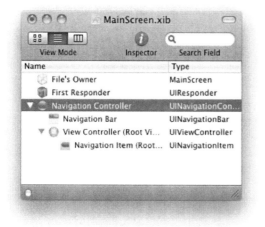

Figure 3–4. *Document window showing the Navigation Controller hierarchy*

3. As I mentioned before, the UINavigationController actually contains a number of different items. Now look at your Designer window, where you'll see the newly added Navigation Controller (Figure 3–5).

Figure 3–5. *Navigation Controller showing a placeholder for your View*

4. While the Navigation Controller comes with a number of controllers and
    views, it doesn't actually contain a view to house your content, so we
    need to add one. Simply drag a UIView control from the Library window
    onto the View placeholder in the Designer window, or onto the View
    Controller in the Document window. Once you've done that, your screen
    should look like Figure 3–6, and your Document window should look like
    Figure 3–7.

Figure 3–6. *Navigation Controller after View has been added*

Figure 3–7. *Document Window showing the added View in the hierarchy*

5. You can change the **Root View Controller** text by double-clicking it. In this case, let's just change it to **Hello World**. After you've changed that text, add two buttons to the view and set their text to **Hello World Screen**, and **Hello Universe Screen**, respectively. Once you're done, your screen should resemble Figure 3–8.

Figure 3–8. *Finished MainScreen.xib*

6. Next, create three outlets:

   - ▓ `btnHelloWorld`
   - ▓ `btnHelloUniverse`
   - ▓ `navMain`

7. Wire the `btn*` outlets up to their respective buttons, and wire `navMain` up to the `Navigation Controller`. See Chapter 2 if you forgot how to make outlets and wire them up.

8. Once you've got your outlets created and wired up, save your work.

HelloWorld and HelloUniverse Screens

Now we're ready to do the two subviews, so let's get started.

1. Open up the `HelloWorldScreen.xib` file in Interface Builder and drop a label on to the screen that says **Hello World!**, as shown in figure 3–9.

Figure 3–9. *Finished Hello World screen*

2. Since this screen will actually have a navigation bar at the top, you can make the Designer window show one as well, by selecting **TopBar➤Navigation Bar** in the **Simulated User Interface Elements** section of the Attributes Inspector, as shown in figure 3–10.

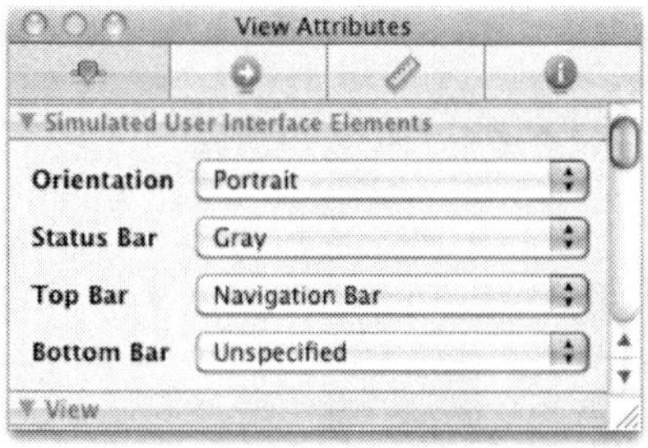

Figure 3–10. *Attributes Inspector showing simulation options*

3. The Designer will now show a simulated top bar when you're designing your screen. Have a look and you can see how much room you have, as shown in figure 3–11.

Figure 3–11. *Simulated navigation bar in the designer*

4. Once you've finshed the Hello World screen, do the same thing with the Hello Universe screen, except set the text of the label to be Hello Universe!.

5. When you're done, save your work, and head back over to MonoDevelop.

Showing Different Screens

Now that we've got our screens created in Interface Builder, let's modify the code in the MainScreen controller to handle our button clicks and show our different screens.

MainScreen.xib.cs

Open up the MainScreen.xib.cs file in MonoDevelop. This file is our controller class for our main screen. The first thing we're going to do is change our default constructor to load our view (as defined in our .xib file) synchronously. The template, in MonoDevelop, for a UIViewController has the following default constructor, shown in Listing 3–1.

Listing 3–1. *Default UIViewController constructor when the view is defined in a .xib file*

```
public [ControllerClassName] () : base("[ControllerClassName]", null)
{
    Initialize ();
}
```

This calls the base class's default constructor and passes the name of the Nib file where we created our view. The base class then deserializes and loads the view from that file. Unfortunately, however, the base class implementation loads the view asynchronously. That is, the actual controls and content on that view aren't available immediately. This is typically not a problem, because the UIViewController has a method called ViewDidLoad that is called once the view has fully loaded.

We'll see in a moment, when we look at our AppDelegate class, why this can be a problem, but for now, replace that constructor with the following, shown in Listing 3–2, which does the same exact thing, but loads the view synchronously (LoadNib doesn't return until the view is loaded).

Listing 3–2. *Default UIViewController constructor that loads the .xib synchronously*

```
public MainScreen ()
{
        Initialize ();
        NSBundle.MainBundle.LoadNib("MainScreen", this, null);
        this.ViewDidLoad();
}
```

We made one other change in here that's important to note as well. If you manually call LoadNib, the ViewDidLoad method will not be called. Instead, we need to call it ourselves, after the view has been loaded.

Next, add the following method, shown in Listing 3–3.

Listing 3–3. *Wiring up event handlers in the ViewDidLoad method*

```
public override void ViewDidLoad ()
{
        base.ViewDidLoad ();
        this.btnHelloUniverse.TouchUpInside += (s, e) => {
                this.navMain.PushViewController (new HelloUniverseScreen (), true); };
        this.btnHelloWorld.TouchUpInside += (s, e) => {
                this.navMain.PushViewController (new HelloWorldScreen (), true); };
}
```

The ViewDidLoad method is called by the view controller after the view is loaded and fully initialized. We'll examine the controller and view lifecycle in more detail in Chapter 5, but ViewDidLoad is a good place to wire up your event handlers because it is only called after your controls are instantiated, and is only called once in a view's lifecycle.

The UINavigationController manages a stack of navigation items, which are typically controllers. To show a new screen, we can simply push a view controller onto the stack via the PushViewController method. Our event handler code does exactly that, when a user clicks one of our buttons.

Next, we need to make our Navigation Controller accessible from our AppDelegate class, so that we can add the view it manages to our window. Let's add a property to do just that, as shown in Listing 3–4.

Listing 3–4. *Exposing our navigation controller*

```
public override UINavigationController NavigationController
{
    get { return this.navMain; }
}
```

You'll notice this property is an override. That's because the `UIViewController` class already exposes a `NavigationController` property. This property will return a `UINavigationController` only if this `View Controller` is currently on a navigation stack. In our case, our `MainScreen.xib` actually contains the Navigation Controller. So we override this property for simplicity.

Next, we're going to change our `AppDelegate` class to load our main screen when the application starts up.

AppDelegate

Open up the `Main.cs` file in MonoDevelop and add the following declaration to your `AppDelegate` class, as shown in Listing 3–5.

Listing 3–5. *Declaring a class-level reference to our MainScreen*

```
MainScreen _mainScreen;
```

> **NOTE:** We've declared a reference to our `MainScreen` as a class-level variable. This is *extremely* important. The garbage collector in MonoTouch is very aggressive, and in a moment we're going to instantiate our `MainScreen` in a method and then add it to the navigation stack. If we declared it within the scope of the method, it could get garbage collected when the method returns. If this were to happen, if we were to try to do anything with it (like handle a button click), the application would crash with a null-reference error.

Then, in the `FinishedLaunching` method, add the code shown in Listing 3–6.

Listing 3–6. *Declaring our MainScreen as a class-level variable*

```
this._mainScreen = new MainScreen ();
window.AddSubview (this._mainScreen.NavigationController.View);
```

The `UINavigationController` is unique, in terms of controllers, in that you can push other controllers onto it. It then adds the view of the controller onto its view hierarchy. However, with most other controllers, and also with the `Window`, you have to add views instead.

The code we added to our `AppDelegate` class does just that. It creates a new `MainScreen` controller, and then adds the Navigation Controller's view onto it.

It's important to note here, if we didn't change our constructor in our `MainScreen` class to be synchronous, our `NavigationController` property would likely be null when we called the `window.AddSubview`, and the application would error on starting.

Now, when we run our application, we should see our main screen load, as shown in figure 3–12.

Figure 3–12. *Application running, displaying the Main Screen*

If you click the **Hello World Screen** button you should get something like figure 3–13.

Figure 3–13. *Application running, displaying a sub screen*

Summary

Congratulations! You know understand how the MVC pattern is used in Cocoa Touch to create multiple screen applications. In our next chapter, we'll extend this concept to build a universal application for both the iPhone and the iPad!

iPad and Universal (iPhone/iPad) Applications

So far we've covered a lot of the basics of making an iPhone application using MonoTouch, including how the MVC pattern fits in, but what about iPad applications? It turns out, building iPad applications is almost exactly like building iPhone applications, and, in fact, you can even extend your iPhone applications to run on both the iPhone and the iPad, and vice-versa.

iPad applications run exactly the same way iPhone (or iPod Touch) applications do. The only appreciable difference is the form factor. The iPad is nearly the size of a standard American sheet of paper.

This means that you can fit a lot more on screen, which has a tremendous impact on how iPad versions of iPhone OS applications differ from their iPhone counterparts. With the larger screen, you can often combine what would be several screens on the iPhone into a single screen in an iPad application.

Because of the larger screen size, Apple has given us a couple of additional controls that are only available on the iPad, the most significant of which is the UISplitViewController, which is used to manage a master/detail view configuration. We'll take a look at that control in more detail in Chapter 8, but other than a couple of controls, building iPad applications is nearly identical to iPhone applications.

There are a few hardware resource differences between the different devices, so I've included a table here of the major differences to give you an understanding of how they differ. Most of the time these differences are negligible, but it's important that, if you intend for your applications to run on older devices, you test your applications on them.

Table 4–1. *iOS device comparison*

Device	Max. OS Version	RAM	Processor Speed	Screen Size + Resolution
iPhone	3.1.3	128MB	412MHZ	480x320 pixels @ 163ppi
iPhone 3G	4.2.1	128MB	412MHZ	480x320 pixels @ 163ppi
iPhone 3GS	4.3+	256MB	600MHZ	480x320 pixels @ 163ppi
iPhone 4G	4.3+	512MB	~1GHZ	960x640 pixels @ 326ppi
iPad	4.3+	256MB	~1GHZ	1024x768 pixels @ 132ppi

There are other capability differences as well, such as the presence of a compass or GPS, which we will examine in later chapters that deal with the particular item. For more information on device particulars, Wikipedia has excellent coverage of the iPhone at en.wikipedia.org/wiki/Iphone, and the iPad at en.wikipedia.org/wiki/Ipad.

In this chapter we're going to walk through creating an iPad application, and then go through a couple of options for creating universal applications that run on both the iPhone and the iPad.

A Note About Resolution on the iPhone

The iPhone 4G has a high-resolution screen (2x the density of the iPhone 3GS and below) known as the Retina Display. This means that, while the resolution is twice that of the earlier iPhone models, the screen size remains the same. We'll examine how we account for this in later chapters, but for now, the answer is largely that we don't have to. Apple has kept the coordinate system the same for both screens, which means that the screen space is still 480x320 "points," whether you're on the 4G iPhone or an earlier version.

The most important difference this makes is when it comes to images. In Chapter 6, when we get introduced to controls, we'll see that when loading images, the iOS will automatically look for images with an "@2x" in the filename suffix and load them (as opposed to images without that suffix) if the current device is a high-density Retina Display.

Creating an iPad-Only Application

Let's look at how to create an application that will only run on the iPad. Create a new solution of type iPad Window-based project under the **C#➤iPhone and iPad** templates, as shown in Figure 4–1.

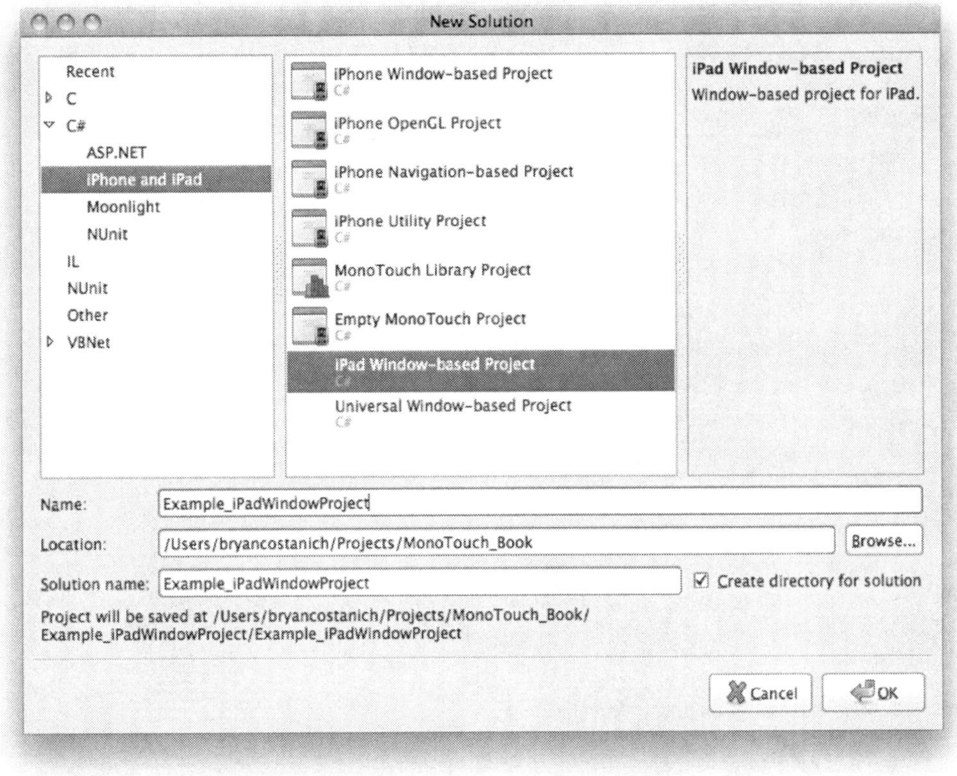

Figure 4–1. *iPad Window-based project template*

The iOS looks for a file named info.plist in your application bundle to determine what iOS versions and devices your application supports. A *.plist file* is a special type of file called a property list. We'll cover .plist files in more detail in Chapter 14, but essentially, a .plist file is a place where application settings and information are stored.

Changing Common Settings in MonoDevelop

Most of the time you don't have to edit the info.plist file directly, because many of the common settings that you might configure are actually available via the **Project Options** dialogue in MonoDevelop. We touched briefly on the Project Options dialog in Chapter 2, when we covered how to set your application name and icons.

When you build your application, MonoTouch automatically creates an info.plist file for you if you do not already have one based on your project options, and if you do have one, it will merge the project options settings with it.

When you create an application using the iPad Window-based project template, it automatically sets the **Target devices** setting to **iPad only,** as shown in Figure 4.2.

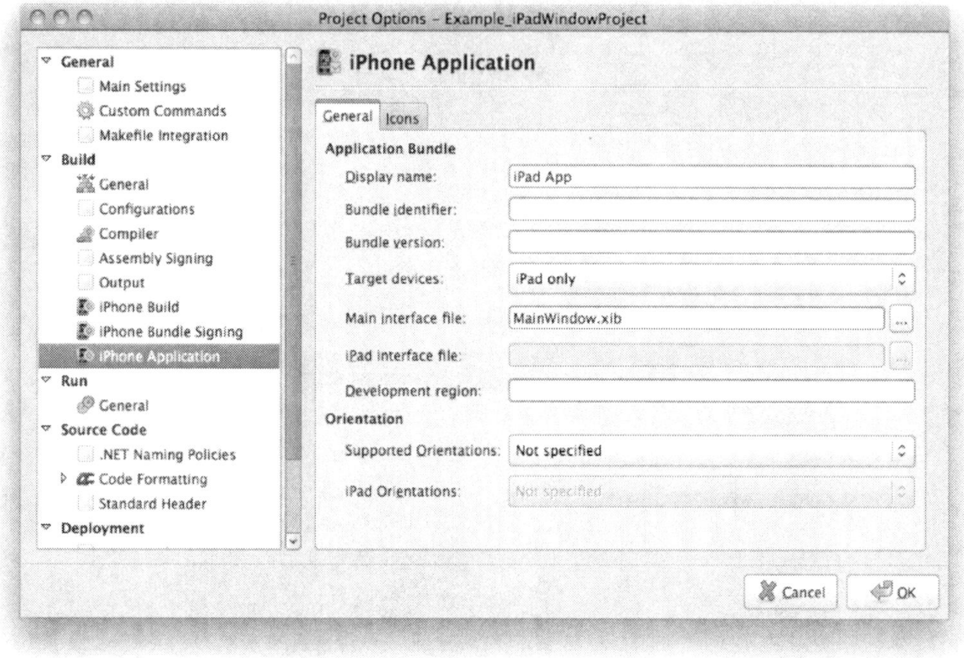

Figure 4–2. *Build settings for an iPad-only application*

It also sets the **Main interface file** setting, which contains your Window. This setting is actually a little confusing, because there is also an **iPad interface file** setting, as seen in Figure 4.2. However, if the **Target devices** setting is set to either **iPhone** or **iPad** only, the only interface file setting that is used is **Main interface file**. If you're building a universal (iPhone and iPad) application, then the **Main interface file** setting will be used for the iPhone application, and the **iPad interface file** setting will be used for the iPad application.

You can also load your Window programmatically, and therefore bypass the interface settings altogether. We'll look at that in just a bit when we talk about universal applications.

iPad Screens in Interface Builder

If you open up your MainWindow.xib file in Interface Builder, you'll notice that nearly everything is the same, except that your Designer window is a lot bigger; now add a UILabel to it, as shown in Figure 4–3. Adding controls is exactly the same as it is for iPhone applications.

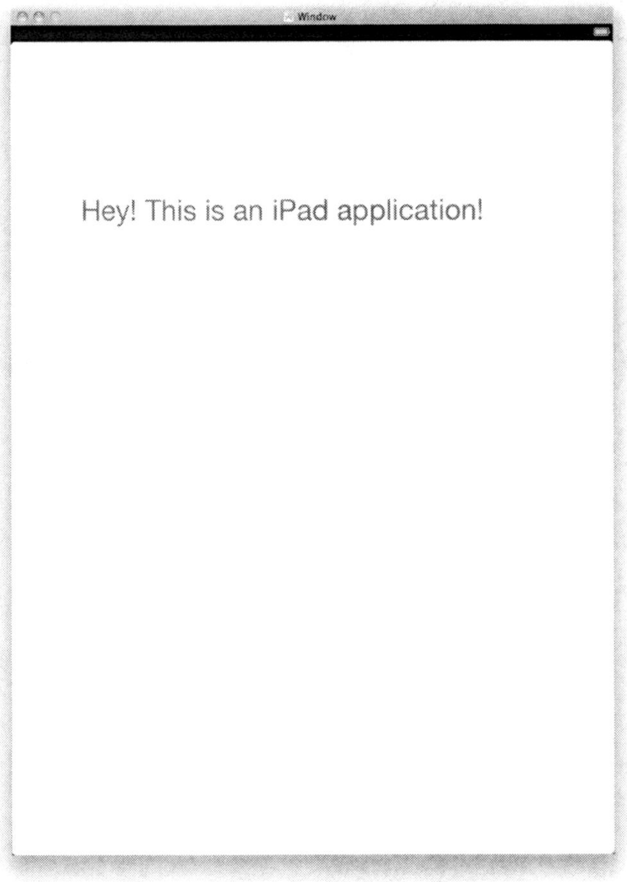

Figure 4–3. *iPad Designer window in Interface Builder*

If you save your work in Interface Builder and then run your application just as you would an iPhone application, the iPhone Simulator will show up, as in Figure 4–4, running your application.

Figure 4–4. *iPhone Simulator running an iPad application*

You'll notice, however, that this time, instead of getting a simulated iPhone, the simulator will simulate an iPad.

As you can see, the technical aspect of creating an iPad application is just as easy as it is for creating an iPhone application.

Now let's take a look at creating applications that run on both the iPhone and the iPad.

Creating a Universal iPhone/iPad Application

There are a couple of ways to create a universal application that will run on both the iPhone and iPad.

- The first and easiest is to use the universal project template in MonoTouch.

■ The second, and much more powerful way, is to detect which device the application is executing on, and programmatically load the appropriate UI for that device.

Let's take a look at using the universal project template first.

Method 1: Universal Project Template

The universal project template can be found in the **New Solution** dialogue with the other templates under **Universal Window-based Project**, as shown in Figure 4–5.

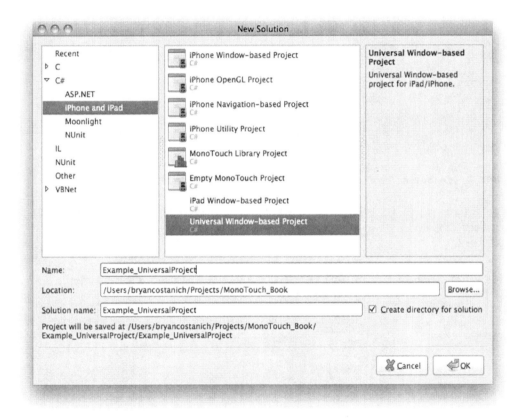

Figure 4–5. *Universal project template*

When you create a new project based on the universal template, you'll notice it creates an AppDelegate class and a MainWindow for both the iPhone and the iPad, as shown in Figure 4–6.

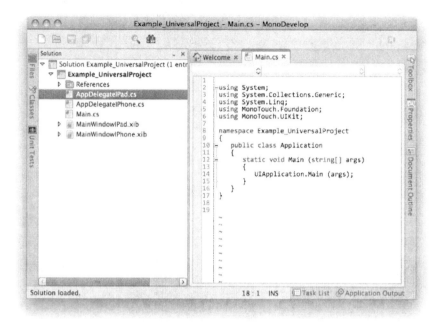

Figure 4–6. *New universal project showing duplicate AppDelegate and MainWindow files*

If you take a look at the build options, you'll notice that **Target Device Setting** is set to **iPhone and iPad**, and that an interface file is specified for both devices, as shown in Figure 4–7.

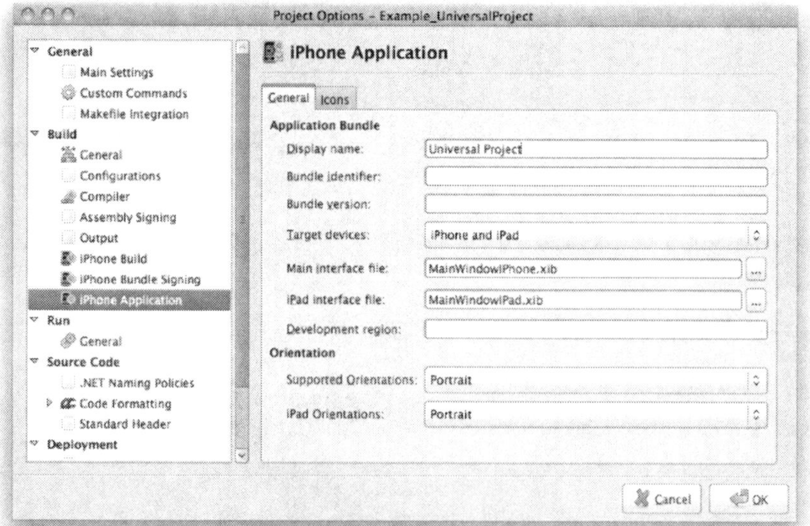

Figure 4–7. *Project options in a universal project template-based application*

To specify which device to simulate when running the application on the simulator, set Project▸iPhone Simulator Target to either the iPhone or the iPad.

This is a very simple and easy way to create a universal application, but since we have duplicate AppDelegate classes, it can lead to redundant code being written. If you wanted to, you could create a single AppDelegate class and reference that class in both your MainWindowIPad.xib and MainWindowIPhone.xib files. Additionally, you could simplify your application even further by creating one window based on the dimensions of the device and loading the appropriate screens based on what device is running, which is exactly what we'll do next.

Method 2: Programmatic Device Detection

To create a universal application from scratch that detects the device type and loads the appropriate screens, start by creating a new **Empty MonoTouch Project**, as shown in Figure 4–8.

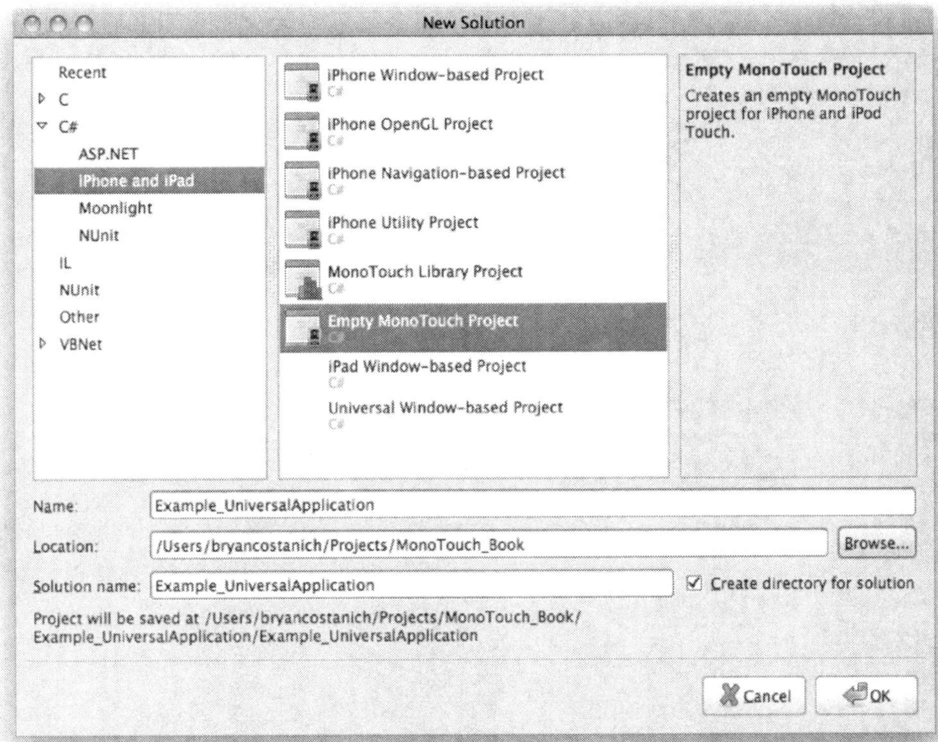

Figure 4–8. *Empty MonoTouch project*

MonoDevelop sets the target device to iPhone by default, so the first thing we need to do is change that to iPhone and iPad. Right-click your project and choose **Options**. Then in the **Build▶iPhone Application** tab, change the **Target devices** setting to **iPhone and iPad**, as shown in Figure 4–9.

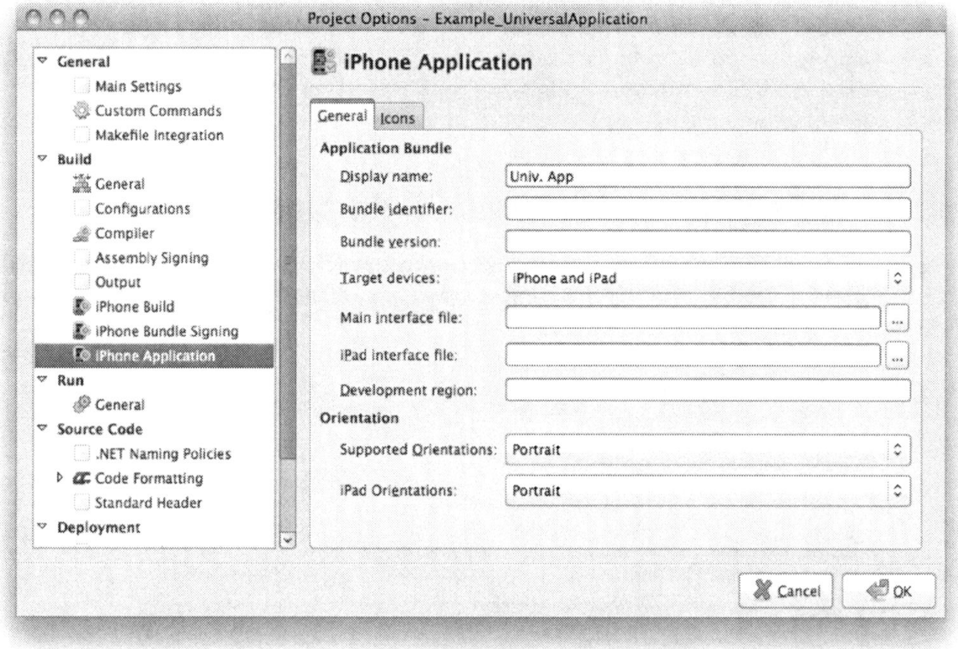

Figure 4–9. *Target devices setting*

Determining the Device Type

Because this is an empty template, we need to create our `Main` method as well as our `AppDelegate` class from scratch. First, however, let's add some classes to help us determine which device is running. First, add an enum called `DeviceType`, with the code shown in Listing 4–1.

Listing 4–1. *DeviceType enumeration*

```
using System;
namespace Example_UniversalApplication
{
    public enum DeviceType
    {
        iPhone,
        iPad
    }
}
```

To add the enum, simply right-click the project and choose **Add**➤**New File** and choose **General**➤**Empty Enumeration**, and name it `DeviceType`.

Next, add a new class called `DeviceHelper`, with the code shown in Listing 4.2.

Listing 4–2. *Deterimining whether the current device is an iPad or an iPhone*

```
using System;
using MonoTouch.UIKit;

namespace Example_UniversalApplication
{
    public static class DeviceHelper
    {
        public static DeviceType DetermineCurrentDevice ()
        {
            //---- figure out the current device type
            if (UIScreen.MainScreen.Bounds.Height == 1024 ||
                UIScreen.MainScreen.Bounds.Width == 1024)
            {
                return DeviceType.iPad;
            } else
            {
                return DeviceType.iPhone;
            }
        }
    }
}
```

`DeviceHelper` has one method, `DetermineCurrentDevice`, which determines what device the application is executing on by checking the size of the screen. If either the height or width (the device may be in portrait or landscape mode) is 1024 pixels, then it must be an iPad. Anything else has to be an iPhone. This seems like a strange way to determine the current deivce, and it is; however, it is the Apple-recommended method, since they do not expose an API to query the device type.

Creating a Custom AppDelegate

Next, we need to create an `AppDelegate` class. If you recall from Chapter 1, the `AppDelegate` class is responsible for handling our application events. Put the following code into your `AppDelegate` class (Listing 4–3).

Listing 4–3. *An AppDelegate class that creates a window and loads the appropriate screen based on the current device*

```
using System;
using MonoTouch.UIKit;
using MonoTouch.Foundation;

namespace Example_UniversalApplication
{
    [Register("AppDelegate")]
    public class AppDelegate : UIApplicationDelegate
    {
        protected UIWindow _window;
```

```
public DeviceType CurrentDevice
{
    get { return this._currentDevice; }
    set { this._currentDevice = value; }
}
protected DeviceType _currentDevice;

public AppDelegate () : base()
{
}

public override bool FinishedLaunching (UIApplication app, NSDictionary options)
{
    //---- create our window
    this._window = new UIWindow (UIScreen.MainScreen.Bounds);
    this._window.MakeKeyAndVisible ();

    //---- are we running an iPhone or an iPad?
    this.DetermineCurrentDevice ();

    switch (this._currentDevice)
    {
        case DeviceType.iPhone:
            // Load the iPhone home screen
            this._iPhoneHome = new HomeScreen_iPhone ();
            this._window.AddSubview (this._iPhoneHome.View);
            break;
        case DeviceType.iPad:
            // Load the iPad home screen
            this._iPadHome = new HomeScreen_iPad ();
            this._window.AddSubview (this._iPadHome.View);
            break;
    }

    return true;
}

protected void DetermineCurrentDevice ()
{
    this._currentDevice = DeviceHelper.DetermineCurrentDevice ();
}
}
}
```

Since we're building this from scratch, there are a couple things to be aware of. The first is the line shown in Listing 4–4.

Listing 4–4. *Register attributes make classes visible to the underlying runtime*

```
[Register("AppDelegate")]
```

In order for the underlying Objective-C runtime to be able to find our class, we need to make it visible via the Register attribute. We need it here because in just a bit we're going to tell iOS to load our AppDelegate in our Main method. If we don't add the attribute, iOS won't be able to locate our class and we'll get an error when we run the application.

Next, we have the following line (Listing 4–5)

Listing 4–5. Declaring our UIWindow

```
protected UIWindow _window;
```

In all of our other examples so far, we've used a xib file for our window, but in this example, we're going to create it programmatically. In our FinishedLaunching method, we have the following line (Listing 4–6).

Listing 4–6. *Instantiating a new UIWindow class based on the current screen resolution*

```
this._window = new UIWindow (UIScreen.MainScreen.Bounds);
```

This creates a window based on the size of the device. The nice thing about doing it this way is that now, no matter what device we're using, whether it's an iPad or an iPhone, our window is created correctly.

Next, we call the DetermineCurrentDevice method that we created earlier in our DeviceHelper class.

Finally, we have a switch block that loads the appropriate screen, based on which device we're running. If you're building this application, you'll want to add the appropriate screens for your device and load them here.

Note that we've exposed the CurrentDevice property as part of our AppDelegate, so we can access that property from anywhere in our application via the following call, shown in Listing 4–7.

Listing 4–7. *Accessing the current application delegate*

```
((AppDelegate)UIApplication.SharedApplication.Delegate).CurrentDevice
```

Creating a Custom Main Method

Finally, we need our static Main method that the iOS calls to run our application. This looks nearly identical to our Main method before, but with one slight change (Listing 4–8).

Listing 4–8. *Custom Main method that loads our AppDelegate class*

```
using System;
using MonoTouch.UIKit;

namespace Example_UniversalApplication
{
    public class Application
    {
        public static void Main (string[] args)
        {
            UIApplication.Main (args, null, "AppDelegate");
        }
    }
}
```

This time, when we tell the iOS to load our application, we need to pass it the name of our AppDelegate. Ordinarily, it would look at our **Main interface file** setting in the info.plist and load whatever application delegate class was specified in our window xib file, but since we don't have a xib file, we have to set this programmatically.

That's all it takes to launch our application programmatically without defining a xib file that contains our window.

One of the nice things about this approach is that instead of being forced to define separate screens for both devices every single time, you are free to combine screens when appropriate. You can even extend this pattern by creating two different screens that implement an interface and then use a single controller to provide unified code-behind for both devices. In fact, some of the applications in this book are written this way, so check them out to see how this is accomplished.

Summary

In this chapter we learned how to build applications for the iPad, as well as two different approaches to building universal applications. You should now have a pretty solid grasp on how iOS applications work, including how to build them from scratch without using a xib file to define your window.

Congratultions, you've finished your MonoTouch 101 course. This is the last chapter we'll go through that will have the walk-through tutorial approach. Most of the rest of this book will take a reference approach to different parts of a MonoTouch iOS application.

Chapter 5

More on Views and Controllers

In Chapter 3 we learned about the MVC pattern in the iOS and we built an application that uses multiple view controllers coupled with views that enabled us to have multiple screens. In this chapter, we're going to explore that relationship a little deeper, which will help us understand how to effectively work with views in our applications.

> **NOTE:** I use the term *control* interchangeably with *view* (`UIView` or its derivatives) throughout this book. This is largely because the "Control" paradigm, as we're used to in the world of Microsoft UI Development, is largely analogous and provides a nice conceptual equality. Additionally, Apple's documentation often refers to various views such as buttons, etc., as controls.

We're also going to explore the lifecycle of controllers and views so that we know where to put our code so that it executes at the proper time. Finally, we'll take a look at how to handle rotation of the device to provide a seamless user experience.

Custom UIViewController and UIView Implementations

Subclassing `UIViewController`, that is, implementing a custom class that inherits from it, is an extremely common task in iOS programming, since you need to do it for nearly every screen. Let's look at a custom `UIViewController` and its `UIView`, to really get a grasp of the relationship between the two. The simplest case is shown in Listings 5–1 and 5–2.

Listing 5–1. *Custom UIViewController class*

```
public class MainViewController : UIViewController
{
        public MainViewController () : base()
        {
        }

        public override void LoadView ()
        {
                //---- replace the default view with our custom view
                this.View = new MainView (UIScreen.MainScreen.ApplicationFrame);
        }
}
```

Listing 5–2. *Custom UIView class*

```
public class MainView : UIView
{
        public MainView (RectangleF frame) : base(frame)
        {
        }
}
```

As you can see, there's not a whole lot to this. We're going to explore the lifecycle more in the next section, but the UIViewController is responsible for managing the view. When creating UIViews that aren't defined in Interface Builder, we override LoadView on the UIViewController, to replace the default view that is baked into UIViewController with our own, custom one.

Default UIView Constructor for a View Defined in a xib file

The default constructor for a view takes a RectangleF that specifies the size and location of the view on the screen. In this case we can simply pass in the MainApplicationFrame, but if you have a tab bar, and/or a navigation controller, you'd have to account for both of those and change the position and size.

If we are defining the UIView in Interface Builder, the pattern is a little different. When a UIView is defined in a xib file, the iOS calls a different constructor in our UIViewController, as shown in Listing 5–3, that passes in the name of the xib file and loads the view from that, rather than code.

Listing 5–3. *Constructor for loading UIView from .xib file*

```
public MainScreen() : base("MainScreen", null)
{
        Initialize ();
}
```

We don't really have to worry about this too much, however, because the default MonoDevelop **View Interface Definition with Controller** template does this for us, as we've seen in the previous exercises. To see an example of this, check out the Example_ViewAndViewControllerInCode sample application.

Manually Loading a UIView Defined in a .xib File

You can also load a UIView directly onto a controller's root view outside of the context of a constructor, as shown in Listing 5–4.

Listing 5–4. *Constructor for loading UIView from .xib file*

```
NSBundle.MainBundle.LoadNib ("LandscapeView", this, null);
```

However, as we saw in Chapter 3, manually loading the .xib yourself means that the ViewDidLoad method is not called, so you should call it manually after loading the view.

UIViewController Event Lifecycle

As you can probably tell from the previous code samples, the UIView is in charge of displaying itself and any views/controls it contains, and the UIViewController is responsible for managing the UIView. As such, there are a number of events that are called during the lifecycle of both classes.

Understanding the lifecycle events in the UIViewController is important because you need to know which ones to override and when, so that your code executes at the proper time in the lifecycle of the controller. It will also help you understand the relationship between the UIViewController and UIView.

Let's take a look at the common UIViewController lifecycle methods.

LoadView

The LoadView method is called by the iOS when a controller's View property is requested, but is null.

You should only override this method if you're defining a custom UIView class in code, rather than in a .xib file that you've created in Interface Builder. As shown in Listing 5–1, LoadView should be used to load your custom UIView class onto the UIViewController.

One important distinction of the LoadView method is that, unlike the other lifecycle events, you should not call base.LoadView() in the override if you are replacing the default view with your own. You should call it, however, if you add your view as a subview, as we'll see in the "Managing More than One View in a Controller" section.

ViewDidLoad

ViewDidLoad is the single most common method to override in a UIViewController. It is called after the view has been initialized and loaded. It's called whether the view has been defined in Interface Builder (as a .xib file), or in code.

ViewDidLoad is where you should place any code that you want to run after the basic view stuff has been loaded. For instance, ViewDidLoad is a good place to add any subviews/controls to your view, wireup event handlers, populate your view with data, etc.

ViewDidUnload

ViewDidUnload is called whenever the view is unloaded. This can happen for a number of reasons:

- *View disposal:* If Dispose is called on the view, or any other time the view is unloaded

- *Low memory:* If the device is running low on memory, it may unload views that are not currently on the navigation stack or screen.

This method is extremely important in Objective-C iOS applications, where memory management is all manually done, but less important with MonoTouch applications because of the garbage collector.

With that said, however, you should override this method if you have resources referenced in association with your view that you want to unload or dereference.

ViewWillAppear

ViewWillAppear is called right before the view is going to become visible. Unlike ViewDidLoad, which only gets called when the view loads, ViewWillAppear will get called everytime the view is about to be presented. For instance, if your view controller is on a navigation stack, the view might go in and out of view, depending on if other views are loaded on top of it, or if yours pops off the stack. However, the view may not unload.

ViewWillAppear is especially useful to refresh any information on your view that might have changed when a user is viewing another screen/view. This applies equally to data on the view and other display tasks, such as orientation, status bar style, and navigation bar customization. Listing 5–5 illustrates hiding the navigation bar when a view appears.

Listing 5–5. *Hiding the Navigation Bar when a view appears*

```
public override void ViewWillAppear (bool animated)
{
        base.ViewWillAppear (animated);
        this.NavigationController.SetNavigationBarHidden (true, animated);
}
```

ViewWillDisappear

ViewWillDisappear is the corollary to ViewWillAppear. It is called every time the view is about to be removed from presentation or covered by another view. You should override this method to undo anything that you might have done to the display in ViewWillAppear. This is also a good method to save any changes that your user might have performed in the view. Listing 5–6 illustrates showing the navigation bar when a view disappears.

Listing 5–6. *Showing the Navigation Bar when a view disappears*

```
public override void ViewWillDisappear (bool animated)
{
        base.ViewWillDisappear (animated);
        this.NavigationController.SetNavigationBarHidden (false, animated);
}
```

Other Methods

In addition to the common methods mentioned here, there are more methods that occur in the UIViewController lifecycle. We'll cover a group of them related to orientation changes when a user rotates a device in the upcoming "Handling Rotation" section. The rest are documented in the UIViewController reference documentation provided by Apple. For the most part, you won't need to use them, except in advanced scenarios.

UIView Event Lifecycle

We've looked at the UIViewController lifecycle and its role in managing UIViews, so let's dig further into the UIView itself now. In addition to the constructor, there are really only two methods in UIView that we usually concern ourself with. They are:

- Draw
- LayoutSubviews

Constructor

In addition to iniatializing fields or data that you might need in your UIView, the constructor is also the correct place to initialize your view heirachy, if one exists.

Custom UIViews are often composed of many subviews. For example, you might create a custom UIView for displaying images that contains a UIImage and a UILabel, showing the caption. In that case, you would add your UIImage and UILabel to your view hierarchy by calling AddSubview from within the constructor.

Draw

The Draw method is called the first time the view is displayed, and anytime after that we tell the iOS that the view needs to be redrawn (by calling SetNeedsDisplay or SetNeedsDisplayInRect). We'll examine this in more detail in Chapter 16, when we discuss CoreGraphics. This is the only time that the iOS allows us direct access to the drawing surface of the view. For example, the code in Listing 5–7 draws the view background white.

Listing 5–7. *Overriding the Draw method in a UIView control to paint the background*

```
public override void Draw (System.Drawing.RectangleF rect)
{
        using (CGContext context = UIGraphics.GetCurrentContext ())
        {
                context.SetRGBFillColor (0.7f, 0.7f, 0.7f, 1f);
                context.FillRect (rect);
        }
        base.Draw (rect);
}
```

The Draw method can also be called at other times as well. For example, anytime the graphics subsystem decides the view is dirty (for instance, something has been drawn above it), iOS will call Draw.

LayoutSubviews

LayoutSubviews is a convenience method (the default base implementation doesn't do anything) that provides you with a known method for modifying the layout (size, location, etc.) of any subviews. It's not called unless you invoke the SetNeedsLayout method on the UIView.

If your view needs to change its layout depending on such alterations as orientation changes and size changes, then you should call the SetNeedsLayout method, which tells the OS to invoke this method when it is appropriate.

Managing More than One View in a Controller

So far we've seen a 1:1 correlation between controllers and views; that is, for every controller, we've had it manage a single view. This is a pretty common pattern, but a controller can actually manage multiple views without having a separate controller for each view. The opposite is not true, however; a single view can only be assigned to one controller. In fact, one of the approaches to handle device rotation is for a single controller to have a view for each orientation, and then switch views when the device rotates. We'll look at this more in a bit when we talk about handling rotation.

Switching Views

If we want to switch views, it's easy: simply set the View property on your controller class to the new UIView. There is a caveat to this, however; if you want to animate the transition between the views, as shown in Figure 5–1, it's a little more complex.

Figure 5–1. *Transitioning between views with a Flip animation*

The problem that arises is that the iOS will only automatically animate property changes to a view, rather than loading/unloading the view itself. To get around this, we have to add our initial view to the root view of the controller, rather than replace it, as shown in Listing 5–8.

Listing 5–8. *Adding a custom UIView as a subview on the root view*

```
public class MainViewController : UIViewController
{
        public override void LoadView ()
        {
                this.View.AddSubview (new MainViewOne (new RectangleF (new PointF (0, 0)
                , UIScreen.MainScreen.ApplicationFrame.Size)));
        }
}
```

You'll notice that we've done something a little different here. When we instantiate the view and pass it the frame, instead of passing the ApplicationFrame, as we did in Listing 5–1, we actually have to modify the origin to be 0,0. If we didn't do this, the view would actually be down farther than it shoud be, and we'd see a blank space the size of the status bar.

This is because the ApplicationFrame has an origin of (0, 20), or 20 points down from the top. It does this because the status bar is 20 points tall. When we add a view to another view, the origin is relative to the view that you're adding it to. So now, if we use the ApplicationFrame, we'd wind up with it putting our subview 20 points down relative to the root view.

Animating the Transition

To get this to animate, we wrap it in an animation block. We'll explore animation in much more detail later in Chapter 17, but animation blocks are very simple, as shown in Listing 5–9.

Listing 5–9. *Animating a subview transition*

```
protected void SwitchViews ()
{
        //---- begin an animation block
        UIView.BeginAnimations ("View Flip");
        UIView.SetAnimationDuration (1.25);
        UIView.SetAnimationCurve (UIViewAnimationCurve.EaseInOut);
        UIView.SetAnimationTransition (UIViewAnimationTransition.FlipFromRight,
        this.View, true);

        this.View.AddSubview (new MainViewTwo (new RectangleF (new PointF (0, 0)
                ,UIScreen.MainScreen.ApplicationFrame.Size)));

        //---- end our animation block
        UIView.CommitAnimations ();
}
```

When using an animation block, which simply call UIView.BeginAnimations, give it a name, then set up our animation properties such as the duration, the animation type, etc., then perform the operation that we want to animate, and finally, call UIView.CommitAnimation. The BeginAnimations and CommitAnimations calls simply tell the iOS that any applicable operations in between should be animated. For a working example of this, take a look at the Example_SwitchingViews companion sample application.

Handling Rotation

One of the nice features of the iPhone, iPod Touch, and the iPad is the inclusion of an accelerometer that tells the OS which way it's oriented in space (among other data). In turn, the OS then tells your application the device has been rotated.

You can see a simple example of this in the Safari Application, shown in Figure 5–2.

Figure 5–2. *The Safari application rotated with the iPhone*

It's your choice whether to build your app to rotate to match the device's orientation. Sometimes it makes sense to have the application support rotation, and sometimes it doesn't. It can be more work to support rotation, but it's generally a good idea if it makes sense for your application, because it can improve your user experience tremendously.

All devices have four distinct directions, starting with the home button at the bottom, and rotating clockwise, they are:

- Portrait
- LandscapeRight
- PortraitUpsideDown
- LandscapeLeft

While it's your choice whether or not you support both landscape and/or portrait mode, if you're creating an application that will run on the iPad, you must support both 180° versions of the particular format you support. For instance, if your app is intended to run only in portrait mode, you should support both Portrait and PortraitUpsideDown.

What orientations your application can support are configured in the project options under the iPhone Application tab, as seen in Figure 5–3.

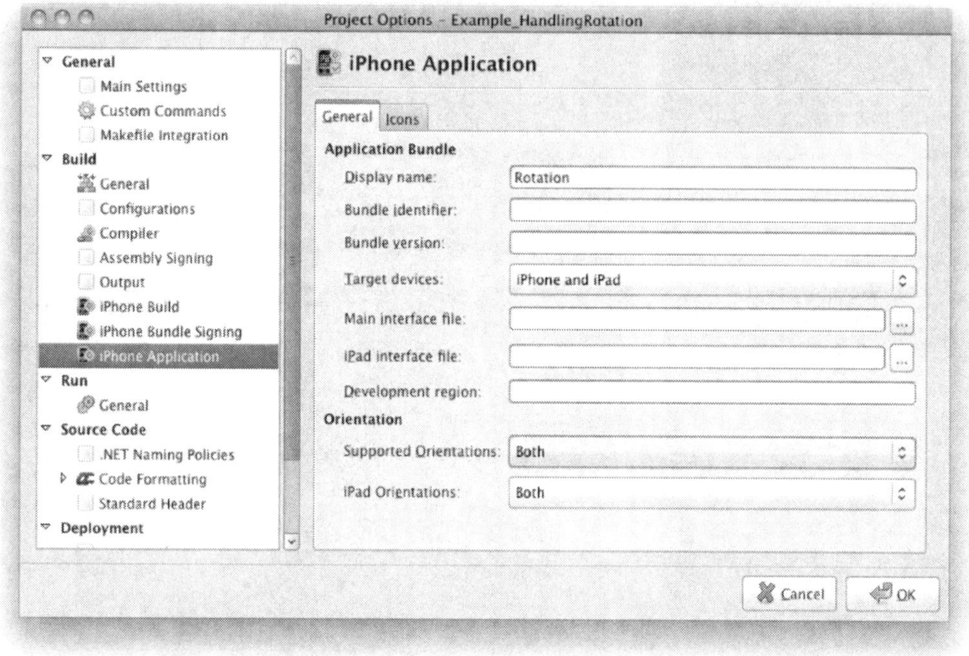

Figure 5–3. *Setting the supported orientations in project options*

Just setting the supported orientations in your project options, however, does not automatically mean that all the screens in your application support those orientations. It may not make sense for every screen to support all orientations. In fact, the OS asks every view controller in your application what orientations it supports. If you support more than just the standard profile view, you need to override the ShouldAutorotateToInterfaceOrientation method, which passes the orientation that the application is switching to, as shown in Listing 5–10.

Listing 5–10. *Specifying what view orientation your view controller supports*

```
public override bool ShouldAutorotateToInterfaceOrientation (UIInterfaceOrientation
toInterfaceOrientation)
{
        switch (toInterfaceOrientation)
        {
                case UIInterfaceOrientation.LandscapeLeft:
                case UIInterfaceOrientation.LandscapeRight:
                case UIInterfaceOrientation.Portrait:
                case UIInterfaceOrientation.PortraitUpsideDown:
                default:
                        return true;
        }
}
```

If you return true, then the OS will try and rotate your view when the device orientation changes to that orientation.

Rotation Lifecycle Events in UIViewController

There are five rotation specific lifecycle events in a UIViewController. Let's take a look at them.

ShouldAutorotateToInterfaceOrientation

As we illustrated in Figure 5–3, ShouldAutorotateToInterfaceOrientation is called by the iOS to determine whether or not your UIViewController supports a particular orientation. If you do not override this method, it assumes that the only orientation your controller supports is portrait mode.

WillAnimateRotation

WillAnimateRotation is where you perform your main rotation logic. It's called right before the iOS is going to perform the rotation and gives you an opportunity to move your controls around or perform any other logic you need to support the rotation of your view. The nice thing about WillAnimateRotation is that it's actually wrapped in an animation block, so you can reposition any controls in this method and they'll automatically move smoothly to their new location, as illustrated in Listing 5–11.

Listing 5–11. *Moving controls during rotation*

```
public override void WillAnimateRotation (UIInterfaceOrientation toInterfaceOrientation,
double duration)
{
        base.WillAnimateRotation (toInterfaceOrientation, duration);

        switch (toInterfaceOrientation)
        {
                //---- if we're switchign to landscape
                case UIInterfaceOrientation.LandscapeLeft:
                case UIInterfaceOrientation.LandscapeRight:
                        //---- reposition your controls
                        this._button1.Frame = new System.Drawing.RectangleF
                        (10, 10, 100, 33);
                        break;

                //---- if we're switching back to portrait
                case UIInterfaceOrientation.Portrait:
                case UIInterfaceOrientation.PortraitUpsideDown:
                        //---- reposition your controls
                        this._button1.Frame = new System.Drawing.RectangleF
                        (10, 10, 100, 33);
                        break;
        }
}
```

WillRotate

WillRotate is called before WillAnimateRotation and provides you with an opportunity to turn off or disable anything that might otherwise cause issues during the rotation animation. Unlike WillAnimateRotation, it is not wrapped in an animation block, so this is a good place to do any processing before you animation occurs.

DidRotate

DidRotate is the corollary to WillRotate. It is called after the rotation animation is perfomed and gives you an opportunity to undo anything that you did in the WillRotate method.

WillAnimateFirstHalfOfRotation and WillAnimateSecondHalfOfRotation

The WillAnimateRotation method was introduced in the 3.0 version of the iOS and provides us with a single method call to perform our rotation animation. Before that, we had to implement a two-step process that involved WillAnimateFirstHalfOfRotation and WillAnimateSecondHalfOfRotation. The new method is much more efficient, and therefore faster, however, if you're performing a specialized animation that requires multiple steps you need to use these two-step method calls.

General Approaches to Rotation

Now that you understand the lifecycle of device rotation, let's look at some general approaches to handling rotation. There are three basic ways to support interface rotation in your app, they are:

- Autosizing
- Moving controls
- Swapping views

Let's look at each of these approaches in detail.

Autosizing

The easiest way to handle rotation is to let your view and subviews (controls) do it for you. In the companion Example_HandlingRotation application, this is how the home screen handles rotation, as seen in Figure 5–4.

Figure 5–4. *Controls that are autosized for rotation*

To rotate the simulator, select **Hardware ➤ Rotate Left** or **Rotate Right** from the menu.

When the application rotates from portrait to landscape, the controls stay centered and expand to fill the screen. This is trivial to configure in Interface Builder, which gives you a lot of options for how you want to autosize your controls. To configure autosizing, select the control, and then, in the Size Inspector window, you can configure the relative position of your control, as well as how it autosizes, as shown in Figure 5–5.

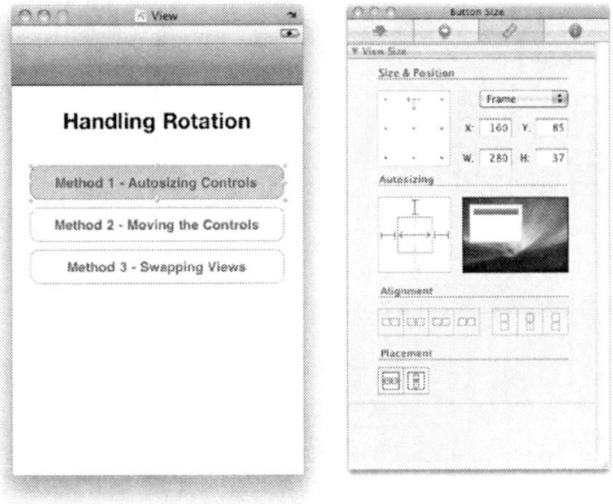

Figure 5–5. *Specifying Autosizing options.*

The Size & Position settings control where the control is anchored, and its initial size. The Autosizing settings control how the control resizes when the window changes size (as happens when the orientation changes). To change the orientation of the view, click the curved arrow at the top right of the designer. In our case, with the above settings, the landscape control positions are shown in Figure 5–6.

Figure 5–6. *Autosized controls after rotation to landscape*

Autosizing is particularly effective for screens where you have a single control that takes up the entire screen and handle resizing automatically, such as a UITableView, as shown in Figure 5–7.

Figure 5–7. *UITableView automatically autosizes*

The autosizing method, while being the easiest, however, is also the method of most limited use and really only works for the simplest of interfaces, as we'll see next.

Moving Controls

Autosizing is very easy to configure, but consider the example in Figure 5–8.

Figure 5–8. *Autosizing doesn't work for all interfaces*

As you can see, the portrait mode interface doesn't lend itself well to rotation without moving the controls around. It's a fairly common scenario to have to change the location of the controls in order to maintain an effective user interface. Consider Figure 5–9, which illustrates the same controls as before, but in a rotatable interface that moves the controls.

Figure 5–9. *Before and after moving controls*

As mentioned previously, the WillAnimateRotation method is the correct place to perform any repositioning of controls for rotation (see Figure 5–4). Because the WillAnimateRotation method is called from within the context of an animation block, your controls will reposition themselves with a smooth, cinematic animation.

Additionally, you should do a check during your ViewDidLoad method and position your controls appropriately based on what position the device is in when the view loads, as shown in Listing 5–12.

Listing 5–12. *Checking the orientation of the device when the view loads*

```
public override void ViewDidLoad ()
{
        base.ViewDidLoad ();

        switch (this.InterfaceOrientation)
        {
                case UIInterfaceOrientation.LandscapeLeft:
                case UIInterfaceOrientation.LandscapeRight:

                        //position your controls for landscape mode
                        ...
                        break;

                //---- we're switch back to portrait
                case UIInterfaceOrientation.Portrait:
                case UIInterfaceOrientation.PortraitUpsideDown:
```

```
                //position your controls for portrait mode
                ...
                break;
        }
}
```

Because this approach is animated, if you can't use autosizing, this should be your goto approach for handling rotation because it gives the smoothest user experience: something that iPhone and iPad users have come to expect.

Swapping Views

Sometimes, you might want to provide a completely different experience in portrait modes than in landscape modes. This is common in iPad applications where if a user changes their orientation, they're presented with a completely different set of options and/or interface.

It's also useful when repositioning controls is just too complex or tedious.

In these cases, it can be helpful to swap views entirely, when the device rotates. Consider Figure 5–10.

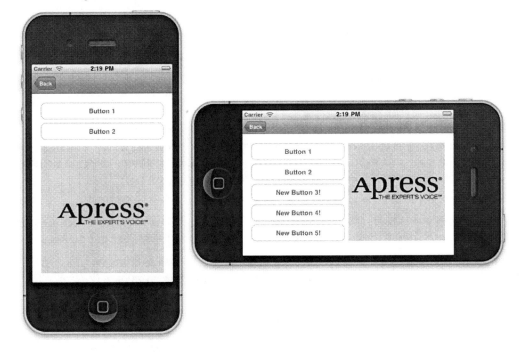

Figure 5–10. *Swapping views during rotation.*

While it would be possible to add those extra buttons programmatically, during the WillAnimateRotation method, it is far easier to simply define a different view, and then load that view when the device rotates.

Listing 5–13 illustrates loading different views (defined in xib files) based on the orientation of the device.

Listing 5–13. *Loading different views from an .xib file, based on the orientation*

```
public override void WillAnimateRotation (UIInterfaceOrientation toInterfaceOrientation,
double duration)
{
        base.WillAnimateRotation (toInterfaceOrientation, duration);

        switch (toInterfaceOrientation)
        {
                //---- if we're switchign to landscape
                case UIInterfaceOrientation.LandscapeLeft:
                case UIInterfaceOrientation.LandscapeRight:

                        NSBundle.MainBundle.LoadNib ("LandscapeView", this, null);

                        break;

                //---- we're switch back to portrait
                case UIInterfaceOrientation.Portrait:
                case UIInterfaceOrientation.PortraitUpsideDown:

                        NSBundle.MainBundle.LoadNib ("PortraitView", this, null);

                        break;
        }
}
```

We use the LoadNib method to load a UIView that has been defined in a xib file, and pass a reference to this (our controller) as the owner. If we're loading a view that has been defined in code, it's even easier: we can just instantiate it without having to do any special loading, as illustrated in the following code snippet:

```
this.View = new PortraitView();
```

While swapping views is an effective approach to handling device rotation, it presents an interesting problem: if the main view has changed, then so have all of our outlets.

There are a couple different ways to deal with this. If your interface changes significantly—that is, controls are added or removed—consider creating a controller for each orientation, and then use your main controller as a parent. That way each orientation has its own controller whereby you can handle view events, do processing, etc.

If your interface changes its layout, but doesn't change its controls, consider creating an Inteface that both views implement so that you can treat them the same in code. For example, if you create an interface called IMyScreen, and on that interface, define your controls, and then in your view, implement that interface, you can keep a class-level reference to your current view as IMyScreen and treat all of your different views the exact same way.

Rotation Review

You can see all three of these approaches to rotation in practice in the Example_HandlingRotation companion application. The approach that you take will necccessarily be the result of a decision based on different tradeoffs between coding simplicity, cinematic experience, and complexity of design. Table 5–1 sums up the pros and cons of each approach.

Table 5–1. *Different approaches to rotation*

Approach	General Use	Pros	Cons
Autosizing	Simple Interfaces	Easy to implement, requires no code, and provides a cinematic user experience	Only works on simple interfaces where controls don't have to move
Repositioning Controls	Moderate Interfaces	Provides a cinematic user experience, does not require complex outlet and action management.	Can be tedious to implement the moving of controls
Swapping Views	Complex/Multiple Interfaces	Only way to handle multiple views	Complex to implement; doesn't provide a cinematic experience

Summary

Whew, that was an intense chapter! There was a lot of stuff in there, and if you're just starting MonoTouch, you're not likely to soak it all in quite yet. As you work with Cocoa Touch more, however, you'll find the things you learned in here invaluable to understanding how to work with views and controllers in MonoTouch, and the theory will become practice. I recommend coming back to this chapter again later, as you become more familiar with building iOS applications, as a lot of the concepts covered here will make more sense.

This is the last chapter in Part 1 of the book. In the next section, we're going to start looking at individual controls and how to use them.

Chapter 6

Introduction to Controls

The concept of a control in MonoTouch is a funny one. In Windows frameworks such as WPF or ASP.NET, there is an actual `Control` class that all controls are derived from. Not so in MonoTouch/CocoaTouch. There is, in fact, a `UIControl` class, but not all controls actually inherit from it; some inherit directly from `UIView`.

In MonoTouch the term control is more conceptual, spanning views, controllers, and even plain old object classes. Ultimately, a control is just an encapsulated object that either displays stuff or manages stuff that gets displayed.

In this chapter, we're going to go through some various concepts that will help complete your understanding of using controls in MonoTouch. Some of these concepts will make more sense after actually using the controls, so it's recommended you take a quick read through this chapter, and then come back to it as a reference as you go through the next three chapters which cover specific controls.

Coordinate System

Many of the controls that you will use or create in MonoTouch are placed in specific locations in views in your application. When placing them, their location is based on a simple x, y Euclidean coordinate space. Each integer on the axis represents one point.

WHAT'S A POINT? Previous to the iPhone 4 (with the Retina Display), all coordinates were based on pixels, rather than points. However, because the Retina Display has a pixel density twice that of previous iPhone devices, a pixel has a different meaning between the iPhone 4 and older iPhone devices. To make things easier, Apple no longer uses the term pixel, and instead uses point, which is a device/resolution independent abstraction that maps 1:1 to pre-iPhone 4 device pixels. As we'll see in just a moment, points are specified by floats (they are represented by the System.Drawing.PointF class), which means that if you need pixel precision on the Retina Display, you can use decimal numbers, e.g. 0.5 to specify a single pixel in the Retina Display.

One caveat to the Euclidean coordinate space, however, is that instead of having the origin (0,0) at the bottom-left and the y-axis increasing as it goes up, the origin is actually at the top-left, and the y-axis increases as it goes down.

You can see this coordinate space in the following screen shot (Figure 6–1).

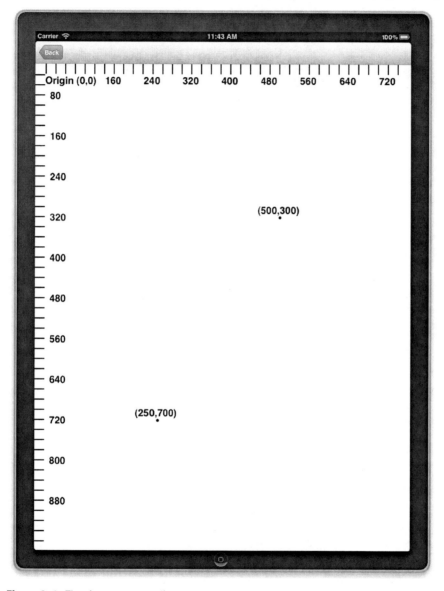

Figure 6–1. *The view-space coordinate system*

Frame

The location and size of controls is set via the `Frame` property, which takes a `RectangleF` object. Many controls take a `Frame` parameter in their constructor so you don't have to set it later. For example, the following code snippet (Listing 6–1) creates a `UILabel` control at the x,y coordinates of (20, 300), with a size of 280 points wide and 40 points tall.

Listing 6–1. *Instantiating a label and setting its frame*

```
this._customLabel = new UILabel (new RectangleF (20, 300, 280, 40));
```

Some controls, such as the `UIPickerView`, size themselves, so you can specify a `RectangleF.Empty` object as their initial `Frame`. This will allow you to not have to specify their size, and if you want to make changes to their location, later on, you can.

Autosizing

We looked at the autosizing stuff briefly in Chapter 5, when talking about handling rotation.

You can set autosizing properties in the **Size Inspector** window in Interface Builder under the **Autosizing** section, as shown in Figure 6–2.

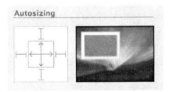

Figure 6–2. *Setting autosizing properties in Interface Builder*

You can click on the red lines to enable or disable the autosizing features. As you set them, the animation on the right will show you how your control will react when the view containing it is resized.

The red lines in the outer square represent the margins on the outside of the control. If they're enabled, the control will try to maintain a fixed margin to the respective side that is enabled.

The red lines in the inner square represent the size of the control. If they're enabled, the control will resize itself in the direction that's enabled.

You can also set these properties in code via the `AutoresizingMask` property on `UIView`. `AutoresizingMask` takes a bit mask that describes which autosizing attributes to apply. You can find the different options in the `UIViewAutoresizing` enumeration. Because it's a bit mask, you can apply several values at once; for example, the following code, shown in Listing 6–2, tells `myControl` that its top margin should be flexible, and that it can resize its width.

Listing 6–2. *Setting autosizing properties in code*

```
myControl.AutoresizingMask =
        UIViewAutoresizing.FlexibleTopMargin | UIViewAutoresizing.FlexibleWidth;
```

Working with Fonts

The iOS comes with quite a selection of high-quality fonts built in that you can choose from. To see a full selection, run the `Example_Fonts` companion application, which enumerates the entire list, as shown in Figure 6–3.

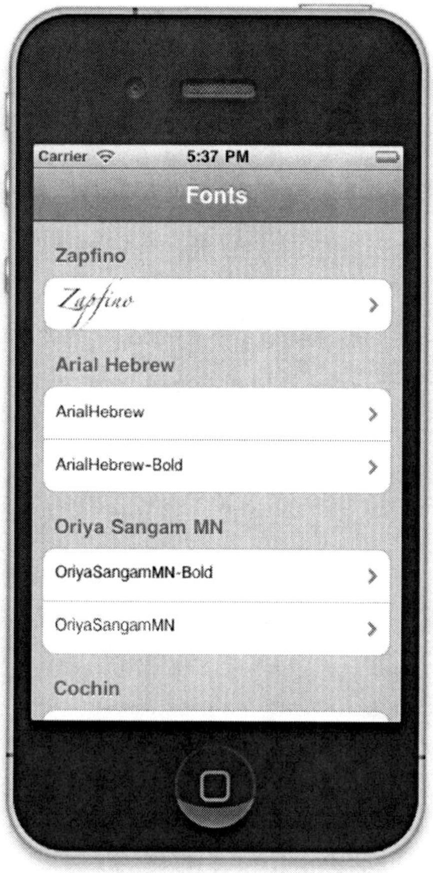

Figure 6–3. *Fonts in the iOS*

A font in MonoTouch is represented by the `UIFont` class, which encapsulates information such as font face, size, etc. `UIFont` objects are created via static factory methods on the `UIFont` class itself. If you want to create a `UIFont` from the default font-face, you can call `SystemFontOfSize` and pass in the size of the font you want. For example, the following code, shown in Listing 6–3, will create the default `UIFont` that's 20 points in height.

Listing 6–3. *Creating the default system font at 20 points in height*

```
UIFont myFont = UIFont.SystemFontOfSize (20);
```

Additionally, you can call `BoldSystemFontOfSize` to create a bold system font, or `ItalicSystemFontOfSize` to create the default italic font.

You can also create a font based on the name via the `FromName` method. For example, to create a 20 pixel high Helvetica-Bold font, you can make the following call (Listing 6–4).

Listing 6–4. *Creating a font from a known name*

```
UIFont myFont = UIFont.FromName ("Helvetica-Bold", 20);
```

Font Sizes

Font sizes are specified by the height of a line of text in points. `UIFont` includes a number of built-in properties that give you default font sizes:

- `SystemFontSize`: The default font size for normal text

- `SmallSystemFontSize`: The default font size for small text

- `ButtonFontSize`: The default font size for buttons

- `LabelFontSize`: The default font size for text labels

These properties return `float` values, so you can use these properties in place of specifying a specific float size. For example, the following code (Listing 6–5) creates a default font face at the default font size.

Listing 6–5. *Creating a default font with the default size*

```
UIFont myFont = UIFont.SystemFontOfSize (UIFont.SystemFontSize);
```

Enumerating Fonts

The font selection varies between devices, so you should make sure that a font is available before trying to use it.

Fonts are categorized by the family that they belong to. For example, the Helvetica family of fonts includes a normal version, a bold version, an oblique (italic) version, and a bold-oblique version. Each one of these font faces has a specific name. For example, the bold version of Helvetica is Helvetica-Bold.

You can enumerate through the font families via the `FamilyNames` property on the `UIFont` class, which returns a string array of every font-family available.

You can enumerate through the fonts in a given family via the `FontNamesForFamilyName` property on the `UIFont`, which takes a string parameter of the family name and returns a string array of each font face in that family.

To see this in action, check out the `Example_Fonts` companion application.

Tags

Unlike in traditional Windows UI frameworks such as WPF, ASP.NET, etc, controls don't have an ID property that you can use to identify them. Instead, the UIView class includes an integer property called Tag that allows you to give them an identifier. You can use this to identify controls that have been dynamically generated, such as cells in a table view.

Control States

Controls that inherit from UIControl have different states. Some states are the direct result of user interaction, such as touching a control, and other states are independent of interaction, such as being disabled.

The various control states are part of the UIControlState enum, and are as follows:

- Normal: The default state of the control, neither selected or highlighted, but enabled

- Highlighted: The state that a control is in during a touch. It exists to let users know they're touching the control. If a control is in this state, its Highlighted property will return true.

- Disabled: When a control is disabled, a user cannot interact with it. You can set a control to be disabled or enabled via the Enabled property.

- Selected: For many controls, this state isn't really implemented, meaning it does nothing. For those controls that do use it, you can access it via the Selected property.

For many controls, you can customize their behavior an appearance per state. For example, if you're using a UIButton, you can set the Title and other properties for each state. In Interface Builder there is a drop-down in the Attributes Inspector that lets you specify state configuration, as shown in Figure 6–4.

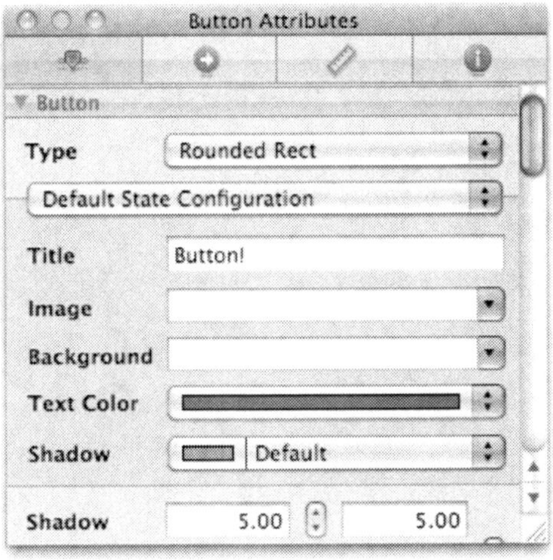

Figure 6–4. Attribute Inspector let's you specify control state properties on controls that support them.

You can also specify them programmatically, for example, the following code (Listing 6–6) sets the Title of a button for the Normal control state.

Listing 6–6. Setting button text programmatically

```
button.SetTitle ("My Button", UIControlState.Normal);
```

Control state is a bit flag, so you can also combine them to refer to more than one state, as shown in Listing 6–7.

Listing 6–7. Combining control state flags

```
button.SetTitle ("My Button", UIControlState.Normal | UIControlState.Disabled);
```

If you don't explicitly a property for a state, the property value from the Normal state is used by default.

Working with Images

It's common to need to customize your interface by displaying images from your project to it. Most of the time this means loading the image and setting it to the Image property (or similar) to a control. This necessitates creating a UIImage object that contains your image.

In order to do this, the UIImage class has two static factory methods, FromFile and FromBundle that can load your image directly from the filesystem. FromFile and FromBundle both take a path to your image but work slightly different, as we'll see in a moment.

When loading files (including images) from your application, you reference them via the same path as they are in your project. For example, if you wanted to load the Lightning_Small.png image from the project, as shown in the following screenshot (Figure 6–5), you would load it via the Images/Lightning_Small.png path.

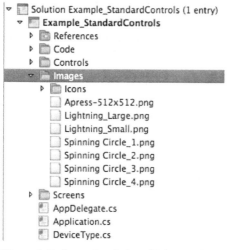

Figure 6–5. *A sample solution with images in it*

For example, the following code (Listing 6–8) uses the FromFile method to do just that.

Listing 6–8. *Loading an image from file*

```
UIImage myImage = UIImage.FromFile("Images/Lightning_Small.png");
```

With that said, there are a couple of gotchas to know:

- **Do not name your folder "Resources":** This causes havoc with CocoaTouch (it's actually banned by the iOS) and your items in that folder won't actually be accessible. Your application might even crash.

- **The device is case-sensitive:** However, the simulator is not. So if you're not careful to watch your case when loading resources, it may work in the simulator but fail in the device.

- **Build Action must be marked as content:** When you add a resource that you want to use within your project such as an image, you must set the Build Action to be Content. You can set this during the add files dialog, or after the file has been added by right-clicking on the file and choosing Build Action ➤ Content.

- **Images don't show up in Interface Builder:** When you set the path to an image in Interface Builder, the image won't show up. This, unfortunately, is a MonoTouch limitation and may be fixed in a later release.

FromFile vs. FromBundle

As mentioned before, there are two standard ways to load an image from a file — FromFile and FromBundle. They are both very similar, but work slightly differently.

FromBundle

FromBundle is a synchronous call that will block the thread while it loads an image. Once loaded, the image is cached by the iOS. This means that if you call FromBundle again, with the same image path, it will pull the image from cache rather than disk.

FromBundle also has a little magic up its sleeve. The iPhone 4G has a screen resolution twice that of the earlier iPhones. To take advantage of the higher resolution, when your application is running on the iPhone 4G, it should use images that are twice the resolution of images used on the older iPhones. However, to do a check every time and load the appropriately sized image would be tedious. Because of this, you can include images in your application that have an @2x name suffix, and FromBundle will automatically load those images if it's being called while on the iPhone 4G. For example, you might have two images that have the same content but different sizes called MyImage.png and MyImage@2x.png.

With all that said, FromBundle has some definite drawbacks.

- First, it caches the images that are loaded, but it doesn't have proper cache management and won't clear images, so it can retain them in memory even after you're finished using them. Many iPhone developers have seen this actually crash their apps because of low memory availability.

- Second, because it's a synchronous (blocking) call, calling it many times at once can significantly slow down your application, especially if you load many at once.

- Third, it can only load images that are contained within your application's sandbox, so if content is stored elsewhere, it cannot access it.

FromFile

Unlike FromBundle, FromFile is an asynchronous, lazy-loading call that won't actually load the image until it is requested, such as when it is needs to be displayed. Additionally, it can load files outside of the application sandbox.

As with FromBundle, FromFile includes some drawbacks.

- First, it doesn't cache images, so additional loads of the same image will still incur a disk-read hit.

- Second, it doesn't include any of the @2x file name magic of FromBundle.

Which One?

Generally, you should use FromFile if you need to load many images at once because of its lazy-loading method. You should use FromBundle if you need to reuse the same image over and over.

If you want to use the @2x suffix that is automatic in FromBundle, but you need to load many images, you should use FromFile instead but add code to do a device check and load the appropriate file based on that.

Subclassing (Creating Custom Controls)

If you've been reading the book up this point, you actually already know a lot about subclassing to create custom controls. Whenever you inherit from UIView or UIViewController, you've subclassed them to perform custom functionality.

There are a couple of things to keep in mind when creating custom controls, however.

Necessary Constructors

In addition to your own constructors that you might want to put on a control, if your control is going to be initialized from a xib file, you need an additional constructor:

Listing 6–9. *NSCoder constructor needed by the Objective-C runtime.*

```
public Foo (NSCoder coder)
```

This constructor is called by the runtime when your control is instantiated from a xib file.

Registering Your Controls

When creating controls and/or classes that need to be used in Interface Builder, you need to register them to be visible to the Objective-C runtime. MonoTouch includes the MonoTouch.Foundation.Register attribute that allows you to give your class an Objective-C visible name. For example, the following code registers the TapZoomScrollView control that is in the Example_StandardControls companion code (Listing 6–10).

Listing 6–10. *Using the Register attribute to make a class visible to the Objective-C runtime*

```
[MonoTouch.Foundation.Register("TapZoomScrollView")]
public class TapZoomScrollView : UIScrollView
{
        // implementation
}
```

Using Your Controls in Interface Builder

If you create a control that inherits from UIView, UIController, or one of the existing controls in the Library window in Interface Builder, such as a UIButton, UILabel, etc., you can use your control in place of the control that you inherited from. Interface Builder is very primitive though, so unlike in traditional Microsoft .NET frameworks such as WPF, there is no provision for giving you any real design time control, other than what's already there for the base control.

To use a custom control, drag the base control (such as a UIView or a UIButton) to the design surface, and then in the **Class** specifier in the **Identity Inspector** window, set your custom control name. For example, in the following screenshot, I have a custom control that inherits from UIView called RoundRectangleGroupView. To use it, I've drug a UIView onto the Designer, and then in the Inspector window, I've set its class name, as shown in Figure 6–6.

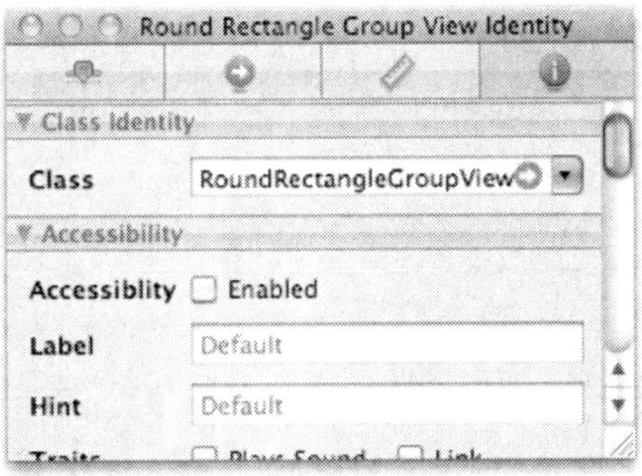

Figure 6–6. *Using a custom control in Interface Builder*

In the Design window, the view just shows up as a normal view, but when I run it on the device or the simulator, I see my customizations.

Prototypes vs. Delegates vs. Events, What?

Objective-C and CocoaTouch have very different conventions for handling user interaction and databinding than traditional .NET models. For example, when binding to a DataGrid in ASP.NET, you set the DataSource property and as long as the data source implements IEnumerable, the grid does the work for you. When a user selects a row, the grid raises an event telling you which row was selected.

In CocoaTouch it's a bit different. For example, if you're working with a table, you assign a data source to your table, but the table calls methods on your data source asking to know how many items are in there, how to build each cell, etc. When a user selects a row on the table, instead of raising an event that you handle, you assign a special class on the table that it calls a method on to let you know that a row is selected. Because of this model, your data source in CocoaTouch has to conform to each type of control that it's binding to. For this reason, the data source takes on a different meaning, and instead of simply holding data, it is actually an engine that knows how to perform databinding. Typically you assign a model (your data) to your data source in CocoaTouch so that it can bridge the gap between just containing data and actually knowing how to databind.

MonoTouch has tried to bridge this gap by preserving the Apple way of doing things while also providing .NET like methods as well. As such, there are several different ways to work with controls.

Protocols

In Objective-C programming, you'll hear a lot about Protocols. In Apple's world, a protocol is similar to an interface in .NET. A protocol defines a contract whereby the caller knows that certain methods will exist on a class that conforms to the contract or interface. For example, you might define an interface, Iperson, that has the following method:

```
Run(int howFar)
```

The difference is, with Apple's API, the methods on a protocol are actually optional. If the runtime doesn't find the Run method, it doesn't matter; the runtime just won't call it.

This raises an interesting problem though; if you're implementing a protocol in MonoTouch, the Objective-C runtime needs to be able to "see" your methods. However, because the iOS doesn't have any intrinsic knowledge of C#, your methods aren't visible to iOS the way they would be if you were writing Objective-C code.

In order to make your methods visible to the underlying Objective-C runtime, you must register them by decorating them the MonoTouch.Foundation.Export attribute. For example, the following code, shown in Listing 6–11, exports a DoSomeRunning method as the Run method to the Objective-C runtime.

Listing 6–11. *Using the Export attribute to make a method visible to the Objective-C runtime*

```
[Export ("Run")]
public void DoSomeRunning(int howFarToRun) {…}
```

Notice that the C# method name doesn't match the exported method name. You can name your method whatever you want, as long as you export it with the method that the runtime expects.

Delegates

Marking all your methods with the Export attribute can be pretty tedious. For one thing, you'd have to know exactly what the method name was that the runtime expects, and second, you'd have to know what the signatures looked like.

MonoTouch tries to make this a bit easier on us by providing strongly typed delegate base classes that already have these methods and their respective Export attributes on them.

To use them, we simply write a class that derives from the appropriate base delegate class, override the methods that we care about, and assign our class to the delegate property of whatever class that needs it.

One of the nice things about this is that, if we're in MonoDevelop, we simply type override in our class that derives from the delegate, and it gives us autocomplete, with options for whatever method we want to override. That way we don't have to remember all the methods and their signatures!

> **NOTE:** When overriding strongly typed delegate class methods, you shouldn't call the base implementations. For example, if you're overriding the `GetView` method, you shouldn't call `base.GetView()` in the overridden `GetView` implementation.

Weak-Delegates

You don't have to use a strongly typed delegates that MonoTouch gives you. You can write your own custom delegate classes and then decorate them with the `Export` attribute on methods you want to expose to handle callbacks. To do this, simply create your class, mark your methods using the `Export` attribute, and then set your custom class to the `WeakDelegate` property of whatever class expects a delegate. For more information, see: `http://monotouch.net/Documentation/API_Design.rf`

When doing things this way, you will need to know the exact name that the runtime expects. Luckily, Miguel de Icaza, the founder of Mono (and MonoTouch) keeps a Rosetta stone updated online that maps between the MonoTouch methods (used on the strongly-typed delegates) and the methods that Apple uses. You can find it here: `http://tirania.org/tmp/rosetta.html`.

> **NOTE:** Apple's "methods" are actually called `selectors` because Objective-C is a message-based language, whereby you pass messages around, rather than call methods. When you use the selector names, you must use the entire string, including the trailing colons (if present). For instance, the following `Export` declaration, shown in Listing 6–12, is correct for the `titleForHeaderInSection` selector that is called by a `UITableView` to get the header text for a row.

Listing 6–12. *When exporting, the selector name must match exactly, including colons.*

```
[Export("tableView:titleForHeaderInSection:")]
protected string GetTitleForHeader(UITableView tableView, int section) {…}
```

Updating Your Controls from the UI Thread

Often times you will find yourself performing long-running operations and separate threads, so that you can keep the UI responsive. For instance, let's say you're writing a newsreader application that pulls down feeds from the Internet. You may want to do that on a background thread so that the user can view or interact with other screens in your application, or you may want to populate the news items as they come in.

This is all well and good until you need to update your UI from those threads. A problem could arise whereby two background processes try to update the UI thread at the same time, or maybe, a background process tries to update the UI while the UI is performing an action. This can cause a thread-lock and an application crash. In the best case, the MonoTouch runtime will actually give you a runtime cross-threading exception telling you that you shouldn't update the UI from a background thread, but you may not even get the courtesy of that: MonoTouch might simply crash with a nonsensical error.

Because of this, you should always update your UI from the main thread (also known as the UI thread). But how do you do that? Well, just like WPF or Winforms development, MonoTouch provides a method to do just that. It's called InvokeOnMainThread and it's available on the UIView class. To use InvokeOnMainThread, simply pass a delegate (or a lambda, or an anonymous method) to it that should run on the main UI thread. The iOS will then queue and run that method as soon as it has a free moment.

For example, the following method (Listing 6–13) is pulled from the ActivityIndicatorAlertView class in the Example_StandardControls companion application.

Listing 6–13. *Invoking a method on the main UI thread*

```
public void Hide (bool animated)
{
        this.InvokeOnMainThread (delegate {
                this.DismissWithClickedButtonIndex (0, animated);
        });
}
```

The ActivityIndicatorAlertView is a custom alert view that shows a spinning activity indicator. It's intended to be shown while a background process is running, and then dismissed from that background process when it's completed its work. Because the background process may be on a different thread, the Hide method makes sure that the alert view is dismissed on the UI thread.

> **NOTE:** You can also use BeginInvokeOnMainThread if you want to make an asynchronous invocation on the main thread. However, unlike the BeginInvoke/EndInvoke pattern in normal .NET programming, there is no underlying support for invocation completion notifications, therefore there is no EndInvorkeOnMainThread or similar.

Summary

This chapter introduced you to controls and gives you some foundation knowledge for working with them, but a lot of the concepts and information in here will make much more sense after you've worked with the controls for a bit. In the next few chapters we'll do just that: we're going to explore nearly every control in CocoaTouch.

Chapter 7

Standard Controls

Building for iOS devices is very different from building traditional desktop or web applications. Users have come to expect a very specific set of interaction metaphors associated with their user experience on the devices. The iOS ships with a number of applications that utilize a common set of controls that users have become very familiar with.

These controls are built with the form factor and the touch metaphor in mind as first-class design considerations. As such, they're different than the standard set of controls available for desktop and web applications.

Most of these controls are included in CocoaTouch's UIKit (aka the `MonoTouch.UIKit` namespace). These controls should be your first choice for creating your application's interface. This will help your application conform to Apple's *Human Interface Guidelines* and make your application feel familiar and understandable.

In this chapter, we're going to look at many of the controls in the UIKit, including:

- `UILabel`
- `UIButton`
- `UIImage`
- `UITextField`
- `UIScrollView`
- `UISegmentedControl`
- `UISwitch`
- `UISlider`
- `UIActivityIndicatorView`
- `UIProgressView`
- `UIPageControl`
- `UIAlertView`
- `UIActionSheet`

- UIDatePicker
- UIPickerView
- UIToolbar

We'll go through each one of these and look at the basic mechanism of usage, plus many of the common advanced scenarios for them. By the end of this chapter, you will have a solid understanding of each one of these, and know how to customize them.

All samples in this chapter are in the Example_StandardControls companion application and code.

UILabel

If you've made it this far in this book, you're already familiar with the UILabel control. The UILabel control displays read-only text for user. A number of label styles are shown in the following screen shot (Figure 7–1).

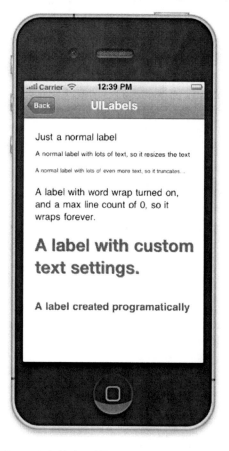

Figure 7–1. *Various UILabel styles*

The UILabel comes with a number of different of customizable properties that change its behavior and appearance.

Text Wrapping Options

UILabel has a property called AdjustFontSizeToWidth which has a default value of true—when the text doesn't fit within the given label space, the text is reduced down to the MinimumFontSize setting and then truncated after that. There are other options, however, that can be set via the LineBreakMode property:

- WordWrap: The text wraps to the next line, breaking in between words.

- CharacterWrap: Same as WordWrap, but the line breaks at individual characters, rather than keeping words together.

- Clip: This cuts off the rendering when the text runs out of space. If it clips where a character is, it will render a partial character.

- HeadTruncation: Truncate the text at the beginning and add an ellipsis in its place.

- MiddleTruncation: Same as HeadTruncation, but truncates the middle of the text.

- TailTruncation: Same as other truncation options, but at the end of the text.

Number of Lines

The UILabel control exposes a property called NumberOfLines that specifies how many lines the label should display. If you want unlimited lines, set it to 0.

UITextField

UITextField is a common control that you're no doubt familiar from other programming environments. It provides a single-line, user-editable text field and is useful for text input, as shown in Figure 7–2.

Figure 7–2. *Various UITextFields with a standard keyboard open*

UITextField derives from UIScrollView, so it includes scrolling functionality as a built-in feature.

Borders

There are a few different border styles for the UITextField:

- RoundedRect: This is the default style and is illustrated in Figure 7–2 in the first text field.

- Line: Line renders a single pixel-thick border around the text field, as illustrated in the second text field in Figure 7–2.

- None: None renders a text field with no border, as illustrated in the third text field in Figure 7–3.

- Bezel: Bezel renders a text field that looks a little like old-school windows controls, as shown in the fourth text field in Figure 7–4.

Text Value

You can get and set the text in the UITextField via the Text property.

Default Placeholder Text

You can specify text that shows up in the text field until a user selects the text field with the PlaceHolder property. This text does not show up in the Text property.

Keyboards

When a user selects a text field to edit, an onscreen keyboard may appear (in iPads, you can use an external keyboard instead, and choose not to show the on-screen one). There are several different types of keyboards, and working with them is discussed in the "Working with Keyboards" chapter (Chapter 10).

UIButton

The button control is an extremely common control that you'll find in a lot of UI frameworks on different platforms. However, the UIButton control has been designed specifically for the iOS, and as such, is slightly different.

Handling 'Clicks'

Instead of having a Click metaphor that is associated with having a mouse input, UIButton exposes touch events. The most common one, and the one you should use to handle "clicks," is called TouchUpInside. TouchUpInside is called when a user touches a button and then releases the touch while still on the button. This allows users to cancel accidental button presses by sliding their finger off and then releasing.

The following code (Listing 7–1) shows an alert popup when a button's TouchUpInside event is raised.

Listing 7–1. *Displaying an alert when a user touches a button*

```
this.btnTwo.TouchUpInside += delegate {
        new UIAlertView ("button two click!", "TouchUpInside Handled", null
                , "OK", null).Show ();
};
```

As per the Apple *Human Interface Guidelines*, nearly all of your button usage should be based on the TouchUpInside event.

Different Types of Buttons

There are a number of different button types, as illustrated in Figure 7–3.

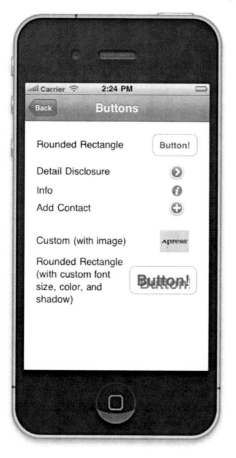

Figure 7–3. *Different types of UIButton controls*

The button type is specified during instantiation. For example, to create a rounded rectangle button, you call the FromType static method on a UIButton class as follows (Listing 7–2).

Listing 7–2. *Creating a rounded rectangle button*

```
UIButton button = UIButton.FromType (UIButtonType.RoundedRect);
```

In Interface Builder, you can specify the type of button in the Type setting on the Attributes Inspector, as shown in Figure 7–4.

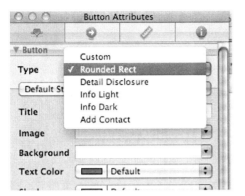

Figure 7–4. *Specifying a rounded rectangle button in Interface Builder*

Button Text

As mentioned in Chapter 6, buttons have multiple states. In order to set the text for a button, you have to set it for a particular state. For example, the following sets the normal text of a button to "MyButton" via the SetTitle method (Listing 7–3).

Listing 7–3. *Setting button text programmatically*

```
button.SetTitle ("My Button", UIControlState.Normal);
```

The Normal state settings are used for any states not explicitly defined.

UIImage

The UIImage control is another familiar control for applications developers. It is just a container control that displays an image (Figure 7–5).

Figure 7–5. *A UIImage control taking up the entire view*

In Interface Builder you can set the image it displays in the Image property, as shown in Figure 7–6.

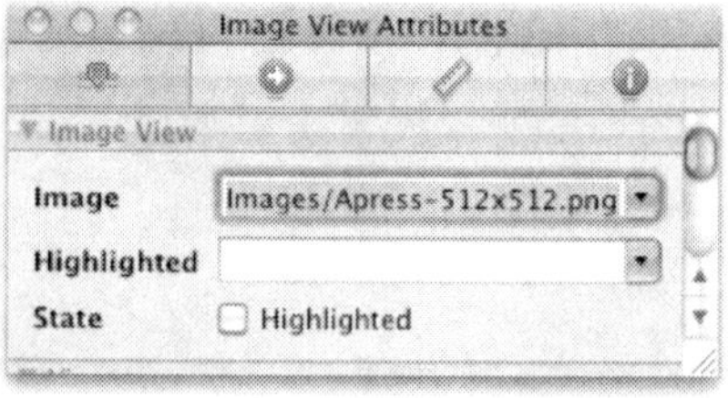

Figure 7–6. *Setting the image to display in Interface Builder*

You can also create image views and assign images to them programmatically. The following code, shown in Listing 7–4, creates an image view control from a UIImage that we load directly from the file system.

Listing 7–4. *Creating an image view in code*

```
this._imageView1 = new UIImageView(
        UIImage. FromBundle ("Images/Icons/Apress-50x50.png"));
this._imageView1.Frame = new RectangleF(
        20, 20, this._imageView1.Image.CGImage.Width
        , this._imageView1.Image.CGImage.Height);
this.View.AddSubview(this._imageView1);
```

> **NOTE**: iOS provides a way to load different images, depending on the current device. This is especially helpful in dealing with the different resolutions of different devices. I covered this extensively in the previous chapter, so if you've missed it, I recommend reviewing the section on Images.

Animating an Image View

One cool thing about the image view is that that you can animate it by providing it an array of UIImage objects on the AnimationImages property and then calling StartAnimating. You can also specify how many times to repeat the animation via the AnimationRepeatCount property (use 0 for endless animation), and the duration of time it takes to cycle through all the images via the AnimationDuration property.

Unfortunately, however, you must set all of the animation properties programmatically, as there is no way to set them in Interface Builder. The following code, shown in Listing 7–5, creates a UIImageView that cycles through four images every half a second, endlessly:

Listing 7–5. *Creating an image view that animates by cycling through a sequence of images*

```
this._imgSpinningCircle = new UIImageView();
this._imgSpinningCircle.AnimationImages = new UIImage[] {
        UIImage.FromBundle ("Images/Spinning Circle_1.png")
        , UIImage.FromBundle ("Images/Spinning Circle_2.png")
        , UIImage.FromBundle ("Images/Spinning Circle_3.png")
        , UIImage.FromBundle ("Images/Spinning Circle_4.png")
};
this._imgSpinningCircle.AnimationRepeatCount = 0;
this._imgSpinningCircle.AnimationDuration = .5;
this._imgSpinningCircle.Frame = new RectangleF(150, 20, 100, 100);
this.View.AddSubview(this._imgSpinningCircle);
this._imgSpinningCircle.StartAnimating ();
```

To see this code in action, checkout the Example_StandardControls companion code.

UIScrollView

The UIScrollView control is a wrapper control that is used to contain views that have content larger than the viewable area and therefore need scrolling functionality to be able to view all of the content.

Additionally it includes functionality for zooming in and zooming out via the pinch-to-zoom gesture multi-touch gesture that the iOS is famous for.

The UIScrollView is the basis for both the UITableView and the UITextView, since both of them need scrolling as a first-class feature.

To use a scroll view, simply add it to your view, and then add the view that needs scrolling to it. Then, set the ContentSize property to be whatever size your content area is.

For example, the code shown in Listing 7–6 creates a scroll view, adds it to the main view on a controller, and then adds an image view to the scroll view.

Listing 7–6. *Using a UIScrollView to show an image*

```
//---- create our scroll view
this._scrollView = new UIScrollView (
        new RectangleF (0, 0, this.View.Frame.Width, this.View.Frame.Height -
this.NavigationController.NavigationBar.Frame.Height));
this.View.AddSubview (this._scrollView);

//---- create our image view
this._imageView = new UIImageView (UIImage.FromFile ("Images/Apress-512x512.png"));
this._scrollView.ContentSize = this._imageView.Image.Size;
this._scrollView.AddSubview (this._imageView);
```

Enabling scrolling is easy. You simply have to set the ContentSize property to be larger than the Frame size of the scroll view and scrolling will be automatically enabled. In the previous code example, we have an image that is larger than the scroll view, so the following code line (Listing 7–7) does just that.

Listing 7–7. *As long as the ContentSize is larger than the frame size, UIScrollView will automatically provide scrolling.*

```
this._scrollView.ContentSize = this._imageView.Image.Size;
```

Zooming

If you want zooming to work, you must implement ViewForZoomingInScrollView callback and return the view to zoom. For example, the code in Listing 7–8 tells our scroll view control from the previous code sample that, when a user tries to zoom, it should zoom in (or out) on the image view it contains.

Listing 7–8. *Implementing the ViewForZoomingInScrollView callback method*

```
this._scrollView.ViewForZoomingInScrollView += delegate(UIScrollView scrollView) {
        return this._imageView;
};
```

Additionally, you also have to set the MaximumZoomScale and a MinimumZoomScale properties so it knows how much it can zoom in or out (Listing 7–9).

Listing 7–9. *Setting zoom limits on a scroll view*

```
this._scrollView.MaximumZoomScale = 3f;
this._scrollView.MinimumZoomScale = .1f;
```

Implementing Tap-to-Zoom

The tap-to-zoom feature—where a user double taps with a finger on something to get it to zoom—in is not enabled by default by the scroll view, but it's not difficult to implement. You simply need to sublass (inherit from) UIScrollView, override the TouchesBegan method, and when a user taps twice, call SetZoomScale on the scroll view. The scroll view will then call your ViewForZoomingInScrollView method to try and zoom your view.

The following code, shown in Listing 7–10, is a complete tap-to-zoom scroll class that you can use in place of the standard UIScrollView control.

Listing 7–10. *Implementing tap-to-zoom*

```
[MonoTouch.Foundation.Register("TapZoomScrollView")]
public class TapZoomScrollView : UIScrollView
{
        public TapZoomScrollView (IntPtr handle) : base(handle) { }
        [Export("initWithCoder:")]
        public TapZoomScrollView (NSCoder coder) : base(coder) { }
        public TapZoomScrollView () { }
        public TapZoomScrollView (RectangleF frame) : base(frame) { }

        public override void TouchesBegan (MonoTouch.Foundation.NSSet touches
                , UIEvent evt)
        {
                base.TouchesBegan (touches, evt);
                UITouch touch = touches.AnyObject as UITouch;
                if (touch.TapCount == 2)
                {
                        if (this.ZoomScale >= 2)
                        {
                                this.SetZoomScale(1, true);
                        }
                        else
                        {
                                this.SetZoomScale(3, true);
                        }
                }
        }
}
```

To change the amount of zoom, simply change the SetZoomScale(3, true) call and pass in a different value for the amount to zoom.

Scroll Paging

The scroll view control has a property called PagingEnabled, that when set to true 'snaps' the scrolling to stop at each page of content. A page of content is defined as the viewable space without scrolling, e.g., the scroll's frame size.

Enabling paging is cool on its own, but is extremely useful when used in conjunction with the UIPagerControl, as we'll see later in this chapter.

UISegmentedControl

The segmented control is a connected set of buttons that, by default, act kind of like a set of radio buttons. When you select one button in the group, the other buttons become unselected. The segmented control is useful for when you want your users to select between a small number of items. It comes in a number of styles, as shown in Figure 7–7.

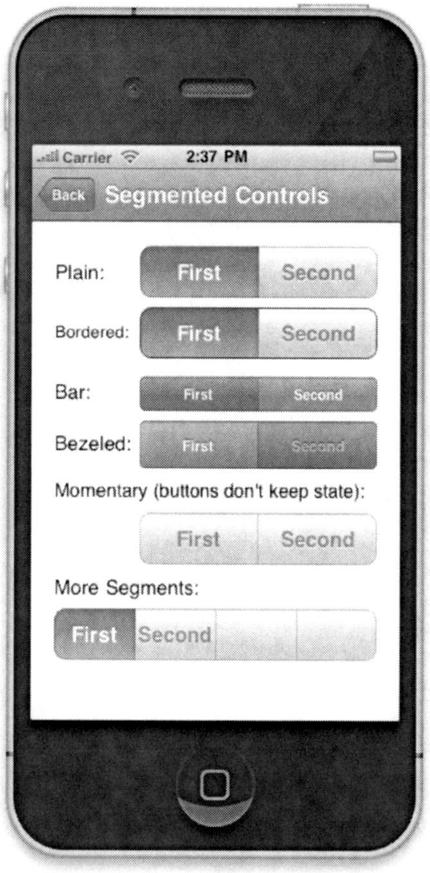

Figure 7–7. *Various segmented control styles and configurations*

In addition to switching between the set of buttons, the segmented control exposes a property called Momentary that makes the segmented control not track state, such that they simply act like buttons. If you set Momentary = false, when you click on one, it doesn't stay selected.

Configuring the Segmented Control

Configuring the segment control is very easy in Interface Builder—it even gives you a drop-down in which you can configure each segment individually, specifying the Title, Image, whether or not it is selected by default, etc., as shown in Figure 7–8.

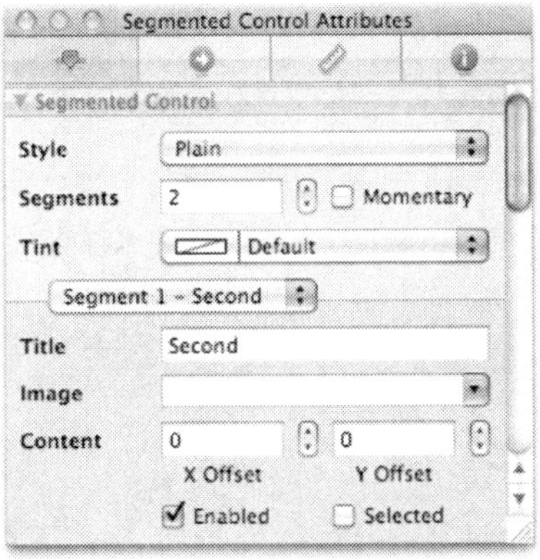

Figure 7–8. *Interface Builder makes configuring a segmented control a snap.*

You can also create and configure segmented controls programmatically. For example, the following code (Listing 7–11) creates a bordered segmented control with two segments.

Listing 7–11. *Creating a segmented control programmatically*

```
this._segControl1 = new UISegmentedControl ();
this._segControl1.ControlStyle = UISegmentedControlStyle.Bordered;
this._segControl1.InsertSegment ("One", 0, false);
this._segControl1.InsertSegment ("Two", 1, false);
this._segControl1.SelectedSegment = 1;
this._segControl1.Frame = new System.Drawing.RectangleF (20, 20, 280, 44);
this.View.AddSubview (this._segControl1);
```

The ControlStyle property sets the style of the segmented control, InsertSegment allows you to add segments at specific locations (you can animate their appearance as well), and SelectedSegment specifies which segment should start out as selected.

Specifying Segment Sizes

When you create a segmented control, by default each button is automatically sized to be of an equal width; however, you can specify sizes for specific buttons, if you want. In Interface Builder, the Size Inspector provides a drop-down in which you can select your segment and set the size, as shown in Figure 7–9.

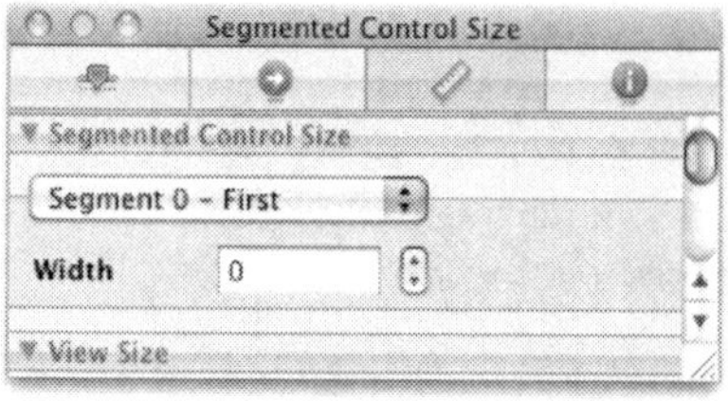

Figure 7–9. *Setting the size of a segment in Interface Builder*

You can also set the width of a segment programmatically via the SetWidth method, which takes a size and the segment index number to specify the size for. For example, to set the second segment (index of 1, because it starts at 0) to be 100 points, you would call the following, shown in Listing 7–12.

Listing 7–12. *Setting the size of a segment programmatically*

```
mySegementedControl.SetWidth (100f, 1);
```

Handling Button Presses

Because the segmented control is a set of connected buttons, to listen for button press, you handle the ValueChanged event and check the SelectedSegment property to determine which button is selected. For example, the following code (Listing 7–13) listens for the button press on a segmented control called _segControl1, and then writes to the console (the Application Output window in MonoDevelop) the segment that was selected.

Listing 7–13. *Handling the ValueChanged event on a segmented control*

```
this._segControl1.ValueChanged += delegate(object sender, EventArgs e) {
        Console.WriteLine ("Item " + (sender as
                UISegmentedControl).SelectedSegment.ToString () + " selected");
};
```

UISwitch

The UISwitch is the iOS equivalent to a check box. It provides a Boolean on/off switch, as shown in Figure 7–10.

Figure 7–10. *UISwitch in the off and on positions*

The current Boolean on/off value can be accessed via the On property, and you can listen for changes on the ValueChanged event. For example, the code shown in Listing 7–14 shows an alert when the switch is changed, and shows the current on/off value.

Listing 7–14. *Listening for a UISwitch change event and displaying the on/off value*

```
this.swchOne.ValueChanged += delegate {
        new UIAlertView ("Switch one change!", "is on: " + this.swchOne.On.ToString (),
                null, "OK", null).Show ();
};
```

UISlider

The slider control provides a mechanism for users to select a numerical value in between two limits. The nice thing about the slider is that it gives a very analog feeling while modifying stuff.

By default, the slider has a plain look, which is essentially a progress bar with a slide button on top, but you can also customize it with images (Figure 7–11).

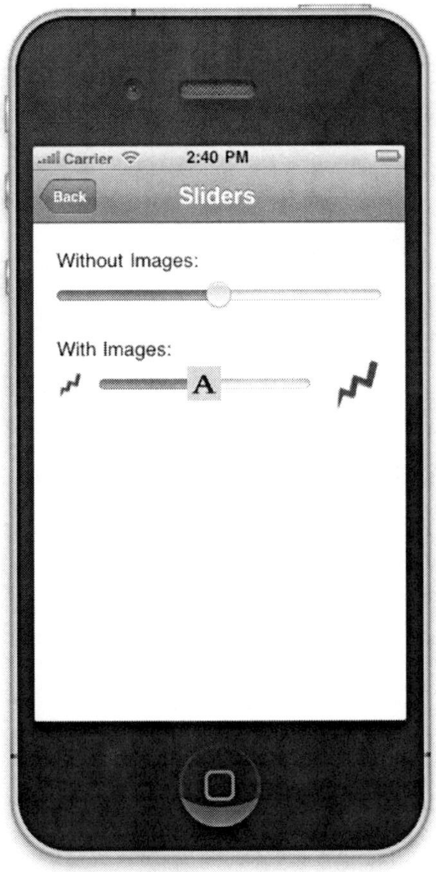

Figure 7–11. *UISlider with and without images*

Images

The image on the left is the `MinValueImage`, and the image on the right is the `MaxValueImage`. You can set both of these in Interface Builder, as shown in the following screenshot (Figure 7–12), but you have to set the thumb button image in code.

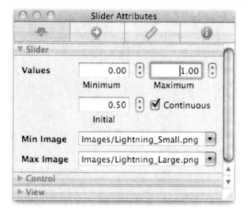

Figure 7–12. *Setting the min and max images for the slider*

To set the thumb image, call `SetThumbImage`, as shown in Listing 7–15.

Listing 7–15. *Setting the thumb image for the slider*

```
this.sldrWithImages.SetThumbImage(UIImage.FromFile("Images/Icons/Apress-29x29.png"),
UIControlState.Normal);
```

Accessing the Value

You can set the minimum and maximum values that each end of the slider has via the `MinValue` and `MaxValue` properties, respectively.

To get the current value of the slider, use the `Value` property.

If you want to listen for the value to change, handle the `ValueChanged` event.

UIActivityIndicatorView

The `UIActivityIndicatorView` control provides a small spinning activity indicator that is intended to be used to let the user know that something is happening.

They're very simple to use. They really have two properties that we care about:

- `IsAnimating`: If `true`, the activity indicator will animate (spin); if `false`, it will not spin.

- `HidesWhenStopped`: If `true`, when the activity indicator is not animating, it will be invisible.

There are three different styles, as shown in Figure 7–13.

Figure 7–13. *The different UIActivityIndicatorView styles (the white style is shown with a brown background for contrast against the white view)*

If you're creating them in code, you have to specify the style in the constructor if you want anything other than the default (Gray style), as shown in Listing 7–16.

Listing 7–16. *Specifying the style when creating an activity spinner*

```
UIActivityIndicatorView spinner = new UIActivityIndicatorView
        (UIActivityIndicatorViewStyle.WhiteLarge);
```

Typically, you set HidesWhenStopped to true, which sets their visibility to hidden when stopped, and then start them just before you make a call that will take some time to complete, and then stop them when the call is completed (Listing 7–17).

Listing 7–17. *Typical activity indicator usage*

```
spinner.HidesWhenStopped = true;
spinner.IsAnimating = true;
// [make long running call, such as a database call, or a web request]
spinner.IsAnimating = false;
```

If you're doing any processing that takes longer than about ten seconds, you should use the UIProgressView instead.

UIProgressView

The UIProgressView provides a mechanism to show progress during long-running processes. It's a very simple control. It has two different styles available via the UIProgressBarViewStyle; Default, and Bar, as shown in Figure 7–14.

Figure 7–14. *UIProgressView styles*

To create a progress control programmatically as a Bar style, you must pass the style into the constructor, as shown in Listing 7–18.

Listing 7–18. *Creating a UIProgressView with the Bar style in code*

```
UIProgressView progressBar = new UIProgressView (UIProgressViewStyle.Bar);
```

Setting the Progress Value

The value of the progress bar is set via the Progress property, which must be a float value from 0.0 to 1.0, inclusive. Progress values are often set when an activity is happening on a separate thread, so, as outlined in Chapter 6, you should make sure to invoke any progress updates on the UI thread. This is not strictly necessary with the progress bar, because it'll accept cross-thread updates; however, it's still a good idea, since many of the other controls require UI-thread updates.

UIPagerControl

The pager control provides users with a way to "page" through screens. It is most effective when combined with a scroll view that has paging enabled. You can see this in use on the home screen of the iPhone and iPad.

With a swiping gesture, you can scroll to the next or previous page of icons, with each page snapping into place. As the pages change, the page indicator at the bottom (the little gray-and-white dots) keeps tabs on your page. A user can also click directly on the pager control to advance the page forwards and backwards by one, as shown in Figure 7–15.

Figure 7–15. *Pager control sample in the Example_StandardControls companion application*

Each"page" that a pager control manages is usually best created as a view with an associated controller, but it doesn't have to be. You can also create one wide view that is in a scroll view.

The multiple view pattern is much better for encapsulating functionality for each page, and also allows you to load/unload them one at a time when they're being displayed in order to minimize memory usage. However, using one big view is much simpler.

In the `Example_StandardControls` companion application, we use controllers that manage a view for each page. The following code (Listing 7–19) loads those controllers and puts them into a collection that we use later.

Listing 7–19. *Using views as pages in a scroll view for the page control*

```
protected void LoadControllers ()
{
        //---- instantiate and add the controllers to our list
        this._controllers.Add (new Controller_1 ());
        this._controllers.Add (new Controller_2 ());
        this._controllers.Add (new Controller_3 ());

        //---- loop through each one
        for (int i = 0; i < this._controllers.Count; i++)
        {
                //---- set their location and size, each one is moved to the
                // right by the width of the previous
                RectangleF viewFrame = new RectangleF (
                        this.scrlMain.Frame.Width * i
                        , this.scrlMain.Frame.Y
                        , this.scrlMain.Frame.Width
                        , this.scrlMain.Frame.Height);
                this._controllers[i].View.Frame = viewFrame;

                //---- add the view to the scrollview
                this.scrlMain.AddSubview (this._controllers[i].View);
        }

        //---- set our scroll view content size (width = number of pages * scroll view
        // width)
        this.scrlMain.ContentSize = new SizeF (
                this.scrlMain.Frame.Width * this._controllers.Count,
                this.scrlMain.Frame.Height);
}
```

After we create the controllers, we add each view as a page by setting the width of the view to be the same width as the scroll view and adding them side-by-side, increasing to the right.

Page Changes via the Pager Control

To listen for page changes performed on the pager control itself, we wire up a handler to the `ValueChanged` event on the pager control. For page changes performed by the user scrolling the view, we handle the `Scrolled` event on the scroll view.

The following code (Listing 7–20) is called in our `ViewDidLoad` method and wires up those handlers and then calls our `LoadControllers` method that we looked at before.

Listing 7–20. *Wiring up the ValueChanged and Scrolled event handlers*

```
//---- wire up our pager and scroll view event handlers
this.pgrMain.ValueChanged += HandlePgrMainValueChanged;
this.scrlMain.Scrolled += HandleScrlMainScrolled;

//---- load our controllers (we'll use one per page)
this.LoadControllers ();
```

Then, in our `ValueChanged` event handler, we scroll to the view that is associated with the page that is selected in the pager control, as shown in Listing 7–21.

Listing 7–21. *Scrolling to a page in the pager control*

```
/// <summary>
/// Runs when a dot on the pager is clicked. Scrolls the scroll view to the appropriate
/// page, based on which one was clicked
/// </summary>
protected void HandlePgrMainValueChanged (object sender, EventArgs e)
{
        //---- it moves page by page. we scroll right to the next controller
        this.scrlMain.ScrollRectToVisible (
                this._controllers[(sender as UIPageControl).CurrentPage].View.Frame,
                true);
}
```

Updating the Pager Control When the Page is Scrolled to Via a Scroll View

When a user scrolls the page via a swipe gesture in the scroll view, you should update the pager control with the page number that was scrolled to. Unfortunately, the scroll view doesn't have any functionality to tell you which page has been scrolled to, so you have to calculate it yourself, as shown in Listing 7–22.

Listing 7–22. *Updating the pager control with what page has been scrolled to*

```
/// <summary>
/// Runs when the scroll view is scrolled. Updates the pager control so that it's
/// current, based on the page
/// </summary>
protected void HandleScrlMainScrolled (object sender, EventArgs e)
{
        //---- calculate the page number
        int pageNumber = (int)(Math.Floor (
                (this.scrlMain.ContentOffset.X - this.scrlMain.Frame.Width / 2)
                 / this.scrlMain.Frame.Width) + 1);

        //---- if it's a valid page
        if (pageNumber >= 0 && pageNumber < this._controllers.Count)
        {
                //---- Set the current page on the pager control
                this.pgrMain.CurrentPage = pageNumber;
        }
}
```

You can set the current page on the pager control via the `CurrentPage` property.

As you can see, the pager control and the scroll view work hand-in-hand. You can use the pager control without the scroll view, but it's generally a much better user experience to combine them.

UIAlertView

`UIAlertView` is a simple pop-up control that allows you to provide a modal window to your users (Figure 7–16).

Figure 7–16. *A simple UIAlertVIew with a cancel button*

Out of the box, you can add buttons to an alert view, or, by inheriting from `UIAlertView`, you can roll your own custom one.

Creating a basic alert is very simple. The following code (Listing 7–23) creates and shows the alert in the previous screenshot.

Listing 7–23. *Creating a simple alert view*

```
UIAlertView alert = new UIAlertView () { Title = "alert title", Message = "this is a
        simple alert" };
alert.AddButton("OK");
alert.Show ();
```

Alerts and Garbage Collection

The garbage collector in MonoTouch is ferocious. If you create an alert view inside of a method, and don't keep a reference to that alert view at your class level, when the method returns, it's a good bet that MonoTouch will garbage collect it. Meaning that if you have any event handlers or delegates wired to it, they'll get a null reference error.

For this reason, if you're creating an alert view and you're also listening to events on it, make sure that you declare it as a class-level variable, so that it sticks around. For example, you might do something like the following, shown in Listing 7–24.

Listing 7–24. *Declaring an alert at the class level*

```
public class foo
{
        UIAlertView _myAlert;
        public void DoSomething()
        {
                this._myAlert = new UIAlertView() …
        }
}
```

We'll see this pattern at work in Listing 7–25.

Working with Buttons

In the previous example, we had only one button, so when the alert was dismissed, we didn't really need to know anything about it. But with the AddButton method we can add more buttons than just one. Consider the following alert, shown in Figure 7–17.

Figure 7–17. *An alert view with more buttons*

Now that we have three buttons, we probably want to know which one gets pressed, so that we can do different things based on which button is pressed. For this, we can handle the `Clicked` event on the `UIAlertView` (Listing 7–25).

Listing 7–25. *Creating a multi-button alert with a Clicked handler*

```
this._alert = new UIAlertView () { Title = "custom buttons alert", Message = "this alert
has custom buttons" };
this._alert.AddButton("custom button 1");
this._alert.AddButton("custom button 2");
this._alert.AddButton("OK");
this._alert.Clicked += delegate(object a, UIButtonEventArgs b) {
        Console.WriteLine ("Button " + b.ButtonIndex.ToString () + " clicked"); };
this._alert.Show ();
```

The `Clicked` delegate contains a `UIButtonEventArgs` parameter, and from that we can get the `ButtonIndex`, which tells us which button was pressed.

Notice in this example we created our alert from `this._alert`, which is a class-level variable (Listing 7–26).

Listing 7–26. *When using callbacks on an alert, you must keep a reference to the alert.*

```
public partial class AlertViewsScreen_iPhone : UIViewController
{
        UIAlertView _alert;
        ...
}
```

As I mentioned before, the reason we created it as a class-level variable is because now that we have a delegate method, we have to keep a reference to the alert around. Otherwise the alert would get garbage collected when the method that we created it in returned. As such, the delegate would also get garbage collected and we'd get a runtime error when the OS tried to call it on click.

Alert Delegate

As discussed in Chapter six, you can also use a class delegate instead of event handlers. The code in Listing 7–27 is an example delegate for a UIAlertView.

Listing 7–27. *Sample UIAlertViewDelegate*

```
/// <summary>
/// This is our custom buttons alert delegate.
/// </summary>
protected class CustomButtonsAlertDelegate : UIAlertViewDelegate
{
        public CustomButtonsAlertDelegate () : base() { }

        public override void Canceled (UIAlertView alertView)
        {
                Console.WriteLine ("Alert Cancelled");
        }

        /// <summary>
        /// Runs when any of the custom buttons on the alert are clicked
        /// </summary>
        public override void Clicked (UIAlertView alertview, int buttonIndex)
        {
                Console.WriteLine ("Button " + buttonIndex.ToString () + " clicked");
        }

        /// <summary>
        /// Runs right after clicked, and before Dismissed
        /// </summary>
        public override void WillDismiss (UIAlertView alertView, int buttonIndex)
        {
                Console.WriteLine ("Alert will dismiss, button "
                        + buttonIndex.ToString ());
        }

        /// <summary>
        /// Runs after Clicked
        /// </summary>
        public override void Dismissed (UIAlertView alertView, int buttonIndex)
        {
```

```
        Console.WriteLine ("Alert Dismissed, button "
                + buttonIndex.ToString ());
        }
    }
```

Customizing the Alert View Even Further

Sometimes you need an alert view that is completely custom. Perhaps you want a pop-up login screen, or a progress screen, or even a simple wait screen (Figure 7–18).

Figure 7–18. *Custom UIAlertView*

If you want to customize a UIAlertView, you can simply create a class that inherits from UIAlertView and override the Draw method. If you want to change the size of the alert, you should override the LayoutSubview method. Listing 7–28 is the complete class for the alert shown in the previous screenshot.

Listing 7–28. *Implementing a custom UIAlertView*

```
[Register("ActivityIndicatorAlertView")]
public class ActivityIndicatorAlertView : UIAlertView
{
        /// <summary>
        /// our activity indicator
        /// </summary>
        UIActivityIndicatorView _activityIndicator;
        /// <summary>
        /// the message label in the window
        /// </summary>
        UILabel _lblMessage;

        /// <summary>
        /// The message that appears in the alert above the activity indicator
        /// </summary>
        public string Message
        {
                get { return this._message; }
                set { _message = value; }
        }
        protected string _message;

        #region -= constructors =-

        public ActivityIndicatorAlertView (IntPtr handle) : base(handle) {}

        [Export("initWithCoder:")]
        public ActivityIndicatorAlertView (NSCoder coder) : base(coder) {}

        public ActivityIndicatorAlertView () { }

        #endregion

        /// <summary>
        /// we use this to resize our alert view. doing it at any other time has
        /// weird effects because of the lifecycle
        /// </summary>
        public override void LayoutSubviews ()
        {
                base.LayoutSubviews ();
                //---- resize the control
                this.Frame = new RectangleF (this.Frame.X, this.Frame.Y,
                        this.Frame.Width, 120);
        }

        /// <summary>
        /// this is where we do the meat of creating our alert, which includes adding
        /// controls, etc.
        /// </summary>
        public override void Draw (RectangleF rect)
        {
                //---- if the control hasn't been setup yet
                if (this._activityIndicator == null)
                {
                        //---- if we have a message
                        if (!string.IsNullOrEmpty (this._message))
```

```
                   {
                           this._lblMessage = new UILabel (
                                   new RectangleF (20, 10, rect.Width - 40, 33));
                           this._lblMessage.BackgroundColor = UIColor.Clear;
                           this._lblMessage.TextColor = UIColor.LightTextColor;
                           this._lblMessage.TextAlignment = UITextAlignment.Center;
                           this._lblMessage.Text = this._message;
                           this.AddSubview (this._lblMessage);
                   }

                   //---- instantiate a new activity indicator
                   this._activityIndicator = new UIActivityIndicatorView
                           (UIActivityIndicatorViewStyle.White);
                   this._activityIndicator.Frame = new RectangleF
                           ((rect.Width / 2)
                           - (this._activityIndicator.Frame.Width / 2)
                           , 50, this._activityIndicator.Frame.Width
                           , this._activityIndicator.Frame.Height);
                   this.AddSubview (this._activityIndicator);
                   this._activityIndicator.StartAnimating ();
               }
               base.Draw (rect);
       }

       /// <summary>
       /// dismisses the alert view. makes sure to call it on the main UI
       /// thread in case it's called from a worker thread.
       /// </summary>
       public void Hide (bool animated)
       {
               this.InvokeOnMainThread (delegate {
                       this.DismissWithClickedButtonIndex (0, animated);
               });
       }
}
```

To see this class in action, take a look at the Example_StandardControls companion code and application.

UIActionSheet

The action sheet is one of the few controls that differs significantly in behavior between the iPhone/iPod Touch and the iPad. In both devices, their use is the same, but their appearance and behavior is different.

Action sheets are functionally very similar to alerts, but are intended to be used when you need to present users with options for actions or making decisions in order to progress through a task.

On iPhone/iPod Touch devices, action sheets are slide-on modal windows. On iPad devices, they're popover windows nearly identical to alert views. For example, the following Figure 7–19 is a screenshot of an action sheet on an iPhone.

Figure 7–19. *An action sheet on an iPhone showing a destructive button (delete), a cancel button (cancel), and two other buttons*

Creating the equivalent action sheet on an iPad will result in something slightly different, as shown in Figure 7–20.

Figure 7–20. *The same action sheet on the iPad*

The first thing that you notice is that there is no Cancel button. The reason is, in the iPad, you can actually cancel the action sheet by clicking outside of it, so you typically don't include a Cancel button.

Creating a Simple Action Sheet

Using an action sheet is very simple, and similar to using an alert view. For example, the following code in Listing 7–29 creates an action sheet that has a Delete and Cancel button (on the iPad, the Cancel button will not be visible).

Listing 7–29. *Creating a simple delete/cancel action sheet*

```
this._actionSheet = new UIActionSheet ("simple action sheet", null, "cancel", "delete",
    null);
this._actionSheet.Clicked += delegate(object a, UIButtonEventArgs b) {
    Console.WriteLine ("Button " + b.ButtonIndex.ToString () + " clicked");
};
this._actionSheet.ShowInView (this.View);
```

As with an alert view, the action sheet raises a `Clicked` event when a user chooses a button. In the event handler delegate for clicked event a `UIButtonEventArgs` object is passed that contains the index of the button that was selected.

NOTE: The action sheet has the same exact issue with garbage collection that the alert view does, in that you must keep a reference to the action sheet if you are subscribing to events. For more information, read through the "Alert View" section earlier in this chapter.

Button Types

An action sheet has three different button types:

- `Cancel`: The button that is used to dismiss the action sheet without selecting an action. The Cancel button is shown as a black button.

- `Destructive`: A button the causes the destruction of an item, such as a Delete button. The destructive button is shown as a red button.

- `Other`: For any other buttons. Other buttons are shown in white on the iPad, and a light gray on the iPhone.

If you're creating an action sheet manually, you can set which button is your destructive button via the `DestructiveButtonIndex` property. For example, the following code (Listing 7–30) sets the first button to be the destructive button.

Listing 7–30. *Setting the destructive button*

```
this._actionSheet.DestructiveButtonIndex = 0;
```

To set your cancel button, you use the `CancelButtonIndex` in the same manner.

Adding Custom Buttons

To add custom buttons to your action sheet, call the AddButton method ((Listing 7–31).

Listing 7–31. *Adding a custom button to an action sheet*

```
this._actionSheet.AddButton ("a different option!");
```

Displaying an Action Sheet

An action sheet can be shown from a toolbar, tab bar, button bar item, or a view. Depending on what device you're on, the animation of its appearance may be different. For instance, on the iPhone/iPod Touch, the action sheet slides up from the bottom of the device, but on the iPad, it will appear anchored over what you've shown it from.

To show the action sheet, use either the ShowInView, ShowFrom, ShowFromTabBar, or ShowFromToolbar methods. For example, the following code (Listing 7–32) specifies an action sheet in the current controller's view.

Listing 7–32. *Showing an action sheet in the current view*

```
this._actionSheet.ShowInView (this.View);
```

Subclassing

One of the most powerful things about the action sheet is using it as an animating control that can display other content. For instance, in the UIPickerView section (coming up), we'll take a look at how to subclass the action sheet to dynamically show a picker view.

UIDatePicker

The date picker control is a slot-machine-like spinner control that provides users a way to enter date and time information, as shown in Figure 7–21.

Figure 7–21. *A UIDatePicker control on an iPhone*

The date picker control has several different operating modes that you can specify with the Mode property:

- DateAndTime: In this mode, you get both the date and the time, as shown in the previous screenshot.

- Time: Only spinners for time data are visible.

- Date: Only spinners for data data are visible.

- CountDownTimer: Only spinners for hours and minutes are visible.

Configuration

The date picker is very easy to configure in Interface Builder (Figure 7–22).

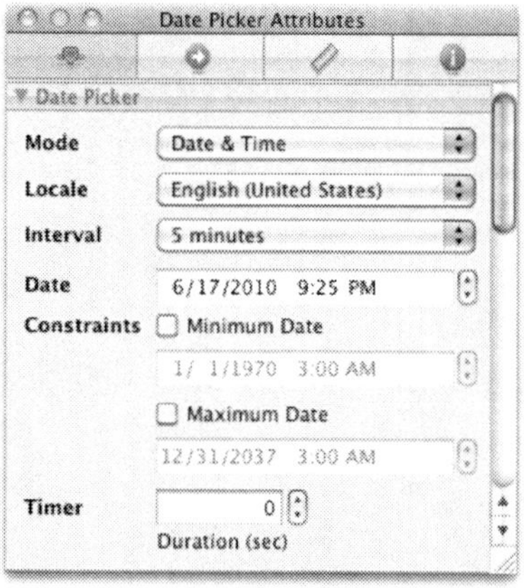

Figure 7–22. *Configuring a date picker in Interface Builder*

You can also configure it programmatically. You can set the minimum and maximum dates shown in the picker via the `MinimumDate` and `MaximumDate` properties. For example, the following code (Listing 7–33) configures a picker to only show a week in the future and a week in the past.

Listing 7–33. *Configuring minimum and maximum dates in code*

```
myDatePicker.MinimumDate = DateTime.Today.AddDays (-7);
myDatePicker.MaximumDate = DateTime.Today.AddDays (7);
```

To get the date or time value, you can access the `Date` property on the picker. For example, the code in Listing 7–34 displays the selected date and time from a date picker on a label.

Listing 7–34. *Accessing the Date property of a date picker*

```
myDateLabel.Text = myDatePicker.Date.ToString ();
```

If you're in countdown timer mode, you can access the `CountDownDuration` property, which gives you the total number of seconds of the timer countdown on the date picker.

Showing Dynamically

One of the most common scenarios with having a date picker is showing it dynamically—like how a keyboard slides up onscreen, rather than having it onscreen at all times. To do this, the easiest way is to modify an action sheet so that it has a picker on it, and then display the action sheet, as shown in the following screenshot (Figure 7–23).

Figure 7–23. *Displaying a picker on an action sheet*

The following code in Listing 7–35 is a control that does just that. This works on the iPhone, but you could extend this to work on the iPad as well.

Listing 7–35. *Action sheet date picker control code*

```
/// <summary>
/// A class to show a date picker on an action sheet. To use, create a new
/// ActionSheetDatePicker, set the Title, modify any settings on the DatePicker
/// property, and call Show(). It will automatically dismiss when the user clicks
/// "Done," or you can call Hide() to dismiss it manually.

/// </summary>
[MonoTouch.Foundation.Register("SlideOnDatePicker")]
public class ActionSheetDatePicker
{
        #region -= declarations =-

        UIActionSheet _actionSheet;
```

```csharp
UIButton _doneButton = UIButton.FromType (UIButtonType.RoundedRect);
UIView _owner;
UILabel _titleLabel = new UILabel ();

#endregion

#region -= properties =-

/// <summary>
/// Set any datepicker properties here
/// </summary>
public UIDatePicker DatePicker
{
        get { return this._datePicker; }
        set { this._datePicker = value; }
}
UIDatePicker _datePicker = new UIDatePicker(RectangleF.Empty);

/// <summary>
/// The title that shows up for the date picker
/// </summary>
public string Title
{
        get { return this._titleLabel.Text; }
        set { this._titleLabel.Text = value; }
}

#endregion

#region -= constructor =-

/// <summary>
///
/// </summary>
public ActionSheetDatePicker (UIView owner)
{
        //---- save our uiview owner
        this._owner = owner;

        //---- configure the title label
        this._titleLabel.BackgroundColor = UIColor.Clear;
        this._titleLabel.TextColor = UIColor.LightTextColor;
        this._titleLabel.Font = UIFont.BoldSystemFontOfSize (18);

        //---- configure the done button
        this._doneButton.SetTitle ("done", UIControlState.Normal);
        this._doneButton.TouchUpInside += (s, e) => {
                this._actionSheet.DismissWithClickedButtonIndex (0, true); };

        //---- create + configure the action sheet
        this._actionSheet = new UIActionSheet () {
                Style = UIActionSheetStyle.BlackTranslucent };

        //---- add our controls to the action sheet
        this._actionSheet.AddSubview (this._datePicker);
        this._actionSheet.AddSubview (this._titleLabel);
        this._actionSheet.AddSubview (this._doneButton);
```

```
        }

        #endregion

        #region -= public methods =-

        /// <summary>
        /// Shows the action sheet picker from the view that was set as the owner.
        /// </summary>
        public void Show ()
        {
                //---- declare vars
                float titleBarHeight = 40;
                SizeF doneButtonSize = new SizeF (71, 30);
                SizeF actionSheetSize = new SizeF (
                        this._owner.Frame.Width, this._datePicker.Frame.Height
                        + titleBarHeight);
                RectangleF actionSheetFrame = new RectangleF (
                        0, this._owner.Frame.Height - actionSheetSize.Height
                        , actionSheetSize.Width, actionSheetSize.Height);

                //---- show the action sheet and add the controls to it
                this._actionSheet.ShowInView (this._owner);

                //---- resize the action sheet to fit our other stuff
                this._actionSheet.Frame = actionSheetFrame;

                //---- move our picker to be at the bottom of the actionsheet
                // (view coords are relative to the action sheet)
                this._datePicker.Frame = new RectangleF (this._datePicker.Frame.X,
                        titleBarHeight, this._datePicker.Frame.Width
                        , this._datePicker.Frame.Height);

                //---- move our label to the top of the action sheet
                this._titleLabel.Frame = new RectangleF (10, 4, this._owner.Frame.Width
                        - 100, 35);

                //---- move our button
                this._doneButton.Frame = new RectangleF (actionSheetSize.Width -
                        doneButtonSize.Width - 10, 7, doneButtonSize.Width,
                        oneButtonSize.Height);
        }

        /// <summary>
        /// Dismisses the action sheet date picker
        /// </summary>
        public void Hide (bool animated)
        {
                this._actionSheet.DismissWithClickedButtonIndex (0, animated);
        }

        #endregion
}
```

You can find this code (and its use) in the companion Example_StandardControls application and code.

UIPickerView

The picker view is very similar to the date picker. In fact, the date picker actually uses a picker view under the hood. The picker view lets you create an arbitrary number of spinners and put text or images into the rows of each one. The following screenshot (Figure 7–24) is a simple custom picker view with just one spinner that shows text items.

Figure 7–24. *A simple custom picker view*

When working with picker views, each spinner is called a component, and each item within the component is called a row.

Populating the Picker

In order to build out its items, and to let your code know when a user interacts with it, you have to implement callback methods that the picker calls. To implement these methods, you have different options. As discussed in Chapter 6, you can use various techniques, such as implementing a strongly-typed-delegate, a weak-delegate, or wiring up event handlers to the picker events.

No matter what method you choose, there are several important callbacks or events that you need to implement in order to populate the items in a picker view:

- GetRowsInComponent: Called by the picker to determine how many items (rows) are in a given spinner (component)

- GetTitle: Called by the picker to retrieve the text for a particular row in a component. If you don't implement this, you need to implement the GetView method.

- GetView: Called by the picker to retrieve the view for a particular row in a component. If you implement GetView, do not implement GetTitle. Use this if you want to use images or other custom things in your picker view. You can use any thing that implements UIView such as a UIImageView if you want to put an image in, or even a custom view.

- GetComponentCount: Called by the picker to determine how many components to render

Additionally there are optional methods that allow you to further customize the picker:

- GetComponentWidth: Used to specify the width of a given component

- GetRowHeight: Used to specify the height of a given row in the specified component

Finally, there are methods to handle user interaction:

- Selected: Called when any of the spinners change value and passes the component index as well as the row

UIPickerViewModel

One of the easiest ways to implement these methods is to create a class that inherits from UIPickerViewModel (which contains all these methods), and then assign it to the Model property on your picker control. For example, Listing 7–36 is a very simple picker view model that manages the data for a picker that has a single component.

Listing 7–36. *A simple picker view model*

```
/// <summary>
/// This is our simple picker model. it uses a list of strings as it's data
/// </summary>
protected class PickerDataModel : UIPickerViewModel
{

        public event EventHandler<EventArgs> ValueChanged;

        /// <summary>
        /// The items to show up in the picker
```

```csharp
/// </summary>
public List<string> Items
{
        get { return this._items; }
        set { this._items = value; }
}
List<string> _items = new List<string>();

/// <summary>
/// The current selected item
/// </summary>
public string SelectedItem
{
        get { return this._items[this._selectedIndex]; }
}
protected int _selectedIndex = 0;

/// <summary>
/// default constructor
/// </summary>
public PickerDataModel ()
{
}

/// <summary>
/// Called by the picker to determine how many rows are in a given spinner item
/// </summary>
public override int GetRowsInComponent (UIPickerView picker, int component)
{
        return this._items.Count;
}

/// <summary>
/// called by the picker to get the text for a particular row in a particular
/// spinner item
/// </summary>
public override string GetTitle (UIPickerView picker, int row, int component)
{
        return this._items[row];
}

/// <summary>
/// called by the picker to get the number of spinner items
/// </summary>
public override int GetComponentCount (UIPickerView picker)
{
        return 1;
}

/// <summary>
/// called when a row is selected in the spinner
/// </summary>
public override void Selected (UIPickerView picker, int row, int component)
{
        this._selectedIndex = row;
        if (this.ValueChanged != null)
        {
```

```
                    this.ValueChanged (this, new EventArgs ());
            }
        }
}
```

To populate the model, we simply add strings to the items collection and then set it to the Source property of the picker object, as shown in Listing 7–37.

Listing 7–37. *Populating the model*

```
this._pickerDataModel = new PickerDataModel ();
this._pickerDataModel.Items.Add ("item the first!");
this._pickerDataModel.Items.Add ("item the second!");
this._pickerDataModel.Items.Add ("item the third!");
this._pickerDataModel.Items.Add ("fourth item!");
this.pkrMain.Source = this._pickerDataModel;
```

To listen for picker changes, we could then handle the ValueChanged event. For example, the following code in Listing 7–38 writes the currently selected item text to a label.

Listing 7–38. *Handling the ValueChanged event*

```
this._pickerDataModel.ValueChanged += (s, e) => {
        this.lblSelectedItem.Text = this._pickerDataModel.SelectedItem;
};
```

UIToolbar

The toolbar control is a placeholder for buttons that perform commands specific to the screen that's displaying. For example, the bar along the bottom with the back, forward, etc. buttons in Mobile Safari is a toolbar, as shown in Figure 7–25.

Figure 7–25. *A toolbar in Mobile Safari*

Toolbars are specific to the screen they're on. If you want to make a toolbar that appears on all screens, use a tab bar instead (see Chapter 8).

Item Types

Toolbars are extremely powerful. When you create a toolbar you assign an array of `UIBarButtonItem` objects to it. Out of the box there are a bunch of different built-in item types, including basic text buttons, buttons with images, and spacing separators. There are a ton of built-in styles, as illustrated by the following screenshot (Figure 7–26), which includes some of them.

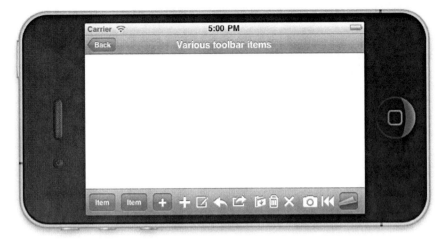

Figure 7–26. *Some of the built-in options for toolbar items*

However, a toolbar item can even be assigned a custom view, so anything that you can build into a view, can go on the toolbar. Because of this, the toolbar is almost infinitely customizable.

Toolbars in Interface Builder

Configuring a toolbar in Interface Builder is very easy, although to do anything fancy, such as using a custom view, you'll have to modify the toolbar items in code.

When putting items on toolbars in Interface Builder, you have three control choices:

- **Bar Button Item:** An extensible button item that can be modified both in Interface Builder and in code

- **Flexible Space Bar Button Item:** A space between items that expands or shrinks based on how much room on the toolbar there is. This is very useful when handling rotation and you want to maintain spacing ratios.

- **Fixed Space Bar Button Item:** A space between items that retains its size, despite toolbar growth or shrinkage

The toolbar controls in Interface Builder are as shown (Figure 7–27).

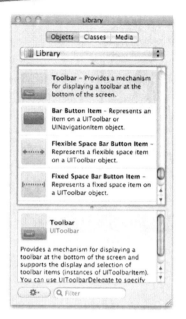

Figure 7–27. *Toolbar controls in Interface Builder*

For example, the following toolbar (Figure 7–28) has (in this order):

- Button : Fixed Space : Button : Flexible Space : Button : Button

Figure 7–28. *A sample toolbar with buttons and spacing in portrait mode*

If we look at the toolbar as designed in Interface Builder, the spacing controls are apparent, as shown in Figure 7–29.

Figure 7–29. *A sample toolbar in Interface Builder*

If we rotate the view, the toolbar will resize and the fixed width spacing control stays the same size, but the flexible size control expands, as shown in Figure 7–30.

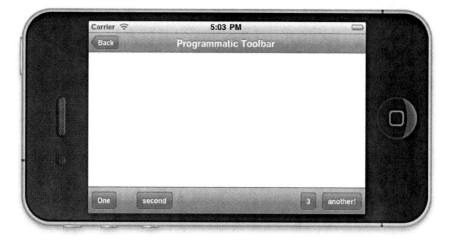

Figure 7–30. *The flexible space control expands with the toolbar.*

Programmatic Creation

You can also create toolbars programmatically. Even though in Interface Builder we had several controls to choose from, all toolbar items are actually `UIBarButtonItem` objects. To set an item to be a preset image or spacing item, we can use a constructor that takes `UIBarButtonSystemItem` type. For example, to create a fixed width space item, we would do the following (Listing 7–39).

Listing 7–39. *Creating a system toolbar item*

```
UIBarButtonItem fixedWidth = new UIBarButtonItem (UIBarButtonSystemItem.FixedSpace);
```

If we want to create a normal button, we use a constructor that takes a `UIBarButtonItemStyle` type. For example, to create a standard button with a label, we would create a new `UIBarButtonItem`, passing in the title of the button, the button style, and the event handler (if there is one), as shown in Listing 7–40.

Listing 7–40. *Creating a normal button toolbar item*

```
string buttonTitle = "One";
UIBarButtonItem btnOne = new UIBarButtonItem (buttonTitle,
UIBarButtonItemStyle.Bordered, null);
```

If we wanted to create an item from a custom view, we can use the constructor that takes a view item, or we could assign the view to the `CustomView` property. For example, the following code in Listing 7–41 creates an item from a view.

Listing 7–41. *Creating a toolbar item that has a custom view*

```
UIBarButtonItem customViewButton = new UIBarButtonItem(new MyCustomView());
```

Once you have all your items created, you put them into an array and then set them on the toolbar (Listing 7–42).

Listing 7–42. *Adding items to a toolbar*

```
UIBarButtonItem[] items = new UIBarButtonItem[] { btnOne, fixedWidth, btnTwo,
    flexibleWidth, btnThree, btnFour };
this._toolbar.SetItems (items, false);
```

There are a number of different constructors for toolbar button items—check out the MonoTouch docs for more info.

Sizing

If you're creating your toolbar in code and you want to support autosizing to handle rotation, you should set the `AutoresizingMask` property, which takes one or more flags describing the resizing behavior. For example, the following code in Listing 7–43 tells the toolbar to automatically move down or up depending on the height of the view and to automatically resize the width to fill up the appropriate space.

Listing 7–43. *Common auto sizing settings for a toolbar*

```
this._toolbar.AutoresizingMask = UIViewAutoresizing.FlexibleTopMargin |
UIViewAutoresizing.FlexibleWidth;
```

Handling Clicks

An important thing to know is that, unlike normal buttons, toolbar items do not raise the TouchUpInside event, but instead raise Clicked events. The CocoaTouch API may be powerful, but is not consistent.

For instance, the following code (Listing 7–44) raises an alert when a button is clicked.

Listing 7–44. *Handling the Clicked event on a toolbar item*

```
btnOne.Clicked += (s, e) => { new UIAlertView ("click!", "btnOne clicked", null, "OK",
    null).Show (); };
```

I've used the C# lambda syntax to save space in the previous code example.

Summary

This was a monster chapter that gave a pretty in-depth introduction to all of the basic controls in CocoaTouch; however, it is by no means exhaustive. We could have gone deeper into nearly every single one of these controls. The UIKit is extremely powerful, and with each subsequent release of the iOS, more controls are added and existing controls become more powerful.

In the next chapter we're going to continue our control review and look at even more controls that deal with managing screens and content.

Chapter 8

Content Controls

In the previous chapter, we looked at the standard controls in the CocoaTouch UIKit. In this chapter, we're going to continue our journey through the UIKit control ecosystem and look at controls whose job it is to manage content, be it other views or controllers. Specifically, in this chapter we're going to cover the following controls:

- Navigation controller
- Tab bar controller
- Split view controller
- Web view
- Map view
- Search bar

We've already used some of these in the example applications, or at least talked about them in examples. In this chapter, we're going to dig into each one of them in more detail, examine their capabilities, and explore how to work with them.

You can find all of the examples in this chapter in the `Example_ContentControls` companion application and code to see these explorations in action.

Navigation Controller

The `UINavigationController` is the easiest way to handle navigation between hierarchical screens in iOS, because it manages the complexity of navigation, breadcrumbing, and display for you. You simply create a new `UINavigationController` and then push a `UIViewController` onto it using the `PushViewController` method. The first one you create is known as the root view controller. When you push a view controller onto a navigation controller, the navigation controller automatically displays the controller's view. To add a new controller, you just call `PushViewController` again. When you push a second view controller onto the stack, the navigation controller automatically adds a `Back` button, which will pop that controller off the view stack when that button is clicked. You can also manually pop a controller off the stack by calling the PopViewController method, although in practice, that's rarely used.

Generally, the Navigation Controller is used to display screens that contain hierarchical data. For example, in the Settings Application, the navigation controller is used to drill down through settings, as shown in Figure 8–1.

Figure 8–1. *A Navigation Controller in the Settings application.*

As you push view controllers onto the navigation stack, their title appears in the navigation bar and a Back button appears with the title of the previous controller. When a user clicks the Back button, the current screen is popped off the stack, which shows the previous screen. It encapsulates all the controls and logic needed to handle all this for you.

Unlike other controllers, it's not meant to be subclassed, but rather you can set properties and call methods on it to modify its behavior and appearance.

Unfortunately, this means that it's not extremely customizable, presumably because Apple wants to control the navigation experience and make it consistent across applications.

Parts of the Navigation Controller

Before we get into using and customizing the navigation controller, let's first examine the different parts of it.

The navigation controller consists of four main components:

- **Navigation view:** This is the entire view presented by the navigation controller and contains all other controls and views. The navigation view is available via the View property on the navigation controller, and is what you add to your window or other parent when you want to actually display the navigation controller.

- **Navigation bar:** The navigation bar is the area at the top of the navigation view that displays any navigation items, such as the Back button, the current controller title, and, optionally, a button on the right. Displaying the navigation bar is optional, and it's very common to hide it when displaying the root view controller, and then animate it into view when the first subcontroller is pushed onto the navigation stack.

- **Navigation toolbar:** The navigation toolbar appears at the bottom of the navigation view and provides a controller-specific set of toolbar items that are relevant for the current controller that's displayed on the stack. The navigation toolbar isn't displayed by default.

- **Content view:** The content view is the main area of the navigation view. It's where the top controller on the view stack's view is displayed.

Figure 8–2 illustrates the relationship between these components.

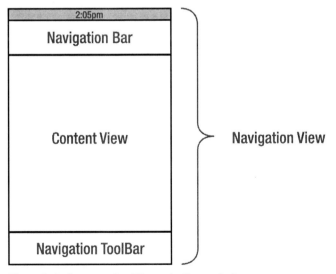

Figure 8–2. *Components of the navigation controller*

Using the Navigation Controller

You can create a navigation controller in Interface Builder, but because it's so simple, and there's very little you can customize in Interface Builder on it, it's far easier to create it in code. The basic pattern for using a navigation controller is as follows:

- Instantiate it.

- Push the root View Controller onto it.

- Add its View to the window or other parent controller (such as a Tab Bar).

Listing 8–1 (from the AppDelegate class in the Example_StandardControls companion code) does just that.

Listing 8–1. *Creating a navigation controller on the window*

```
...
this._mainNavController = new UINavigationController ();
...
this._mainNavController.PushViewController (this._iPhoneHome, false);
...
this._window.AddSubview (this._mainNavController.View);
```

When you add view controllers to a navigation controller, you can get a reference to the navigation controller (to push more controllers onto, or to modify it) via the NavigationController property on the UIViewController that has been pushed on it. For example, Listing 8–2 is in a custom view controller that sets the transparency of the navigation bar.

Listing 8–2. *Accessing the navigation controller from a view controller that is on its stack*

```
this.NavigationController.NavigationBar.Translucent = true;
```

When designing screens in Interface Builder that are meant to be used in a navigation controller, you can simulate the navigation controller so you get a more accurate idea of the screen size that your view will have by setting the **Simulated User Interface Elements** settings, as shown in Figure 8–3.

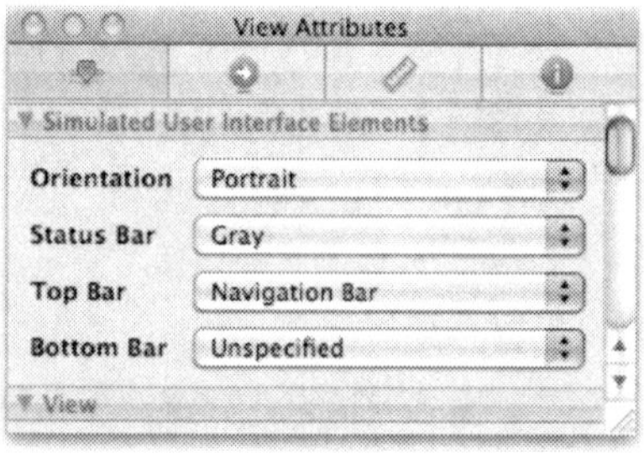

Figure 8–3. *Simulating the navigation controller components in Interface Builder*

After you change these settings, you'll see the appropriate element simulated in the designer window, shown in Figure 8–4.

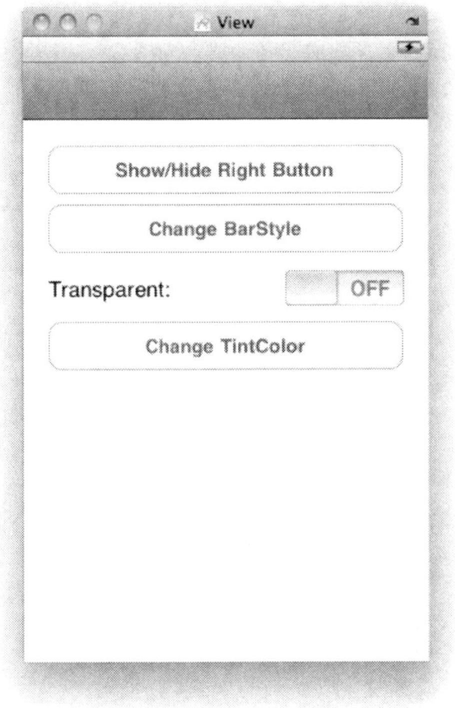

Figure 8–4. *Simulated navigation bar in Interface Builder*

Because it's simulated, it only gives you a blank area of the appropriate size.

Modifying the Navigation Bar

The navigation controller allows you to modify a few things on the navigation bar, including the following:

- Title text

- Navigation bar style

- Navigation bar color

- Transparency of the navigation bar

- Right button

Title

By default, the title text comes from the Title property of the UIViewController that is topmost on the view stack (the currently displayed one). However, you can also set it directly via the Title property on the navigation controller's NavigationItem. See Listing 8–3.

Listing 8–3. *Setting the navigation item title*

```
this.NavigationItem.Title = "Customizing Nav Bar";
```

Setting it directly is useful when you want it to differ from title text that appears elsewhere, such as when you're using the tab bar controller, which we'll explore later.

Style

The navigation bar itself can be set to one of two styles, Default, or Black, which are included in the UIBarStyle enumeration. See Figure 8–4.

Figure 8–5. *Default and Black navigation bar styles*

Default gives the bar and its buttons a gray-blue theme, and `Black` gives the bar and its buttons a black/dark-gray theme. To set the style, set the `BarStyle` property of the navigation bar to a value from the UIBarStyle enumeration (see Listing 8–4).

Listing 8–4. *Setting the navigation bar style to black*

```
this.NavigationController.NavigationBar.BarStyle = UIBarStyle.Black;
```

TintColor

In addition to the two color choices in the `BarStyle` property, you can set the navigation bar to use a specific color via the `TintColorProperty`. See Figure 8–6.

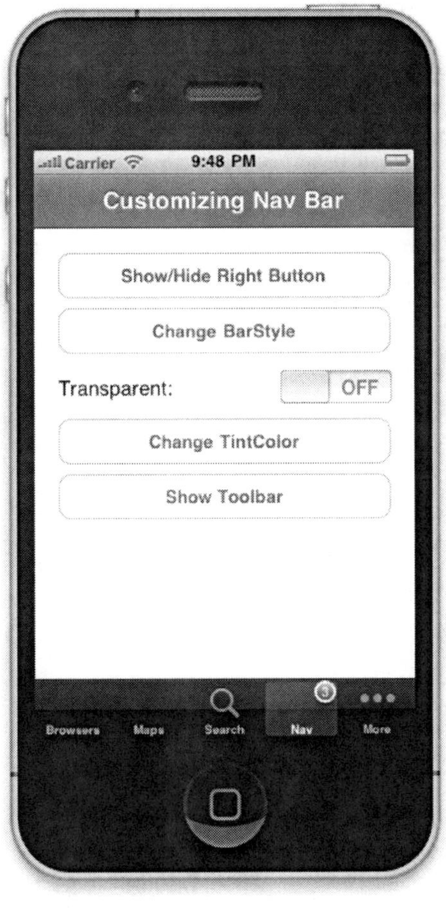

Figure 8–6. *Custom tint color for the navigation bar*

For example, Listing 8–5 sets the bar tint color to be red.

Listing 8–5. *Setting the navigation bar tint to red*

```
this.NavigationController.NavigationBar.TintColor = UIColor.Red;
```

To reset the color back to the default, simply set the `TintColor` property to `null`.

Opacity

You can specify the navigation bar to take on a partially transparent quality by setting the `Translucent` property to true (see Listing 8–6).

Listing 8–6. *Making the navigation bar translucent*

```
this.NavigationController.NavigationBar.Translucent = true;
```

However, when you do this, the content view area of the navigation controller is enlarged to also include the top bar area; so if you have any controls at the top of the view, they will appear behind the top bar! To account for this, make sure to leave extra room at the top of your view. If you're designing your view in Interface Builder, you can set the Top Bar property of the **Simulated User Interface Elements** section to **Translucent Black Navigation Bar** to see what this looks like.

Right Button

In addition to the Back button and the title on the navigation bar, you can add a custom button to the right-hand portion of the bar. This is especially useful if you want to add an `Edit` button or the like. To set the button, call the `SetRightBarButtonItem` on the navigation item and pass in a `UIBarButtonItem`, and determine whether you want it to animate on or off (via a fade). You can either use a custom `UIBarButtonItem`, or you can use one of the built-in ones via the `UIBarButtonSystemItem` enumeration as shown in Listing 8–7.

Listing 8–7. *Adding a button to the navigation bar*

```
this.NavigationItem.SetRightBarButtonItem(
        new UIBarButtonItem(UIBarButtonSystemItem.Action, null), true);
```

To remove the button, call the method again, but pass in a null for the button (see Figure 8–8).

Listing 8–8. *Removing a button from the navigation bar*

```
this.NavigationItem.SetRightBarButtonItem(null, true);
```

Navigation Toolbar

The navigation controller can optionally show a toolbar at the bottom of view. The toolbar works exactly the same way the regular toolbar does, as described in the last chapter. The only difference is that the navigation controller gets its toolbar items from the toolbar items collection on the current view controller that is displayed. For example, Listing 8–9 crates the toolbar items collection on a custom `UIViewController`.

Listing 8–9. *Creating a toolbar items collection on a UIViewController for use in a navigation controller's toolbar*

```
this.SetToolbarItems( new UIBarButtonItem[] {
        new UIBarButtonItem(UIBarButtonSystemItem.Refresh)
        , new UIBarButtonItem(UIBarButtonSystemItem.FlexibleSpace) { Width = 50 }
        , new UIBarButtonItem(UIBarButtonSystemItem.Pause)
}, false);
```

You can then show the toolbar by setting the ToolbarHidden property on the navigation controller to false, and it will show the items (see Listing 8–10).

Listing 8–10. *Showing a navigation controller's toolbar*

```
this.NavigationController.ToolbarHidden = false;
```

Tab Bar Controller

The navigation controller works great for hierarchal navigation across screens, but sometimes you want to split your application into different areas. The UITabBarController is designed to do just that. It allows you to separate your application into different areas and navigate between them. You can even combine the use of the tab bar controller with the navigation controller and you can have different tabs control different groups of hierarchal screens.

The tab bar controller resides at the bottom of the device, and displays a set of tabs that you define. See Figure 8–7.

Figure 8–7. *Tab bar controller in the iPhone*

It also provides functionality for reordering the tabs. See Figure 8–8.

Figure 8–8. *Tab bar reordering is a built-in feature of the tab bar controller*

You can have up to five items on the tab bar at any one time. If you add more, it puts a **More** tab on the tab bar and, when you click it, you get a navigation table with the other tabs. See Figure 8–9.

Figure 8–9. *The More tabs screen*

Creating a Tab Bar Controller

Using the tab bar controller is very straightforward. You simply subclass it, set its ViewControllers property with an array of view controllers, and then add its view to a window. You do not manage the tabs directly; instead, you set the TabBarItem properties on each of your controllers that are associated with the tab bar controller, and the tab bar controller picks up those items and displays them.

As with the navigation controller, it's much easier to use programmatically rather than in Interface Builder. In fact, for a variety of reasons, Apple encourages you to use it programmatically.

To create a custom tab bar controller, define a new class that inherits from UITabBarController, then override the ViewDidLoad method, instantiate your controllers, and add them to the class via the UITabBarController's ViewControllers property. For example, Listing 8–11 is a custom tab bar controller that has two tabs: one contains a navigation controller, and the second tab contains just a custom view controller screen.

Listing 8–11. *A custom tab bar controller*

```
public class MyTabBarController : UITabBarController
{
        //---- screens
        UINavigationController _browsersTabNavController;
        Browsers.BrowsersHome _browsersHome;
        Search.SearchScreen _searchScreen;

        public override void ViewDidLoad ()
        {
                base.ViewDidLoad ();

                //---- browsers tab
                // in this case, we create a navigation controller and then add our
                // screen to that
                this._browsersTabNavController = new UINavigationController();
                this._browsersTabNavController.TabBarItem = new UITabBarItem();
                this._browsersTabNavController.TabBarItem.Title = "Browsers";
                this._browsersHome = new Browsers.BrowsersHome();
                this._browsersTabNavController.PushViewController(this._browsersHome,
                        false);

                //---- search
                this._searchScreen = new Search.SearchScreen();
                this._searchScreen.TabBarItem = new
                    UITabBarItem(UITabBarSystemItem.Search, 1);
                //---- create our array of controllers
                var viewControllers = new UIViewController[] {
                        this._browsersTabNavController,
                        this._searchScreen,
                };

                //---- attach the view controllers
                this.ViewControllers = viewControllers;
```

```
                              //---- set our selected item
                              this.SelectedViewController = this._browsersTabNavController;
               }
}
```

When using a navigation controller with a tab controller (as with the first tab item we just looked at), the navigation controller should always be a child of the tab bar controller.

Tab Bar Items

The tab bar picks up the tab bar item information from each controller you add to it via the TabBarItem property. When creating tab bar items, you can create them from built-in system items, or you can create them from scratch, specifying the title text and the image. You can find the available system items in the UITabBarSystemItem enumeration.

Using a Custom Tab Bar Controller

Once you've defined your custom tab bar controller, using it is very easy. Simply instantiate it and then add its view to your window or view, just as you would if you were using a navigation controller. For example, the example application delegate in Listing 8–12 uses the custom tab bar controller we defined as the root view controller on a window.

Listing 8–12. *Using a tab bar controller as the root view controller in an application*

```
public class AppDelegate : UIApplicationDelegate
{
        protected UIWindow _window;
        protected MyTabBarController _tabs;

        …
        public override bool FinishedLaunching (UIApplication app, NSDictionary options)
        {
                //---- create our window
                this._window = new UIWindow (UIScreen.MainScreen.Bounds);
                this._window.MakeKeyAndVisible ();

                this._tabs = new MyTabBarController();
                this._window.AddSubview (this._tabs.View);

                return true;
        }
}
```

User Customizable Tabs

As mentioned before, the tab bar controller supports user rearranging of the tabs out of the box. This is accomplished via the CustomizableViewControllers property of the tab bar controller. Any controllers that are a part of this collection are reorderable. If you don't set this property directly, it automatically gets its values from the ViewControllers property. If you want to make only a subset of your tabs rearrangeable, then you need to specify which ones are customizable. For example, Listing 8–13 specifies that only the third and fourth items in the view controllers should be customizable.

Listing 8–13. *Specifying only certain controller as customizable*

```
var customizableControllers = new UIViewController[] {
        viewControllers[2],
        viewControllers[3]
};
this.CustomizableViewControllers = customizableControllers;
```

Tab Badges

The tab bar controller allows you to add a badge to tab bar items in order to bubble up information to the user that pertains to that particular tab. The badges show up as a red circle with white text on the upper-right portion of the tab icon. See Figure 8–10.

Figure 8–10. *Badges on tab bar items*

To specify a badge value, the tab bar item exposes a property called BadgeValue that takes a string. See Listing 8–14.

Listing 8–14. *Setting a badge value*

```
myController.TabBarItem.BadgeValue = "3";
```

Simply set your value to that property and a badge will appear on the tab bar item.

Split View Controller

The `UISplitViewController` is a specialized controller available only on the iPad that allows you to present a master-detail view where in landscape view, two views are shown onscreen, and in portrait view, one view is shown with the option to show the second view. See Figures 8–11 and 8–12.

Figure 8–11. *Split view controller in landscape mode, showing the master and detail views.*

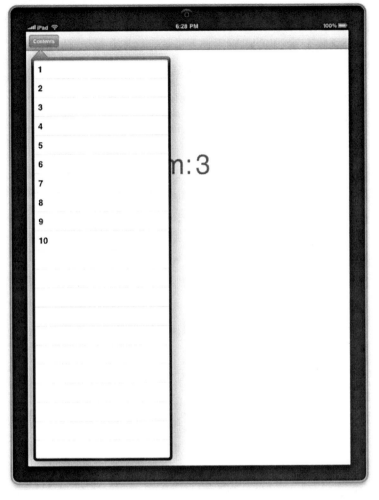

Figure 8–12. *Split view controller in portrait mode, showing the master overlayed on the detail view.*

The split view was created specifically for the iPad to take advantage of its screen size being larger than that of the iPhone and iPod Touch.

The master/detail user interface pattern exploits the metaphor that in a user interface you have a master view that allows you to choose from a number of detail views. In the example given in the Example_SplitView companion code and application, there is a table view as the master view. When you click on an item in that table, the detail view changes to reflect the selection. As you can see in figure 8–12 both the master and the detail view are automatically shown in landscape view. However, by default when you rotate your device to portrait mode, the master view is hidden.

The split view is meant to be used such that in portrait mode, you provide a button that your users can touch to show the master view in a UIPopover control. The split view provides you with events (or delegate methods) that provide you with a button that is already wired up to show the master view; you just have to consume them and add the button to your detail view.

Using the Split View

Like other controllers, the split view is easiest to use in code. Simply create a class that subclasses `UISplitViewController` and assign your controllers that it will manage to the `ViewControllers` property. The `ViewControllers` takes an array of two controllers: the first one being the controller that contains the master view, and the second one containing the detail view. For example, the custom split view class in Listing 8–15 comes from the `Example_SplitView` companion code and application.

Listing 8–15. *Implementing a custom split view and assigning the views to it*

```
public class MainSplitView : UISplitViewController
{
        protected Screens.MasterView.MasterTableView _masterView;
        protected Screens.DetailView.DetailViewScreen _detailView;

        public MainSplitView () : base()
        {
                //---- create our master and detail views
                this._masterView = new Screens.MasterView.MasterTableView ();
                this._detailView = new Screens.DetailView.DetailViewScreen ();

                //---- create an array of controllers from them and then assign it
                // to the controllers property
                this.ViewControllers = new UIViewController[] { this._masterView,
                        this._detailView };

                …
        }
}
```

Creating Views for the Split View

If you're using Interface Builder to create your master and detail view controllers, it will automatically size your views appropriately if you change the **Split View** setting in the **Simulated User Interface Elements** in the **Attributes Inspector**. See Figure 8–13.

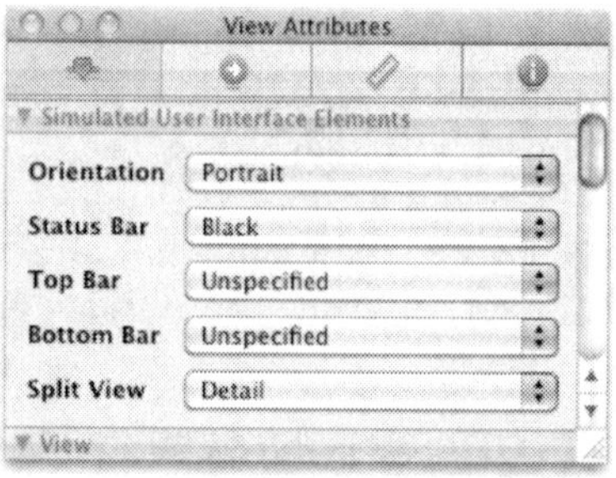

Figure 8–13. *Changing the Split View setting will automatically resize your view in Interface Builder*

That way, your view is automatically sized to simulate the actual size it will be in the split view.

Showing and Hiding the Button to Show the Master View

Out of the box, the split view doesn't automatically add the button to your detail view that shows the master view. However, it does provide an event that gives you a button that is already wired up to show the view in a popover controller. In order to use this button, you should first define a place for it in your detail view, and then provide a method to add the button to that place. For example, in Listing 8–16, I put a toolbar at the top of the detail view, and then provided the following methods to add and remove the button.

Listing 8–16. *Providing methods in a detail view controller to add and remove the button to show the master view*

```
public void AddContentsButton (UIBarButtonItem button)
{
        button.Title = "Contents";
        this.tlbrTop.SetItems(new UIBarButtonItem[] { button }, false );
}
public void RemoveContentsButton ()
{
        this.tlbrTop.SetItems(new UIBarButtonItem[0], false);
}
```

How and where you add the button is your choice, but for consistency purposes, it's a good idea to show it in the upper left corner.

Next, in your split view controller, you should handle the WillHideViewController and WillShowViewController events to call the methods that you define in your detail view controller.

```
this.WillHideViewController += (object sender, UISplitViewHideEventArgs e) => {
        this._detailView.AddContentsButton(e.BarButtonItem);
};
this.WillShowViewController += (object sender, UISplitViewShowEventArgs e) => {
        this._detailView.RemoveContentsButton();
};
```

You could also handle this in the delegate, but in this case it's simplest to use the events. WillHideViewController is raised when the device is rotated into portrait mode, and therefore the master view will be hidden, so in that event handler you should call your method to show the button.

WillShowViewController is raised when the device is rotated into landscape mode, and therefore the master controller will be shown, so in that event handler you should call your method to remove/hide the button.

Communicating Between the Master and Detail View

Once you have your master and detail view up and running, it quickly becomes necessary to formulate a way for them to communicate with each other. There are a couple ways to handle this, depending on your needs. One way is to pass a reference to the other controller in each controller; however, the problem with this is that when something occurs in one of the controllers – say a button click that should affect the other controller – the split view controller doesn't know that anything has occurred.

Therefore, the best practice is to raise events in each controller, and then have the split view controller handle them and call the appropriate methods on the appropriate controller, thereby acting as a controller/mediator between the two child controllers. For example, in Listing 8–17, when a user clicks on a row in the master view, I raise an event that is handled in the split view controller and sets the appropriate data on the detail controller.

Listing 8–17. *Handling an event on the split view controller to affect the detail controller*

```
this._masterView.RowClicked +=
        (object sender, MasterView.MasterTableView.RowClickedEventArgs e) => {
        this._detailView.Text = e.Item;
};
```

The nice thing about this pattern is that, because the split view controller is the main controller, you can then swap out detail controllers based on what's happening in the master controller. For instance, say you had several different options on the master view, that when clicked, each one should show a different detail view.

Web View

The iOS has one of the best built-in mobile browsers available. It ships with Mobile Safari, which bases its rendering engine on WebKit, the same rendering engine used in Safari, Google Chrome, and others.

Apple makes the core browser functionality available via the UIWebView control. With it, it's easy to integrate a full-featured browser directly into your application. Not only can you use it to display web pages, but it also provides a rich document display engine. You can display HTML documents complete with images, JavaScript, and other content, directly from your application. Taking it one step further, you can package your content as XML and use the XSL transform feature in .NET to style your content and display it to your users.

Additionally, the web view also supports a number of non-web document formats, including Microsoft Word, Microsoft Excel, Rich Text Format (RTF), Portable Document Format (PDF), and a number of other document formats.

In this chapter, we'll take a look at how to use the web view, including loading web pages, navigation, handling interaction, and so on. Then we'll cover loading local content, other document types, and finally, I'm going to talk about some magic that we can do to listen for events on the page and actually run JavaScript that allow you to deeply interact with the web view to use it as a powerful content rendering engine.

Using the Web View

Using the web view control is very easy, all you have to do is add it to your view controller and call LoadRequest, passing a URL and it will load your web page (see Listing 8–18).

Listing 8–18. *Loading a web request of www.google.com in a web view*

```
myWebView.LoadRequest (new NSUrlRequest (new NSUrl ("http://www.google.com")));
```

The hardest part about loading a web page is actually constructing a URL. LoadRequest takes an NSUrlRequest object. The NSUrlRequest only has one interesting constructor, and that takes an NSUrl object. Let's take a moment to look at NSUrl.

NSUrl

NSUrl represents a URL in CocoaTouch and has a couple of different constructors, depending on what kind of URL you're creating. If you just want to do a plain-old web URL, you can use it by simply supplying the fully qualified web address (in this case, www.google.com.)

We'll look at some of the other constructors in just a bit.

Navigation

Just like a browser, the web view control shares the concept of navigating backward and forward through page history. To this end, it exposes two methods, GoBack and GoForward, which navigate backward and forward in the page history. Before you call them, you should check the CanGoBack and CanGoForward properties to see if navigation in that particular direction is allowed. For example, Listing 8–19 handles the back and forward button clicks in the web browser example in the Example_ContentControls companion application and code:

Listing 8–19. *Navigating backwards and forwards in a web view control*

```
this.btnBack.TouchUpInside += (s, e) => {
        if (this.webMain.CanGoBack) { this.webMain.GoBack (); } };
this.btnForward.TouchUpInside += (s, e) => {
        if (this.webMain.CanGoForward) { this.webMain.GoForward (); } };
```

If you want to stop a request while it's loading, you can call the StopLoading method on the web view. For example, Listing 8–20 handles the stop button click in the sample web browser.

Listing 8–20. *Stopping the loading of a request*

```
this.btnStop.TouchUpInside += (s, e) => { this.webMain.StopLoading (); };
```

Events

The web view exposes events related to loading that allow you to respond to various states and inform users of the loading process. As with other controls, you can either choose to handle them as events, assign a strongly-typed delegate, or use a weak delegate (see chapter 6 for more information on this pattern). The events are described in the following sections.

LoadStarted

LoadStarted is raised at the beginning of the request. You can handle this event to let your user know that the request is loading by showing an activity spinner, or other indicator. For example, the handler in Listing 8–21 is from the web browser sample. It enables the Stop button, enables the navigation buttons based on navigation availability, and starts the animation of an activity spinner.

Listing 8–21. *Handling the LoadStarted method*

```
public void LoadStarted (object source, EventArgs e)
{
        this.btnStop.Enabled = true;
        this.SetBackAndForwardEnable ();
        this.imgBusy.StartAnimating ();
}
protected void SetBackAndForwardEnable ()
{
        this.btnBack.Enabled = this.webMain.CanGoBack;
        this.btnForward.Enabled = this.webMain.CanGoForward;
}
```

LoadingFinished

LoadingFinished is raised when the request has completed loading. You can handle this event to stop or hide any activity indicator that you may have shown while the request was loading. For example, Listing 8–22 is from the web browser sample. It disables the Stop button (since the request is no longer loading), enables the Back and Forward button based on navigation availability (see previous code sample for the SetBackAndForwardEnable method), and then stops the activity spinner.

Listing 8–22. *Handling the LoadingFinished method*

```
public void LoadingFinished (object source, EventArgs e)
{
        this.btnStop.Enabled = false;
        this.SetBackAndForwardEnable ();
        this.imgBusy.StopAnimating ();
}
```

LoadError

The LoadError event is raised when there is a problem with the request. This most commonly happens if the device does not have connectivity. As per the *Apple Human*

Interface Guidelines, you are required to handle this event and notify the user if they do not have connectivity. If you load internet requests, Apple will test your application with and without connectivity, and if you don't fail gracefully and let your user know that they don't have connectivity, your application is almost certain to be rejected.

For example, Listing 8–23 is again from the web browser sample. It alerts the user with the reason why their web request failed to load.

Listing 8–23. *Handling the* LoadError *method*

```
public void LoadError (object sender, UIWebErrorArgs e)
{
        this.imgBusy.StopAnimating ();
        this.btnStop.Enabled = false;
        this.SetBackAndForwardEnable ();
        //---- show the error
        UIAlertView alert = new UIAlertView ("Browse Error"
                , "Web page failed to load: " + e.Error.ToString ()
                , null, "OK", null);
        alert.Show ();
}
```

Running this with no Internet connectivity will result in the alert shown in Figure 8–14.

Figure 8–14. *Alerting the user that there is no Internet connection*

Loading Local Content

One of the most powerful uses of the web view control is to use it as a content rendering engine. You can format your content as HTML and then display it in the web view. Because it's a full-featured browser engine, it supports everything that would normally work in Mobile Safari, such as rich CSS integration, JavaScript, and the like.

You can even take it one step further and store your content as XML and then use .NET's built-in support for applying XSL style sheets to transform the XML into XHTML, and then display it in the web view. As you can imagine, with this technique, you could build content-rich applications very easily.

There are two ways to load local content: you can either call LoadRequest and give it a path to a file, or you can load content directly from a string. When you pass a path to load from, you should use the BundlePath property of the MainBundle object to get the local directory of your application. From there, you can append the path to your content as it appears in your project file. For example, Listing 8–24 loads the Home.html file from the Content directory of the project.

Listing 8–24. *Loading local content in a web view*

```
string homePageUrl = NSBundle.MainBundle.BundlePath + "/Content/Home.html";
this.webMain.LoadRequest (new NSUrlRequest (new NSUrl (homePageUrl, false)));
```

When storing and loading content, there are two things that you should keep in mind: first, while the simulator is not case-sensitive, the device is, so make sure you have all your casing correct; otherwise, it'll work in the simulator but not on your device. Second, you content must have a build action of Content, or it won't get compiled into your application.

When you load HTML content into the web view directly from a string, you call LoadHtmlString and pass your HTML as well as a path in which you want it to execute in. For example, Listing 8–25 loads a page of HTML directly from a string, and sets the base directory to be the Content directory, so any links from the page will be relative to that directory.

Listing 8–25. *Loading content directly from a string of HTML*

```
string contentDirectoryPath = NSBundle.MainBundle.BundlePath + "/Content/";
this.webMain.LoadHtmlString ("<html><a href=\"Home.html\">Click Me</a>"
        , new NSUrl (contentDirectoryPath, true));
```

In this case, we used a different NSUrl constructor where the second parameter is a boolean value indicating whether or not the path was a directory.

Interacting with Page Content

While the web view makes a great content rendering engine, there are times in which it would be really nice if you could interact with the content. For instance, say you want to run a script on the page, or you want to listen for a user click on an element to launch something in the application.

Apple makes the first scenario very easy by allowing us to run a script on the page, but the second scenario is a little more complex. Let's look at the first scenario.

Running JavaScript

The web view exposes a method called EvaluateJavascript that allows you to run JavaScript code within the context of the page. You can pass the function any executable script in the method and the web view will run it. This can be extremely effective if you have methods that you want to call on the page. For instance, say that you have the JavaScript shown in Listing 8–26 in your page.

Listing 8–26. *Executing JavaScript in the web view*

```
<script language="javascript">
        function RunAction()
        {
                alert('RunAction javascript method called');
        }
</script>
```

You can run that script by calling:

```
myWebView.EvaluateJavascript ("RunAction();");
```

Listening for Events

Unfortunately, the web view doesn't give us an easy way to listen for events the way it allows us to run JavaScript, so we have to get a little crafty.

The web view exposes an event called ShouldStartLoad that we can use for just this purpose. You can use ShouldStartLoad to intercept load requests by the web view, figure out what the request is, and then return false if you want to handle the request, instead of letting the browser do it. For example, let's say that we have the following link, and we want to handle it by loading a screen in the application:

```
<a href="//LOCAL/Action=Image">action test</a>
```

One of the parameters of ShouldStartLoad is a UIWebViewNavigationType enumeration which tells us whether the request was from a link, a form submission, or something else. It'll even tell us if the user is navigating backward or forward (via the GoBack or GoForward methods). You can then use this, in conjunction with the NSUrlRequest parameter, to parse the request and then handle it in the application. For example, Listing 8–27 looks for the link that we just defined and shows an alert when it's clicked:

Listing 8–27. *Handling a link click in a web view by your application*

```
public bool HandleStartLoad (UIWebView webView, NSUrlRequest request
        , UIWebViewNavigationType navigationType)
{
        Console.WriteLine (navigationType.ToString ());

        //---- first, we check to see if it's a link
        if (navigationType == UIWebViewNavigationType.LinkClicked)
        {
```

```
                        //---- next, we check to see if it's a link with //LOCAL in it.
                        if(request.Url.RelativeString.StartsWith("file://LOCAL"))
                        {
                                new UIAlertView ("Action!", "You clicked an action.", null,
                                        "OK", null).Show();
                                //---- return false so that the browser doesn't try to navigate
                                return false;
                        }
                }
                //---- if we got here, it's not a link we want to handle
                return true;
        }
```

Loading Non-Web Documents

In addition to HTML, the web view supports the rendering of the following document types:

- Microsoft Excel (.xls)

- Microsoft Word (.doc)

- Microsoft PowerPoint (.ppt)

- Apple Numbers (.numbers and .numbers.zip)

- Apple Keynote (.keynote and .keynote.zip)

- Apple Pages (.pages and .pages.zip)

- Portable Document Format (.pdf)

- Rich Text Format (.rtf)

- Rich Text Format Directory (.rtfd.zip)

You can load these documents just as you would any other local content. Simply call LoadRequest and pass the path to the file.

Map View

CocoaTouch UIKIt includes the UIMapView control, which gives you the same powerful, easy to use map control that is used in the Maps Application. See Figure 8–15.

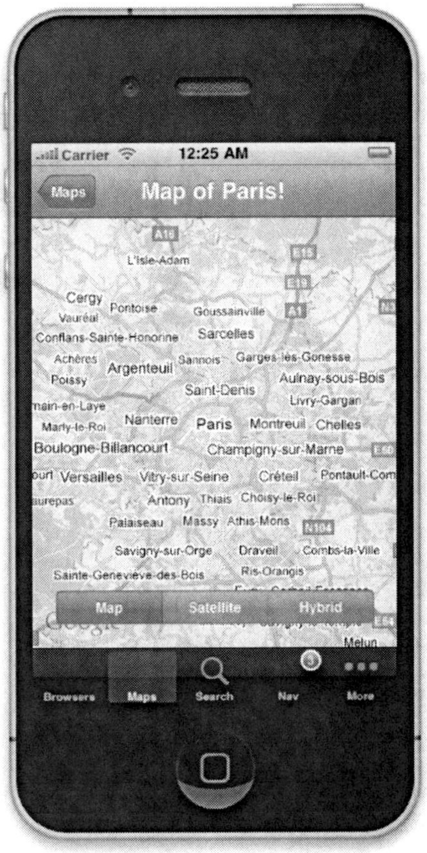

Figure 8–15. *Map view control in an application*

Just like with the Maps Application, the map control supports pinch and zoom touches, as well as scrolling via touch. By default, both zooming and scrolling are enabled, but you can turn them off via the ZoomEnabled and ScrollEnabled properties.

Using the Map View

Using the map view is easy. Simply drop the view into your controller and set the Region property, passing in a CLLocationCoordinate2D that specifies the latitude/longitude of the center of the map, and an MKCoordinateSpan that specifies the size of the area to zoom to. For example, Listing 8–28 displays the map of Paris.

Listing 8–28. *Setting the map to display Paris, with a zoom level of 20 miles*

```
//---- create our location and zoom for paris
CLLocationCoordinate2D coords = new CLLocationCoordinate2D(48.857, 2.351);
MKCoordinateSpan span = new MKCoordinateSpan(
        MilesToLatitudeDegrees(20), MilesToLongitudeDegrees(20, coords.Latitude));
```

```
//---- set the coords and zoom on the map
this.mapMain.Region = new MKCoordinateRegion(coords, span);
```

Creating an MKCoordinateSpan requires the degrees, in latitude and longitude, of the area to display (thus creating the zoom level); however, if you want to convert miles to degrees, you can use the methods shown in Listing 8–29.

Listing 8–29. *Converting miles to latitudinal and longitudinal degrees*

```
public double MilesToLatitudeDegrees(double miles)
{
        double earthRadius = 3960.0;
        double radiansToDegrees = 180.0/Math.PI;
        return (miles/earthRadius) * radiansToDegrees;
}
public double MilesToLongitudeDegrees(double miles, double atLatitude)
{
        double earthRadius = 3960.0;
        double degreesToRadians = Math.PI/180.0;
        double radiansToDegrees = 180.0/Math.PI;

        //---- derive the earth's radius at that point in latitude
        double radiusAtLatitude = earthRadius * Math.Cos(atLatitude * degreesToRadians);
        return (miles / radiusAtLatitude) * radiansToDegrees;
}
```

Different Map Modes

The map view supports the display of the map in the following three modes, contained in the MKMapType enumeration:

- **Regular:** The normal map mode that displays geographic features in an illustrated depiction.

- **Satellite:** Renders the map using satellite images of the area.

- **Hybrid:** A mix between Regular and Satellite, Hybrid mode renders the map using satellite images and then overlays geographic information, annotating the satellite view.

You can set the current map view mode via the MapType property. For example, Listing 8–30 handles the ValueChanged even on a button segment control and updates the map display to the appropriate type, depending on which segment is selected.

Listing 8–30. *Updating the map display type depending on what is selected*

```
this.sgmtMapType.ValueChanged += (s, e) => {
        switch(this.sgmtMapType.SelectedSegment)
        {
                case 0:
                        this.mapMain.MapType = MKMapType.Standard;
                        break;
                case 1:
                        this.mapMain.MapType = MKMapType.Satellite;
                        break;
```

```
        case 2:
                this.mapMain.MapType = MKMapType.Hybrid;
                break;
    }
};
```

When Hybrid is selected, the view looks like Figure 8–16.

Figure 8–16. *The map view in Hybrid mode showing a satellite image with features overlayed.*

Using Device Location

The map can automatically display the location of the device by setting the
ShowsUserLocation property to true (see Listing 8–31).

Listing 8–31. *Centering the map at the device location*

```
this.mapMain.ShowsUserLocation = true;
```

The map will then center on the location of the device; as the device moves, the map will
update, keeping the map centered on the device location.

Annotating the Map

You can add annotations to the map such as pins that mark locations on the map. See Figure 8–17.

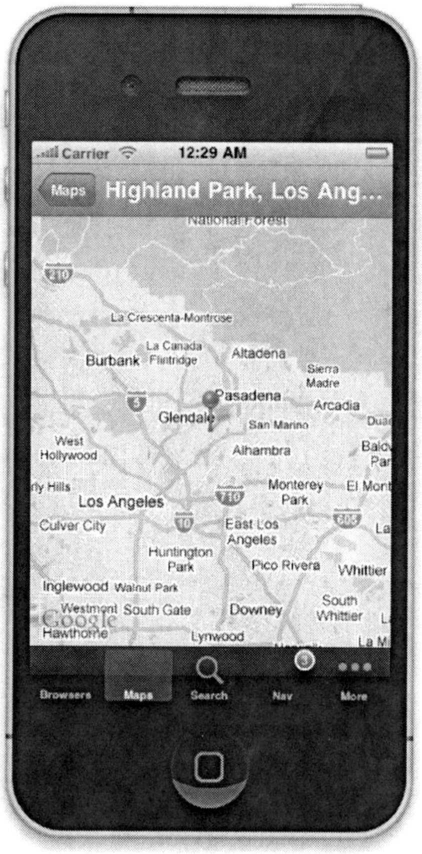

Figure 8–17. *A pin annotation on the map view*

To add an annotation to the map view, first create a class that subclasses the MKAnnotation class. See Listing 8–32.

Listing 8–32. *A custom MKAnnotation class*

```
/// <summary>
/// MonoTouch doesn't provide even a basic map annotation base class, so this can
/// serve as one.
/// </summary>
protected class BasicMapAnnotation : MKAnnotation
{
        /// <summary>
        /// The location of the annotation
        /// </summary>
        public override CLLocationCoordinate2D Coordinate { get; set; }
```

```
/// <summary>
/// The title text
/// </summary>
public override string Title
{ get { return this._title; } }
protected string _title;

/// <summary>
/// The subtitle text
/// </summary>
public override string Subtitle
{ get { return _subtitle; } }
protected string _subtitle;

/// <summary>
///
/// <summary>
public BasicMapAnnotation (CLLocationCoordinate2D coordinate, string title,
        string subTitle)
        : base()
{
        this.Coordinate = coordinate;
        this._title = title;
        this._subtitle = subTitle;
}
}
```

MKAnnotation has the following three properties that are important:

- **Coordinate:** The only required property, Coordinate specifies the location of the annotation.

- **Title:** Optional, Title specifies the first line of text in an annotation callout.

- **SubTitle:** Optional, Subtitle specifies the second line of text in an annotation callout.

You can then add your annotation objects to your map view via the AddAnnotation method, shown in Listing 8–33.

Listing 8–33. *Adding an annotation to a map view*

```
this.mapMain.AddAnnotation(new BasicMapAnnotation(
        new CLLocationCoordinate2D(34.120, -118.188), "Los Angeles", "City of Demons"));
```

You should add all of your annotations when you create your map view; the map view will handle cleaning them up when they go off screen, and re-adding them when they come back into view.

GetViewForAnnotation

The previous example will get you a basic annotation, but to really customize it, you need to implement an MKMapViewDelegate and override the GetViewForAnnotation method. GetViewForAnnotation is exactly like the GetCell method in the table delegate, but instead returning a cell, you return an MKAnnotationView object.

GetViewForAnnotation is called by the map view whenever an annotation needs to be retrieved to display on the screen. This can happen quite often, as a user scrolls around on the map because just as with table cells, when the annotation goes out of view, the iOS scavenges its object and puts it in a pool so that it can be reused for other annotations.

Listing 8–34 is a sample map view delegate that implements the GetViewForAnnotation method and returns an MKPinAnnotationView as the annotation view.

Listing 8–34. *Implementing* GetViewForAnnotation *in a custom map delegate*

```
protected class MapDelegate : MKMapViewDelegate
{
        protected string _annotationIdentifier = "BasicAnnotation";

        public override MKAnnotationView GetViewForAnnotation (
                MKMapView mapView, NSObject annotation)
        {
                //---- try and dequeue the annotation view
                MKAnnotationView annotationView =
                        mapView.DequeueReusableAnnotation(this._annotationIdentifier);

                //---- if we couldn't dequeue one, create a new one
                if (annotationView == null)
                {
                        annotationView =
                        new MKPinAnnotationView(annotation, this._annotationIdentifier);
                }
                else //---- if we did dequeue one for reuse, assign the annotation to it
                { annotationView.Annotation = annotation; }

                //---- configure our annotation view properties
                annotationView.CanShowCallout = true;
                (annotationView as MKPinAnnotationView).AnimatesDrop = true;
                (annotationView as MKPinAnnotationView).PinColor =
                        MKPinAnnotationColor.Green;
                annotationView.Selected = true;

                return annotationView;
        }
}
```

The pattern in this code example is almost exactly the same pattern for table cells. The iOS keeps a pool of annotation view objects for the map, and you can reuse them via the DequeueReusableAnnotation method in conjunction with a reuse identifier (for more context see Chapter 9). To understand the rest of the code, though, we need to examine annotation views.

Annotation Views

An MKAnnotationView object is different from an MKAnnotation in that it contains the callout view that the annotation displays when it's selected, as well as the MKAnnotation object that specifies the coordinates. When you create an MKAnnotation, you pass it your MKAnnotation (it can later be found on the read-only Annotation property), and a reuse identifier. The reuse identifier is used to identify the type of annotation view so that you can reuse them like templates.

The easiest way to customize an annotation view is to set properties on it that control its display. For example, the following are some common properties that you can set on an annotation view:

- CanShowCallout: Whether the callout will be displayed when a user clicks on the marker on the map.

- Image: You can specify an image that will be displayed in the callout via the Image property. If you provide an image, the callout will automatically resize itself to fit the image.

- RightCalloutAccessoryView and LeftCalloutAccessoryView: These two properties allow you to set a custom view on either the right or left side of the annotation view.

For example, setting the properties shown in Listing 8–35 will result in a callout similar to the one in Figure 8–18.

Listing 8–35. *Customizing an annotation view*

```
annotationView.CanShowCallout = true;
annotationView.RightCalloutAccessoryView =
UIButton.FromType(UIButtonType.DetailDisclosure);
annotationView.LeftCalloutAccessoryView =
        new UIImageView(UIImage.FromBundle("Images/Apress-29x29.png"));
```

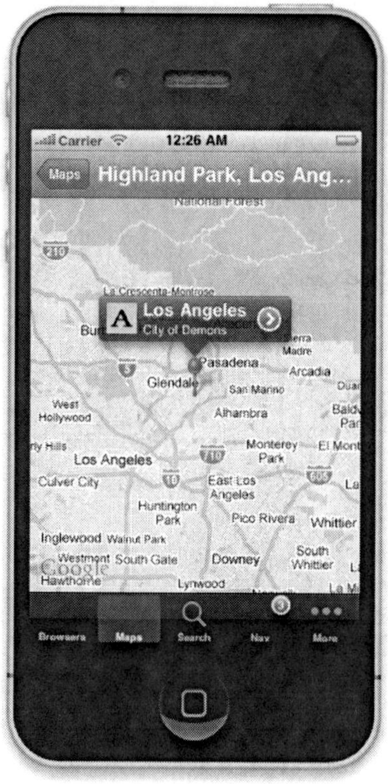

Figure 8–18. *A customized annotation view with left and right accessories set*

If the basic annotation view isn't quite enough for what you need, you can also subclass it and do the rendering yourself during the Draw method.

MKPinAnnotationView

In the delegate in figure 8–18, we created an MKPinAnnotationView. MKPinAnnotationView is a specialized that annotation view that gave us a few more options. Specifically, by using a pin annotation, we were able to do the following (see Listing 8–36).

Listing 8–36. *An MKpinAnnotationView gives us a little more control over the marker on the map.*

```
(annotationView as MKPinAnnotationView).AnimatesDrop = true;
(annotationView as MKPinAnnotationView).PinColor = MKPinAnnotationColor.Green;
```

If you set the AnimatesDrop property to true, when the map is first displayed, the annotation marker (pin) will drop onto the map.

The PinColor property allows us to select from three different colors for the pin, available in the MKPinAnnotationColor enumeration (Red, Green, and Blue).

Handling Annotation Callout Clicks

In figure 8–18, we gave the annotation view a detail disclosure button as its right accessory view. The detail disclosure indicates that clicking on the button will result in a detail information screen for that particular item. To handle the click, simply add a handler as you would any other button. For instance, Listing 8–37 creates the button, adds a handler that shows an alert when clicked that displays the coordinates, and then adds that button as the right callout accessory view.

Listing 8–37. *Handling user interaction on a callout*

```
UIButton detailButton = UIButton.FromType(UIButtonType.DetailDisclosure);
detailButton.TouchUpInside += (s, e) => { new UIAlertView("Annotation Clicked", "You
clicked on " +
        (annotation as MKAnnotation).Coordinate.Latitude.ToString() + ", " +
        (annotation as MKAnnotation).Coordinate.Longitude.ToString() , null, "OK",
        null).Show(); };
annotationView.RightCalloutAccessoryView = detailButton;
```

Clicking on the detail disclosure button would then result in the alert shown in Figure 8–19.

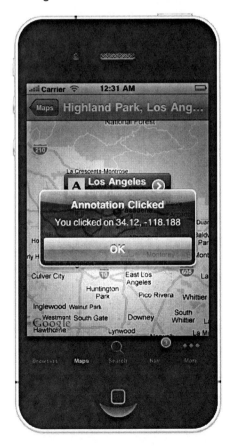

Figure 8–19. *Showing an alert when an annotation has been clicked.*

Annotation Performance Considerations

Because the map allows an unlimited number of annotations, there are two optimizations that you should consider to ensure a responsive map view as well as a pleasant user experience.

- **Annotation Reuse:** When implementing GetViewForAnnotation, make sure to make use of the DequeueReusableAnnotation so that your annotation objects are put in the pool when not onscreen, and are reused when they come into view.

- **Annotation Display:** Because a user can zoom in and out on the map view, you should consider overriding the RegionChanged method in the map view delegate and managing the number of annotations that are on the map via the AddAnnotation and RemoveAnnotation methods. For example, as a user zooms out (and more of the map becomes visible), you may want to reduce the number of annotations displayed. This not only helps with performance, but also provides a much nicer experience for the user, because they aren't inundated with too many pins when they zoom out, and when they zoom in, they're able to see more detail.

User Overlays

Overlays are a special kind of annotation that allow you to draw shapes on the map, such as lines, circles, rectangles, polygons, and so on, and then optionally fill them in. For example, Figure 8–20 shows the Pyramids at Giza with a circle overlay.

Figure 8–20. *A circle overlay above the Pyramids at Giza.*

Overlays are available in iOS 4.0 and later and are useful in showing all kinds of data that is best illustrated on a map such as routes, population distribution, and the like.

Overlays are similar to annotations, and in fact, under the hood they're treated nearly identically. The general pattern to using overlays is as follows:

1. Create an overlay shape.

2. Add the overlay to the Map view.

3. Implement the `GetViewForOverlay` delegate.

Creating the Overlay

When creating an overlay, you can choose from a number of built-in shapes, or you can define your own custom shape. The built-in overlay shapes are contained in the following classes:

- `MKCircle`: Defines a circular area that can optionally be filled. You create an `MKCircle` via the static `Circle` method on the `MKCircle` class.

- MKPolygon: Defines a polygon area that can optionally be filled. You can mask out areas within the polygon by adding interior polygons via the InteriorPolygons property. You created an MKPolygon via the static FromPoints or FromCoordinates methods on the MKPolygon class.

- MKPolyline: Defines a multi-segment line. You create an MKPolyline from the static FromCoordinates method on the MKPolyline class.

For example, Listing 8–38 is from the Example_ContentControls companion code and application and creates the circle overlay seen in figure 8–20.

Listing 8–38. *Creating a circle overlay*

```
CLLocationCoordinate2D coords = new CLLocationCoordinate2D(29.976111, 31.132778);
this._circleOverlay = MKCircle.Circle(coords, .5);
```

In addition to the built-in shapes, you can define your own via a CGPath object and then use the MKOverlayPathView class in the GetViewForOverlay method. For more information on how to use a CGPath, see Chapter 14.

Adding the Overlay

Once you've created your overlay shape, you can add it to the map view via either the AddOverlay method, or the AddOverlays method if you have more than one overlay to add. For example, Listing 8–39 adds the circle overlay we just created.

Listing 8–39. *Adding a circle overlay to a map view*

```
this.mapMain.AddOverlay(this._circleOverlay);
```

Implementing GetViewForOverlay

Once you've created and added your overlay to the map view, you need to implement the GetViewForOverlay method as part of your map view delegate (or handle the GetViewForOverlay event, and so on). GetViewForOverlay is different than GetViewForAnnotation in that there is no template reuse, so you don't have to worry about the deque reusable calls or reuse identifiers.

Instead, you simply have to instantiate a view that contains your shape. Each shape has an associated view class: MKCircleView, MKPolygonView, and MKPolylineView. If you're using a custom CGPath, then you use an MKOverlayPathView object. For example, Listing 8–40 uses a Lamda delegate to handle the GetViewForOverlay event.

Listing 8–40. *Implementing* `GetViewForOvlerlay` *to configure the view to hold our circle overlay*

```
this.mapMain.GetViewForOverlay += (m, o) => {
        if(this._circleView == null)
        {
                this._circleView = new MKCircleView(this._circleOverlay);
                this._circleView.FillColor = UIColor.LightGray;
        }
        return this._circleView;
};
```

In this code, we create a view for the shape, assign any display properties we want, such as fill color, line width, color, and so on, and then return that view. In this case, I've defined the view at the class level, so that I check to see if it's already been initialized, and if it hasn't I configure it.

Of course, as specified in Chapter 6, you could also implement a map view delegate and override the `GetViewForOverlay` method in there as well.

Search Bar

The UISearchBar control is a very simple control that is really just a text box with a magnifier glass icon and an "x" button. It's commonly paired with a table control to display search results. See Figure 8–21.

Figure 8–21. *Search bar with a table view displaying results*

Despite its name, the search control doesn't actually provide any search functionality. It's really just a fancy text box. To use it, you simply listen for the TextChanged event and display (in your choice of format) the appropriate search results to the user. For example, in the Example_ContentControls companion code and application, I've paired the search bar with a table view and when the text changes, I update the table based on the value of the Text property. See Listing 8–41.

Listing 8–41. *Updating a table with search results when the text changes in a search bar*

```
this.srchMain.TextChanged += (s, e) => {
        //---- select our words
        this._tableSource.Words = this._dictionary
                .Where(w => w.Contains(this.srchMain.Text)).ToList();

        //---- refresh the table
        this.tblMain.ReloadData();
};
```

You can also use the SearchButtonClicked event to show results; however, it is much better to give instant feedback by updating the results more during editing. Then, when a user clicks the search button, simply dismiss the keyboard, so that the results are in view. See Listing 8–42.

Listing 8–42. *Dismissing the keyboard when a user clicks the search button*

```
this.srchMain.SearchButtonClicked += (s, e) => { srchMain.ResignFirstResponder(); };
```

Summary

With this chapter, we've finished off the last of the controls in MonoTouch. If you've been reading this book through from front to back you should now have a solid understanding of nearly every control in the UIKit, how to use them and, when appropriate, how to extend them. In the next chapter, we're going to finish our journey through the user experience layer by examining working with keyboards.

Chapter 9

Working with Tables

Tables are the workhorse control of iOS applications. In fact, it's hard to find a non-game application that doesn't use tables in some manner. And because they're so customizable, you may not even know that you're using a table!

Although tables certainly aren't a new invention by any means in terms of application development, tables in iOS are very specific. Unlike tables in other application development frameworks that you might be familiar with, tables in iOS can have many rows, but only one column. This may seem like a limitation, but you can actually put just about anything you want in a row, so you can actually imitate columns, if need be.

In this chapter we're going to first look at the different parts of a table, as well as the common classes you use to work with them. Next, we'll cover how to customize tables, and finally, we're going to look at how to make them editable. By the end of the chapter there will be very little about tables we haven't covered.

Parts of the UITableView

When working with tables, it's important to understand the constituent parts, as tables in iOS are a bit different than tables you might be used to. Tables in iOS consist of the following pieces:

- Sections
- Rows
- Headers
- Footers

These pieces are seen in the following screen shot (Figure 9–1).

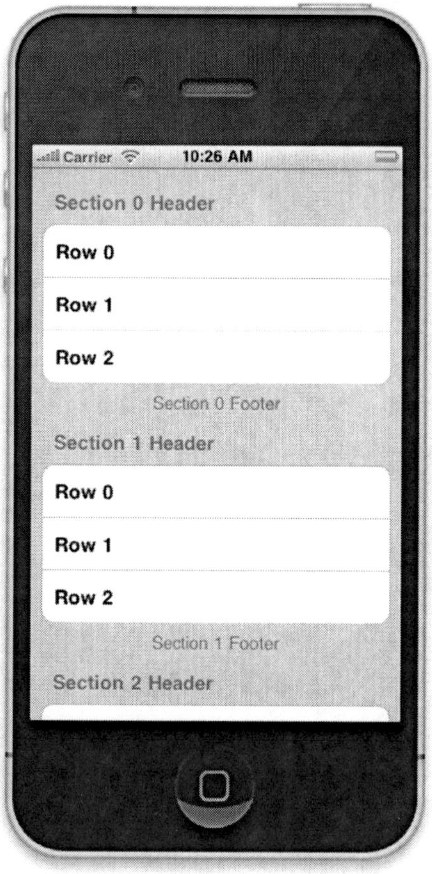

Figure 9–1. *The constituent parts of a table*

While Rows, Headers, and Footers are a common occurrence in tables across platforms, Apple introduces the Section concept as something that is fairly proprietary to their control set. Sections provide a way to logically group rows together. This concept extends beyond just the display of the table on screen to the underlying data source. When you bind data to a table in MonoTouch, you provide sections, which contain rows.

Populating a Table

To populate a table you have to provide a data source to it. I mentioned, in Chapter 6, that a data source in CocoaTouch is a little different. Unlike in traditional .NET UI frameworks, where a data source is typically just a collection of domain objects that implements IEnumerable, a data source in CocoaTouch is a specialized interface that that implements specific methods that tell the OS how to handle the binding and display of data.

In MonoTouch, there are two base classes that provide the framework for implementing a data source—they are UITableViewDataSource and UITableViewDelegate. The table view populates itself by calling methods on these two classes. It's actually a bit confusing, because while UITableViewDelegate is intended to be used to support user interaction, such as when a user clicks on a row, UITableViewDelegate actually contains a number of methods that also pertain to databinding.

The MonoTouch team has gone pretty far in simplifying this by combining the UITableViewDataSource and UITableViewDelegate into one class called UITableViewSource.

UITableViewSource

By using UITableViewSource you don't need two different classes to handle your table binding logic (as well as your user interaction).

When subclassing UITableViewSource, there are a number of methods that you can override to provide data binding functionality. There are also a number of other methods on UITableViewSource that cover other aspects of working with tables, such as allowing rows to be edited, moved, and deleted, as well as methods that pertain to user interaction. We'll cover those methods in their respective sections in this chapter, but for the sake of simplicity, the following methods only include databinding/display functionality:

- RowsInSection: Called by the table view to determine how many cells to create for that particular section. **This method is required**.

- GetCell: Called by the table view to get the actual UITableViewCell to render for the particular section and row. **This method is required**.

- NumberOfSections: Called by the table view to determine how many sections (groups) there are.

- TitleForHeader: Called by the table view to retrieve the header text for the particular section (group).

- TitleForFooter: Called by the table view to retrieve the footer text for the particular section (group).

- GetHeightForRow: Override this method if you need to specify a custom height for a row.

- GetHeightForFooter: Similar to GetHeightForRow, override if you need a custom height for a footer row.

- GetHeightForHeader: Similar to GetHeightForFooter, override if you need a custom height for a header row.

- GetViewForFooter: If you want to provide a custom view for your footer, you can override this method.

■ GetViewForHeader: Same as GetViewForFooter, except it gets a custom view for the header.

To use the UITableViewSource base class, you simply create a class that inherits from it, and then override the methods you want to provide implementation for.

For example, let's say we wanted to create a simple class that represents table data, whereby each row is represented as a string, and we wrap those items in a item group, as shown in the following class in Listing 9–1.

Listing 9–1. *Sample table item data object*

```
public class TableItemGroup
{
        public string Name { get; set; }
        public string Footer { get; set; }

        public List<string> Items
        {
                get { return this._items; }
                set { this._items = value; }
        }
        protected List<string> _items = new List<string> ();
}
```

We've also made a variable for the footer and header text in this class. This is of course, just a simple class to store data. You could use whatever class you want to store your data, but this simple example will give us a good example of how to use it with a data source to perform the actual databinding.

To populate the data as shown in Figure 9–1, we would do the following (Listing 9–2).

Listing 9–2. *Populating our sample data*

```
List<TableItemGroup> tableItems = new List<TableItemGroup> ();

//---- declare vars
TableItemGroup tGroup;

//---- Section 1
tGroup = new TableItemGroup() { Name = "Section 0 Header", Footer = "Section 0
        Footer" };
tGroup.Items.Add ("Row 0");
tGroup.Items.Add ("Row 1");
tGroup.Items.Add ("Row 2");
tableItems.Add (tGroup);

//---- Section 2
tGroup = new TableItemGroup() { Name = "Section 1 Header", Footer = "Section 1
        Footer" };
tGroup.Items.Add ("Row 0");
tGroup.Items.Add ("Row 1");
tGroup.Items.Add ("Row 2");
tableItems.Add (tGroup);

//---- Section 3
tGroup = new TableItemGroup() { Name = "Section 2 Header", Footer = "Section 2
        Footer" };
```

```
tGroup.Items.Add ("Row 0");
tGroup.Items.Add ("Row 1");
tGroup.Items.Add ("Row 2");
tableItems.Add (tGroup);
```

Given the previous data, we can then create a UITableViewSource as follows (Listing 9–3).

Listing 9–3. *A sample* UITableViewSource *that uses our TableItemGroup class*

```
public class TableSource : UITableViewSource
{
        protected List<TableItemGroup> _tableItems;
        protected string _cellIdentifier = "TableCell";

        public TableSource (List<TableItemGroup> items) { this._tableItems = items; }

        public override int NumberOfSections (UITableView tableView) { return
                this._tableItems.Count; }

        public override int RowsInSection (UITableView tableview, int section)
        {
                return this._tableItems[section].Items.Count;
        }

        public override string TitleForHeader (UITableView tableView, int section)
        {
                return this._tableItems[section].Name;
        }

        public override string TitleForFooter (UITableView tableView, int section)
        {
                return this._tableItems[section].Footer;
        }

        public override UITableViewCell GetCell (
                UITableView tableView, MonoTouch.Foundation.NSIndexPath indexPath)
        {
                //---- declare vars
                UITableViewCell cell = tableView.DequeueReusableCell
                        (this._cellIdentifier);

                //---- if there are no cells to reuse, create a new one
                if (cell == null)
                {
                        cell = new UITableViewCell
                                (UITableViewCellStyle.Default, this._cellIdentifier);
                }

                //---- set the item text
                cell.TextLabel.Text =
                        this._tableItems[indexPath.Section].Items[indexPath.Row];

                return cell;
        }
}
```

The code is fairly simple—we only needed to override a few of the methods mentioned earlier to get all the functionality we needed. The only tricky thing is the `GetCell` call, so let's look at that in detail in Listing 9–4. The first line is a little strange.

Listing 9–4. *Dequeing a cell*

```
UITableViewCell cell = tableView.DequeueReusableCell (this._cellIdentifier);
```

Because iDevices have limited processing power, if we had to create a new `UITableViewCell` control each time one needed to be displayed, there would be tremendous processing overhead and memory usage when trying to render long lists. To counteract this, under the hood, the `UITableView` control keeps a pool of `UITableViewCell` controls, and when a cell scrolls out of view, it goes into the pool for reuse. By calling `DequeueReusableCell` we can attempt to pull an already initialized cell out of the reuse pool.

This is also where our `_cellIdentifier` comes into play. By giving our cell an identifier, they essentially become templates that we can reuse by pulling them out of the cell pool. At first, there won't be any cells to reuse, however, so in the next line, we check to see if the cell is `null`, and if it is, we create a new `UITableViewCell` control, specifying its style, and the `CellIdentifier`.

Finally, we set our properties on the cell. In this case we simply set the text that is displayed, but as we'll see in the "Customizing Tables" section, we can actually do quite a bit here to customize each cell if we wanted to.

That's all there is to creating a `UITableViewSource` or `UITableViewDataSource`. Of course this is just the basics, and you can take it much further, as we'll see in the following sections.

To see a table source in action, checkout the `Example_TableParts` companion code and application.

Responding to User Interaction

Oftentimes, just populating a table is only part of the battle; you also need to respond to when users click on items, etc. As part of the contract defined by `UITableViewDelegate` (and therefore also `UITableViewSource`), there are a number of methods that are related to user interaction. They are as follows:

- `RowSelected`: Called when a user touches a row. Use this method to respond to row selection.

- `WillSelectRow`: Called just before `RowSelected`. This method is useful if you need to modify the selection index that gets passed to `RowSelected`.

- `RowDeselected`: Called when a row loses selection. This happens when another row is selected.

■ WillDeselectRow: Called just before RowDeselected. Just as with WillSelectRow, this method gives you an opportunity to modify the selection index that gets passed to RowDeselected.

When the selection methods are called, they're passed an NSIndexPath that contains Section and Row properties that describe what was selected/deselected.

To see this in action, check out the Example_TableParts companion code and application.

UITableViewController

UIKit includes a controller built specifically to manage table views called UITableViewController. The UITableViewController is a specialized UIViewController that contains a UITableView as its root view, accessible via its TableView property.

In the Objective-C world, the UITableViewController implements the UITableViewDataSource and UITableViewDelegate protocols, so you can add your binding methods directly to a subclass of the controller. Unfortunately, however, in MonoTouch, this is not the case. While this is a limitation, it's easy enough to simply add a UITableViewSource class to your UITableViewController so that you can have that functionality built in, as shown in the following code snippet (Listing 9–5).

Listing 9–5. *Adding a UITableViewSource to a UITableViewController*

```
public class HomeScreen : UITableViewController
{
        …
        public override void ViewDidLoad ()
        {
                base.ViewDidLoad ();
                this.TableView.Source = new TableSource();
                // populate table source with data
                …
        }

        public class TableSource : UITableViewSource
        {
                // TableViewSource implementation
                …
        }
}
```

Generally, when working with tables, it's a good idea to use a UITableViewController, rather than a UITableView directly, because you can encapsulate your databinding and user interaction code into the controller.

Refreshing the Table When Data Changes

If the underlying data that is used to populate your table changes, you can refresh the table by calling the ReloadData method, as shown in Listing 9–6.

Listing 9–6. *Refreshing a table when the underlying data changes*

```
this.tblMain.ReloadData();
```

As with all UI updates, however, you should make sure the ReloadData method is called on the main UI thread. For more information about cross-thread UI updates, see Chapter 6.

Customizing the Appearance of a Table View

Tables in CocoaTouch are incredibly powerful because they're extremely customizable. You have several options for controlling the appearance of tables:

- Table Styles
- Cell Styles
- Custom Cells

Table styles and cell styles require no custom code, they're simply style properties that are applied. With custom cells, you actually create your own custom cell views that are displayed.

All code for customizing the appearance of a table can be found in the Example_TableAndCellStyles companion code and application.

Let's look at each one of the options in detail.

Table Styles

Tables in CocoaTouch come in two flavors, plain and grouped. The plain table style is a more space-efficient style because it takes up the entire table area and there is little unused space; however, the grouped style is more effective in visually separating sections (groups) of rows, as shown in Figure 9–2.

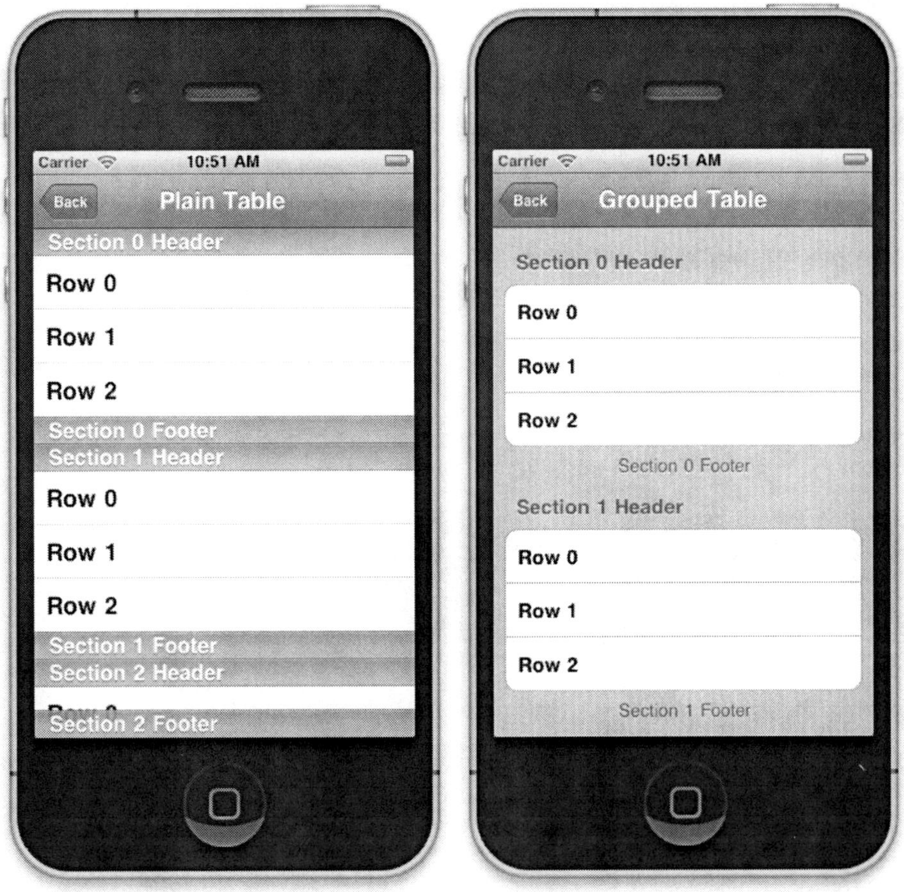

Figure 9–2. *Plain table style and Grouped table style, respectively*

In either style, the headers and footers are optional, but I included them in the previous screenshot to show how they display.

To specify the table style in IB, select the table view and change the **Style** in the Attribute Inspector window, as shown in Figure 9–8.

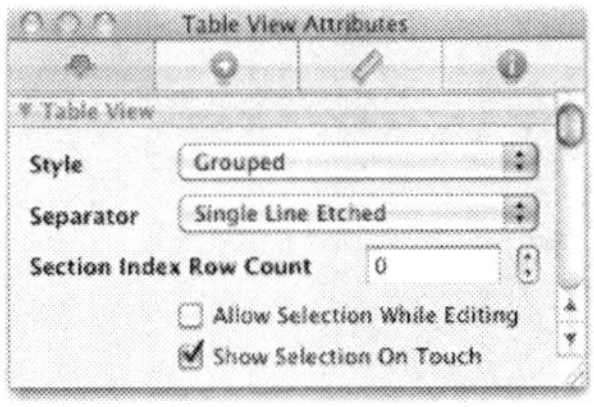

Figure 9–3 *Specifying table style in Interface Builder.*

To set a table style in code, you need to set it in the constructor of the table view, or the table view controller. For example, the following constructor is for a custom

UITableViewController that takes a UITableViewStyle parameter and passes it to the base implementation (Listing 9–7).

Listing 9–7. *Specifying the table style in a UITableViewController constructor*

```
public SimpleTableScreen (UITableViewStyle tableStyle) : base (tableStyle) {}
```

The following code in Listing 9–8 creates a new UITableView with the specified UITableViewStyle.

Listing 9–8. *Specifying the table style on a UITableView*

```
UITableView myTableView = new UITableView(this.View.Frame, UITableViewStyle.Grouped);
```

Providing a Table Index

You can provide a table index for your users, which is a list of clickable section indexes that runs down the right side of the table, as shown in Figure 9–3.

Figure 9–4. *Table indexes*

In order to provide a table index, there are two methods that should be implemented in your table delegate (or table source):

- SectionIndexTitles: Called by the table view to retrieve a list of titles to display on the index list. This method should return an array of string values that it will use to populate the index list.

- SectionFor: Called by the table view to retrieve the section number for the given index title and section number. This method should return an integer that maps to the appropriate section number in your table for the passed in title and/or index number.

Your section index titles don't need to map 1:1 to your actual sections. This is why the SectionFor method exists. SectionFor gives you an opportunity to map whatever indices are in your index list to whatever sections are in your table. For example, you may have a "z" in your index, but you may not have a table section for every letter, so instead of "z" mapping to 26, it may map to 25 or 24, or whatever section index "z" should map to.

For example, we can extend the data source that we created in Listing 9–2 to support a table index, as shown in Listing 9–9.

Listing 9–9. *Extending the data source from 9–2 to support a table index*

```
public class TableSourceWithIndex : TableSource
{
        Dictionary<string, int> _indexSectionMap = null;

        public TableSourceWithIndex (List<TableItemGroup> items
                , Dictionary<string, int> indexSectionMap)
        {
                this._tableItems = items;
                this._indexSectionMap = indexSectionMap;
        }

        public override string[] SectionIndexTitles (MonoTouch.UIKit.UITableView
                tableView)
        {
                return new List<string>(this._indexSectionMap.Keys).ToArray();
        }

        public override int SectionFor (MonoTouch.UIKit.UITableView tableView, string
                title, int atIndex)
        {
                return this._indexSectionMap[title];
        }
}
```

In this example we store our index list as a Dictionary<string, int> that contains the section names and the section index they map to. In the SectionIndexTitles method, we return the list of keys as a string array. Then, in the SectionFor method, we look up the section title and return the index of the section for that title.

To see this code in action, checkout the Example_TableAndCellStyles companion code and application.

Cell Styles

We've seen that you can change the overall style of the table via table styles, but you can also change the style of each individual row (or cell). There are several different cell styles out of the box. They are contained in the UITableViewCellStyle enumeration, which has the following values:

- Default: Allows for an image, a heading, and a cell accessory

- Subtitle: The same as the default style, except that it allows for a subheading below the main text

- Value1: Also known as the Right-Aligned Subtitle style, this style is the same as the Subtitle style, except that the subheading is in the right portion of the cell, rather than under the main text.

- Value2: Also known as the Contact style, this style doesn't support images, but it supports main text and a subheading. The main text is on the left and is small and blue, the subheading text is on the right in bold.

These four cell styles are shown in the following illustration (Figure 9–4).

Figure 9–5. *Default, Subtitle, Value1, and Value2 cell styles*

You set the style of a table cell via the style parameter in the UITableCellView constructor. Typically, this is done during the GetCell method on your UITableViewDataSource, when you create your cells. For example, the following code in Listing 9–10 creates a new subtitle style table style with the identifier of mySubtitleCellTemplate.

Listing 9–10. *Specifying a style when creating a table cell*

```
UITableViewCell myTableCell = new UITableViewCell(UITableViewCellStyle.Subtitle
    , "mySubtitleCellTemplate");
```

Cell Accessories

All of the out-of-the-box cell styles support an accessory view on the cell. An accessory view is a control that appears to the right of the main cell content, as shown in Figure 9–5.

Figure 9–6. *Standard table cell construction*

If the cell isn't in editing mode (which we'll talk about in the "Editable Tables" section), you can set either a custom view as the accessory via the AccessoryView property, or you can set a built in accessory via the Accessory property. The Accessory property takes a value from the UITableViewCellAccessory enumeration, which has several options:

- Checkmark: Puts a check mark in the accessory view. Used to display row selection for checked lists.

- DetailDisclosureButton: Puts a blue circle with a white chevron in the accessory view. Used to indicate that selecting the row will result in getting a detail view screen for the item being clicked.

- DisclosureIndicator: Puts a gray chevron in the accessory view. Used to indicate that selecting the row will result in another table of options.

These three options are shown in their respective order in the following screen shot (Figure 9–6).

Figure 9–7. *Built-in Accessory view options*

One important thing to know: when a user clicks an accessory view, the `RowSelected` method in the table delegate is not called. Instead, if you want to respond to accessory selection, you should override the `AccessoryButtonTapped` method in your table delegate (or `UITableViewSource`). For example, the following method in Listing 9–11 writes out the section and row to the console when an accessory view is clicked.

Listing 9–11. *Handling an accessory click*

```
public override void AccessoryButtonTapped (UITableView tableView
        , NSIndexPath indexPath)
{
        Console.WriteLine("Accessory for Section, " + indexPath.Section.ToString()
                + " and Row, " + indexPath.Row.ToString() + " tapped");
}
```

Other Cell Customizations

Since the 3.0 release of iOS, Apple has exposed APIs to customize a number of other things including `TextColor`, `SelectedTextColor`, `SelectedImage`, `BackgroundView`, `SelectedBackgroundView`, and others.

Custom Cells

The built-in cell styles, in conjunction with the customizable properties, provide a pretty flexible palette with which to work; however, sometimes you need something that is just not possible out of the box.

Fortunately for us, Apple gives us a pretty easy way to do this by allowing us to create our own custom `UITableViewCell` controls and use them in our table views.

You can define your custom cells in either Interface Builder as `.xib` files, or you can create them completely in code.

The basic pattern is to create a view controller that manages a `UITableViewCell` as its view, then, in your `GetCell` method in your data source, you return the table cell that you've defined in the custom view controller.

There is a bit of trickiness with this however. When using a controller to manage your cell, you have to keep track of the controllers in your datasource because while the table contains a collection of cells, it doesn't maintain the controllers that own them. This is easier to understand if we look at the code needed to support this pattern.

First, in your data source class, you should create some kind of collection that will hold your cell controllers, as shown in Listing 9–12.

Listing 9–12. *A generic dictionary that tracks cell controllers*

```
protected Dictionary<int, CustomCellController> _cellControllers =
        new Dictionary<int, CustomCellController>();
```

In the previous code sample, I've defined a generic `Dictionary` that contains a collection of `CustomCellController` (the class name of my custom cell controller) obects and is indexed by integers. I use an int index because I will create a unique index for each one via `Environment.TickCount`.

Then, the `GetCell` method looks like the one we created before when we talked about data sources, except this time we store and retrieve our custom cell controllers and utilize our custom cells (Listing 9–13).

Listing 9–13. *A sample GetCell implementation when using custom cells*

```
public override UITableViewCell GetCell (UITableView tableView, NSIndexPath indexPath)
{
        //---- declare vars
        UITableViewCell cell = tableView.DequeueReusableCell (this._cellIdentifier);
        TableItem item = this._tableItems[indexPath.Section].Items[indexPath.Row];
        CustomCellController1 cellController = null;

        //---- if there are no cells to reuse, create a new one
        if (cell == null)
        {
                cellController = new CustomCellController1();
                cell = cellController.Cell;
                cell.Tag = Environment.TickCount;
                this._cellControllers[cell.Tag] = cellController;
        }
        else //---- if we did get one, we also need to lookup the controller
        {
                cellController = this._cellControllers[cell.Tag];
        }

        //---- set the properties on the cell
        cellController.Heading = item.Heading;
        cellController.SubHeading = item.SubHeading;

        //---- if the item has a valid image
        if(!string.IsNullOrEmpty(item.ImageName))
        {
                if(File.Exists(item.ImageName))
                { cellController.Image = UIImage.FromBundle(item.ImageName); }
        }

        return cell;
}
```

Let's examine how to create our actual cell controller. First we'll look at defining one in a .xib file using Interface Builder, and then we'll look at how to create them directly in code.

Creating a Custom Cell in Interface Builder

To create a custom cell controller in Interface Builder:

1. Start with an **iPhone View with Controller** (or iPad, it doesn't matter) template.

2. Next, delete the default view that's in there and add a `UITableViewCell` from the Library window, as shown in Figure 9–7.

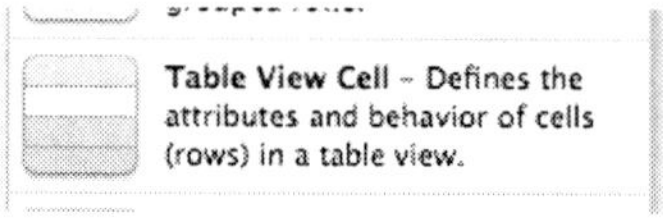

Figure 9–8. *A table cell in the Library window*

3. Once you've added your cell view, you can put controls on it as you would any other view, as shown in Figure 9–8.

Figure 9–9 *A custom table cell and controller in Interface Builder*

4. In order for the cell to be reused as a template, you should set the cell identifier. To set it in Interface Builder, there is an `Identifier` property in the Attributes Inspector, as shown in Figure 9–9.

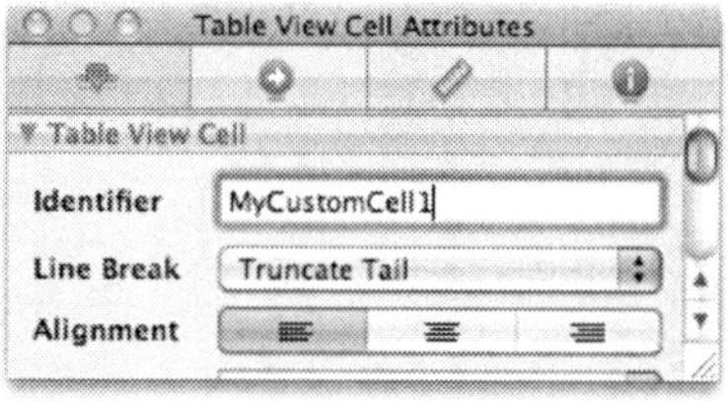

Figure 9–10. *Setting the cell identifier in Interface Builder*

5. Add outlets in Interface Builder and wire them up to any controls you want to be able to access.

6. Next, in your controller, expose your cell view (and any other properties you want), as shown in Listing 9–14.

Listing 9–14. *Exposing the custom cell in a controller (and other properties)*

```
public partial class CustomCellController1 : UIViewController
{
        public UITableViewCell Cell
        {
```

```
                get { return this.celMain; }
        }
        public string Heading
        {
                get { return this.lblHeading.Text; }
                set { this.lblHeading.Text = value; }
        }
        public string SubHeading
        {
                get { return this.lblSubHeading.Text; }
                set { this.lblSubHeading.Text = value; }
        }

        public UIImage Image
        {
                get { return this.imgMain.Image; }
                set { this.imgMain.Image = value; }
        }
        ...
}
```

7. Finally, as we've done with other controllers (and we talked about in Chapter 5), we need to make the .xib constructor synchronous (blocking) rather than asynchronous, a shown in Listing 9–15.

Listing 9–15. *Forcing the default constructor to be synchronous*

```
public CustomCellController1 ()
{
        //---- this next line forces the loading of the xib file to be synchronous
        MonoTouch.Foundation.NSBundle.MainBundle.LoadNib ("CustomCellController1", this
                , null);
        Initialize ();
}
```

If we left it asynchronous (public CustomCellController1 () : base("CustomCellController1", null), when we accessed any of the controls that were defined in the .xib after we instantiated it, we would get a null reference exception. For instance, on these lines in our GetCell method, we would get an error when cell.Tag was accessed because the .xib hadn't fully loaded yet, as shown in Listing 9–16.

Listing 9–16. *When we make our constructor synchronous, this won't error.*

```
cellController = new CustomCellController1();
cell = cellController.Cell;
cell.Tag = Environment.TickCount;
```

That's all that is needed to create and use a custom cell that we created in Interface Builder. Using the same data as before, but with the custom cell, our table now looks like the following (Figure 9–10).

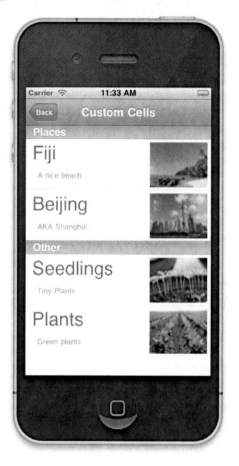

Figure 9–11. *A table with custom cells*

Next, let's look at how to do the same thing, but in code.

Creating a Custom Cell in Code

Creating a custom cell without Interface Builder is a little more difficult in terms of laying out your controls because you don't have a designer to work with. On the other hand, when you create a custom cell in code, you don't have to worry about the asynchronous .xib constructor, since you're not loading your interface from a file.

Other than that, it's the exact same thing. Simply create a new class that inherits from UIViewController and manages a UITableViewCell as its view. One thing to note, if you want to specify the cell identifier so that you can reuse your cells, you must do it in the cell constructor, as shown in Listing 9–17.

Listing 9–17. *Specifying a cell identifier in the cell constructor*

```
UITableViewCell _cell = new UITableViewCell(UITableViewCellStyle.Default
    , "CustomCell2");
```

To create the same cell controller that we built before in Interface Builder, but in code, all we need is the following (Listing 9–18).

Listing 9–18. *Creating a custom cell controller in code*

```
using System;
using MonoTouch.UIKit;
using System.Drawing;

namespace Example_TableAndCellStyles.Code.CustomCells
{
        public class CustomCellController2 : UIViewController
        {
                UILabel _lblHeading = new UILabel(new RectangleF(11, 0, 195, 46));
                UILabel _lblSubHeading = new UILabel(new RectangleF(20, 45, 186, 30));
                UIImageView _imgMain = new UIImageView(new RectangleF(214, 5, 100, 75));

                public UITableViewCell Cell
                { get { return this._cell; } }
                UITableViewCell _cell =
                        new UITableViewCell(UITableViewCellStyle.Default,
                        "CustomCell2");

                public string Heading
                {
                        get { return this._lblHeading.Text; }
                        set { this._lblHeading.Text = value; }
                }
                public string SubHeading
                {
                        get { return this._lblSubHeading.Text; }
                        set { this._lblSubHeading.Text = value; }
                }

                public UIImage Image
                {
                        get { return this._imgMain.Image; }
                        set { this._imgMain.Image = value; }
                }

                public CustomCellController2 () : base()
                {
                        base.View.AddSubview(this._cell);
                        this._cell.AddSubview(this._lblHeading);
                        this._cell.AddSubview(this._lblSubHeading);
                        this._cell.AddSubview(this._imgMain);

                        this._imgMain.AutoresizingMask =
                                UIViewAutoresizing.FlexibleLeftMargin;
                        this._lblHeading.TextColor = UIColor.Brown;
                        this._lblHeading.Font = UIFont.SystemFontOfSize(32);
                        this._lblSubHeading.TextColor = UIColor.DarkGray;
                        this._lblSubHeading.Font = UIFont.SystemFontOfSize(13);

                }
        }
}
```

Editable Tables

Tables in iOS have an edit mode that allows you to insert, delete, and re-order rows. When you put a table in edit mode, the cell width is shortened horizontally, an edit control (such as a "+" for insertion, or "-" for deletion) appears to the left of the cell content, and a reordering control appears to the right of the cell content, as shown in Figure 9–11.

Editing control   Cell content   Reordering control

Figure 9–12. *A cell in edit mode*

The controls appear regardless of whether the table is set to the plain or the grouped style (Figure 9–12).

Figure 9–13. *Tables in edit mode*

To put a table into editing mode, call the `SetEditing` method on the table view. For example, the following code in Listing 9–19 toggles the edit mode of a table.

Listing 9–19. *Toggling the edit mode of a table*

```
myTable.SetEditing (!myTable.Editing, true);
```

The first parameter is whether or not the table should be put into edit mode, and the second parameter is whether or not to animate the transition.

Editing Methods

There are a number of methods related to table editing that are defined in the table view delegate contract:

- `CanEditRow`: Called by the table view to determine whether or not the given row is editable, and therefore should get an editing control

- `CanMoveRow`: Called by the table view to determine whether or not the given row is moveable, and therefore should get a reordering control

- `TitleForDeleteConfirmation`: Called by the table view to determine the title for the delete confirmation button during swipe-to-delete gestures

- `EditingStyleForRow`: Called by the table view to determine whether the editing style for the given row should be insertion or deletion. Return either `UITableViewCellEditingStyle.Insert` or `UITableViewCellEditingStyle.Delete`. If you don't implement this method, the iOS will assume that the editing method should always be `Delete`.

- `CommitEditingStyle`: Called by the table view after a user has clicked on the editing control. Gives you an opportunity to edit the table and your underlying data source in response to the action.

- `MoveRow`: Called by the table view after a user has reordered a row. Gives you an opportunity to modify your underlying data source to stay in sync with the user's action

As with the other methods mentioned earlier in this chapter, they are all defined in the `UITableViewSource` base class, so the easiest way to implement them is to subclass that and override the methods.

Most of the methods are pretty simple, but a couple of them—`CommitEditingStyle` and `MoveRow`—can be tricky.

CommitEditingStyle Method

The CommitEditingStyle method is passed an enumeration value that describes the edit that was made, an NSIndexPath describing what row and section the edit was made on, and a reference to the table that was edited.

The basic pattern for implementing this method is to:

- Determine what kind of edit was made
- Modify the underlying data source in response to the edit
- Modify the table based on the edit

For example, the following method uses the same data structure we've used throughout the chapter to handle Delete and Insert edits on a table, as shown in Listing 9–20.

Listing 9–20. *Sample implementation of CommitEditingStyle*

```
public override void CommitEditingStyle (UITableView tableView,
UITableViewCellEditingStyle editingStyle, MonoTouch.Foundation.NSIndexPath indexPath)
{
        switch (editingStyle)
        {
                case UITableViewCellEditingStyle.Delete:
                        //---- remove the item from the underlying data source
                        this._tableItems[indexPath.Section].Items
                                .RemoveAt (indexPath.Row);
                        //---- delete the row from the table
                        tableView.DeleteRows (new NSIndexPath[] { indexPath }
                                , UITableViewRowAnimation.Fade);
                        break;

                case UITableViewCellEditingStyle.Insert:
                        //---- create a new item and add it to our underlying data
                        this._tableItems[indexPath.Section].Items.Insert (indexPath.Row
                                , new TableItem ());
                        //---- insert a new row in the table
                        tableView.InsertRows (new NSIndexPath[] { indexPath }
                                , UITableViewRowAnimation.Fade);
                        break;

                case UITableViewCellEditingStyle.None:
                        Console.WriteLine ("CommitEditingStyle:None called");
                        break;
        }
}
```

It's important to note that you need to call the DeleteRows and InsertRows methods on the table manually— the table does not do it automatically. This is so you can have control over what rows are inserted or deleted.

MoveRow Method

When MoveRow is called, the method is passed the index of a row before and after it was moved. Unlike CommitEditingStyle, the table handles the moving of the item in the table as part of the user interaction (the user actually drags the item from one spot to another). However, you still need to implement the logic to move your item from one spot to another. For example, the following implementation in Listing 9–21 handles moving of items in response to the source and destination index.

Listing 9–21. *Sample implementation of the MoveRow method*

```
public override void MoveRow (UITableView tableView, NSIndexPath sourceIndexPath,
NSIndexPath destinationIndexPath)
{
        //---- get a reference to the item
        var item = this._tableItems[sourceIndexPath.Section].Items[sourceIndexPath.Row];
        int deleteAt = sourceIndexPath.Row;

        //---- if we're moving within the same section, and we're inserting it before
        if ((sourceIndexPath.Section == destinationIndexPath.Section)
                && (destinationIndexPath.Row < sourceIndexPath.Row))
        {
                //---- add one to where we delete, because we're increasing the index by
                // inserting
                deleteAt = sourceIndexPath.Row + 1;
        }

        //---- copy the item to the new location
        this._tableItems[destinationIndexPath.Section].Items
                .Insert (destinationIndexPath.Row, item);

        //---- remove from the old
        this._tableItems[sourceIndexPath.Section].Items.RemoveAt (deleteAt);

}
```

Deleting Items

It's important to note that there are two ways to delete rows in a table. The first way is as we've seen in the previous screen shot, that is, put the table in edit mode and click the "-" button.

The second way is known as the *swipe-to-delete* gesture. If the editing method for a row is Delete and the table isn't in edit mode, then you can swipe your finger horizontally across a row, which will show a **Delete** button, as shown in Figure 9–13.

Figure 9–14. *Delete confirmation button after a swipe-to-delete gesture*

The text of the Delete button is specified in the TitleForDeleteConfirmation method.

Advanced Table Editing

We've covered basic table editing, but there's one more editing trick up the iOS's sleeve. If you've ever edited a contact in the iOS, you may have noticed that when you put the contact table into edit mode, new rows magically appear. For instance, after the phone numbers, a new row appears, giving you a chance to add another phone number, as shown in Figure 9–14.

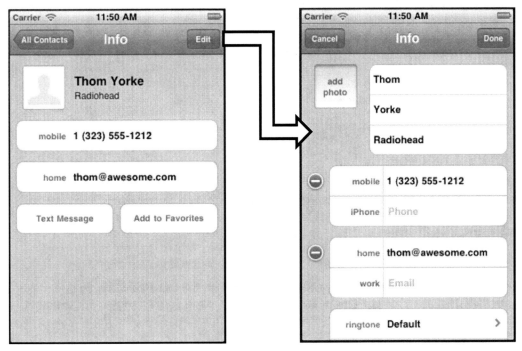

Figure 9–15. *When editing a contact, some rows change and new rows appear.*

This functionality can be extremely useful in certain situations; however, on first glance there doesn't appear to be any way to accomplish it. The problem is, when you put a table into edit mode, it doesn't raise any event or call any methods letting you know that it is changing modes.

The workaround here is to implement these methods yourself and then call them when you toggle the table editing mode. For example, if I define the following methods on my table source, I can modify the table when it goes in and out of editing mode (Listing 9–22).

Listing 9–22. *Adding methods to be notified when a table's edit mode is changed*

```
public void WillBeginTableEditing (UITableView tableView)
{
        …
}
public void DidFinishTableEditing (UITableView tableView)
{
        …
}
```

Then, in the same method that toggles the edit mode of the table (in our case, the handler for the button click), you can call those methods, as shown in Listing 9–23.

Listing 9–23. *Manually calling methods on the table source to let it know when it is going in or out of editing mode*

```
this.btnEdit.Clicked += (s, e) => {
        this.tblMain.SetEditing (!this.tblMain.Editing, true);

        if (this.tblMain.Editing)
        { this._tableSource.WillBeginTableEditing (this.tblMain); }
        else
        { this._tableSource.DidFinishTableEditing (this.tblMain); }
};
```

Implementing the table changes within those methods then becomes just like implementing the `CommitEditingStyle` method; you make any relevant changes to the table, and then the same changes to the underlying data source. The only difference is that, if you want your changes to be animated (and you should, to create a cinematic user experience), you need to wrap your edits in a table update animation.

To animate your edits, you simply call `BeginUpdates` on the table view before you make your changes, and then call `EndUpdates` after you've made your changes. For example, the following code in Listing 9–24 inserts a new row into the table (just like in the contacts application) with a smooth animation.

Listing 9–24. *Wrapping manual table changes in an animation block*

```
public void WillBeginTableEditing (UITableView tableView)
{
        //---- start animations
        tableView.BeginUpdates ();

        //---- insert a new row in the table
        tableView.InsertRows (new NSIndexPath[] { NSIndexPath.FromRowSection (1, 1) }
                , UITableViewRowAnimation.Fade);
        //---- create a new item and add it to our underlying data
        this._tableItems[1].Items.Insert (1, new TableItem ());

        //---- end animations
        tableView.EndUpdates ();
}
```

Hopefully, one day, the MonoTouch team will add these methods to the `UITableViewDelegate` and wrap them in an animation block so we don't have to do them manually, but for now at least we have a workaround.

Table Performance Considerations

While tables are probably the most versatile tool in CocoaTouch, they're also where you can get in the most trouble in terms of performance, if not done properly. This is especially true if you have many rows. While the iDevices get more and more powerful with each successive generation, you still have to optimize your code to get that responsiveness and cinematic feel that users have come to expect from iOS applications. This is especially true with older generation iDevices, where the display of rows in a table can be downright taxing.

It is advisable to deploy to the device early and often to evaluate the performance of your table. The simulator is just that, a simulator, and not the actual device. It operates much faster than the device does, and if you rely on it to gauge the performance of your application, you will almost certainly be disappointed when you deploy to the device.

Furthermore, when you do test your tables, if the users can add their own rows, you should test your application with many more rows than you expect a user to add. If it is still snappy and responsive, you know that you've built it correctly, and your users won't be disappointed with its performance.

Let's examine a number of performance optimizations for tables.

Cell Reuse

Cell reuse is the first technique to employ to have a responsive table. This is especially true if you have lots of rows. If you do not reuse your cells, the iOS has to instantiate new ones each time one is displayed. This can become a huge problem very quickly. In order to determine if your cells are being reused, it is advisable to use a `Console.WriteLine` call in your cell-reuse code to write out to the application console as a cell is being reused when it scrolls onto the page. Make sure you have enough rows that some first appear off the screen, so that when they scroll onto the screen the OS has an opportunity to reuse old ones that have already scrolled off. The examples in this chapter show how to properly reuse cells; if your cells aren't being reused, study the code samples and make sure your implementation is correct.

Cache the Row Height

The table can request the height of your rows quite often. In fact, it will likely request it at least every time the cell is created, and in some cases can request it more often than that. If you are calculating the row height based on cell contents, be sure and cache that value, so you don't have to recalculate it. You may want to create a property on your custom cell controller that calculates and then caches it.

Cache Images

If you're using images, consider caching them so that they don't have to be loaded from a file each time they're displayed. If your cells share images, consider putting them into a `Dictionary` object and pull them from there. Be wary of loading too many, though. It's not unusual to only have half of the device's useable memory at your disposal, so if you have a lot of images, you may have no choice but to load them from file, or at least have a collection where you only store a certain number, and load the least-used from files.

Avoid Transparency

One of the most expensive operations to perform in the iOS is the rendering of transparency. There are two drawing systems on the iOS, CoreGraphics, and CoreAnimation. CoreGraphics utilizes the GPU and CoreAnimation utilizes either the main processor, or the GPU, depending on what it thinks will be fastest, and usually this is the GPU. The problem with this is that the device GPU is not optimized for blending. Because of this, you should try and avoid transparency where possible. If you absolutely cannot avoid transparency, you should do the drawing yourself, which we'll examine next.

Manually Draw the Cell

As a last-ditch effort for performance, you can do the drawing yourself by subclassing UITableViewCell and overriding the Draw method so that you can do the drawing manually. This technique has its drawbacks, however.

- First, it can be technically complex.
- Second, if you're using Draw to create an image and paint it on the view, it can utilize a LOT of memory if you have lots of rows.

For more information on this technique, check out the fifth example in Apple's sample app TableViewSuite, noted below.

Avoid Complex Graphical Computations

As with the transparency issue, stay away from graphical elements that require computation, such as a gradient that isn't already baked into the image you're displaying.

Create Your Cell in Code

If you're running out of optimizations, and you're still needing a performance boost, you can scrap the custom UITableViewCell that you created in Interface Builder altogether and hand-create the controls programmatically.

Further Optimizations

For more examples showing performance optimizations, check out Apple's TableViewSuite example application at
http://developer.apple.com/iphone/library/samplecode/TableViewSuite/index.html.

Summary

This was a lot of content for a single control, but at this point it should be clear why. The table view is the single most versatile and useful control in the entire CocoaTouch UIKit. Not only does it have quite a bit of flexibility out of the box, but you can create your own custom cells to take customization to the next level.

Chapter 10

Working with Keyboards

iOS devices are equipped with software keyboards that automatically appear onscreen when a control that can receive text input receives focus. Additionally, all iDevices support hardware keyboards via Bluetooth or the 30pin accessory connector. When a hardware keyboard is attached to an iPad, users can configure the onscreen (software) keyboard to not show.

There are three main tasks associated with the onscreen keyboard:

- **Configuring the correct keyboard**
- **Scrolling to the input control**
- **Dismissing the keyboard when editing is finished**

In this chapter, we're going to examine all three of these items, plus show you how to customize the keyboard. First, let's take a look at the different types of keyboards and text input mechanisms.

Keyboard/Input Properties

The keyboard automatically appears for input controls so you don't ever use it directly. However, you can modify properties on your input controls that determine which keyboard to use. In Interface Builder you can find these properties in the Attributes Inspector under **Text Input Traits**. See Figure 10–1.

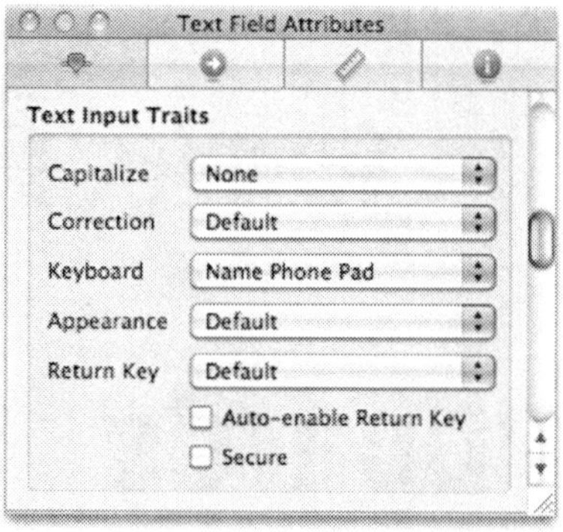

Figure 10–1. *Text Input Traits control the keyboard appearance and type.*

Capitalization

The capitalization setting controls whether (and how) characters that are input are to be capitalized.

The capitalization setting can also be set programmatically via the AutocapitalizationType property, and has the following options (available via the UITextAutocapitalizationType enumeration):

- **AllCharacters:** When set to AllCharacters, every character entered will be capitalized.

- **None:** When set to None, text entered will be unchanged.

- **Sentences:** When set to Sentences, the first word after a sentence's termination punctuation will have its first letter capitalized.

- **Words:** When set to Words, every word will have the first letter capitalized.

Correction

The correction setting determines whether the text input will be given word correction options. You can also set it programmatically via the AutocorrectionType property, and it has the following options (available via the UITextAutocorrectionType enumeration):

- **Default:** When set to Default, correction will occur on most input types.

- **No:** When set to No, correction will not occur.

- **Yes:** When set to Yes, correction will occur.

Keyboard

The keyboard setting specifies what type of keyboard is displayed. The iOS provides several different keyboards that are specific to the input task; for example, there is a URL keyboard that includes keys specific to URLs such a ".com."

You can also set the keyboard type programmatically via the KeyboardType property, which has the following options (available via the UIKeyboardType enumeration):

- **Default:** When set to Default, the keyboard is typically the standard QWERTY layout.

- **ASCIICapable:** ASCIICapable is the keyboard that is usually shown when Default is set, and shows a standard QWERTY keyboard.

- **NumbersAndPunctuation:** When set to NumbersAndPunctuation, the keyboard shows numbers and various punctuation symbols. This keyboard is also accessible via the ASCII keyboard when the "123" button is pressed.

- **URL:** When set to URL, the keyboard shows a QWERTY layout with the addition of common URL characters such as "." and even ".com."

- **NumberPad:** When set to NumberPad, the keyboard shows 0-9 and a backspace key.

- **PhonePad:** When set to PhonePad, the keyboard shows the Number Pad with a "+*#" key that brings up common phone punctuation.

- **NamePhonePad:** When set to NamePhonePad, the keyboard shows a standard QWERTY layout with a "123" button that brings up a Number Pad keyboard. This keyboard is intended to be used for entering phone numbers and names.

- **EmailAddress:** When set to EmailAddress, the keyboard shows a standard QWERTY layout along with an "@" and a "." key.

Figure 10–2 illustrates several of these keyboard types.

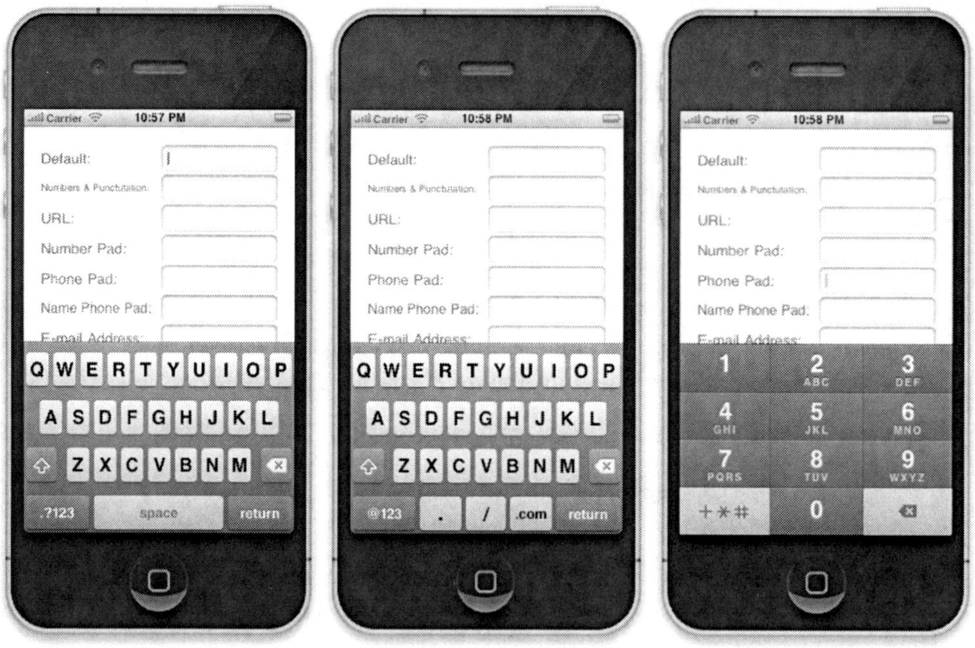

Figure 10–2. *The ASCIICapable, URL, and PhonePad keyboards*

Return Key

In addition to the different keyboard types, you can further customize the keyboard by specifying the type of key that inhabits the "return" key's spot. You can also set the return key via the ReturnKeyType property, which has the following options (available via the UIReturnKeyType enumeration):

- **Default**
- **Go**
- **Google**
- **Join**
- **Next**
- **Route**
- **Search**
- **Send**
- **Yahoo**
- **EmergencyCall**

Changing the return key type has no effect on the behavior of the keyboard; it simply changes the appearance of the return key.

Languages

In addition to the different keyboard types, users can configure additional keyboard languages in the iOS settings application. When any of the non-number type keyboards are displayed, a globe button is shown on the keyboard that allows the user to switch to different languages. The keyboards in different languages can be radically different from the English ones, and even can have multiple steps to input a single character. Some example keyboards are shown in Figure 10–3.

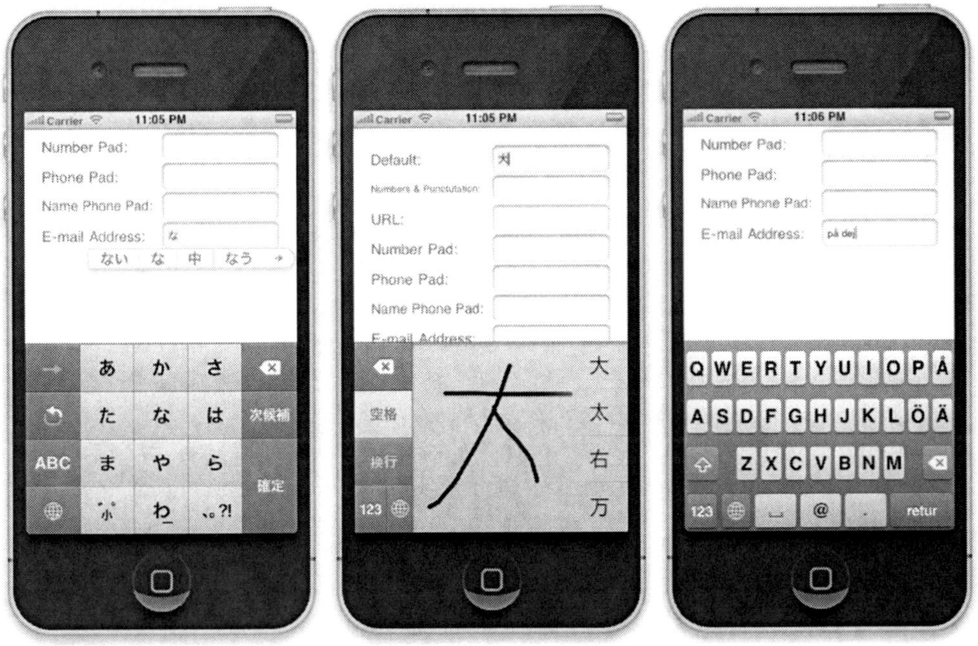

Figure 10–3. *The Japanese Kana, Chinese Handwriting, and Swedish keyboards*

You don't have to worry about doing anything special generally for these keyboards, but you should know that they exist and make sure that, if you are developing applications for a multi-lingual audience, you always save your text data in Unicode. See the .NET documentation on localization for more information on international encoding.

Hiding the Keyboard

While the keyboard appears automatically, it doesn't automatically disappear when the return key is pressed. Instead, you need to call the `ResignFirstResponder` method on the input that has focus when the `ShouldReturn` method is raised. For example, Listing 10–1 uses an anonymous method (passed as a Lambda expression) to hide the keyboard when the return key is pressed while the txtDefault text field has focus:

Listing 10–1. *Dismissing the keyboard when the return key is pressed*

```
this.txtDefault.ShouldReturn += (textField) => { textField.ResignFirstResponder();
    return true; };
```

Making Input Fields Visible When the Keyboard Covers Them

When the keyboard slides up on the screen, it can hide input controls that are underneath it. If a control that has focus is underneath, it might be hidden, which means the user won't be able to see what they're typing. If the control in question is in a table, this isn't an issue, because the table has built-in functionality to scroll the control into the viewable space automatically. However, if it's not in a table, you have to manage this yourself.

The basic pattern to accomplish this is as follows:

- **Use a scroll view:** Your controls should be in a scroll view so you can scroll them into view when the keyboard appears.

- **Handle keyboard events:** The iOS raises notifications when the keyboard is about to appear or disappear. You should listen for these notifications in order to adjust your controls.

- **Resize the scroll view frame:** When the keyboard pops up, you should adjust the frame of the scroll view to shrink to the smaller display area. The iOS automatically centers the control that has focus in the frame; however, if you don't resize the view, the center will be under the keyboard. When the keyboard goes away, you can reset your scroll view frame back to normal.

For example, Listing 10–2 is from the Example_Keyboards companion code and application, and does just that.

Listing 10–2. *Resizing the scroll view when the keyboard is shown or hidden*

```
public partial class HomeScreen : UIViewController
{
        /// <summary>
        /// Track the content size so we can reset to this
        /// </summary>
        RectangleF _contentViewSize = RectangleF.Empty;

        ...

        void Initialize ()
        {
                this._contentViewSize = this.View.Frame;
                this.scrlMain.ContentSize = this._contentViewSize.Size;
        }
```

```
#endregion

public override void ViewDidLoad ()
{
        base.ViewDidLoad ();

        …

        //---- wire up our keyboard events
        NSNotificationCenter.DefaultCenter.AddObserver
                (UIKeyboard.WillShowNotification, delegate(NSNotification n) {
                this.KeyboardOpenedOrClosed (n, "Open"); });
        NSNotificationCenter.DefaultCenter.AddObserver
                (UIKeyboard.WillHideNotification, delegate(NSNotification n) {
                this.KeyboardOpenedOrClosed (n, "Close"); });

}

/// <summary>
/// resizes the view when the keyboard comes up or goes away, allows our
/// scroll view to work
/// </summary>
protected void KeyboardOpenedOrClosed (NSNotification n, string openOrClose)
{
        //---- if it's opening
        if (openOrClose == "Open")
        {
                //---- declare vars
                RectangleF kbdFrame = UIKeyboard.BoundsFromNotification (n);
                double animationDuration =
                        UIKeyboard.AnimationDurationFromNotification (n);

                //---- get the current view's bounds
                RectangleF newFrame = this.View.Bounds;
                //---- shrink the frame's height
                newFrame.Height -= kbdFrame.Height;

                //---- apply the size change
                UIView.BeginAnimations ("ResizeForKeyboard");
                UIView.SetAnimationDuration (animationDuration);
                this.scrlMain.Frame = newFrame;
                UIView.CommitAnimations ();
        }
        else //---- if it's closing, resize
        {
                //---- declare vars
                double animationDuration =
                        UIKeyboard.AnimationDurationFromNotification (n);

                //---- reset the content size back to what it was before
                UIView.BeginAnimations ("ResizeForKeyboard");
                UIView.SetAnimationDuration (animationDuration);
                this.scrlMain.Frame = this._contentViewSize;
                UIView.CommitAnimations ();
        }
}
```

```
public override void DidRotate (UIInterfaceOrientation fromInterfaceOrientation)
{
        base.DidRotate (fromInterfaceOrientation);
}

public override bool ShouldAutorotateToInterfaceOrientation (
        UIInterfaceOrientation toInterfaceOrientation)
{
        return true;
}
```

```
}
```

Wow! That was a wall of code. Let's break it down and examine it in pieces. The first thing we do is create a class level variable to hold our content frame (see Listing 10–3).

Listing 10–3. *Creating a variable to track our scroll view's content size*

```
RectangleF _contentViewSize = RectangleF.Empty;
```

During the Initialize method (which is called by the constructors), we then initialize that variable with the view's frame and then set the content size on the scroll view from it (see Listing 10–4).

Listing 10–4. *Setting the scroll view's content size*

```
this._contentViewSize = this.View.Frame;
this.scrlMain.ContentSize = this._contentViewSize.Size;
```

We do this for two reasons; first, we track the content size in a variable so that we can reset the scroll view size back to it when the keyboard goes away. Second, in order for the scroll view to work, you have to set the content size. In this case, the content size is the same as the view size. For more information on the scroll view, check out Chapter 7, where the scroll view is covered.

Next, we wire up handlers for our keyboard events (see Listing 10–5).

Listing 10–5. *Adding observers to the notification center for keyboard events*

```
NSNotificationCenter.DefaultCenter.AddObserver (UIKeyboard.WillShowNotification
        , delegate(NSNotification n) { this.KeyboardOpenedOrClosed (n, "Open"); });
NSNotificationCenter.DefaultCenter.AddObserver (UIKeyboard.WillHideNotification
        , delegate(NSNotification n) { this.KeyboardOpenedOrClosed (n, "Close"); });
```

Keyboard events are interesting, because there is no accessible keyboard object and therefore you can't just add an event handler directly. Instead, you have to add an observer via the AddObserver method on the NSNotificationCenter. The notification center is an application-wide event subscription manager. System notifications occur on the DefaultCenter. When you register your observer, you pass a delegate method that has a single NSNotification parameter.

In this case, we're calling our KeyboardOpenedOrClosed method and pass either "Open" or "Close" as a parameter, depending on whether the keyboard is opening or closing.

Finally, the real work is done during the KeyboardOpenedOrClosed method. If the keyboard is opening, we get our keyboard from the notification parameter via the code in Listing 10–6.

Listing 10–6. *Getting the keyboard frame information from the notification*

```
RectangleF kbdFrame = UIKeyboard.BoundsFromNotification (n);
```

Next, we create a new RectangleF to hold the new frame of the scroll view and then resize the height to account for the keyboard (see Listing 10–7).

Listing 10–7. *Creating a new frame size for the scroll view that takes into account the keyboard*

```
RectangleF newFrame = this.View.Bounds;
newFrame.Height -= kbdFrame.Height;
```

We pull the frame from the Bounds property of the view, because during rotation, the Bounds property changes, but the frame size stays the same.

Finally, we apply the new frame size to the scroll view and wrap it in an animation block that has the same duration as the keyboard appearance (see Listing 10–8).

Listing 10–8. *Applying the new size to the scroll view*

```
double animationDuration = UIKeyboard.AnimationDurationFromNotification (n);
UIView.BeginAnimations ("ResizeForKeyboard");
UIView.SetAnimationDuration (animationDuration);
this.scrlMain.Frame = newFrame;
UIView.CommitAnimations ();
```

If the keyboard is going away, it's much simpler; you don't need to calculate the new size, you simply pull it from the variable we declared earlier to reset it (see Listing 10–9).

Listing 10–9. *Resetting the scroll view size when the keyboard goes away*

```
double animationDuration = UIKeyboard.AnimationDurationFromNotification (n);
UIView.BeginAnimations ("ResizeForKeyboard");
UIView.SetAnimationDuration (animationDuration);
this.scrlMain.Frame = this._contentViewSize;
UIView.CommitAnimations ();
```

Again, we wrap it in an animation block so that the scrolling happens smoothly with the keyboard's animation.

Summary

With this chapter, we bring the second part of the book to a close. If you've been reading from the beginning, you should now have a very solid understanding of how to build applications for the iOS with MonoTouch. You should now have a comprehensive understanding of how projects are set up, the ins and outs of building applications, and a nearly exhaustive knowledge of the UIKit.

The next chapter begins section three, in which we'll examine a number of specialized topics for building iOS applications.

Congratulations, you're halfway through!

Chapter 11

Multitasking

It's hard to imagine a modern computing device that doesn't allow you to run multiple applications at one time; however, up until v4.0 of the iOS for the iPhone and iPod Touch, and v4.2 for the iPad, you could only run one application at a time. Because of this, multitasking was one of the most aniticipated updates that have come out for the iOS.

Multitasking in the iOS is a different than the traditional concept of multitasking, in which multiple applications can be open at the same time and have equal access to computing resources. Instead, in the iOS, when an application is put into the background because another application has been brought to the foreground (or if the device receives a phone call), the application running in the background has a tightly controlled set of things it can do.

This design is intentional, and serves two purposes. First, as the iOS devices have limited processing power, this assures that the foreground application gets enough access to it to remain snappy and responsive. Second, it helps to conserve the battery by reducing power consumption.

Because of this design, unlike traditional applications, your application has certain design guidelines and responsibilities that it must adhere to in order to play well in the iOS playground.

The iOS has a mixed model for allowing programs in the background to perform tasks. When developing iOS applications that need to perform background processing, there are three different models:

- **Register as a Background Neccesary Application:** There are three types of applications that are allowed continuous background processing; Location, Audio, and VOIP applications.

- **Register a Task with iOS that Needs to be Completed:** You can tell the iOS that a particular task needs time to complete, and request that it not put that task to sleep if the application moves to the background.

- **Notifications:** You can also either schedule a local notification, or send a remote notification (from a server application) that will give the option to the user to bring the application to the foreground.

Notifications are covered in Chapter 18. In this chapter we're going to take a look at the various ways that an application can perform tasks while in the background, and the various responsibilities it has in the iOS framework.

All samples in this chapter can be found in the Example_BackgroundExecution companion application and code.

Application States

Prior to the multitasking iOS update, there were only three states an application could be in:

- Running/Active: The application is running in the foreground.

- Inactive: The application has been interrupted and is "paused." An interruption can happen when a user receives a phone call or a text message, or an alert is raised by the iOS. If you don't accept accept the interruption, it goes back to the active state.

- Terminated/Not Running: The application has either not yet been launched, or it was terminated by accepting an interruption (such as a phone call), or the user has closed it by hitting the home button.

However, with the multitasking update, applications got a new state known as background or suspended. The background state means that the application is still loaded, but is not generally allowed to do any processing. As we'll explore in this chapter, however, there are ways to actually prevent an application from going into a suspended state, or even continuing to do processing, if it has.

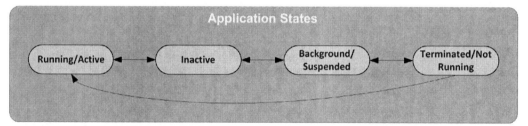

Figure 11–1. *Multitasking application states in the iOS*

This fundamentally changed the behavior of applications. Prior to multitasking, if a user hit the Home button or accepted an interruption, the application was shut down completely.

After the multitasking update, however, when the user clicks the Home button or accepts an interruption, the application will enter a background state whereby the application can actually continue processing, if it received permission from the iOS.

Additionally, by double-clicking the home button, you can switch between running applications. Only one application can be in the active state at any one time, however, and that designation goes to the application whose interface is currently displayed in the window, or the application that is currently being used.

Understanding Background Tasks

Before we get into how to actually develop for background execution, first we need to understand the options and limitations. There are a few different approaches on how to execute while in the background. The first approach is to tell the iOS that you need background processing time to perform a particular task.

By doing this, the iOS will treat your application in a certain way, depending on the particular task that allows your application to be able to accomplish what it needs to do.

The following task categories are available in the iOS:

- **Audio:** Audio applications are allowed to continue processing as long as they're playing audio. When they stop playing audio, the iOS will suspend them.

- **Location:** Location applications will continue to receive location updates from the iOS and, depending on the application, can either be suspended between updates, or remain running.

- **VoIP:** Voice Over Internet Protocol (VoIP) applications are given opportunities to respond at registered intervals in order to keep their connection alive to the VoIP services that power them. Additionally, many VoIP applications also need the privileges extended to Audio applications in order to process audio while in the background.

We'll take a look at each of these in more detail later in this chapter.

Checking for Multitasking Capability

Because multitasking support is dependent on both OS version and hardware, if your application relies on it and must change its behavior if multitasking support is not available, you can check to see availability via the IsMultitaskingSupported property on the UIDevice class, as shown in Listing 11–1.

Listing 11–1. *Determining if multitasking support is available*

```
if(UIDevice.CurrentDevice.IsMultitaskingSupported)
{
        // code dependent on support
}
```

Application Delegate Methods

The iOS notifies your application of changing application states via event methods in the AppDelegate class. You handle these just as you would the other ones, such as the FinishedLaunching method. The following application delegate methods are relevant to state changes:

- OnResignActivation: This method is called when the application is about to enter the inactive state, either because it's being temporarily inactivated (due to an event such as a phone call), or it's going into a background state. If your application is a game, this is the time to pause it and throttle down your frame rates while the application waits to either become active again, or go into the background.

- DidEnterBackground: If the device your application is running on supports multitasking, this method is called instead of WillTerminate. You should use this method to stop updating the interface and save any state that is necessary to resume the application where it was left off, should it get terminated. You have approximately 5 seconds to finish this method or your application or your application's process will be killed. Also, once your application is in background mode, any attempt to update the interface (or make an OpenGL ES call), will also cause the process to be killed.

- WillEnterForeground: This method is called when your application is about to transition from the background to the inactive state. You should use this method to reverse any teardown and rehydrate any state saved during the DidEnterBackground state.

- `OnActivated`: This method is called when the application is moved to the active state by either being launched by the user, or when an interruption (such as a phone all or an SMS message) is ignored. `OnActivated` is the place to start updating your applications interface again; for example, if you're building a game, this is the method to throttle your frame rates back up and present your user with the option to resume (unpause).

- `WillTerminate`: If the device the application is running on does not support multitasking, this method is called when the user closes the application, either because they've hit the Home button, or they've accepted an interruption. If the device does support multitasking, it's rare for this method to be called, but not unheard of, as the iOS might need to free up resources. You should use this method to save any data, release any resources, etc. As with `DidEnterBackground`, you have approximately 5 seconds to complete this method, otherwise your application's process could be killed.

As you can see, Apple is serious about applications conforming to their restrictions and will terminate your application's process if it does not behave well. This is to ensure that the device will be responsive to users, regardless of what your application is doing.

Multitasking Guidelines and Requirements

In addition to the previous notes, there are other behaviors and requirements that your application should adhere to in order to be a good citizen with the iOS. The following guidelines should be adhered to when building iOS applications that rely on background processing:

- **Don't update your UI or make OpenGL ES calls while in the Background state:** While in the background state, if you attempt to udate the UI, your application will likely be terminated without warning. Likewise, if you attempt to make an `OpenGL ES` call while in the background state, the same thing will happen.

- **Save application state before moving to Background:** In order to provide your users with a seemless experience, make sure to save enough application state before moving to the background to be able to rehydrate the application in a state that makes sense. Ideally, this means that when your application is moved back into the foreground, it starts right where it left off.

- **Stop using shared resources when moving to Background:** Applications that are in the active state have priority access to shared resources such as the Address Book, etc. If your application attempts to access a shared resource while in the background state, it will likely be terminated.

- **Remove sensitive information from View:** The iOS takes a snapshot of the window when it moves into the background state (right after `DidEnterBackground` is called). When the application transitions out of the background state, the system shows that that snapshot briefly. During the `DidEnterBackground` method, make sure to hide or obscure any sensitive information such as passwords.

- **Cancel/close network service calls:** When your application moves to the background (during `DidEnterBackground`), it should close any network connections and unregister from any Bonjour-related services. This is not a requirement, however, if you've registered your application as either an Audio or VOIP background application.

- **Be prepared for network connection failures:** If you have any sockets open, you should not rely on them continuing to be open when your application goes into the background state. Good programming practice dictates that you should always check a connection before using it; so as long as you adhere to that principle, your application should be OK.

- **Register and respond to external accessory notifications:** If your application uses the External Accessory Framework, you should make sure to register for the disconnect notification which will be called when your application moves to the background state. Likewise, when your application transitions into the active state, it will receive a reconnect notification if registered. You should make sure to handle these appropriately in your application, based on the notion that accessories will be disconnected when the application is suspended.

- **Do minimal processing when in the background:** If your application is registered for a particular task, such as playing audio, it should do just enough work to accomplish that task and save non-essential processing for when your application is in the foreground/active state. If your application has asked permission to finish a long-running task, it should finish that task and then not do any more processing. If your application is seen by the iOS to be consuming excessive processing power, it will be terminated. Apple doesn't define what that threshold is, so it's best to err on doing the least amount of work possible.

- **Handle alert state:** When applications move into the inactive state, their alerts and action sheets are not dismissed. However, if the application then transitions into the background state, those views will be dismissed. Therefore, during `DidEnterBackground`, you should save enough state such that, when the application moves out of the background state, you can show the alert or action sheet (if appropriate).

Following these guidelines is important not only to to have a well-functioning application, but, if you're submitting to the App Store, your application will also be tested for compliance and, if it does not pass, it won't be accepted. Therefore, it's a good idea to be pre-emptive and follow these guidelines the first time, rather than getting rejected and having to resubmit.

Asking the iOS for Time to Complete a Task

If you have a long-running process that you want to complete before the application shuts down, you can ask the iOS for time to finish that task. To request that a task be allowed to complete before putting the application into a backgroud state, you make a call to the static BeginBackgroundTask method on the UIApplication object, which returns you an integer that represents a unique task identifier. Then, when your task is complete, you call the EndBackgroundTask method (again, on UIApplication) and pass the id of the task that you received when you started it.

If you make a call to BeginBackgroundTask to register your task, the iOS will then generally not suspend your application (it will, however, suspend the UI thread —so UI updates are generally not possible) until all your registered tasks are completed. That means that you can start a task and, if the user clicks the Home button, your application will become inactive, but not suspended.

The following code in Listing 11–2 illustrates this pattern.

Listing 11–2. *Registering a task that will prevent the application from being suspended while it finishes*

```
int taskID = UIApplication.SharedApplication.BeginBackgroundTask(
        () => { /* code to run when remaining time is low*/ });
// perform your task
//---- tell the iOS you're done
UIApplication.SharedApplication.EndBackgroundTask(taskID);
```

> **NOTE**: You must couple any BeginBackgroundTask call with an EndBackgroundTask call. If you don't call EndBackgroundTask, your application will be terminated, rather than put into a background state.

Task Execution Expiration Time

Notice how, in the preceding sample, we passed in an anonymous lambda delegate when we called BeginBackgroundTask. That's because the method expects an expiration parameter that takes a block of code that will execute when the time allotted for your application to complete tasks is nearly up. This is set up this way because the iOS only gives your application a limited amount of time to complete tasks. Just before that time expires, it lets you know by executing the code in the expiration block. This allows you to cancel your long-running task and clean up any resources associated with it.

Generally, the iOS will give you 600 seconds (10 minutes) to finish background tasks, but you're not guaranteed that amount. You can check to see how much time you have remaining by accessing the static BackgroundTimeRemaining property of the UIApplication class. That property will return the number of seconds that you have before the iOS will put your application into the background state. For example, the code in Listing 11–3 writes the amount of time remaining to the Application Output window.

Listing 11–3. *Determining how much time your application has before the iOS puts it into the background state*

```
Console.WriteLine("Background time remaining: "
        + UIApplication.SharedApplication.BackgroundTimeRemaining.ToString());
```

Task Completion Patterns

There are two general places that you would want to tell the iOS that you want to allow your application to complete tasks:

- **During uninterruptable processes:** Anywhere that you're performing a long-running task that you don't want interrupted in the case that the app might move to the background, such as downloading a file.

- **During DidEnterBackground:** If your application is entering a background state (your DidEnterBackground method is called), and you know that you have to do some work that will take longer than 5 seconds (the execution threshold for that method before your app is terminated), then you can register and invoke long-running tasks. Examples of such tasks might be releasing resources, uploading scores to a server (in the case of a game), or long-running cleanup.

The first scenario is rather straightforward to implement: you simply wrap your calls in the BeginBackgroundTask/EndBackgroundTask methods, as shown in Listing 11–4. The second scenario requires that you spawn your tasks on a new thread, so that DidEnterBackground can return. The following example illustrates this pattern:

Listing 11–4. *Scheduling a long running task when the application is about to enter the background state*

```
public override void DidEnterBackground (UIApplication application)
{
        //---- register a long running task, and then start it on a new thread so that
            this method can return
        int taskID = UIApplication.SharedApplication.BeginBackgroundTask(
            () => {});
        Thread task = new Thread(new ThreadStart(()=>
            { FinishLongRunningTask(taskID);}));
        task.Start();
}

protected void FinishLongRunningTask(int taskID)
{
        Console.WriteLine("Starting task " + taskID.ToString());

        //---- sleep for 5 seconds to simulate a long running task
        Thread.Sleep(5000);

        Console.WriteLine("Task " + taskID.ToString() + " finished");

        //---- call our end task
```

```
                    UIApplication.SharedApplication.EndBackgroundTask(taskID);
}
```

If you put that code in your application delegate, launch your application, and click the Home button, the `Application Output` window in MonoDevelop should output something similar to the following (Listing 11–5).

Listing 11–5. *Application Output from Listing 11–4*

```
App entering background state.
Thread started:
Starting task 1
Task 1 finished
```

As you can see, even though the Home button was clicked, to put your application in the background state, the registered task was still allowed to complete.

Registering Your Application to be Allowed to Perform a Particular Background Task Category

Registering long-running tasks is fine for certain scenarios such as one-off task processing, but sometimes you're building an application in which you need constant background processing based around a specific task, without your application moving to a background state. Apple has made a concession for certain types of applications to be allowed to do just that.

In order to let the iOS know what knd of task(s) you want to be able to execute in the background, you must add a `UIBackgroudnModes` key (array type) to the `info.plist` file and specify at least one of the following values:

- audio
- voip
- location

To edit the `info.plist` file, double-click it in the project explorer and Xcode's Property List Editor will open up. Add a new key by clicking **Add Child**. You'll need to type in the UIBackgroundModes key by hand, because it likely won't be in the list of values you can select. After you've named the key, you need to right-click it and change the Value Type to `Array` (Figure 11–2).

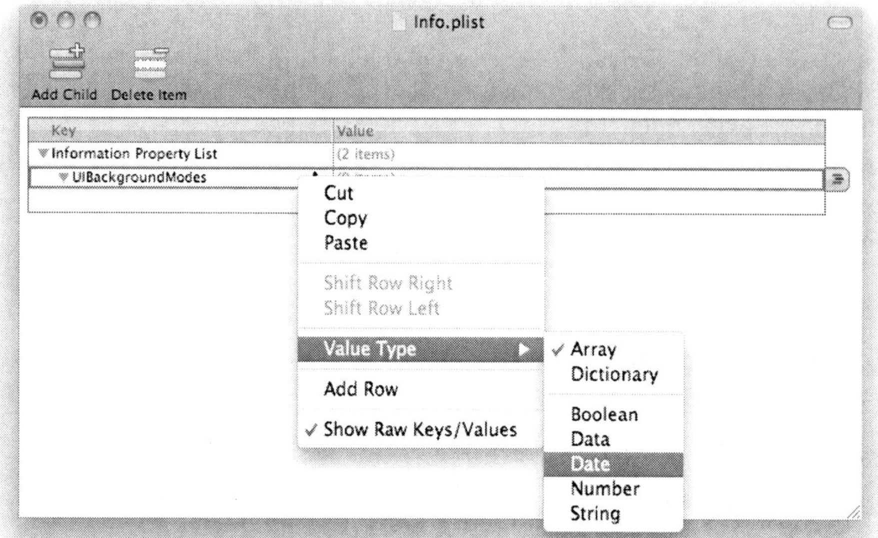

Figure 11–2. *Specifying a UIBackgroundModes key as an array type*

After you've created the key and specified its type, you can then add your values by clicking on the arrow to the left of the key to expand it, and then clicking on the + button on the right. Your info.plist should then look something like Figure 11–3.

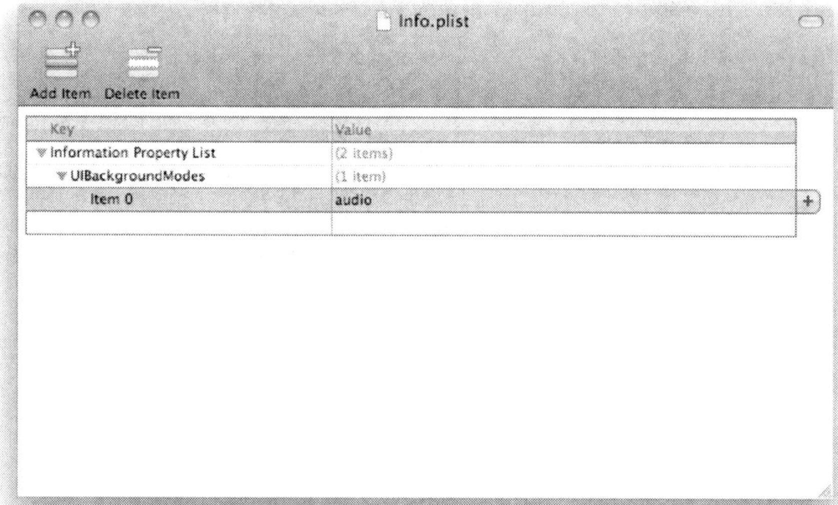

Figure 11–3. *Specifying an "audio" type application*

The property list editor is not one of Apple's finest software products, hence the convoluted steps necessary to do simple tasks.

Audio Applications

As long as audio is specified in the UIBackgroundModes array, and your application is playing audio, the iOS will keep your application running in the inactive state and will not move it to the background. This means that all audio callbacks will operate normally, and for all intents and purposes, your application will, generally, operate normally. For instance, if your application requires that it download music from a server, it can continue to do so.

Because of this, however, it's especially important not to update your UI and adhere to all the other guidelines outlined previously.

> **NOTE:** There are some caveats to this. Audio applications are given a lot of flexibility in what they're allowed to do. For instance, you can access network resources (specifically so that you can play audio from network and Internet locations). However, you can't use Mono/.NET Sockets. Instead you have to use the NSStream class for network streams.

Location Applications

Location applications are applications that depend on location updates to function. There are two general categories of background operational behavior that an application can follow:

■ **Significant location changes only:** Your application can be notified only when a significant change in location occurs. This is only available in iOS v4.0-and later-on devices that have a cellular radio (iPhone, iPad 3G, etc.). In this mode, you do not need to register your application as a location tasked application in the info.plist file. Your application will be moved to the background state normally, and then automatically be woken up when significant changes occur, as long as you subscribe with the StartMonitoringSignificantLocationChanges method on the CLLocationManager class. For more information on this, see Chapter 13 ("Core Location").

■ **Continuous location updates:** Your application can continuously receive location updates and, generally, will never get moved to the suspended state. In order to utilize the mode of operation, your application must register a location value in the UIBackgroundModes key in the info.plist file.

Location services is one of the most draining tasks you can perform on an iOS device; therefore, unless your application needs continuous, precise location information, the recommended approach is to subscribe to signification location changes only while in the background. This method allows the device to power down the radio hardware necessary to receive precise location data, and instead rely on cell tower changes to indicate a significant change in location.

One of the main advantages of subscribing to significant location changes is that the iOS will actually move your application to the inactive state so that it can handle location updates if it's in the background state. If the application has been terminated, it will actually relaunch the application as pass in the location changes in via the options parameter in the FinishedLaunching method in your application delegate.

For more information on working with location services. see Chapter 13.

VoIP Applications

VoIP applications require that a persistent connection be kept between the device and the service that powers it; that way the VoIP account can retain its "online" status, even if the application is not the active application. In order to facilitate this, the iOS provides several allowances and abilities specifically for VoIP applications to keep a connection open.

In order to let the iOS know that your application is a VoIP application, you must specify a voip value in the UIBackgroundModes key in the info.plist file. Additionally, if your application needs to play sound while in the background (as some VoIP applications do), you should also include the audio value.

By registering your application as a VoIP application, you get another benefit—the iOS will actually launch your application when the device is rebooted, so that your user can remain online with your VoIP service.

VoIP Socket Handling

If your application is registerd as a VoIP application, the system will automatically manage the underlying socket if your application is suspended. This means that if new data arrives and your application is suspended, it will move your application to the inactive state so your application can process the data. Typically, if the data that has been received is a phone call or other message that needs user notification, your application should schedule an immediate local notification so that the user is presented with an option answer the call, or handle the message. If the user accepts the notification, then the application will be moved to the active state.

VoIP Keep-alive

In order to keep an "online" status with a VoIP service, VoIP applications typically need to contact the service periodically to keep the connection alive. In order to facilitate this, the iOS has a method that you can call, called SetKeepAliveTimeout, that will wake your application (move it to the inactive state) if it's been suspended and allow you to execute code to keep your connection online:

```
bool SetKeepAliveTimout (double timeout, NSAction handler);
```

When you call this method, you pass in the duration of time (in seconds) between calls, and an anonymous delegate (which is automatically converted to an NSAction) containing the code to run when the time is up. Typically, you would call this method in the DidEnterBackground method, as shown in Listing 11–

Listing 11–6. *Specifying a keep-alive handler and scheduling it*

```
public override void DidEnterBackground (UIApplication application)
{
        UIApplication.SharedApplication.SetKeepAliveTimeout(600, () => {
                /* keep alive handler code*/ });
}
```

You should set the timeout parameter to be the largest amount possible, which must be at least 600 seconds (10 minutes). The iOS guarantees that your handler will be called before the expiration timeout has been met, but it might be called considerably sooner because it is typically batched up with a number of other system calls in order to conserve battery.

Additionally, your handler has 30 seconds to complete, otherwise your application will be terminated, and so you may want to set a timeout on your network calls to be less than that.

Summary

In this chapter we learned that mutlittasking in the iOS means something different than traditional computing and that with it comes certain responsibilities and requirements that we must adhere to in order to play well with other applications. We also covered the various types of background tasks you can perform and how to register with the iOS in order to be able to do them.

In the next chapter, we're going to take a look at storage in the iOS.

Chapter 12

Working with Touch

Probably the single most renown feature of the iPhone and other iOS devices is the capacitive touch screen. Instead of using a mouse that has a constant cursor on the screen, the iOS devices respond to touches directly on the device itself. You can use one or more fingers and perform complex moves that translate into application actions, or gestures.

This carries with it a number of interesting implications and differences from traditional computing. For one, there is no mouseover state, since there is no cursor on the screen, so a touch can occur anywhere. Furthermore, it introduces a whole set of possibilities that would be impossible with a mouse. For instance, pinch-to-zoom (whereby a user can pinch or expand two fingers to zoom out and in) has become a staple of iOS interaction, yet something as basic as that (in iOS terms) would be impossible with a traditional mouse.

To deal with this, the CocoaTouch API has been created to specifically handle touch. Originally, the API consisted of a set of methods that were called when specific touch events occurred (such as touch start, touch move, and so on), but the iOS v3.2 release included a much higher-level API based around *Gesture Recognizers*, which encapsulated the lower-level events and provided a much simpler way to deal with complex touch interactions. The iOS ships with a number of common built-in gesture recognizers, and it allows you to create your own custom ones when you need something that doesn't already exist.

In this chapter we're going to look at when it's appropriate to use which method and, of course, how to use them. All of the examples in this chapter can be found in the Example_Touches companion code and application.

When to Use Which?

With the two options of how to handle touches – either working with the events or using gesture recognizers – the question is, which one do should you use?

The answer is that you should use gesture recognizers everywhere. However, if there isn't a stock recognizer for the gesture that you want to allow your users to use, you need to understand the touch events so that you can build your own custom gesture recognizers.

One of the biggest advantages of using gesture recognizers is their encapsulation. You define a gesture recognizer as a discrete class, which gives you major advantages over using touch events. First, because it's a class, you can reuse it across multiple screens. With touch events, if you want to provide the same touch functionality across multiple views, you'd have to copy your touch event handling code to each view. With a gesture recognizer, however, you can define it in one place and then use it across many views. Second, the recognizer pattern encapsulates gesture events into a single callback for recognition events, rather than multiple events, allowing you consume them with much less code.

We're going to take a look at touch events first, since they're the foundation of handling touch in the iOS. But before that, we need to cover something very important: enabling touch.

Enabling Touch

By default, many of the controls in the UIKit do not have touch enabled. This can be especially frustrating – I've spent many an hour trying to figure out why my touches don't work. To enable touch in Interface Builder, you need to check the User Interaction Enabled checkbox in the Interaction section of the Attribute Inspector, shown in Figure 12–1.

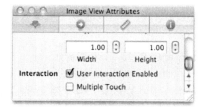

Figure 12–1. *Enabling touch on a control in Interface Builder*

If you're building things in code, you should set the UserInteractionEnabled property on your UIView class to true.

Also, if you set enable touch on a control in Interface Builder and then duplicate or copy and paste that control, it will lose the enabled value. Therefore, if something isn't working, check this first.

Okay, now that we've got that out of the way, let's look at the touch events.

Touch Events

There are three phases of touch (and one cancel event) in the iOS that occur when a user touches a view, moves their finger(s), or removes their finger(s). When these phases occur, the iOS calls their associated methods on the UIView and UIViewController. You can override these methods to intercept the event and handle it accordingly.

- **TouchesBegan:** This is called when a user's finger(s) first touches the screen.

- **TouchesMoved:** This is called when the location of the touch changes, but the finger(s) hasn't been lifted from the screen (as in sliding the finger around the screen).

- **TouchesEnded:** This is called when the user's finger(s) is lifted off the screen.

- **TouchesCancelled:** This is called when iOS cancels the touch. This can occur for a number of reasons, including putting the device near the face (in the case of the phone devices), the application entering a background state (for instance, if the device is a phone and the user receives a call), or terminating in response to a low-memory situation.

Touch events bubble down through the stack, meaning that the touch event occurs on the topmost UIView or UIViewController, and then get called on the UIViews and UIViewControllers below them.

The UITouch Class

When a touch event occurs, a set of UITouch objects are passed to the method that handles the event. The iOS creates a UITouch object for every finger that is on the screen of the device. The UITouch object includes a rather useful set of methods that allow you to determine where the touch occurred (and where the previous touch occurred, if there was one), whether the user tapped more than once, and whether the touch was a swipe (and in what direction), among other things.

Using Touch Events

When you override a touch event, you should first call the base implementation, and then the next thing you typically need to do is to get the touch information. Often, you only want the first touch, so you call the AnyObject method on the touches set to return the root touch object, and then do a null check, just to make sure for some reason the touch event was valid. See Listing 12–1.

Listing 12–1. *Overriding a touch event method and retrieving the root touch*

```
public override void TouchesBegan (NSSet touches, UIEvent evt)
{
        base.TouchesBegan (touches, evt);
        UITouch touch = touches.AnyObject as UITouch;
        if (touch != null)
        {
                //code here to handle touch
        }
}
```

Multi-Taps

The iOS automatically recognizes successive quick touches on the device as a tap and aggregates it as one event. If you need to determine if the touch was a double-tap, you can simply check the TapCount property on the UITouch object, as shown in Listing 12–2.

Listing 12–2. *Getting the number of taps of a touch*

```
if(touch.TapCount == 2)
{…}
```

This greatly simplifies having to count touch events on your own.

Multi-Touch

The iOS supports multiple fingers at the same time. This is why the touches are passed as a set. However, multiple touch is disabled on controls by default, so if you need to support it, you have to enable it. To enable multi-touch in Interface Builder, select your control that you want to receive multiple touches, and then in the Attributes Inspector, under the Interaction heading, enable **Multiple Touch** (see Figure 12–2).

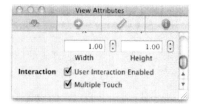

Figure 12–2. *Enabling multi-touch in Interface Builder for your view*

You can also enable multi-touch programmatically via the MultipleTouchEnabled property (see Listing 12–3).

Listing 12–3. *Enabling multi-touch programmatically for your view*

```
this.View.MultipleTouchEnabled = true;
```

You can get the number of fingers touching via the Count property on the touches parameter, and of course if you want to do something with more than just the first touch, you don't have to call AnyObject to get just one.

Determining Touch Location

UITouch has a method called LocationInView that will return a PointF object that contains the coordinates in the particular view that you pass in (views can have different coordinate spaces). Additionally, you can test to see if that location is within a control by calling the Contains method on the Frame. For example, to test whether the touch occurs on an image view, you could use the code snippet in Listing 12–4.

Listing 12–4. *Testing to see if a touch occurred on an image view*

```
if (this.imgTouchMe.Frame.Contains (touch.LocationInView (this.View)))
{ … }
```

Now that you understand the constituent parts of the touch events and the UITouch object, let's actually put it all together.

Example Application

The best way to understand how to use the touch events is to look at the code. In the example application, we have a screen that has three images: a Touch Me image, a Double-Tap Me image, and a Drag Me image. See Figure 12–3.

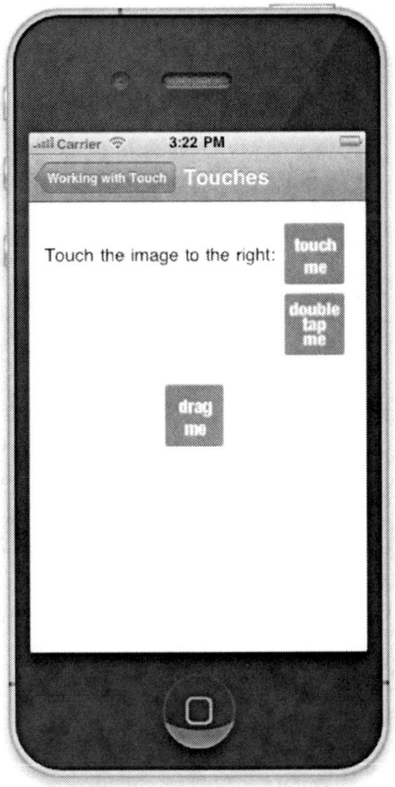

Figure 12–3. *The Example_Touches companion application and code*

For each one of these images, we're going to use the events differently.

- **Touch Me:** When a touch event occurs on this image, we'll write out to the screen what event is happening.

- **Double-Tap Me:** When this image is double-tapped, it will switch to another image, showing a highlighted state.

- **Drag Me:** When a finger is placed on this image and then the finger is moved, it will move the image along with the finger.

Touch Me Image

In order to determine what event is firing on the Touch Me image, we use the code in Listing 12–5.

Listing 12–5. *Handling different touch events*

```
public override void TouchesBegan (NSSet touches, UIEvent evt)
{
        base.TouchesBegan (touches, evt);
        UITouch touch = touches.AnyObject as UITouch;
        if (touch != null)
        {
                if (this.imgTouchMe.Frame.Contains (touch.LocationInView (this.View)))
                { this.lblTouchStatus.Text = "TouchesBegan"; }
        }
}
public override void TouchesMoved (NSSet touches, UIEvent evt)
{
        base.TouchesMoved (touches, evt);
        UITouch touch = touches.AnyObject as UITouch;
        if (touch != null)
        {
                if (this.imgTouchMe.Frame.Contains (touch.LocationInView (this.View)))
                { this.lblTouchStatus.Text = "TouchesMoved"; }
        }
}
public override void TouchesEnded (NSSet touches, UIEvent evt)
{
        base.TouchesEnded(touches, evt);
        UITouch touch = touches.AnyObject as UITouch;
        if (touch != null)
        {
                if (this.imgTouchMe.Frame.Contains (touch.LocationInView (this.View)))
                { this.lblTouchStatus.Text = "TouchesEnded"; }
        }
}
```

Nothing should be too surprising here. We've overridden the three main touch events, and in each one we've done the following:

1. Retrieved the Root (First) Touch.

2. Tested for null.

3. Tested to see if the Touch Occurred within the Bounds of the Control.

4. Updated a Label to Show Touch Status.

If you run the application, you should see the label to the left of the Touch Me image updated with the current event.

Double-Tap Me Image

In order to change the Double-Tap Me image when it's double-tapped, we use the code shown in Listing 12–6.

Listing 12–6. *Changing an image when it's double-tapped*

```
protected bool _imageHighlighted = false;
public override void TouchesBegan (NSSet touches, UIEvent evt)
{
        base.TouchesBegan (touches, evt);
        UITouch touch = touches.AnyObject as UITouch;
        if (touch != null)
        {
                if(touch.TapCount == 2 && this.imgTapMe.Frame.Contains(
                        touch.LocationInView(this.View)))
                {
                        if(this._imageHighlighted)
                        { this.imgTapMe.Image =
                                UIImage.FromBundle("Images/DoubleTapMe.png"); }
                        else { this.imgTapMe.Image =
                                UIImage.FromBundle("Images/DoubleTapMe_Highlighted.png")
                        ; }
                        this._imageHighlighted = !this._imageHighlighted;
                }
        }
}
```

As with before, we get our touch and do the null check, but then we check to see if the TapCount is equal to 2, and if the touch occurred on the Tap Me image. If yes, we check out bool flag to see whether we're displaying the normal or the highlighted image, and simply show the other one.

Drag Me Image

Dragging is a little bit more complicated, because we have to track state across touch events. Specifically, we need to track whether a touch began in a particular object (that is going to be dragged), then move the object when the touch moves, and finally, reset our state when the touch ends or is cancelled.

Dragging also requires knowledge of where the touch was in the previous TouchesMoved event so that we can calculate the change in location and apply that change to the object. For that, we can use the PreviousLocationInView method on the UITouch object, which works exactly like LocationInView, except that it gives us the most recent updated location before the current.

For example, Listing 12–7 supports dragging by checking whether a touch started in the particular object we want to move (in this case, the `imgDragMe` image view); then when the touch moves, it moves the object along with the touch.

Listing 12–7. *Using touch events to drag an image view around the main view*

```
protected bool _touchStartedInside;
public override void TouchesBegan (NSSet touches, UIEvent evt)
{
        base.TouchesBegan (touches, evt);
        UITouch touch = touches.AnyObject as UITouch;
        if (touch != null)
        {
                if (this.imgDragMe.Frame.Contains(touch.LocationInView (this.View)))
                { this._touchStartedInside = true; }
        }
}
public override void TouchesMoved (NSSet touches, UIEvent evt)
{
        base.TouchesMoved (touches, evt);
        //---- get the touch
        UITouch touch = touches.AnyObject as UITouch;
        if (touch != null)
        {
                if (this._touchStartedInside)
                {
                        //---- move the shape
                        float offsetX = touch.PreviousLocationInView(this.View).X
                                - touch.LocationInView(this.View).X;
                        float offsetY = touch.PreviousLocationInView(this.View).Y
                                - touch.LocationInView(this.View).Y;
                        this.imgDragMe.Frame = new System.Drawing.RectangleF(
                                new PointF(this.imgDragMe.Frame.X - offsetX
                                , this.imgDragMe.Frame.Y - offsetY),
                                this.imgDragMe.Frame.Size);

                }
        }
}
public override void TouchesEnded (NSSet touches, UIEvent evt)
{
        base.TouchesEnded(touches, evt);
        this._touchStartedInside = false;
}
public override void TouchesCancelled (NSSet touches, UIEvent evt)
{
        base.TouchesCancelled (touches, evt);
        this._touchStartedInside = false;
}
```

In this example, we also utilized the `TouchesCancelled` event method to reset our `_touchStartedInside` flag, in the event that the touch was cancelled.

As you can see, this required quite a bit of code just to drag an object. We had to override all four of the touch event methods in order to accomplish it. It's for this very reason that Apple created gesture recognizers, which simplify this process considerably.

Gesture Recognizers

Gesture recognizes greatly simplify performing actions in your applications in response to complicated touches, because they encapsulate them into a single touch event, called a gesture. The iOS has a number of built-in gestures that it understands, which are encapsulated in various `UIGestureRecognizer` classes. The built-in gesture recognizers include the following:

- **UITapGesturesRecognizer:** For taps, one or more
- **UIPinchGestureRecognizer:** Pinching and spreading apart fingers (to zoom, for example)
- **UIPanGestureRecognizer:** Panning or dragging
- **UISwipeGestureRecognizer:** Swiping in any direction
- **UIRotationGestureRecognizer:** Rotating two fingers (like spinning an image)
- **UILongPressGestureRecognizer:** Press and hold

Additionally, you can define your own gesture recognizers for custom touch actions and use them as you would the built-in gestures recognizers.

Using Gesture Recognizers

Always use gesture recognizers for the actions for which they were designed, because users expect them to work a certain way. For example, the pinching gesture should zoom out, or have similar functionality, and the rotation gesture should rotate an object or the screen in some way. This doesn't mean that you can't get creative with them, but if you stray too far away from their intended use, Apple could reject your application. Plus, if you use them the way they were intended, your users will find your app more intuitive, and that could go a long way to making your app successful in terms of adoption.

Gesture recognizers are applied to views in which they listen to touch events, and when a gesture occurs they call a method (known as a target) that you've wired up to handle the event. It's not that different from the standard .NET eventing model, but since the underlying mechanism is Objective-C, as we'll see, it's a little strange.

The basic pattern to using gesture recognizer is as follows:

1. **Create the gesture recognizer:** Simply declare the type of gesture you want to recognize and instantiate it.

2. **Configure target:** Gesture recognizers can execute code, known as a target, that you configure when the status of gesture recognition occurs. You can have a gesture call many targets; you're not limited to just one. Within that target, you should check to see what it's status is (via its State property, which we'll examine shortly), and update your application accordingly.

3. **Configure any gesture settings:** Depending on the gesture, there might be properties that you'll want to set. For example, if you're using a swipe gesture, you would specify which direction of swipe you want to recognize; if you're using a tap gesture, you might want to tell it how many taps to listen for.

4. **Enable it:** Once the gesture is configured, you must tell it that it's okay to receive touches.

5. **Add it to the view:** The final step is to add the gesture recognizer to the actual view that you want to listen for gestures on. For example, if we want to listen for the pan/drag gesture on an image view to move it when the user moves his finger, we would add it to the image view.

Let's take a look at each one of these steps in more detail.

Creating the Gesture Recognizer

Creating a gesture recognizer is easy: simply declare the gesture, whether built-in or custom, and instantiate it. See Listing 12–8.

Listing 12–8. *Declaring and instantiating a gesture*

```
UITapGestureRecognizer tapGesture = new UITapGestureRecognizer();
```

A reference to the gesture recognizer will get attached to the view that you add it to later, so it's kept around by the MonoTouch runtime and won't be garbage collected until the view is gone. Therefore, you don't have to worry about creating it as a class-level variable.

Configuring the Gesture

After you've instantiated the gesture recognizer, you should configure any properties that you need to control the gesture's recognition behavior. Tables 12–1 through 12–4 list a set of common properties for the built-in gesture recognizers that have configurable properties.

Table 12–1. *UITapGestureRecognizer*

Property Name	Purpose
NumberOfTapsRequired	Specifies the number of times a user taps the view in order to fire the gesture. The Default is one.
NumberOfTouchesRequired	Specifies the number of fingers required to qualify as a tap. The Default is one.

Table 12–2. *UIPanGestureRecognizer*

Property Name	Purpose
MinimumNumberOfTouches	The minimum number of fingers necessary for the gesture to be recognized. Typically one finger should be used to drag an object or to scroll, and two fingers should navigate or flip pages, and so on. The Default is one.
MaximumNumberOfTouches	The maximum number of fingers allowed to qualify as a pan gesture.

Table 12–3. *UISwipeGestureRecognizer*

Property Name	Purpose
Direction	The direction of the swipe necessary to be recognized as the gesture. Valid values are Up, Down, Left, and Right, and are contained the in the UISwipeGestureRecognizerDirection enumeration.
NumberOfTouchesRequired	Specifies the number of fingers required to qualify as a swipe. The Default is one.

Table 12–4. *UILongPressGestureRecognizer*

Property Name	Purpose
MinimumPressDuration	The minimum time interval, in seconds, of the touch required before the gesture is recognized. The default is 0.4 seconds.
NumberOfTouchesRequired	The number of fingers necessary for the gesture to be recognized. The default is one.
NumberOfTapsRequired	The number taps necessary for the gesture to be recognized. The default is one.
AllowableMovement	The allowed movement of the fingers (in pixels) before the gesture is cancelled. The default is 10 pixels.

Configuring the Target

When a gesture has been recognized, iOS will call each target that is wired up to execute. A target is a lot like an event handler – however, because the iOS is responsible for managing gestures and Objective-C doesn't have the concept of eventing, it's a little different. Instead of the traditional .NET handler syntax (+=), you have to call the AddTarget method on the gesture recognizer and pass it one of the following two things:

- **An Anonymous Delegate or Lambda**

- **An Objective-C Selector**

The easiest (and most .NET-like) way is to use an anonymous delegate or Lambda, but I'll cover both methods.

Using an Anonymous Delegate or Lambda

Configuring an anonymous delegate or Lambda to execute when a gesture is recognized is very easy, and it works conceptually just like an event. One of the overloads of AddTarget takes an NSAction. MonoTouch has an implicit conversion from delegate to NSAction, so you can pass your delegate (or in the case of the following code, a Lambda), directly to the AddTarget method. For example, Listing 12–9 updates a label when a tap gesture is recognized.

Listing 12–9. *Adding a Lambda target to a gesture*

```
tapGesture.AddTarget(() => {
        this.lblGestureStatus.Text = "tap me image tapped @" +
                tapGesture.LocationOfTouch(0, this.imgTapMe).ToString();
});
```

Using the Selector Pattern

If you want to configure an Objective-C selector to execute when the gesture is recognized, it's a little more complicated.

A selector is simply a method that is visible to the underlying iOS runtime. Objective-C doesn't have the concept of methods and parameters; instead, it has selectors to which messages are passed. In order to make a method visible to the runtime, MonoTouch includes an ExportAttribute with which you decorate your method. See Listing 12–10.

Listing 12–10. *Making your method visible to the underlying Objective-C runtime as a selector*

```
[Export("HandleTap")]
public void HandleTap(UITapGestureRecognizer recognizer)
{
        ...
}
```

If you read the first section of this book, this should look familiar to you, because this is how outlets are made visible to .xib files.

Once you've created your handler and attributed it, you can add it as a target, and simply create a new Selector object with the name of the handler. See Listing 12–11.

Listing 12–11. *Wiring up a selector target for the gesture recognizer to call when it occurs*

```
tapGesture.AddTarget(this, new Selector("HandleTap"));
```

In this case, the first parameter is a reference to the current view controller, where our HandleTap method resides.

Enabling Gesture Recognition

Gestures will only be enabled if touch interactions are enabled on the view that you're adding a gesture to. See the "Enabling Touch" section in the beginning of this chapter for more information.

Adding the Gesture to a View

The final step in using gesture recognizers is to add the gesture to the view that you actually want the gesture to be recognized on. To do this, simply call the AddGestureRecognizer on the view object that you want to listen for the gesture on, and pass your configured gesture. See Listing 12–12.

Listing 12–12. *Adding a gesture recognizer to a view*

```
this.imgDragMe.AddGestureRecognizer(gesture);
```

That's it! Now you can use your gesture recognizer. Now let's look at what information we get when a gesture occurs, so we can have an idea of how to actually create our handlers, and then we'll walk through a couple examples of actually using them.

Retrieving Gesture Information

When the gesture target event handler/subscriber is called, a reference to the gesture that occurred is passed to the handler. Depending on the gesture type, you can get different information about the gesture via properties and methods on that gesture object. Tables 12–5 through 12–8 list the common information available on the built-in gestures.

Table 12–5. *UIPinchGestureRecognizer*

Name	Type	Purpose
Scale	Property	The scale factor of how far the user moved their fingers.
Velocity	Property	The speed at which the user moved their fingers.

Table 12–6. *UIPanGestureRecognizer*

Name	Type	Purpose
TranslationInView	Method	Returns a System.Drawing.PointF object describing the offset of movement from the original location in the coordinate system of the view passed in.
VelocityInView	Method	The speed at which the user moved their fingers in both the horizontal and vertical directions. Also returns a System.Drawing.PointF object; however, instead of coordinate values, the X and Y properties represent the velocity along those axis.

Table 12–7. *UISwipeGestureRecognizer*

Name	Type	Purpose
LocationInView	Method	Returns a System.Drawing.PointF object describing the center of the touch (or touches) in the coordinate system of the view passed in.
LocationOfTouch	Method	Returns a System.Drawing.PointF object describing the location of a given touch.

Table 12–8. *UIRotationGestureRecognizer*

Property Name	Purpose
Rotation	The angle, in radians, of the rotation of the gesture.
Velocity	The speed in which the fingers were moved.

In addition to the information just referenced, all gestures have a property called State that gives you important information on what their status is.

Gesture Recognizer States

Gesture recognizers are state machines. That's really just a fancy way of saying that they have various states and they keep track of what state they are currently in. Gesture recognizer state is important, because every time it changes, the iOS calls its subscribing method (or Selector) giving it an update. In fact, if you're creating a custom gesture and you never change the state, the subscriber is never called, thereby making the gesture recognizer useless.

The states that a gesture can have are dependent on what type of gesture it is recognizing, either discrete or continuous. A discrete gesture is a gesture that fires once after it has been recognized, and a continuous gesture is a gesture that continues to fire as it changes. For example, a tap gesture is discrete because once the tap(s) occur, the gesture recognizer's target event handler/consumer is called one time. On the other hand, the pan gesture is continuous, because once it begins, it continues to fire and send updates as the user moves her finger around.

The states that a gesture recognizer can exist in are contained in the UIGestureRecognizerState enumeration and include the following:

- **Possible:** This is state that all gesture recognizers start in. If you're creating a custom gesture, you don't have to set this yourself in your derived class, because the base class starts in Possible.

- **Began:** When a continuous gesture is first recognized, the state is set to Began, so that the subscribers to that gesture can differentiate between data when the gesture recognition started, and when it changed. This is important for features like dragging, when you need to know when the gesture began so that you can cache the original location of the object you're moving. We'll look at this in a bit.

- **Changed:** After a continuous gesture has begun, but hasn't finished, the state will be set to Changed every time a touch moves or changes, as long as it's still within the expected parameters of the gesture.

- **Cancelled:** The Cancelled state should be set if the recognizer went from Began to Changed, but then the touches changed in such a way as to no longer fit the pattern expected for the gesture.

- **Recognized:** When a recognizer detects a set of matching touch data for the particular gesture for which it's listening, it will change its state to Recognized, which tells the consuming handler that the gesture has finished.

- **Ended:** The Ended state is an alias for the Recognized state, and therefore does the same thing.

- **Failed:** When the touches don't match the particular gesture a recognizer is listening for, the state will change to Failed, which means that the iOS will continue to try and recognize other gestures and call touch events.

The possible state transitions are illustrated as shown in Figure 12–4.

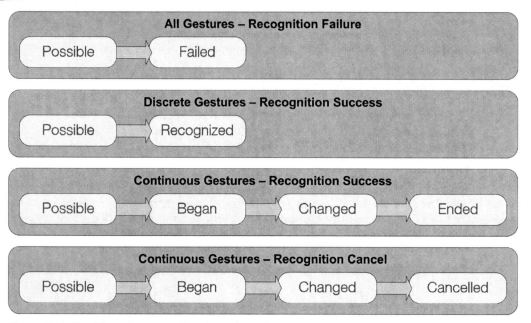

Figure 12–4. *Possible gesture recognition states, depending on gesture type.*

Example Using the Tap Gesture

Now that you understand the pieces of using a gesture recognizer, let's put it all together and look at a couple examples. This first example creates a tap gesture recognizer that requires a double-tap and then updates a label with the location of the touch (in the local coordinate system of the image view) when it fires. See Listing 12–13.

Listing 12–13. *Setting up a tap gesture recognizer*

```
UITapGestureRecognizer tapGesture = new UITapGestureRecognizer();
tapGesture.AddTarget(() => {
        this.lblGestureStatus.Text = "tap me image tapped @"
                + tapGesture.LocationOfTouch(0, this.imgTapMe).ToString();
});
tapGesture.NumberOfTapsRequired = 2;
this.imgTapMe.AddGestureRecognizer(tapGesture);
```

As you can see, using gesture recognizers can greatly simplify handling touch actions as compared to handling the events yourself.

Example Using the Pan Gesture to Drag an Object

Earlier, we looked at how to handle dragging of objects using touch events. Now let's do the same thing, except with a gesture recognizer. For dragging, we'll use the UIPanGestureRecognizer, which recognizes when a finger touches the screen and is then moved around.

Unfortunately, the pan gesture recognizer doesn't give us the previous touch location, so instead, every time the gesture begins, we have to cache the location of the object we want to move and then calculate the offset. As such, the first thing we need to do is declare a class-level variable to cache our object location. See Listing 12–14.

Listing 12–14. *Creating a class variable to cache our object's location*

```
System.Drawing.RectangleF _originalImageFrame = System.Drawing.RectangleF.Empty;
```

Next, we create, configure, enable, and add the gesture recognizer to our image. See Listing 12–15.

Listing 12–15. *Creating a class variable to cache our object's location*

```
UIPanGestureRecognizer gesture = new UIPanGestureRecognizer();
gesture.AddTarget(() => { HandleDrag(gesture); });
this.imgDragMe.AddGestureRecognizer(gesture);
```

Finally, in our HandleDrag method, we check move our object based on the state of the recognizer. See Listing 12–16.

Listing 12–16. *Moving an object during a pan gesture recognizer handler method*

```
protected void HandleDrag(UIPanGestureRecognizer recognizer)
{
        //---- if it's just began, cache the location of the image
        if(recognizer.State == UIGestureRecognizerState.Began)
        { this._originalImageFrame = this.imgDragMe.Frame; }

        if(recognizer.State != (UIGestureRecognizerState.Cancelled
                | UIGestureRecognizerState.Failed
                | UIGestureRecognizerState.Possible))
        {
                //---- move the shape by adding the offset to the object's frame
                System.Drawing.PointF offset
                        = recognizer.TranslationInView(this.imgDragMe);
                System.Drawing.RectangleF newFrame = this._originalImageFrame;
                newFrame.Offset(offset.X, offset.Y);
                this.imgDragMe.Frame = newFrame;
        }
}
```

There we have it! We've successfully implemented dragging without having to handle the event methods ourselves and keep track of state, and so on.

Working with Multiple Gesture Recognizers

Sometimes you need to apply multiple gesture recognizers to a single view. For example, you might want allow both panning and pinching gestures on scroll view to allow users to move the view about and also zoom in/out. When working with multiple gestures in one view, there are a few considerations and opportunities.

Allowing Simultaneous Gesture Recognition

By default, gesture recognizers do not run simultaneously. That is, if you have two gesture recognizers attached to a view, each one is given the opportunity to receive touch events in a non-deterministic order, but they won't receive events simultaneously. If, in the rare instance, you do want them to have the opportunity to operate simultaneously, you must override the ShouldRecognizeSimultaneously property and return true. See Listing 12–17.

Listing 12–17. *Allowing a gesture recognizer to operate simultaneously*

```
gesture.ShouldRecognizeSimultaneously += (UIGestureRecognizer r) => { return true; };
```

Note, however, that returning true will guarantee that the recognizer can operate concurrently with other recognizers, but returning false does not guarantee non-concurrent operation, because other recognizers can return true, allowing them to operate concurrently.

Disabling Another Gesture

Sometimes you may want to prevent a gesture recognizer from functioning. For example, you may have multiple gesture recognizers attached to a view, but depending on what's going on in the view, you may only want certain gestures to be recognized at any given time. Also, sometimes you want even finer control, in which you wish to allow what touches another gesture receives, or even how it processes the touches.

Because of this, gesture recognizes implement two delegate properties that allow you to examine the state of your application and of the current touch events and make decisions on how and whether to recognize gestures. These two events are the following:

- **ShouldReceiveTouch:** The ShouldReceiveTouch delegate method is called right before the recognizer is passed a touch event and allows you to examine the touches and decide whether each one can be sent to the recognizer. One possible use of this is if you have two gesture recognizers and you want to enable simultaneous recognition, but you want to split the touches between the gestures. You can also use this method to disable a gesture recognizer altogether, by simply returning false without being discriminate about the particular touch.

- **ShouldBegin:** The ShouldBegin delegate method is called when a recognizer attempts to change state from Possible, to another state. Returning false will force the state to be changed to Failed, no matter what state it was getting changed to. This provides you with an opportunity to examine the state of your application and the gesture, and cancel the recognition event at the last possible moment.

You can override these methods via a strongly typed UIGestureRecognizerDelegate class, a weak delegate (with the proper Selector Export attributes), or you can simply bind via the event handler syntax. For example, Listing 12–18 overrides the

ShouldReceiveTouch method to disable the recognition by preventing any touch events from reaching it.

Listing 12–18. *Preventing a recognizer from receiving any touches*

```
gesture.ShouldReceiveTouch += (UIGestureRecognizer r, UITouch t) => { return true; };
```

Requiring Another Gesture to Fail Before One Succeeds

Sometimes, as a requirement of a gesture recognition succeeding, you might want another to fail. For instance, say you have a two gesture recognizers on a single view; one that recognizes a single tap, and one that recognizes a double-tap. You likely don't want the single tap gesture to succeed unless the double-tap gesture fails.

To require another gesture to fail before a gesture succeeds, you can call the RequireGestureRecognizerToFail method and pass in the gesture that must fail. See Listing 12–19.

Listing 12–19. *Requiring another gesture to fail before the current one succeeds*

```
gesture.RequireGestureRecognizerToFail(otherGesture);
```

Allowing Gestures and Touch Events Simultaneously

If you add a gesture recognizer to a view, the view (and any views below it) will not receive touch events. This can especially be a problem if you have layered views in which you want a transparent view on top to listen for gestures, but you need to listen for touch events on a view underneath. In order to allow touch events simultaneously with gestures, you need to set the CancelsTouchesInView property on the gesture to false, as in Listing 12–20.

Listing 12–20. *Enabling touch events even when a gesture recognizer is enabled*

```
this._tapGesture.Recognizer.CancelsTouchesInView = false;
```

Creating a Custom Gesture

Although the built-in gesture recognizers cover a lot of the common tasks, sometimes you want to create a custom gesture recognizer that doesn't exist. For example, let's say you want to create a checkmark gesture, whereby a user makes a "V" with their finger. In this section you're going to learn how to do just that.

Creating a custom gesture recognizer is actually fairly easy if you understand the touch events, because it's little more than a wrapper around them. You simply inherit from UIGestureRecognizer, override the touch event methods, and then bubble up your recognition status via the base class' State property.

Checkmark Gesture Recognizer Example

Let's take everything that we've learned about touch and put it together in a custom gesture recognizer that recognizes "V" gestures for checkmarks. We create a custom class that inherits from UIGestureRecognizer and overrides the touch events, keeping track internally of the actual gesture movements. See Listing 12–21.

Listing 12–21. *A custom gesture recognizer for checkmarks*

```
public class CheckmarkGestureRecognizer : UIGestureRecognizer
{
        //---- declarations
        protected bool _strokeUp = false;
        protected PointF _midpoint = PointF.Empty;

        public CheckmarkGestureRecognizer () { }

        /// <summary>
        /// Is called when the fingers touch the screen.
        /// </summary>
        public override void TouchesBegan (MonoTouch.Foundation.NSSet touches,
                UIEvent evt)
        {
                base.TouchesBegan (touches, evt);
                //---- we want one and only one finger
                if(touches.Count != 1)
                { base.State = UIGestureRecognizerState.Failed; }
        }

        /// <summary>
        /// Called when the fingers move
        /// </summary>
        public override void TouchesMoved (MonoTouch.Foundation.NSSet touches,
                UIEvent evt)
        {
                base.TouchesMoved (touches, evt);

                //---- if we haven't already failed
                if(base.State != UIGestureRecognizerState.Failed)
                {
                        //---- get the current and previous touch point
                        PointF newPoint = (touches.AnyObject as UITouch)
                                .LocationInView(this.View);
                        PointF previousPoint = (touches.AnyObject as UITouch).
                                PreviousLocationInView(this.View);

                        //---- if we're not already on the upstroke
                        if(!this._strokeUp)
                        {
                                //---- if we're moving down, just continue to set the
                                // midpoint at whatever point we're at. when we start
                                // to stroke up, it'll stick as the last
                                // point before we upticked
                                if(newPoint.X >= previousPoint.X
                                        && newPoint.Y >= previousPoint.Y)
                                { this._midpoint = newPoint; }
```

```
                            //---- if we're stroking up (moving right x and up y
                            // [y axis is flipped])
                            else if (newPoint.X >= previousPoint.X
                                    && newPoint.Y <= previousPoint.Y)
                            { this._strokeUp = true; }
                            //---- otherwise, we fail the recognizer
                            else { base.State = UIGestureRecognizerState.Failed; }
                    }
                }
        }

        /// <summary>
        /// Called when the fingers lift off the screen
        /// </summary>
        public override void TouchesEnded (MonoTouch.Foundation.NSSet touches,
                UIEvent evt)
        {
                base.TouchesEnded (touches, evt);
                //---- if the gesture is possible, and it stroked upwards, we
                // recognized!
                if(base.State == UIGestureRecognizerState.Possible && this._strokeUp)
                { base.State = UIGestureRecognizerState.Recognized; }
        }

        /// <summary>
        /// Called when the touches are cancelled due to a phone call, etc.
        /// </summary>
        public override void TouchesCancelled (MonoTouch.Foundation.NSSet touches,
                UIEvent evt)
        {
                base.TouchesCancelled (touches, evt);
                //---- we fail the recognizer so that there isn't unexpected behavior
                // if the application comes back into view
                base.State = UIGestureRecognizerState.Cancelled;
        }

        /// <summary>
        /// Called when the state transitions to ended or recognized
        /// </summary>
        public override void Reset ()
        {
                base.Reset ();

                this._strokeUp = false;
                this._midpoint = PointF.Empty;
        }
}
```

If you've been reading this chapter from the beginning, nothing here should be surprising, except for one override method, Reset.

Reset Method

The Reset method is called when the State property changes to either Recognized or Ended, the Reset method is called, giving you a chance to reset any internal state that you've set in your custom gesture recognizer. That way your class can start fresh when the user interacts with the application again and it can be ready to re-attempt at recognizing the gesture.

Using the Custom Gesture Recognizer

The custom gesture recognizer can be used just as you would any of the built-in recognizers. Listing 12–22 toggles an image between checked and unchecked, every time the user makes a checkmark gesture on it.

Listing 12–22. *Using a custom gesture recognizer*

```
this._checkmarkGesture = new CheckmarkGestureRecognizer();
this._checkmarkGesture.AddTarget(() => {
        if(this._checkmarkGesture.State == (UIGestureRecognizerState.Recognized
                | UIGestureRecognizerState.Ended))
        {
                if(this._checked)
                { this.imgCheckmark.Image =
                        UIImage.FromBundle("Images/CheckBox_Unchecked.png"); }
                else { this.imgCheckmark.Image =
                        UIImage.FromBundle("Images/CheckBox_Checked.png"); }
                this._checked = !this._checked;
        }
});
this.imgCheckmark.AddGestureRecognizer(this._checkmarkGesture);
```

If you run the Example_Touches companion application, click Custom Gesture Recognizer on the home page, it takes you to a screen where you can test out the checkmark recognizer to toggle the image. See Figure 12–5.

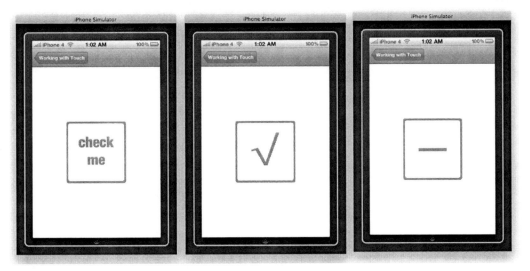

Figure 12–5. *Custom gesture recognizer in action*

As you can see, you can add some pretty cool functionality to your applications using custom gesture recognizers which can be reused across pages.

Summary

The iOS includes two different ways to handle touch interactions: via events and gesture recognizers. In this chapter we looked at working with both, as well as how to create custom gesture recognizers when you need to recognize a gesture that isn't built in.

Chapter 13

Working with Shared Resources

iOS contains a number of shared resources that you can access from your application. In this chapter, we're going to look at using the following iOS resources:

- **File system**
- **Battery**
- **Contacts**
- **Photos and camera**
- **Network indicator**
- **Accelerometer**

File System

Working with the file system in iOS is not unlike working with the file system in .NET from Windows. You can still use the System.IO classes that you're used to working with, such as Directory, File, and the like, but there are a few restrictions to be aware of. Additionally, it's important to understand the directory structure specific to iOS applications in order to know where and when to store things.

Case-Sensitivity

Before delving into the file system, an important point should be noted: although the simulator's file system is case-insensitive, the device's file system is case-sensitive. For this reason, it's very important to pay attention to file casing and to test on an actual device early and often in the development cycle.

Application Sandbox

When your application is installed, iOS creates a directory for it from a GUID and then copies in the .app package, which contains your application source and any embedded resources. It also creates a number of key directories, which we'll look at in the next section.

The directory to which your application is installed is part of the Application Sandbox. The sandbox is a general set of rules and restrictions. For example, say your application is given a sandbox in which it can play, but it can do limited things outside of that sandbox. In the case of iOS, you can read and write files to your application directory (and sub-directories), but you can generally only read files from other locations.

This is part of Apple's security model, and it's intended to prevent malicious programs and code from compromising the integrity of other applications and system data.

Application Directories

The directories listed in Table 13–1 are created in your application's root directory when the application is installed and they're available for your application to use.

Table 13–1. *Application Directories*

File Location	Description
[ApplicationName].app	This is your applications bundle. It contains your application executable and all resources included in the build. You can get the path to this directory via the NSBundle.MainBundle.BundlePath property.
Documents	Use this directory to store documents and application data files. This directory can be made available for access and sharing via iTunes so that users can copy files to and from it from their computer. In order to enable sharing on this directory, add a UIFileSharingEnabled boolean key to your info.plist file and set it to true/yes.
	You can get the path to this directory via an Environment.GetFolderPath (Environment.SpecialFolder.MyDocuments) call.
Library	This is the top-level directory for two other important directories: Preferences and Caches. You can put files in this directory that you don't want shared via iTunes. You can also create other directories in here if you need them to support your application.

File Location	Description
Library/Preferences/	The preferences directory is where iOS stores your application settings. You shouldn't access this directory directly; instead, you should use the settings API. See Chapter 14 for more information.
Library/Caches/	The Caches directory should be used for transient files that need to be persisted in between launches, but not backed up.
	For instance, if you're creating an RSS feed reader that caches RSS feeds, this would be a good folder in which to store them.
	Files in this directory will be removed when a device is restored, so you should always check for an expected file's existence and be able to rebuild them if they've been deleted.
	Additionally, files in this folder aren't deleted unless the device is restored, so your application is responsible for deleting these files when they're no longer needed.
tmp	The tmp directory should be used for temporary files that don't need to be retained between application launches.
	For instance, if your application downloads files from the Internet, this is a good folder in which to store the files during download, until they're finished and you've moved them to their appropriate place.
	Generally, you should delete files placed in this directory when they're no longer needed; however, iOS may remove them when your application isn't running.

Backup/Restore

When a user backs up their device in iTunes, all directories except for the following are backed up:

- **Application Bundle**
- **Library/Caches**
- **tmp**

Backing up large files can take a considerable amount of time, so if your application creates large files that can be recreated, you should consider putting them in the Library/Caches folder instead of the Documents folder.

Application Updates

When a new version of your application is downloaded, iOS installs the application into a new folder, moves the following folders over, and then deletes the old installation:

- **Documents**
- **Library**

Other folders and data may be moved over, but they're not guaranteed, so you should make sure that you put any data or documents that need to be persisted across updates in those folders.

Device Battery

You can check the current status of the battery, including its charge amount, as well as whether it's plugged in and charging. In order to make battery information available to your application, you must first enable battery monitoring setting the BatteryMonitoringEnabled property on the UIDevice class. See Listing 13-1.

Listing 13-1. *Enabling battery monitoring*

```
UIDevice.CurrentDevice.BatteryMonitoringEnabled = true;
```

Battery Level

Once you've enabled battery monitoring, you can get the current charge level via the BatteryLevel property. Listing 13-2 comes from the Example_SharedResources application and sets a progress bar to match the current battery level.

Listing 13-2. *Retrieving the battery charge level*

```
this.barBatteryLevel.Progress = UIDevice.CurrentDevice.BatteryLevel;
```

The value returned is a float value between 0 and 1, with 0 being empty, 1 being completely charged, and .5 being 50% charged. If monitoring hasn't been enabled, it will return -1. Figure 13-1 is a screenshot from the Example_SharedResources application showing the battery charge level and battery state.

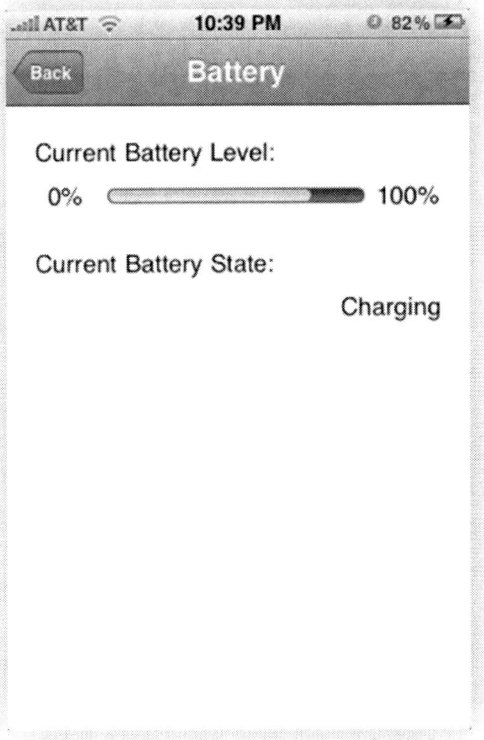

Figure 13–1. *Battery charge level and current battery state shown*

Battery State

You can get the current state of the battery via the BatteryState property on the UIDevice class, which will return one of the following UIDeviceBatteryState enumeration values:

- **Charging:** The device is plugged in and actively charging.
- **Full:** The device has a fully-charged battery, it may or may not be plugged in.
- **Unknown:** The battery status is unknown; this happens if you haven't enabled monitoring.
- **Unplugged:** The device is unplugged and is not charging.

Listing 13–3 comes from the Example_SharedResources application and sets a text label to show the current battery state.

Listing 13–3. *Retrieving the current battery state*

```
this.lblBatteryState.Text = UIDevice.CurrentDevice.BatteryState.ToString();
```

Getting Battery Change Notifications

You can receive notifications when the battery level or the battery state changes from iOS. Unfortunately, it's not as easy as just subscribing to an event. Instead, you must add an Observer to the NSNotificationCenter class and listen for BatteryLevelDidChangeNotification or BatteryStateDidChangeNotification notifications. For example, Listing 13–4 is from the Example_SharedResources application, and updates the battery level and state, respectively, when they change.

Listing 13–4. *Subscribing to battery change notifications*

```
//---- add a notification handler for battery level changes
NSNotificationCenter.DefaultCenter.AddObserver
(UIDevice.BatteryLevelDidChangeNotification
        , (NSNotification n) => {
        this.barBatteryLevel.Progress = UIDevice.CurrentDevice.BatteryLevel;
        n.Dispose();
});
//---- add a notification handler for battery state changes
NSNotificationCenter.DefaultCenter.AddObserver
(UIDevice.BatteryStateDidChangeNotification
        , (NSNotification n) => {
        this.lblBatteryState.Text = UIDevice.CurrentDevice.BatteryState.ToString();
        n.Dispose();
});
```

Address Book/Contacts

iOS has a concept of a shared contact database known as the Address Book. Address book/contact data is shared across many different applications that ship with iOS including the Contacts Application, Mail, and even the Phone Dialer (for those devices that include cellular support).

iOS offers the following two ways to work with the shared address book:

- **Utilize the address book controllers:** You may have noticed that all of the built-in applications share many of the same screens for contact searching and editing. Apple makes available these screens via built-in controllers that you can create and show, much as you would your own custom screens, but they encapsulate all of the functionality for working with the address book and simplify contact management greatly.

- **Access the address book directly:** In addition to the screens that iOS provides you, there is a lower-level API, called the Address Book API, that allows you to query and modify the address book directly.

For most scenarios, using the address book controllers is the recommended way. They're very powerful and give you a ton of functionality for free. However, sometimes it's inappropriate to show the standard screens; or, in some cases, you simply need to query the address book database. For that scenario, you should use the API directly.

In this section, we're going to look at the different types of address book controllers and how to use them, and then we're going to explore the address book API, for when the controllers don't do what you need.

Address Book Controllers

There are four main controllers that you can invoke from your application and each one is designed for a specific address book related task:

- **ABPeoplePickerNavigationController:** Also known as the contact picker, this controller is used to allow your users to choose a contact from the address book. After the user chooses a contact, it's returned to your application.

- **ABPersonViewController:** The person view controller is used to display a single contact and, optionally, to allow edits.

- **ABNewPersonViewController:** The new person view controller is used to add a new contact to the address book.

- **ABUnknownPersonViewController:** The unknown person view controller shows a screen with limited contact data that gives the option to add the data to an existing contact, or create a new contact, and then manages the screens that enable those tasks.

All these controllers can be found in the `MonoTouch.AddressBookUI` namespace.

Let's take a look at each one of these in detail.

People Picker View Controller (Contact Picker)

The contact picker view controller presents the same view as the home screen of the Contacts Application (minus the "groups" button), shown in Figure 13–2.

Figure 13–2. *The people picker view controller showing a list of contacts*

When using the address book controllers, you should declare them as class-level variables, so that they (and their associated event handlers) don't get garbage-collected when the method that declares them returns. See Listing 13–5.

Listing 13–5. *You should declare your address book controllers as class-level members*

```
public partial class MyScreen : UIViewController
{
        protected ABPeoplePickerNavigationController _ addressBookPicker;
        …
}
```

To use the contact picker, instantiate an `ABPeoplePickerNavigationController` and then display it by calling `PresentModalViewController` on the `UIViewController` that represents your current screen.

For example, Listing 13–6 comes from the `Example_SharedResources` application, and shows the contact picker when a button is touched.

Listing 13–6. *Presenting the contact picker when a button is pressed*

```
this.btnChooseContact.TouchUpInside += (s, e) => {
        this._addressBookPicker = new ABPeoplePickerNavigationController();
        this.NavigationController.PresentModalViewController(this._addressBookPicker
                , true);
};
```

There are two important events exposed by the contact picker: the `Cancelled` and `SelectPerson` events. Let's take a look at each of these.

Cancelled Event

The cancelled event is raised when the user clicks the **Cancel** button in the contact picker. The contact picker will not dismiss itself, so you should handle the Cancelled event and call the `DismissModalViewControllerAnimated` method to dismiss the contact picker (see Listing 13–7).

Listing 13–7. *Dismissing the contact picker when cancel is clicked*

```
this._addressBookPicker.Cancelled += (sender, eventArgs) => {
        this.NavigationController.DismissModalViewControllerAnimated(true); };
```

SelectPerson Event

The SelectPerson event is raised when a contact is clicked and the selected person is passed to the event handler via the `Person` property of the `ABPeoplePickerSelectPersonEventArgs` object. As with the `Cancelled` event, the picker will not dismiss itself, so you should dismiss it as part of the event handler. For example, Listing 13–8 comes from the `Example_SharedResources` companion code, and shows populates text fields with the first and last name of the selected contact and then dismisses the picker when the SelectPerson event is raised.

Listing 13–8. *Handling the SelectPerson event*

```
this._addressBookPicker.SelectPerson += (object sender,
ABPeoplePickerSelectPersonEventArgs args) => {
        ABPerson selectedPerson = args.Person;
        this.lblFirstName.Text = selectedPerson.FirstName;
        this.lblLastName.Text = selectedPerson.LastName;
        this.NavigationController.DismissModalViewControllerAnimated(true);
};
```

Person View Controller

The person view controller is likely familiar to you as well; it shows contact details and allows you to edit them, just as in the contact application. See Figure 13–3.

Figure 13–3. *The person view controller in detail and edit mode*

Using the person view controller is even easier than the contact picker, because it manages its own dismissal. However, because it has a nested screen, you must use it in conjunction with a navigation controller, and push it onto the navigation stack via the PushViewController method.

To use the person view controller, instantiate a new ABPersonViewController, set the ABPerson you want to display on the DisplayedPerson property, and then push the controller onto your screen's navigation controller. Additionally, if you want to allow users to edit the contact, you should enable editing by setting the AllowsEditing property to true.

For example, Listing 13–9 comes from the Example_SharedResources application, and shows an editable person view controller when a button is clicked.

Listing 13–9. *Showing an editable person view controller when a button is clicked*

```
this.btnViewSelectedContact.TouchUpInside += (s, e) => {
        this._addressBookViewPerson = new ABPersonViewController();
        this._addressBookViewPerson.DisplayedPerson = this._selectedPerson;
        this._addressBookViewPerson.AllowsEditing = true;
        this.NavigationController.PushViewController(this._addressBookViewPerson, true);
};
```

New Person View Controller

The new person view controller presents a New Contact screen that you can optionally pre-populate with data. See Figure 13–4.

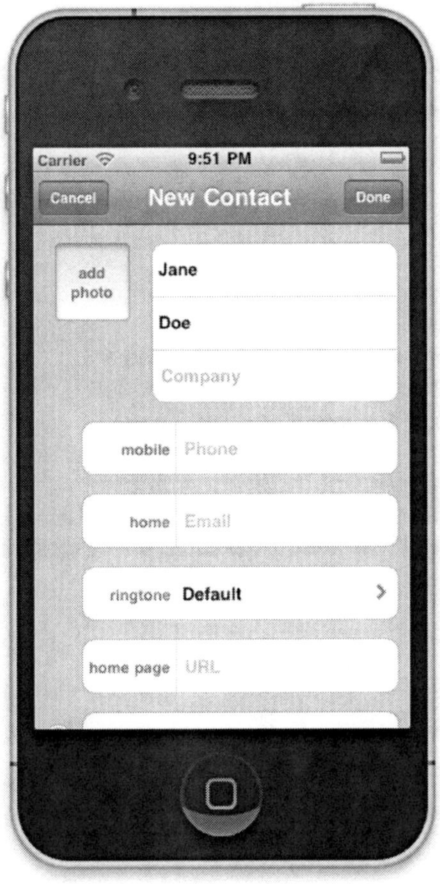

Figure 13–4. *The new person view controller*

As with the person view controller, the new person view controller requires a navigation controller to function properly; without one, the **Cancel** and **Done** buttons will not be displayed. However, unlike the person view controller, the new person view controller needs to manually be dismissed.

To use it, instantiate a new ABNewPersonViewController, push it onto the navigation stack via PushViewController, and handle the NewPersonComplete event. See Listing 13–10.

Listing 13–10. *Showing the new person view controller when a button is clicked*

```
this.btnCreateNewContact.TouchUpInside += (s, e) => {
        this._addressBookNewPerson = new ABNewPersonViewController();
        this.NavigationController.PushViewController(this._addressBookNewPerson, true);

        this._addressBookNewPerson.NewPersonComplete += (object sender
                , ABNewPersonCompleteEventArgs args) => {
                this.NavigationController.PopViewControllerAnimated(true);
        };
};
```

Additionally, you can prepopulate the controller with contact data by creating a new ABPerson object and assigning it to the DisplayedPerson property. See Listing 13–11.

Listing 13–11. *Showing an editable the person view controller when a button is clicked*

```
ABPerson person = new ABPerson();
person.FirstName = this.txtFirstName.Text;
person.LastName = this.txtLastName.Text;
this._addressBookNewPerson.DisplayedPerson = person;
```

NewPersonComplete Event

The NewPersonComplete event is raised when either the **Cancel** or **Done** buttons are clicked. If a new contact has been created, it can be found in the Person property of the ABNewPersonCompleteEventArgs parameter passed to the event handler, however, because the user could have cancelled out of the new person screen, it may be null. For this reason, you should check the Completed property of the event args before accessing the contact information. For example, the event handler in Listing 13–12 displays the new contact ID in an alert box if the new contact was created successfully.

Listing 13–12. *Showing the new person view controller when a button is clicked*

```
this._addressBookNewPerson.NewPersonComplete += (object sender
        , ABNewPersonCompleteEventArgs args) => {
        if(args.Completed)
        {
                new UIAlertView("Alert", "New contact created, ID: "
                        + args.Person.Id.ToString(), null
                        , "OK", null).Show();
        }
        this.NavigationController.PopViewControllerAnimated(true);
};
```

Unknown Person View Controller

The unknown person view controller has the following two purposes.

- It can be used to take contact data that isn't in the address book, and either use it to create a new contact or add the data to an existing contact.

- It can be used to share a contact via e-mail by bundling the contact into a .vcf file and attaching it to an e-mail.

If the user chooses to create a new contact, they're presented with the new contact screen, pre-populated with whatever data has been set. If they choose to add to an existing contact, they are presented with the contact picker controller, which allows them to choose a contact. That data is then merged with the existing contact. If the user chooses to share the contact, the edit e-mail screen is shown with the contact information attached as a .vcf file.

You can configure the unknown person view controller to allow users to add to the address book, to share contacts, or both. Figure 13–5 shows the first screen of it with both address book adding and sharing enabled.

Figure 13–5. *The unknown person contact controller presents a choice to add the contact or share it*

The unknown person view controller works much like the person view controller in that it needs to be pushed onto a navigation controller to work properly, and it handles its own dismissal.

To use the unknown person view, instantiate a new ABUnknownPersonViewController, specify any known contact data via the DisplayedPerson property, and then push the controller onto your navigation controller via the PushViewController method.

Additionally, you should set at least AllowsAddingToAddressBook or AllowsActions to true, in order to display the **Create/Add** or **Share** buttons on the controller.

For example, Listing 13–13 comes from the Example_SharedResources application, and shows the unknown person view controller when a button is pressed. It sets a first and last name and allows both adding to the address book, as well as sharing, and the like.

Listing 13–13. *Showing the unknown person view controller when a button is pressed*

```
this.btnPromptForUnknown.TouchUpInside += (s, e) => {
        this._addressBookUnknownPerson = new ABUnknownPersonViewController();

        ABPerson person = new ABPerson();
        person.FirstName = this.txtFirstName.Text;
        person.LastName = this.txtLastName.Text;
        this._addressBookUnknownPerson.DisplayedPerson = person;

        this._addressBookUnknownPerson.AllowsAddingToAddressBook = true;
        this._addressBookUnknownPerson.AllowsActions = true;

        this.NavigationController.PushViewController(this._addressBookUnknownPerson
                , true);
};
```

PersonCreated Event

The PersonCreated event is similar to the NewPersonComplete event on the new person view controller. It's actually raised when either the **Cancel** or **Done** button is clicked in the new person screen and the contact that was created is passed in via the Person property on the ABUnknownPersonCreatedEventArgs parameter. However, unlike the NewPersonComplete event, there is no Completed property passed to check to see if a person was actually created, so you should do a null check on the property before trying to access it. For example, Listing 13–14 is from the Example_SharedResources code, and displays an alert with the ID of the contact that was created from the unknown person view controller.

Listing 13–14. *You should always do a null check on the Person property when handling the PersonCreated event*

```
this._addressBookUnknownPerson.PersonCreated += (object sender
        , ABUnknownPersonCreatedEventArgs args) => {
        if(args.Person != null)
        {
                new UIAlertView("Alert", "New contact created, ID: "
                        + args.Person.Id.ToString(), null
                        , "OK", null).Show();
        }
};
```

Working Directly with the Address Book

The Address Book Controllers give you quite a bit of functionality for free; however, sometimes you need to go to the metal, as they say, and need to work with the address book directly. For example, you might want to query the address book without ever opening a controller and displaying options to the user. For this reason, iOS exposes an API for querying and updating the address book database directly.

There are the following four main classes that you'll need to understand in order to work with the address book API directly:

- **AddressBook:** Represents the database of contacts available on an iOS device.

- **Records:** Each entry in the address book is represented by a record, which contains data for that particular contact or group.

- **Single-Value Properties:** Single-value properties are simple properties on a record, such as FirstName.

- **Multivalue Properties:** Multivalue properties are special collections for properties that can have multiple values. For instance, a contact can have many phone numbers associated with it, each with its own label such as "Home" or "Mobile." This data is stored as multivalue properties.

Working with address book data typically requires you to work with each one of these classes in that order; first you need to get a reference to the address book, then you typically retrieve a particular record for a contact (or loop through them), and then you access the properties. Let's look at each one of these classes and steps in detail.

Address Books (ABAddressBook)

In order to work with the address book, you need to instantiate a new ABAddressBook object, which creates a connection to the underlying database. From there you can query, update, and so on. Changes that you make to the address book are journaled. That is, If you make changes that you wish to push back to the database, you must call the Save method for them to be committed. If you want to revert any changes back to the original state, you can call Revert. The basic pattern is illustrated in Listing 13–15.

Listing 13–15. *Pattern for working with the address book database*

```
//---- instantiate a reference to the address book
using(ABAddressBook addressBook = new ABAddressBook())
{
        //---- make changes
        // code

        //---- save changes
        addressBook.Save();
        //---- or cancel them
        addressBook.Revert();
}
```

Notice that I used the using statement. ABAddressBook implements IDisposable, because it keeps an unmanaged connection open to the underlying database. The using statement will ensure that the connection is closed via the Dispose method on the object when the using block completes.

> **NOTE:** When using the address book in a multi-threaded scenario, you must create a separate connection (ABAddressBook instance) for each thread you wish to access it on. This goes for objects that are created from it as well. For instance, you cannot pass a record across a thread boundary. Instead, you should pass the ID of the record and get a new reference to it via the ABAddressBook instance created in that thread. Failure to isolate instances between threads will cause a crash in your application. This is a limitation in the underlying Objective-C runtime and you will experience it regardless of whether you're coding in C# with MonoTouch, or Objective-C.

Change Notifications

Because the address book is a shared resource, data in it can be changed by iOS or by other applications. When a change occurs, the ExternalChange event is raised. See Listing 13–16.

Listing 13–16. *Handling external address book changes.*

```
addressBook.ExternalChange += (object sender, ExternalChangeEventArgs e) => {
        // code to deal with changes
};
```

If you have unsaved changes and you want to save them, iOS will attempt to merge your changes with the other changes; however, it's not guaranteed that your changes will go into effect.

In practice, you can avoid having to worry about this by not keeping address book connections open. You should simply get a reference, query/make changes, and dispose of the reference. This will minimize the opportunity for external changes impacting your code.

However, if you do keep a persistent connection to the contacts database open, you can make sure that you have the latest changes by calling Revert, which will update your connection to point to the latest version of the database.

Records

Once you have a reference to the address book, you'll see that it implements IEnumerable with each item being an ABRecord. See Listing 13–17.

Listing 13–17. *The address book implements IEnumerable; every item is an ABRecord.*

```
foreach(ABRecord item in addressBook)
{
        if(item.Type == ABRecordType.Person)
        {
                // do something
        }
}
```

A record can either be a Group or a Person record. You can test via the Type property, which is an ABRecordType enumeration.

Record Properties

Many of the properties on records are simple single-value properties such as FirstName, LastName, and so on. However, for items that can have multiple values, such as phone numbers, they're exposed as ABMultiValue properties. Multivalue properties are similar to arrays of dictionaries. An ABMultiValue object implements IEnumerable and exposes a collection of ABMultiValueEntry objects that contain Label and Value properties. They're exposed via get methods, such as the GetPhones method to retrieve a contact's phone numbers.

For example, Listing 13–18 loops through each record in the address book. If a record is a person record, it writes each contact's name and each of their phone numbers to the application console.

Listing 13–18. *Writing contact names and phone numbers to the Application Output console*

```
//---- for each record
foreach(ABRecord item in addressBook)
{
        Console.WriteLine(item.Type.ToString() + " " + item.Id);
        //---- there are two possible record types, person and group
        if(item.Type == ABRecordType.Person)
        {
                //---- since we've already tested it to be a person, just create a
                // shortcut to that type
                ABPerson person = item as ABPerson;
                Console.WriteLine(person.FirstName + " " + person.LastName);

                //---- get the phone numbers
                ABMultiValue<string> phones = person.GetPhones();
                foreach(ABMultiValueEntry<string> val in phones)
                {
                        Console.Write(val.Label + ": " + val.Value);
                }
        }
}
```

In looking at this code, working with multivalue properties seem pretty straightforward – until you want to make changes. The problem is, they're immutable (unchangeable), so the Label and Value properties are read only, and there's no way to add or remove items from the collection.

In order to make changes, you actually have to copy the ABMultiValue object to an
ABMutableMultiValue object via the ToMutableMultiValue method, make your changes,
and then call the Set method to attach them back to the record. For example, Listing
13–19 comes from the Example_SharedResources application, and adds a phone number
to a contact.

Listing 13–19. *Adding a phone number to a contact*

```
//---- get a reference to the contact
using(ABAddressBook addressBook = new ABAddressBook())
{
        //---- get the contact
        ABPerson contact = addressBook.GetPerson(this._contactID);

        //---- get the phones and copy them to a mutable set of multivalues
        // (so we can edit)
        ABMutableMultiValue<string> phones = contact.GetPhones().ToMutableMultiValue();

        //---- add the phone number to the phones via the multivalue.Add method
        phones.Add(new NSString(this.txtPhoneLabel.Text)
                , new NSString(this.txtPhoneNumber.Text));

        //---- attach the phones back to the contact
        contact.SetPhones(phones);

        //---- save the address book changes
        addressBook.Save();
}
```

If this isn't more proof that Apple hates us, I'm not sure what is.

Deleting is similar (see Listing 13–20).

Listing 13–20. *Deleting a phone number from a contact*

```
using(ABAddressBook addressBook = new ABAddressBook())
{
        ABPerson contact = addressBook.GetPerson(this._contactID);

        //---- get the phones and copy them to a mutable set of multivalues
        // (so we can edit)
        ABMutableMultiValue<string> phones = contact.GetPhones().ToMutableMultiValue();

        //---- loop backwards and delete the phone number
        for(int i = phones.Count - 1; i >= 0 ; i--)
        {
                if(phones[i].Identifier == phoneNumberID)
                { phones.RemoveAt(i); }
        }

        //---- attach the phones back to the contact
        contact.SetPhones(phones);

        //---- save the changes
        addressBook.Save();
}
```

Once you understand this pattern, working with the address becomes a lot easier.

Photos and Camera

Just like with the address book, there are two ways to work with the camera and photos: you can use the built-in UIImagePickerController, which allows you to pick from existing photos in the user photo library and take pictures, or you can use the AV Foundation Framework, which provides a set of API calls to access photos/videos and the camera directly.

We're going to take a look first at the UIImagePickerController, and then we'll take a quick look at the AV Foundation Framework.

UIImagePickerController

In addition to being It also allows you to customize the camera view so you can provide a custom photo taking experience.

To use the image picker, you generally use the following pattern:

- **Determine support:** Not all devices have the same features – some have front cameras, some have camera flash, some allow video recording, and on and on. Before you try to use the image picker, you should determine if the device supports what you want to do with it.

- **Instantiate the picker:** An instance of the `UIImagePickerController` needs to be created in order to be used.

- **Configure the picker:** Once you've instantiated the picker, you need to tell it which interface to display by setting its `MediaTypes` property and set any other options.

- **Provide a custom camera view (optional):** You can optionally show a custom view on top of the camera screen. This gives you the opportunity to customize the picture taking/video recording experience.

- **Present the controller:** After you've configured the picker, you show it by calling `PresentModalController` on your view controller and passing it the picker object.

- **Implement a picker celegate:** After the picker is displayed, the user can either cancel out of it or, depending on how you've configured it, take a photo or a video, or select an existing photo or video. When any of these things happen, an appropriate method on the picker delegate will be called to notify the application. If the user hasn't cancelled, you likely want to do something with the resulting video or photo.

Let's take a look at each of these steps in more detail.

Determining Support

There are the following three basic things that you check before trying to use the image picker:

- **Sources**
- **Cameras and flash**
- **Media types**

If you attempt to configure an image picker with an item that is unsupported, when you display the picker controller, your application will likely crash; you should therefore make sure you check to see if that particular item is available on the device that your application is running on. Let's take a look at each of these items in more detail.

Sources

There are three sources from which you can pull images and media: the Cameras (back, and front), the Photo Library, and the Saved Albums Photos. Each one of these items is available via the UIImagePickerControllerSourceType enumeration, and to check if it's available, you call the static IsSourceTypeAvailable method on the UIImagePickerController class. For example, Listing 13–21 checks to see if a picker controller can be created that takes photos.

Listing 13–21. *Determining whether a particular source is available*

```
bool isCameraAvailable = UIImagePickerController.IsSourceTypeAvailable(
        UIImagePickerControllerSourceType.Camera);
```

Cameras and Flash

The location and availability of cameras and camera flash varies between devices. For example, the iPhone 3Gs and below only have a rear camera, and don't have a flash. The iPhone 4, however, has both a front and a rear camera, as well as a rear flash. The first generation iPad doesn't have a camera at all. To determine whether a particular camera or flash is available, you call the static IsCameraDeviceAvailable and IsFlashAvailableForCameraDevice methods, respectively, which are available on the UIImagePickerController class. You pass a value from the UIImagePickerControllerCameraDevice enumeration that contains Front and Rear values. For instance, Listing 13–22 determines whether or not the rear flash is available on the current device.

Listing 13–22. *Determining whether flash is available*

```
bool isRearFlashAvailable = UIImagePickerController.IsFlashAvailableForCameraDevice(
        UIImagePickerControllerCameraDevice.Rear);
```

Media Types

iOS supports two media types: still images and videos. The availability of each is dependent on the source. For example, first generation iPhones are able to play video, but not record it. Therefore, in order to determine what media type is available, you have to specify the source. To get the available media types, call the static `AvailableMediaTypes` method on the `UIImagePickerController` class and pass in a source type available in the `UIImagePickerControllerSrouceType` enumeration. See Listing 13–23.

Listing 13–23. *Determining which media types are available from the camera*

```
string[] mediaTypes = UIImagePickerController.AvailableMediaTypes(
        UIImagePickerControllerSourceType.Camera);
```

We'll see in just a moment how we can use these types when we configure the image picker.

Creating the Image Picker

Once you've determined feature availability, you need to instantiate the picker controller. Creating a picker controller is very easy, but you should declare it at the class level so it doesn't get garbage collected when your method that instantiates it returns. See Listing 13–24.

Listing 13–24. *Creating an image picker controller*

```
public partial class ImagePickerScreen : UIViewController
{
        protected UIImagePickerController _imagePicker;

        ...
        protected void SomeMethod()
        {
                this._imagePicker = new UIImagePickerController();
                ...
        }
}
```

Configuring the Image Picker

There are a number of different settings and configurations that you can specify on the image picker, each of which affects its behavior, including the following:

- **Media source**
- **Allowable media types**
- **Whether to show camera controls**

Source

The first thing you should set is the source of the media you'd like to access, such as from the Camera or from the Photo Library. You specify the source via the `SourceType` property, which takes a UIImagePickerControllerSourceType enumeration value. What you specify for here determines what picker screen comes up and you have three options:

- **Camera:** Specifying camera will bring up the camera screen with the appropriate camera you've configured.

- **PhotoLibrary:** Specifying photo library will bring up the thumbnail view controller showing images and videos in the user's photo library.

- **SavedPhotosAlbum:** Specifying saved photos album will bring up the thumbnail view controller showing images and videos from the user's camera roll.

For example, Listing 13–25 configures the image picker to bring up the camera view.

Listing 13–25. *Configuring the image picker to show the camera controller screen*

```
this._imagePicker.SourceType = UIImagePickerControllerSourceType.Camera;
```

Media Types

Once you've configured your media source, you should configure which media types you want your user to be able to select. You can set this via the MediaTypes property, and if you want to allow a user to be able to select whatever is available, you can use the AvailableMediaTypes method from before. For example, Listing 13–26 allows a user to select either video or images from the photo library.

Listing 13–26. *Configuring the media types*

```
this._imagePicker.MediaTypes = UIImagePickerController.AvailableMediaTypes(
        UIImagePickerControllerSourceType.PhotoLibrary);
```

If you need to specify only either images or video, you can specify public.image or public.video, respectively.

Camera Controls

If you've specified that the media source should be from the camera, you can specify whether the user gets camera controls via the ShowsCameraControls property. See Listing 13–27.

Listing 13–27. *Disabling camera controls*

```
this._imagePicker.ShowsCameraControls = false;
```

The default is true and you should only set it to false if you're going to provide custom controls in a custom camera view overlay.

Providing a Custom Camera Overlay

The image picker also allows you to customize the camera view so you can provide a custom photo taking experience. If you set the SourceType to UIImagePickerControllerSourceType.Camera, you can set a custom overlay view that gets layered on top of the camera view. To specify an overlay view, all you have to do is set the CameraOverlayView property to the initialized view that you want to display. See Listing 13–28.

Listing 13–28. *Disabling camera controls*

```
this._imagePicker.CameraOverlayView = overlay;
```

If you choose to display the camera controls (ShowsCameraControls = true), you should make sure that don't cover them up so they can still be used.

If you choose to display your own controls you can take a picture when a user clicks your picture button by calling TakePicture on the image picker. Additionally, if you want to implement a zoom, or change the camera viewport, you can create a CGAffineTransformation and assign it to the CameraViewTransform property on the image picker controller.

Displaying the Image Picker

After you've configured your image picker, when you're ready to display it, simply call PresentModalViewController on your screen view controller (or navigation controller), to display it. See Listing 13–29.

Listing 13–29. *Disabling camera controls*

```
this.NavigationController.PresentModalViewController(this._imagePicker, true);
```

Handling Image Picker Events

As with most controls, you have a few options for handling image picker events; you can either wire up the events directly, or implement either a strong or a weak delegate (see Chapter 6 for more information on delegates).

Either way, there are two important events/methods that you should handle, which represent the different paths a user can take via the picker:

- **Canceled**

- **FinishedPickingMedia**

NOTE: There is an additional method called FinishedPickingImage that is called when a photo is picked, but it has been deprecated in v3.0 of iOS. You should instead use FinishedPickingMedia which will be called when either an image or a video is chosen.

Implementing a UIImagePickerControllerDelegate

Implementing the picker controller delegate is like implementing any other delegate –
simply create a class that inherits from UIImagePickerControllerDelegate and override
the methods that you care about. See Listing 13–30.

Listing 13–30. *Implementing an image picker delegate*

```
protected class PickerDelegate : UIImagePickerControllerDelegate
{
        public override void Canceled (UIImagePickerController picker)
        {
                Console.WriteLine("picker canceled");
        }

        public override void FinishedPickingMedia (UIImagePickerController picker
                , NSDictionary info)
        {
                Console.WriteLine("User picked a video.");
        }
}
```

You should declare you delegate at the class level so that it doesn't get garbage
collected. See Listing 13–31.

Listing 13–31. *Declaring an image picker delegate*

```
public partial class ImagePickerScreen : UIViewController
{
        protected PickerDelegate _pickerDelegate;
        …
}
```

And then when you configure your picker, you can attach the delegate. See Listing 13–32.

Listing 13–32. *Attaching an image picker delegate to the image picker*

```
this._pickerDelegate = new ImagePickerScreen.PickerDelegate();
this._imagePicker.Delegate = this._pickerDelegate;
```

Let's take a look at each of the delegate/event methods in more detail.

Canceled Event/Method

The Canceled event (or method if you're using a delegate) is raised when the user
cancels out of the picker screens without picking any media. You should use the
Canceled method to dismiss the picker. See Listing 13–33.

Listing 13–33. *Dismissing the picker when the user cancels out of it*

```
this._imagePicker.Canceled += (s,e) => {
        this._imagePicker.DismissModalViewControllerAnimated(true);
};
```

FinishedPickingMedia Event/Method

The FinishedPickingMedia event (or method if you're using a delegate) is raised when the user picks or takes either a video or an image. The method is passed a reference to the image picker that was used, and an info parameter of type NSDictionary that contains information and content pertaining to the chosen/taken media.

The info dictionary parameter the contains the following keys, which can be found as static properties on the UIImagePickerController:

- **MediaType:** Let's you know whetherthe item chosen is an image or a video. The value is an NSString that evaluates to either public.image or public.video, respectively.

- **ReferenceUrl:** An NSUrl of the location in the filesystem of the original version of the picked item. For example, if the item is edited (such as cropping an image, or editing a movie) in the controller, the ReferenceUrl value points to the unedited item.

- **OriginalImage:** If the item is an image, the OriginalImage key points to the UIimage value of the actual image before it was edited.

- **EditedImage:** Similar to OriginalImage, except that it points to the UIImage after it has been cropped.

- **CropRect:** A System.Drawing.RectangleF describing the crop that was applied to the original image.

- **MediaMetadata:** MediaMetadata points to an NSDictionary of metadata information if an image was chosen.

The general pattern in accessing the info parameter is to extract the value via the key, cast to the appropriate underlying object, and then test for null. For example, Listing 13–34 grabs the MediaUrl value and writes it out to the console.

Listing 13–34. *Accessing the info parameter's data*

```
NSUrl mediaURL = info[UIImagePickerController.MediaURL] as NSUrl;
if(mediaURL != null)
{
        Console.WriteLine(mediaURL.ToString());
}
```

AV Foundation Framework

The AV Foundation Framework is a set of APIs that allow you to directly access the audio/visual capabilities and libraries (including the user's iTunes/iPod library) in the iOS. It allows you a lot more control when dealing with multimedia in the iOS.

The first pieces of the AV Foundation Framework was introduced in iOS v3.0, but really didn't fully mature until v4.1. With the AV Foundation Framework, you can do a number of things, including:

■ Query, enumerate, and write to a user's media (photo and video) albums.

■ Get direct access to iDevice cameras and tweak settings for both still photos and video recording. As well as have direct access to the output.

■ Edit multimedia assets such as videos and audio.

Unfortunately, because the MonoTouch wrapping of the AV Foundation Framework (which is now complete, at the time of writing), happened very near the end of writing this book, I'm only going to briefly introduce it. For a more complete introduction, see the AV Foundation Framework Programming Guide in the Apple Developer Documentation at: http://developer.apple.com/library/ios/#documentation/AudioVideo/Conceptual/AVFoundationPG/Articles/00_Introduction.html.

In this section, we're going to examine how to enumerate multimedia assets instead of using the UIImagePickerController.

Enumerating User Albums

In order to enumerate user photos and videos in the iOS, you must first create an instance of the ALAssetsLibrary class, which provides access to user albums. See Listing 13–35.

Listing 13–35. *Instantiating a reference to the ALAssetsLibrary*

```
this._assetsLibrary = new ALAssetsLibrary();
```

Once you have a reference to the ALAssetsLibrary, you call the Enumerate method, which will loop through each album on the iDevice, passing in:

■ The type of assets to enumerate

■ A delegate method to execute for each item

■ A delegate to execute in the case of an error

For example, the call in Listing 13–36 enumerates all the albums on a user's device. For each album, the GroupsEnumerator method is invoked, and in the case of an error, the anonymous lambda delegate is executed that writes out the error to the console.

Listing 13–36. *Calling the Enumerate method on the ALAssetsGroup to get a list of all the user photo/video albums*

```
this._assetsLibrary.Enumerate(ALAssetsGroupType.All
        , this.GroupsEnumerator
        , (NSError e) => { Console.WriteLine("Could not enumerate albums: " +
                e.LocalizedDescription); });
```

The GroupsEnumerator method is passed a reference to the ALAssetsGroup, which represents an album, and a Boolean reference parameter allowing you to halt the enumeration if you want.

Once you have a group (album) reference, you can then enumerate through the individual items in that group, by calling the Enumerate method on the Group object, and passing a delegate to execute for the asset enumeration.

For example, the method in Listing 13–37 will write out the name of the group and then enumerate the assets within that group.

Listing 13–37. *A method that executed for each asset group/album enumerated*

```
protected void GroupsEnumerator(ALAssetsGroup group, ref bool stop)
{
        //---- when the enumeration is completed, this method is invoked with group set
        // to null
        if (group != null)
        {
                //---- don't stop, baby
                stop = false;

                //---- write out the group type and name
                Console.WriteLine("Group found: " + group.Type.ToString());
                if(group.Name != null) { Console.WriteLine("Group Name: "
                        + group.Name); }

                //---- photos and videos. could also pass AllVideos, AllVideos, etc.
                group.SetAssetsFilter(ALAssetsFilter.AllAssets);
                //---- enumerate each asset within the group
                group.Enumerate(this.AssetEnumerator);
        }
        else
        { Console.WriteLine("Group enumeration completed."); }
}
```

The method is called for each album/group, and then will be called one additional time, passing a null reference for the group, to signal that it has finished.

The delegate called for each asset is similar to the group enumeration delegate, except that instead of being passed a reference to the group, it's passed an ALAsset object, which is a reference to the photo or video in the album. See Listing 13–38.

Listing 13–38. *A method that is executed for each asset within an album*

```
protected void AssetEnumerator(ALAsset asset, int index, ref bool stop)
{
        //---- when the enumeration is completed, this method is invoked with group set
        // to null
        if(asset != null)
        {
                Console.WriteLine("Found asset: " + index.ToString());
                //---- keep going
                stop = false;
        }
        else { Console.WriteLine("Asset enumeration completed."); }
}
```

When enumerating the individual assets, you can get a reference to the thumbnail of the item via the Thumbnail property on the ALAsset object. This allows you to create your own custom asset display screens. For example, in the Example_SharedResources companion code and application, I display a list of albums and their items in tables. See Figure 13–6.

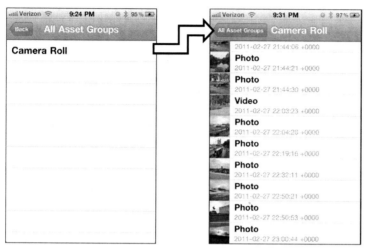

Figure 13–6. *Listing albums and their assets (photos and videos)*

As I mentioned, this is just the tip of the iceberg of what you can do with the AV Assets Framework, I encourage you to take a look at the documentation on it for more information.

Network Activity Indicator

iOS devices have a network activity indicator in the status bar that informs the user that a network operation is taking place. See Figure 13–7.

Figure 13–7. *Network activity indicator in the on state*

Apple recommends that if your application performs a network activity that takes more than a couple of seconds, you should turn the activity indicator on. You can enable it by simply setting the NetworkActivityIndicatorVisible property on the UIApplication class to true. See Listing 13–39.

Listing 13–39. *Turning the network activity indicator on*

```
UIApplication.SharedApplication.NetworkActivityIndicatorVisible = true;
```

This works just fine when you only have one network activity happening at any on time; however, many times you might have several asynchronous activities at once and you don't want to turn off the network activity indicator when one finishes but the others are still active. For this reason, you should keep an application wide counter that you increment and decrement, depending on whether an activity is happening. For example, the AppDelegate class in Listing 13–40 exposes a method called SetNetworkActivityIndicator that does just that.

Listing 13–40. *Managing the network activity indicator based on a reference counter*

```
public class AppDelegate : UIApplicationDelegate
{
        protected int _networkActivityCount = 0;
        ...
        public void SetNetworkActivityIndicator(bool onOrOff)
```

```
    {
            //---- increment or decrement our reference count
            if(onOrOff)
            { this._networkActivityCount++; }
            else { this._networkActivityCount--; }

            //---- set it's visibility based on whether or not there is still
            // activity
            UIApplication.SharedApplication.NetworkActivityIndicatorVisible =
                    (this._networkActivityCount > 0);
    }
}
```

Then, you can call the method and pass whether or not you want to turn the activity indicator on or off.

```
(UIApplication.SharedApplication.Delegate as AppDelegate).SetNetworkActivityIndicator(
        this.swtchActivityIndicator2.On);
```

When as long as the count is greater than zero (any activities are executing) then the indicator will show, but when it drops to zero (no activities are executing), then the activity indicator will no longer be visible.

> **NOTE**: As with most controls, you should set the activity indicator's visibility on the main thread. For more information, see Chapter 6.

Accelerometer

All iOS devices contain a 3-axis accelerometer, which measures g-forces in 3-axis. See Figure 13–8.

Figure 13–8. *Accelerometer axis*

The forces are reported in the direction that the force is being exerted, for example, an iPhone at rest on it's back would experience the following g-forces:

- **X = 0**
- **Y = 0**
- **Z = -1**

This is because "down" would be felt in the Z-axis, in the negative direction (toward the back).

These forces are represented by a `UIAcceleration` object that contains X, Y, and Z properties, containing the g-force in their respective axis.

The accelerometer is accessible via the static `SharedAccelerometer` property of the `UIAccelerometer` class. In order to use it, you simply handle the Acceleration event, which passes you the `UIAcceleration` object as the `Accleration` property on the `UIAccelerometerEventArgs`. For example, the following code writes the real-time 3-axis acceleration forces to label. See Listing 13–41.

Listing 13–41. *Handling the Acceleration event*

```
UIAccelerometer.SharedAccelerometer.Acceleration += (object sender,
UIAccelerometerEventArgs e) => {
        this.lblX.Text = e.Acceleration.X.ToString();
        this.lblY.Text = e.Acceleration.Y.ToString();
        this.lblZ.Text = e.Acceleration.Z.ToString();
};
```

Additionally, you can optionally specify how often you want to receive updates by specifying a value, in milliseconds to the `UpdateInterval` property. For example, Listing 13–42 tells iOS that every 100 milliseconds (10 times a second), it should raise the Acceleration event.

Listing 13–42. *Specifying the acceleration update interval*

```
UIAccelerometer.SharedAccelerometer.UpdateInterval = 100;
```

Shake Gesture

The shake gesture has become a staple of iOS applications, especially for iPhone and iPod touch. Since iOS v3.0, Apple has made it easy to recognize a shake of the device by listening for it and then notifying you when it occurs, rather than you having to manually listen for acceleration events and calculate movement. Unfortunately, however, it's not quite as easy as just listening for an event, so there are several things you have to do in order to handle the shake gesture. Specifically you need to override the following four items in your UIViewController:

- **CanBecomeFirstResponder:** `CanBecomeFirstResponder` is a property that tells iOS whether or not your view controller can receive touch events and action messages (such as motion events). You must override this property and return a true value.

- **ViewDidAppear:** In the ViewDidAppear method, you must call BecomeFirstResponder so that your controller will receive motion events.

- **ViewWillDisappear:** In your ViewWillDisappear, you should call ResignFirstResponder so that your controller releases it's subscription to motion events and allows other controllers to get them.

- **MotionEnded:** The MotionEnded event runs after iOS determines if the motion the device experienced was just noise (such as walking up stairs), and recognizes the motion as a gesture. You must override this method and check the UIEventSubtype enumeration parameter to see if it's of the type MotionShake.

For example, Listing 13–43 comes from the Example_SharedResources companion application's ShakeScreen.cs UIViewController class. It registers itself as a first responder and then updates a label on the screen when the controller experiences a shake event.

Listing 13–43. *Recognizing shake events*

```
public override bool CanBecomeFirstResponder { get { return true; } }
public override void ViewDidAppear (bool animated)
{
        base.ViewWillAppear (animated);
        this.BecomeFirstResponder();
}
public override void ViewWillDisappear (bool animated)
{
        base.ViewWillDisappear (animated);
        this.ResignFirstResponder();
}
public override void MotionEnded (UIEventSubtype motion, UIEvent evt)
{
        base.MotionEnded(motion, evt);
        if(motion == UIEventSubtype.MotionShake)
        {
                this.lblShakeStatus.Text = "Shook!";
        }
}
```

Summary

In this chapter we looked at a number of shared resources, how to use them, and your responsibilities when using them. In the next chapter we're going to shift gears a bit and cover application settings.

Chapter 14

User and Application Settings

When you build an application of any complexity, you often quickly realize a need to allow users to set preferences and settings for how the application is configured and behaves. In Mac programs, these are usually found in the menu under the program name, and then in **Preferences**. In Windows, it's often under **Tools➤Options**.

iOS applications are no different in their need for application settings and preferences; however, the way users set preferences can be slightly different. In iOS applications, there are usually two ways to set preferences. First, you can provide your users a screen or set of screens in the application to change settings, and second, Apple gives us a special application called Settings that allow users to edit preferences when their application is not running.

In this chapter we'll look at how to work with application settings in the iOS, with and without using the Settings Application. By the end of the chapter you will be able to use the NSUserDefaults API to access settings, and also to register them to show up in the Settings Application, if you like.

You can find code for this chapter in the Example_AppSettings companion code and application.

Working with Settings in the iOS

Apple's recommendation is that, generally, for settings that are set once for the lifecycle of the application, you use the Settings Application, and for things that change often, or that the user may need to change while using the application, you should provide users with an interface within the application.

Let's say that, for instance, you're building an e-mail application. Account settings like username and password would probably go into the Settings Application, whereas if you allowed your users to change between application skins, you would probably put that inside the application.

Regardless of where you allow users to edit settings, whether in the Settings Application, in your application (using custom screens), or both, you work with the settings API the same way.

You can find the Settings Application on the home screen of your device. If you've used your device much at all, you're probably familiar with this screen (Figure 14–1).

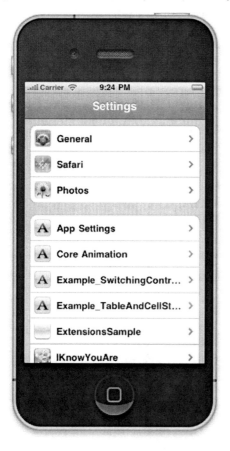

Figure 14–1. *Settings Application showing applications below iOS settings*

If you scroll down, however, you'll see that there are also application-specific settings. If you click an application you will get application settings, as seen in Figure 14–2 for the iPhone, and Figure 14–3 for the iPad.

Figure 14–2. *Settings for an application on the iPhone*

Figure 14–3. *Settings for an application on the iPad*

While there are generally two ways for the user to configure settings, as a developer, Apple provides us a single, unified API, called NSUserDefaults, in which to retrieve and persist them. So whether the user configures a particular setting in the Settings Application, or within your application, you still access it the same way. This means that you can even allow the user to configure a particular setting in either location.

For example, in the Example_AppSettings companion application and code, I provide a screen that allows a user to edit a subset of the settings that are also editable in the Settings Application, as shown in Figure 14–4.

Figure 14–4. *Some settings should be able to be changed in your application*

Registering Settings with the Settings Application

You get the Settings Application UI for free with your application as part of the iOS, but you have to create and configure a special XML file, named Root.plist, in order for your settings to show up in there. **You can still use the API to save and retrieve settings, even if they're not in this XML file, but they will only show up in the Settings Application if they're in this file.**

The steps to create this file are as follows.

1. Create a Settings.bundle folder in your project.

2. Add a file named Root.plist in Settings.bundle.

3. Edit the file in the property list editor and save as XML.

4. Mark the Root.plist file's build-type as content.

Creating a Settings Bundle

The iOS looks in your application bundle for a settings bundle. A settings bundle is just a folder with the name Settings.bundle. To create one, simply right-click your project in MonoDevelop and create a new folder with that name, as shown in Figure 14–5.

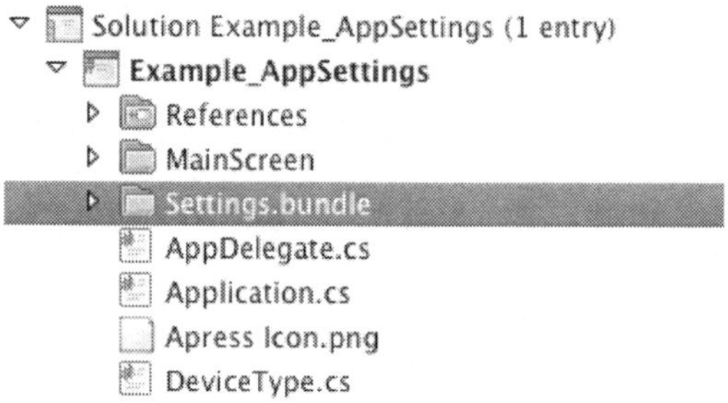

Figure 14–5. *Settings.bundle in a MonoTouch project*

If you look at your project folder in the Finder, you'll notice something strange (Figure 14–6).

Figure 14–6. *Settings.bundle in the Finder*

The Finder shows it not as a folder, but as a file. It is still just a folder, however, and you can even right-click it and choose **Show Package Contents** to view what's inside of it. OSX is just collapsing it in the UI.

Creating the Property List File

Once you've created your Settings.bundle folder, you need to create a new, empty text file called Root.plist in it. To do this, right-click the folder in MonoDevelop and create a new text file, and then rename it Root.plist.

The iOS looks for this file to find your settings. As soon as you create this file, MonoDevelop will automatically open it up in the Property List Editor application that ships with Xcode. When you create a new plist file, it will be blank, but the following screenshot (Figure 14–7) shows what the editor looks like with settings added.

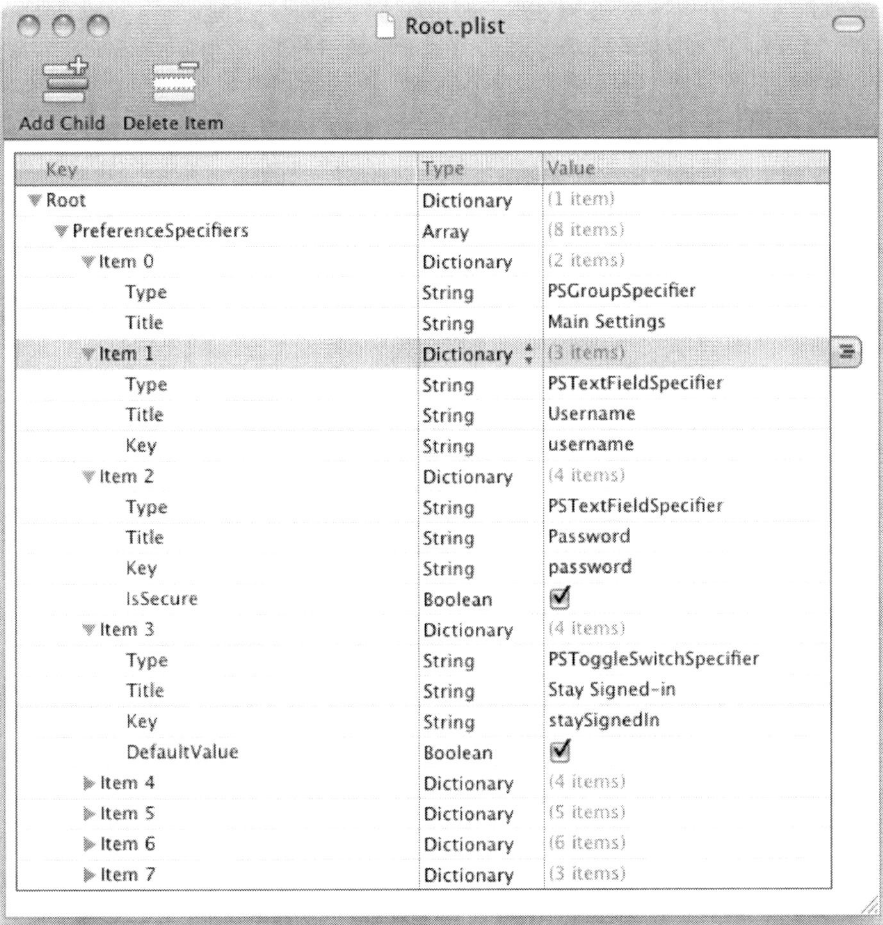

Figure 14–7. *Property List Editor with settings specified*

Property list (.plist) files are Apple's way of storing settings and properties for applications. In fact, in your application bundle there is an Info.plist file that has settings such as what the name of your application is, what icon to use for it, etc.

For settings, you must follow a specific schema in order for the iOS to parse this file correctly. Your file must start with a key called Root, of type Dictionary, which has a child node called PreferenceSpecifiers, of type Array.

All your properties go under the PreferenceSpecifiers node. Every setting is stored as a Dictionary item that contains a set of of key/value pairs that describe that setting.

Plist files are stored by default in a format that is not compatible with the iOS, so in order for them to work, you need to save them as XML by choosing **File▶Save As** in the menu, and choosing **XML Property List** as the file format (Figure 14–8).

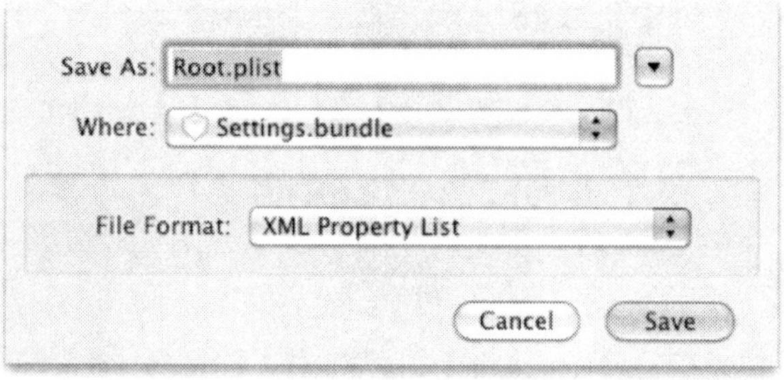

Figure 14–8. *Saving a property list file as XML*

Because this file is a plain-text XML file, you can also edit it in any text editor. For example, the sample application for this chapter has the following content in its Root.plist file, as shown in Listing 14–1.

Listing 14–1. *A sample settings file showing the raw XML*

```xml
<?xml version="1.0" encoding="UTF-8"?>
<!DOCTYPE plist PUBLIC "-//Apple//DTD PLIST 1.0//EN"
"http://www.apple.com/DTDs/PropertyList-1.0.dtd">
<plist version="1.0">
<dict>
        <key>PreferenceSpecifiers</key>
        <array>
                <dict>
                        <key>Type</key>
                        <string>PSGroupSpecifier</string>
                        <key>Title</key>
                        <string>Main Settings</string>
                </dict>
                <dict>
                        <key>Type</key>
                        <string>PSTextFieldSpecifier</string>
                        <key>Title</key>
                        <string>Username</string>
                        <key>Key</key>
                        <string>username</string>
                </dict>
                <dict>
                        <key>Type</key>
                        <string>PSTextFieldSpecifier</string>
                        <key>Title</key>
                        <string>Password</string>
                        <key>Key</key>
                        <string>password</string>
                        <key>IsSecure</key>
                        <true/>
                </dict>
                <dict>
                        <key>Type</key>
```

```
                        <string>PSToggleSwitchSpecifier</string>
                        <key>Title</key>
                        <string>Stay Signed-in</string>
                        <key>Key</key>
                        <string>staySignedIn</string>
                        <key>DefaultValue</key>
                        <true/>
                </dict>
                … (Code Omitted)
        </array>
</dict>
</plist>
```

Each setting must have a Type key that specifies what kind of setting it is, followed by other fields that describe things like the title and default value. Let's look at the different setting types that we can use.

Property Specifier Schema

The following setting types are available for use in the Settings Application.

- **Group (PSGroupSpecifier):** Adding a group combines a set of items into a grouped table. Groups are not nested, so they are just specified sequentially, e.g., any settings that are specified after a group specifier will get put into that group. When you want to add another group, you simply add another group specifier item.

- **Text Field (PSTextFieldSpecifier):** A simple text field where the user can enter a string of text

- **Title (PSTitleValueSpecifier):** A read-only line of text that has a title on the left and optional text on the right

- **Slider (PSSliderSpecifier):** A slider control

- **Toggle Switch (PSToggleSwitchSpecifier):** A Boolean (on/off) toggle switch control

- **Multi-Value (PSMultiValueSpecifier):** A multiple-value option that, if you click it, it opens a new screen and allows you to make a choice from different values

- **Child Pane (PSChildPaneSpecifier):** Gives you another, nested, settings screen on which you can put additional settings. For each child pane, you need an associated .plist file. As part of the setting parameters, you specify the name of the file that holds the child settings.

Each settings type uses different keys to define the options in that setting, as described in the following sections.

One very important thing to know is that, even though you can provide default values for your settings, the iOS won't load them until you access them from the Settings

Application. So even though you specify DefaultValue keys, they will actually be null the first time your application runs! There is a way around this, however, which we'll discuss in the "Initializing Settings" section, just a bit later in this chapter.

PSGroupSpecifier

Table 14–1. *PSGroupSpecifier schema*

Key Name	Data Type	Description
Type (required)	String	The value should always be PSGroupSpecifier.
Title	String	The title of the group. If you don't specify a title, a gap will appear between settings items.

PSTextFieldSpecifier

Table 14–2. *PSTextFieldSpecifier schema*

Key Name	Data Type	Description
Type (required)	String	The value should always be PSTextFieldSpecifier.
Title	String	The text that will display to the left of the text field. If you don't specify a title, the text field will expand to fill the entire row.
Key (required)	String	The identifier that is used to retrieve the setting
DefaultValue	String	The default value of the setting
IsSecure	Boolean	Whether or not the text field will be in password-mode, whereby text typed is replaced with bullet characters in the UI
KeyboardType	String	Type of keyboard to use for the text field. Available options are: Alphabet, NumbersAndPunctuation, NumberPad, URL, and EmailAddress. If not specified, Alphabet is used.
Autocapitalization-Type	String	The style of capitalization to apply to the entered text. Available options are: None, Sentences, Words, and AllCharacters. If not specified, None is used.
AutocorrectionType	String	The auto-correction option to apply to the entered text. Available options are: Default, No, and Yes. If not specified, Default is used, which means Yes, unless it's configured as IsSecure.

PSTitleValueSpecifier

Table 14–3. *PSTitleValueSpecifier schema*

Key Name	Data Type	Description
Type (required)	String	The value should always be `PSTitleValueSpecifier`.
Title	String	The title of the group. If you don't specify a title, a gap will appear between settings items.
Key (required)	String	The identifier that is used to retrieve the setting
DefaultValue (required)	String	The default value of the setting. If you have specified a list of values, this should match one of the items in the `Values` list. Otherwise, the text that you specify in `DefaultValue` will display.
Titles	Array	An array of strings that are used for the possible text strings that can be displayed to the right of the title
Values	Array	An array of strings that are used as keys for the `Titles`. There must be the same number of `Values` as `Titles`.

When using the `Title` setting, if you specify `Titles` and `Values`, you can set a title to a predefined string by setting its value key. If you don't want to include the `Titles` and `Values`, however, it's easier just to set the `DefaultValue` key.

You can also use the `Title` setting to insert gaps into a group of settings, although generally, it's better to simply group them via a `Group` setting.

PSSliderSpecifier

Table 14–4. *PSSliderSpecifiers schema*

Key Name	Data Type	Description
Type (required)	String	The value should always be `PSSliderSpecifier`.
Key (required)	String	The identifier that is used to retrieve the setting
DefaultValue (required)	String	The default value of the setting

Key Name	Data Type	Description
MinimumValue (required)	Number	The value when the slider is all the way to the left
MaximumValue (required)	Number	The value when the slider is all the way to the right
MinimumValueImage	String	The path to the image to display on the left side of the slider. The image should be 21x21 pixels for non-retina displays, and 42x42 pixels for retina display.
MaximumValueImage	String	The path to the image to display on the right side of the slider. The image should be 21x21 pixels for non-retina displays, and 42x42 pixels for retina display.

The Slider setting doesn't allow for a title, so it's a good idea to put a Title setting before it so your users know what the slider is for.

PSToggleSwitchSpecifier

Table 14–5. *PSToggleSwitchSpecifier schema*

Key Name	Data Type	Description
Type (required)	String	The value should always be PSToggleSwitchSpecifier.
Title (required)	String	The title of the group. If you don't specify a title, a gap will appear between settings items.
Key (required)	String	The identifier that is used to retrieve the setting
DefaultValue (required)	Any	The default value of the setting. It's generally a good idea to use the same data type as your TrueValue and FalseValue keys.
TrueValue	Any Scalar Type	The value returned when the toggle switch is in the ON position
FalseValue	Any Scalar Type	The value returned when the toggle switch is in the OFF position

PSMultiValueSpecifier

Table 14–6. *PSMultiValueSpecifier schema*

Key Name	Data Type	Description
Type (required)	String	The value should always be PSMultiValueSpecifier.
Title (required)	String	The text that will appear as the setting name. This string will also be used as the title of the sub-page that is displayed with the values that you can select from.
Key (required)	String	The identifier that is used to retrieve the setting
DefaultValue (required)	String	The default value of the setting. If you have specified a list of values, this should match one of the items in the Values list. Otherwise, the text that you specify in DefaultValue will display.
Titles	Array	An array of strings that are used for the possible text strings that will be displayed as value options
Values	Array	An array of strings that are used as keys for the Titles. There must be the same number of Values as Titles

The items that a user can choose from on a Multi-Value setting are displayed on a sub-screen.

PSChildPaneSpecifier

Table 14–7. *PSChildPaneSpecifier schema*

Key Name	Data Type	Description
Type (required)	String	The value should always be PSChildPaneSpecifier.
Title (required)	String	The text that will appear as the setting name. This string will also be used as the title of the sub-page that will display the settings specified in the File key.
File (required)	String	The name of the .plist file (minus the .plist file extension) that contains the settings that will be used to populate the child pane

For every Child Pane setting you have, you must create a .plist file that it will use.

Accessing Settings

Application settings are accessed via the StandardUserDefaults property of the NSUserDefaults object. There are two ways of accessing any setting. You can access the StandardUserDefaults directly as a dictionary, which returns NSObject objects, or you can use helper methods on it to retrieve your settings already cast as a type.

If you access the dictionary directly, you must check to see if the value is null, as in Listing 14–2.

Listing 14–2. *You should check for null when accessing the settings directly.*

```
if (NSUserDefaults.StandardUserDefaults["password"] != null)
{
        this.txtPassword.Text = NSUserDefaults.StandardUserDefaults["password"]
                .ToString ();
}
```

If you access the data via one of the typed calls, e.g., StringForKey, BoolForKey, you don't have to do a null check first, as in the following example (Listing 14–3).

Listing 14–3. *If you access the settings via the typed calls, you don't have to check for null.*

```
this.txtUsername.Text = NSUserDefaults.StandardUserDefaults.StringForKey ("username");
```

If the setting is empty or doesn't exist, you will get the default value for that type, e.g., String.Empty if it's a string, or false, if it's a Boolean, etc.

Saving Settings

If you're providing an in-application interface for users to edit settings, it's important to be able to not only read settings, but also to save them. To save a setting, call the Set[Type] methods on the StandardUserDefaults property, as in the following example (Listing 14–4).

Listing 14–4. *Saving settings using the user defaults API*

```
NSUserDefaults.StandardUserDefaults.SetString ("bryancostanich", "username");
NSUserDefaults.StandardUserDefaults.SetBool (true, "staySignedIn");
```

Initializing Settings

As I mentioned before, even if you set defaults, the iOS won't load them until the Settings Application is accessed for your application.

To get around this, we need to initialize our defaults before they're accessed. One of the easiest places to do this is in your AppDelegate constructor, because it runs when your application starts up.

You can use the following class (Listing 14–5) to load your app settings directly from your settings file.

Listing 14–5.

```
public static class UserDefaultsHelper
{
        /// <summary>
        /// Loads the default settings from the Settings.bundle/Root.plist file. Also
        /// calls nested settings (referred to in child pane items) recursively, to
        /// load those defaults.
        /// </summary>
        public static void LoadDefaultSettings ()
        {
                //---- check to see if they've already been loaded for the first time
                if (!NSUserDefaults.StandardUserDefaults
                        .BoolForKey ("__DefaultsLoaded"))
                {
                        string rootSettingsFilePath = NSBundle.MainBundle.BundlePath
                                + "/Settings.bundle/Root.plist";

                        //---- check to see if there is event a settings file
                        if (System.IO.File.Exists (rootSettingsFilePath))
                        {
                                //---- load the settings
                                NSDictionary settings =
                                        NSDictionary.FromFile (rootSettingsFilePath);
                                LoadSettingsFile (settings);
                        }

                        //---- mark them as loaded so this doesn't run again
                        NSUserDefaults.StandardUserDefaults
                                .SetBool (true, "__DefaultsLoaded");
                }
        }

        /// <summary>
        /// Recursive version of LoadDefautSetings
        /// </summary>
        private static void LoadSettingsFile (NSDictionary settings)
        {
                //---- declare vars
                bool foundTypeKey;
                bool foundDefaultValue;
                string prefKeyName;
                NSObject prefDefaultValue;
                NSObject key;

                //---- get the preference specifiers node
                NSArray prefs = settings.ObjectForKey (
                        new NSString ("PreferenceSpecifiers")) as NSArray;

                //---- loop through the settings
                for (uint i = 0; i < prefs.Count; i++)
                {
                        //---- reset for each setting
                        foundTypeKey = false;
                        foundDefaultValue = false;
                        prefKeyName = string.Empty;
                        prefDefaultValue = new NSObject ();
```

```
//----
NSDictionary pref = new NSDictionary (prefs.ValueAt (i));

//---- loop through the dictionary of any particular setting
for (uint keyCount = 0; keyCount < pref.Keys.Length; keyCount++)
{
        //---- shortcut reference
        key = pref.Keys[keyCount];

        //---- get the key name and default value
        if (key.ToString () == "Key")
        {
                foundTypeKey = true;
                prefKeyName = pref[key].ToString ();
        }
        else if (key.ToString () == "DefaultValue")
        {
                foundDefaultValue = true;
                prefDefaultValue = pref[key];
        }
        else if (key.ToString () == "File")
        {
                NSDictionary nestedSettings =
                        NSDictionary.FromFile
                        (NSBundle.MainBundle.BundlePath
                        + "/Settings.bundle/"
                        + pref[key].ToString () + ".plist");
                LoadSettingsFile (nestedSettings);
        }

        //---- if we've found both, set it in our user preferences
        if (foundTypeKey && foundDefaultValue)
        {
                NSUserDefaults.StandardUserDefaults[prefKeyName]
                        = prefDefaultValue;
        }
    }
   }
  }
}
```

You can find this code in `Example_AppSettings` companion code. It loads the `Root.plist` file, loops through all the settings and saves the defaults. It then calls itself recursively for any settings stored in other files that are referenced via Child Pane settings. Call it in your `AppDelegate` constructor, as in Listing 14–6.

Listing 14–6. *Loading default settings when the application starts*

```
public AppDelegate () : base()
{
        //---- set any user default values
        UserDefaultsHelper.LoadDefaultSettings ();

        //---- initialize our user settings, which loads them from the file
        // (if they exist)
        NSUserDefaults.StandardUserDefaults.Init ();
}
```

After you load your application defaults, you should also call the Init method on the StandardUserDefaults class, as shown in the following example (Listing 14–7).

Listing 14–7.

```
NSUserDefaults.StandardUserDefaults.Init ();
```

This loads any settings that have been saved. It's important to call it after your defaults have been loaded, so that any saved changes override the defaults.

Summary

In this chapter you learned how to persist and retrieve user settings, as well as how to register settings to display in the Settings Application.

In the next chapter we're going to take a look at one of the most powerful libraries baked into the iOS, CoreAnimation, which provides us a rich framework for providing complex animations with very little code.

Chapter 15

Working with CoreLocation

The iOS utilizes several hardware and software technologies to allow you to locate it in the world, tell you which way you're traveling, and know which way the phone is pointing. The underlying technologies are fairly complex, but Apple abstracts most of this complexity away and gives us an easy API called `CoreLocation` to get location and heading information.

In this chapter, we're going to look at working with the location features in the iOS via the CoreLocation API.

All the code in this chapter is taken from the `Example_CoreLocation` companion code and application. While this example is simple, the application possibilities for this data are endless. For example, you could write an application that computes the distance and direction to known locations from where the user is, or you could create an application that shows which stars are in the sky based on the user's location and heading. The applications that can be built are limited only by your imagination.

Under the Hood

Under the hood, the iOS utilizes the following location technologies:

- **Wi-Fi Positioning Service (WPS):** Available on all iPhones since an early OS update, and all iPad devices. WPS uses a database lookup of nearby Wi-Fi access point MAC addresses with known locations. It then computes the location based on a proprietary algorithm. In a densely packed urban center, with lots of Wi-Fi access points, the accuracy of WPS is often 20–30 meters.

■ **Global Positioning System (GPS):** Available since the iPhone 3G and iPad 3G models, GPS uses a system of orbiting satellites that broadcast time and location signals to Earth. GPS receives these signals and then performs triangulation based on the latency of the signals. GPS is much more reliable than WPS in that it will work anywhere in the world where the GPS receiver has an unobstructed view of at least three satellites. The accuracy of GPS is usually within 20 meters, since the year 2000, when the U.S. government stopped degrading location data for civilian use.

■ **Compass:** Available since the iPhone 3Gs and all iPad models, the compass enables the device to know its orientation to the magnetic poles (magnetic heading). Coupled with its location information, it can also tell you its true heading, based on the known magnetic variation of the location.

Having to work with these directly would be pretty tedious, but fortunately for us, all of this functionality is wrapped up in the CoreLocation API. MonoTouch exposes this API via the MonoTouch.CoreLocation namespace, and the most important class is CLLocationManager.

Usage Pattern

The general pattern for working with CoreLocation is as follows:

1. Instantiate a CLLocationManager object.

2. Configure any settings on CLLocationManager, such as the level of accuracy you want.

3. Wire up event handlers to the update methods on the CLLocationmanager object to handle the location updates (or assign a CLLocationManagerDelegate if you want to use the delegate pattern as described in Chapter 6).

4. Tell CLLocationManager to start feeding you location and/or heading updates.

5. Do something interesting with the location information.

6. Tell CLLocationManager to stop updating you with information (this saves on battery, as we'll examine later).

Instantiating CLLocationManager

The CLLocationManager class is the workhorse of the CoreLocation API, but it's very easy to instantiate, as it has no arguments in its constructor. For example, Listing 15–1 comes from the Example_CoreLocation companion code and application.

Listing 15–1. *Creating a new CLLocationManager Object*

```
public class MainViewController : UIViewController
{
        CLLocationManager _iPhoneLocationManager = null;
        ...

        public override void ViewDidLoad ()
        {
                ...
                this._iPhoneLocationManager = new CLLocationManager ();
        }
}
```

Configuring the Location Manager

Once you've instantiated the location manager object, the next step is to configure any custom settings. There are two main settings that you can configure:

- Update Threshold
- Accuracy

Update Threshold

By default, location and heading data will be updated constantly. You can set a threshold level for how often you want the location and heading to be updated. CLLocationManager exposes the DistanceFilter and HeadingFilter properties, to set location and heading update threshold, respectively.

- **CLLocationManager.DistanceFilter:** The value, in meters, of how far the device has to move laterally before a location update is sent. A value of -1 will cause it to update continuously.

- **CLLocationManager.HeadingFilter:** The value, in degrees, of how far the device has to rotate before a heading update is sent. A value of -1 will cause it to update continuously.

Listing 15–2 tells the location manager to not update until it's either moved 10 meters or the heading has changed by 3 degrees.

Listing 15–2. *Setting the update threshold on the location manager*

```
this._iPhoneLocationManager.DistanceFilter = 10;
this._iPhoneLocationManager.HeadingFilter = 3;
```

Accuracy

By default, the location data given by the iOS will strive to be as accurate as possible. This may mean trying to poll more satellites, resolving more Wi-Fi access points, and so on. You can control what accuracy level the location manager tries to achieve via the

DesiredAccuracy property. It expects a setting in meters; so setting it to 1,000 will give it kilometer-level accuracy. Setting to -1 will force it to be as accurate as possible. For example, Listing 15–3 sets the location manager to a desired accuracy of 1 kilometer.

Listing 15–3. *Setting the desired accuracy to 1 kilometer*

```
this._iPhoneLocationManager.DesiredAccuracy = 1000;
```

There are also the following static properties on the CLLocation object that you can use:

- **AccuracyBest:** Returns -1, for the best possible accuracy.

- **AccuracyNearestTenMeters:** Returns 10.

- **AccuracyHundredMeters:** Returns 100.

- **AccuracyKilometer:** Returns 1,000 (1 kilometer).

- **AccuracyThreeKilometers:** Returns 3000 (3 kilometers).

For example, Listing 15–4 sets the desired accuracy to 10 meters.

Listing 15–4. *Setting the desired accuracy using the typed properties*

```
this._iPhoneLocationManager.DesiredAccuracy = CLLocation.AccuracyNearestTenMeters;
```

The more accurate you tell the location manager to be, the faster it will drain battery, so you should set your desired accuracy level to the most that you will need. For example, if you are trying to determine location to a street level, you should set the accuracy to best (-1). However, if you're building an application that only needs to locate users within a city, you should consider setting it to three kilometers or more.

Listening for Updates

The location manager object exposes two events, UpdatedLocation and UpdatedHeading, that give you location and heading information, respectively.

UpdatedLocation

The UpdatedLocation event is raised when new location information is received, and from it we get things like location coordinates, altitude, and if we're moving, a course and heading. The UpdatedLocation event passes a CLLocationUpdatedEventArgs parameter, which contains two properties: NewLocation and OldLocation. Both are of type CLLocation. The NewLocation property has the latest location data, and OldLocation contains data from the previous update.

CLLocation

The CLLocation class exposes a number of useful properties including the following:

- **Altitude:** The height of the current location in meters above sea level.
- **Coordinate:** The latitude and longitude coordinates of the current location.
- **Course:** The current direction of travel in degrees.
- **Speed:** The current speed of travel in meters per second.
- **HorizontalAccuracy:** The accuracy of the coordinate data in meters.
- **VerticalAccuracy:** The accuracy of the altitude data in meters.

In addition to the location properties, you can use the CLLocation class to determine the distance between two points via the `DistanceFromLocation` method.

For example, Listing 15–5 updates some labels with current location information, as well as the distance, in kilometers, from the current location to Paris, France, when the UpdatedLocation event is raised.

Listing 15–5. *Handling UpdatedLocation to display current location information*

```
this._iPhoneLocationManager.UpdatedLocation += (object sender
        , CLLocationUpdatedEventArgs e) => {
    this._mainScreen.LblAltitude.Text = e.NewLocation.Altitude.ToString ()
            + "meters";
    this._mainScreen.LblLongitude.Text = e.NewLocation.Coordinate.Longitude
            .ToString () + "º";
    this._mainScreen.LblLatitude.Text = e.NewLocation.Coordinate.Latitude
            .ToString () + "º";
    this._mainScreen.LblCourse.Text = e.NewLocation.Course.ToString () + "º";
    this._mainScreen.LblSpeed.Text = e.NewLocation.Speed.ToString () + "meters/s";
    this._mainScreen.LblDistanceToParis.Text = (e.NewLocation.DistanceFrom(
            new CLLocation(48.857, 2.351)) / 1000).ToString() + "km";
};
```

UpdatedHeading

The UpdatedHeading method is called when new heading information is received (which comes from the compass), and passes a `CLHeadingUpdatedEventArgs` parameter, which has a `NewHeading` property that is a `CLHeading` class.

Unlike UpdatedLocation, it only gives us our current heading, and not the last heading as well, so if you want to track changes, you'll have to store them yourself. Fortunately that's not a common need.

CLHeading

The CLHeading class exposes a number of useful properties including the following:

- **HeadingAccuracy:** The accuracy, in degrees, of the heading data.

- **MagneticHeading:** The heading, in degrees, relative to magnetic north.

- **TrueHeading:** The heading, in degrees, relative to true north.

For example, Listing 15–6 handles the UpdatedHeading event and updates the interface with the magnetic and true headings.

Listing 15–6. *Handling the UpdatedLocation and UpdatedHeading events*

```
this._iPhoneLocationManager.UpdatedHeading += (object sender
        , CLHeadingUpdatedEventArgs e) => {
    this._mainScreen.LblMagneticHeading.Text = e.NewHeading.MagneticHeading
            .ToString () + "º";
    this._mainScreen.LblTrueHeading.Text = e.NewHeading.TrueHeading
            .ToString () + "º";
};
```

Starting the Location Service Updates

Once you're ready to receive location and heading information, you call StartUpdatingLocation or StartUpdatingHeading on your configured location manager class. However, before we look at that, we must look at one very important thing: capabilities.

Capabilities

The iPhone/iPad user can turn off location services altogether from the Settings application, or they can disallow them in specific applications. Some users do this for privacy or battery life reasons. Additionally, the compass is not available on iPhone models previous to the 3Gs.

Because of this, before you tell the iOS to start updating you with location and/or heading information, you should first check to see whether these capabilities are available.

For this reason, the CLLocationManager exposes two static properties, LocationServicesEnabled and HeadingAvailable, to give you information regarding CoreLocation feature availability.

- **LocationServicesEnabled:** If it is false, the user has this turned off, and if your application attempts to access location information via StartUpdatingLocation, the user will be given a prompt to allow the application to use location services.

■ HeadingAvailable: This is false on the versions of the iPhone that do not have a built-in compass. If it's false, then you won't be able to get any meaningful heading data. Unlike the location services, the compass cannot be turned off; this property will only be false if there is no compass.

Because the location services may not be available, you should check them before starting your updates. See Listing 15–7.

Listing 15–7. *Checking for feature availability before attempting to use them*

```
if (CLLocationManager.LocationServicesEnabled)
{ this._iPhoneLocationManager.StartUpdatingLocation (); }
if (CLLocationManager.HeadingAvailable)
{ this._iPhoneLocationManager.StartUpdatingHeading (); }
```

Once you've started your location updates, it can take a second or two for the location manager to acquire location and heading information before it starts updating.

If you run this in the simulator, it doesn't actually have access to location and heading information, so it gives you simulated data, which returns the lat/long of Apple's headquarters in Cupertino, California, and made up data for the rest. See Figure 15–1.

Figure 15–1. *Location data in the simulator shows Cupertino, CA.*

If you were to deploy this to an actual device, however, you would get actual location information, as shown in Figure 15–2.

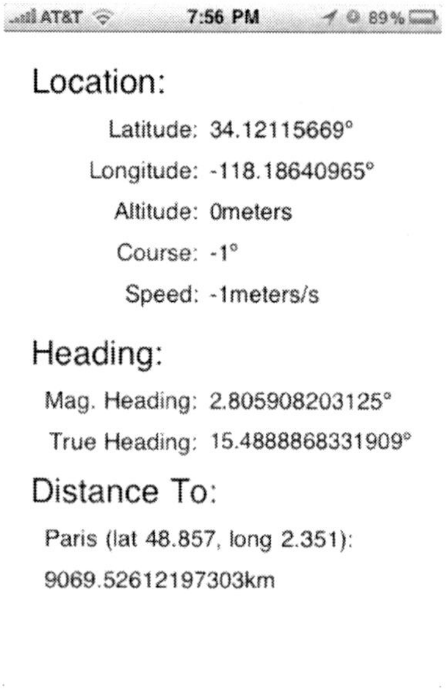

AT&T 📶   7:56 PM   ✦ ⊙ 89% 🔋

Location:

    Latitude: 34.12115669°

    Longitude: -118.18640965°

    Altitude: 0meters

    Course: -1°

    Speed: -1meters/s

Heading:

    Mag. Heading: 2.805908203125°

    True Heading: 15.4888868331909°

Distance To:

    Paris (lat 48.857, long 2.351):

    9069.52612197303km

Figure 15–2. *Location data in the iPhone shows actual location data.*

Stopping Updates

In addition to the StartUpdatingHeading and StartUpdatingLocation methods, there are corresponding StopUpdatingHeading and StopUpdatingLocation methods that you should call when you no longer need heading and/or location data. The location services can be a tremendous drain on battery life and prudent use of these methods will help you to cut down on battery drain.

Battery Drain

I've mentioned battery drain in this chapter several times. This is because location services is one of the most draining features on the iDevice.

Because of this, it's important to use it as little as possible. Performing the following can help reduce usage, and therefore battery drain:

- **Only check when needed:** By calling StartUpdatingLocation and StartUpdatingHeading only when you need the information, and calling StopUpdatingLocation and StopUpdatingHeading when you're finished with the data, the iOS can actually turn off the underlying hardware that makes these calls. This can make the battery last significantly longer.

- **Set your accuracy:** By setting the desired accuracy to the lowest you need, you can cut down considerably on battery drain, because the iOS will reduce the number of datapoints and potentially the actual hardware used to determine location.

Summary

In this chapter, you saw just how easy it is to get location information from the CoreLocation API. In the next chapter, we're going to look at one of the most powerful libraries in the iOS – CoreGraphics, which you can use to do 2D drawing, image manipulation, and the like.

Chapter 16

Drawing with CoreGraphics

Up until this point, any graphics we've drawn have been intrinsically handled by the controls we've used. For example, we've created plenty of buttons, but we've never had to draw them ourselves. Sometimes, however, we need to do custom drawing beyond what the controls offer out of the box. For example, let's say that you want to build a view that has a rounded rectangle border. You could do this with images, but for maximum configurability, you could draw the lines and corners using CoreGraphics. That way, you could vary the radius of the corners, as well as the color and thickness of the lines, without having to do new images every time.

We have several options to do custom drawing, including CoreGraphics, OpenGL, and the XNA Toolkit. CoreGraphics is the simplest option, as it is designed only for 2D drawing. We will explore CoreGraphics in this chapter.

CoreGraphics is also known as the Quartz drawing system, as it inherits its design and functionality from the Quartz framework on the Mac OS.

Entire books have been written on Quartz, and while this chapter will give a solid foundation on how to use CoreGraphics in MonoTouch, as well as introduce you to its common features, it is by no means exhaustive. The Quartz API is massive. Covering it in detail goes far beyond the scope of this book. With that said, however, if you're looking for a more thorough reference once you're through this chapter, check out *Apple's Quartz 2D Programming Guide*. It's part of the documentation that ships with the Xcode SDK, and is an invaluable asset for advanced drawing tasks.

If you're familiar with System.Drawing, you'll no doubt find Quartz API similar, but it is exponentially more powerful. This chapter will get you well on your way with Quartz. By the end, you'll have a good, solid grasp on all the important fundamentals, and be able to do most common drawing tasks.

You can find examples of all the code in this chapter in use in the Example_Drawing companion application.

Let's first look at some fundamental concepts of CoreGraphics, and then we'll dig into some code.

Painter's Model

CoreGraphics uses what is known as the painter's model. As you draw, each subsequent drawing operation is applied on top of the previous one.

Unlike layers in programs such as Photoshop, once you have drawn something, you can't undraw it, or pull layers out. If you want to build an application like that, you either need to store a list of your draw operations and then re-draw each of the ones that you want to apply, or use multiple drawing surfaces, which we will explore in the "Drawing Context" section later in this chapter.

If you've used System.Drawing, or any other modern 2D drawing frameworks, this model will be very familiar to you. And in fact, many of the same techniques and tools apply.

Performance

Another important thing to know about CoreGraphics is that, while it is highly optimized for the iPhone, it is not guaranteed to use hardware acceleration. The iPhone and iPad have a dedicated GPU to handle drawing operations, and some operations that you do in CoreGraphics might be accelerated (handled by the GPU), but you never know what will be accelerated and what won't.

For most uses, this doesn't matter, as the iPhone and iPad handle drawing operations quite well. However, for high-performance 2D or 3D drawing, like the kind you see in games, you should instead use OpenGL or the XNA Toolkit for MonoTouch (which also uses OpenGL under the hood). These toolkits have a number of other features that make them much more suitable for game development. Unfortunately, they're also more complicated, which is why CoreGraphics is very useful.

Colors

Most of the time, when doing computer graphics, we deal in what's known as the RGB color space, or color model. If you've done much modern programming, you're likely to be at least somewhat familiar with the RGB color model. But if you're not, or you want to know it better, a little color theory is helpful.

A Bit o' Color Theory

If you look very closely at an LCD screen, you'll see that each individual pixel is actually made up of three distinct colors – red, green, and blue (hence, RGB). These are known as the three additive primary colors. Combining varying amounts of light in this color triangle creates the largest number of colors available (gamut) that are visible to the human eye. The RGB model is called an additive model because of the varying degrees of light that are added to create the range of colors.

Similarly, most tube televisions and computer monitors use a cathode ray tube (CRT) that has three-color guns of red, green, and blue that emit light toward the front of the screen.

You may have been taught in school that the three primary colors were red, yellow, and blue; however, this notion predates modern color theory and is actually derived from light absorption (subtracting light) by mixing pigments as you would in painting or printing. For this reason, they are often called the historical subtractive primary colors.

We still use a subtractive model when printing, because we're mixing pigments rather than light, but the most common one is the cyan, magenta, yellow, and key black (CMYK) model, which is similar to the historical model.

There are a number of different additive models, but by far the most commonly used one in computers is RGB, because of its direct mapping to display technology.

We refer to each portion of our color as a channel or a component, interchangeably. For example, we might reference the red channel, or the red component, which simply refers to the amount of red light in a particular color representation.

Each component is defined by a float value between 0.0 and 1.0, inclusive. 1.0 means that the component should include as much light of that color as possible. A component value of 0.0 means that there is no light of that color added.

Alpha RGB

Most of the code that we will look at uses an alpha RGB or an alpha RGB (ARGB) model. I mentioned that CoreGraphics uses what's known as the painter's model. The alpha channel specifies how much transparency/opacity to use when drawing on top of something.

An alpha value of 0.0 means that the color application should be completely transparent (the colors underneath will show through 100%). An alpha value of 1.0 means that it should be applied completely opaquely (the colors underneath will be completely covered by the color applied on top).

Often, as a developer, you're given hexadecimal values from designers for colors, because RGB colors are specified in hex values in web development. Colors specified in hex are base-16 representations of a value between 0–255. In order to convert them to RGB values that we can use in MonoTouch, we have to first convert from base-16 (hex) to base-10 (decimal), and then divide by 255. We do this for each channel.

To convert from hex to decimal, we can use the Calculator program provided in OSX. You can get change it into Programmer View by selecting **View ▶ Programmer** in the menu. Select the **16** button in the upper right for hex mode, and **10** for decimal mode. If you enter a value in either mode, it will be automatically converted when you switch modes.

For example, the color #ffcc00 can be converted by splitting it up into its constituent RGB channels: ff, cc, and 00. ff in hex is 255 in decimal. When we divide it by 255, we get 1, so the red component is 1.0. Doing this for cc and 00 get us 0.8 and 0.0, respectively. Therefore, ffcc00 converts to 1.0, 0.8, 0.0 RGB component values.

UIColor and CGColor

For most MonoTouch programming, we use the UIColor class when we want to specify a color. However, when working with CoreGraphics, many calls require a CGColor object. Fortunately though, UIColor wraps CGColor, so anytime you need a CGColor and you have UIColor, you can simply use the CGColor property of the UIColor object.

Drawing Context

Whenever you draw in CoreGraphics, you must draw onto some kind of surface. In CoreGraphics, that surface is a CGContext. You can think of it kind of like the canvas in our painter's model. Like a canvas, it has parameters such as size, but it also has other things, such as what colors are available to you.

There are generally two places you can create a context to draw on: onscreen or off-screen. When you draw onscreen, your drawing happens directly on your view. When you draw off-screen, you create a canvas (or canvases) in memory and then draw onto that.

You might be asking yourself why you would ever want to draw off-screen. You might do so in the following instances:

- **When creating images:** You might sometimes want to use CoreGraphics to create an image for use in other places. If you draw off-screen, you can then save whatever you've drawn as an image when you're done and use it elsewhere.

- **When you want multiple copies:** In CoreGraphics there is an off-screen drawing object called a CGLayer that is used when you want to draw multiple copies of the same item. The iOS caches your layer so it's much faster to draw multiple copies of the same item by using a CGLayer.

- **When drawing to a PDF:** In addition to images, CoreGraphics allows you to create PDF files and draw directly to them.

You can draw off-screen anytime you want by simply creating a new CGContext (or CGLayer from an existing CGContext) and setting its properties. However, if you want to draw onscreen, you must do it during the Draw method of your UIView, because the drawing lifecycle is tightly controlled, and it's the only place you can get a reference to the onscreen context.

Drawing Onscreen

In order to create the onscreen context, you call UIGraphics.GetCurrentContext in the Draw method of your UIView. See Listing 16–1.

Listing 16–1. *Creating a CGContext in the Draw method*

```
public override void Draw (RectangleF rect)
{
        base.Draw (rect);
        using (CGContext context = UIGraphics.GetCurrentContext ())
        {
                // do your drawing
        }
}
```

This will allow you to draw directly on the view. We'll look at how to do the actual drawing in just a moment.

Notice that we're using a using statement. This is because CGContext implements IDisposable and is a non-managed resource. By wrapping our context in a using statement, we've made sure that it gets properly disposed and we don't have any memory leaks.

Drawing Off-Screen

There are two ways to draw off screen. The first is to create a CGBitmapContext class, do your drawing on that context, convert it to an image, and then draw that image onto your screen (or save to a file). The second is to create a CGLayer, do your drawing on that, and then draw that layer onto either an off-screen CGBitmapContext or your onscreen CGContext.

CGBitmapContext

Creating a drawing context from a view is very easy, because all of the properties for the context are pulled from the view, such as the size, the colorspace, and so on. However, creating a context off-screen involves a few more steps, because you need to tell the OS exactly how your in-memory drawing surface needs to be set up.

Listing 16–2 creates a new 32-bit RGB CGBitmapContext.

Listing 16–2. *Creating a 32bit RGB CGBitmapContext*

```
IntPtr data = IntPtr.Zero;
SizeF bitmapSize = new SizeF (200, 300);
int bitsPerComponent = 8;
int bytesPerRow = (int)(4 * bitmapSize.Width);
CGColorSpace colorSpace = CGColorSpace.CreateDeviceRGB ();
CGImageAlphaInfo alphaType = CGImageAlphaInfo.PremultipliedFirst;

using(CGBitmapContext context = new CGBitmapContext (data, (int)bitmapSize.Width,
        (int)bitmapSize.Height, bitsPerComponent, bytesPerRow, colorSpace, alphaType))
{
        // do any drawing
}
```

Let's look at each line in more detail.

1. The first line is a zeroed-out IntPtr. When you create an off-screen context, the first parameter takes an intPtr to existing data. You can create a CGBitmapContext from an existing in-memory data structure. However, doing so has a big drawback: since the release of iOS 4.0, CoreGraphics will try to render your context using OpenGL (which is hardware-accelerated), but if you do it this way, CoreGraphics won't use OpenGL to render your context. This means that any hardware acceleration that you might have had won't happen. Because of this, you'll nearly always want to pass a zero IntPtr for the data parameter.

2. The next line is just setting up the size that we're going to use for the context.

3. Next we specify our number of bits per component. Because we're using an ARGB space, there are four components, or channels: alpha (the transparency), red, green, and blue. If we specify 8 bits per channel, and have 4 channels, that's a 32-bit color space.

4. Line 3 is bytes per row. Since there are 8 bits in a byte, and we have 4 components in each pixel, we have 4 bytes per pixel (32bits = 4bytes). To determine how many bytes we'll need for each row, we multiply the number of pixels by how many bytes are in each pixel.

5. In line 4 we specify that we want to create a standard RGB color space, using the device's RGB profile.

6. The next parameter that we store is the CGImageAlphaInfo. This specifies how the transparency is used. Since we're going to use the ARGB space, where the alpha component is first, we use PremultipliedFirst. PremultipliedLast would be RGBA, which means the last component alpha. There are a number of other alpha options, but we're not concerned with them, because this is the one you'll likely use 99% of the time.

7. The final line is instantiating the CGBitmapContext with all our parameters.

Obviously you can collapse all of this code into a single line, but I've broken it out so you can see what each parameter is.

After you've created your CGBitmapContext object, you can draw on it, just as you would an onscreen CGContext.

When you're ready to use what you've drawn, you can use the ToImage method to convert your CGBitmapContext into an image that you can display onscreen or save to a file.

CGLayer

CGLayers are useful when you want to make multiple copies of what you've drawn in a layer, because they're cached. For instance, let's say you want to draw a star, and then reuse it over and over. See Figure 16–1.

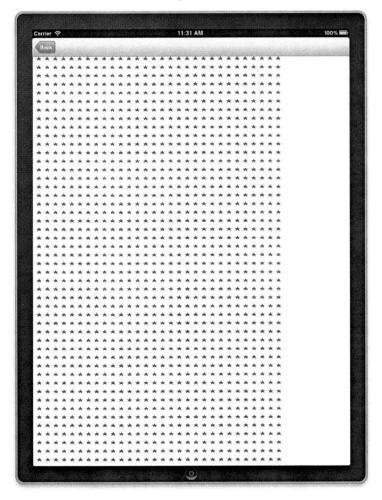

Figure 16–1. *Creating a CGContext in the Draw method*

Creating a CGLayer is very easy, but it must be created from an existing context. See Listing 16–3.

Listing 16–3. *Creating a CGLayer from an existing context*

```
using (CGLayer starLayer = CGLayer.Create (context, rect.Size))
{
        // do your drawing on starLayer.Context
}
```

Once you create a `CGLayer`, it contains a `Context` property that you can draw on, just as you would a `CGContext` or a `CGBitmapContext`.

To use a layer, you must draw it onto another context, using the `DrawLayer` method. Listing 16–4 draws a layer onto an existing context at the point (0,0).

Listing 16–4. *Drawing a* `CGLayer` *onto a context*

```
context.DrawLayer (starLayer, new PointF (0, 0));
```

CoreGraphics Coordinate System

In Chapter 6, we talked about the coordinate system of CocoaTouch. If you recall, coordinates are specified in (x,y). When working in views, the origin (0,0) is at the top left, the x-axis increases to the right, and the y-axis increases as you go down, as shown in Figure 16–2.

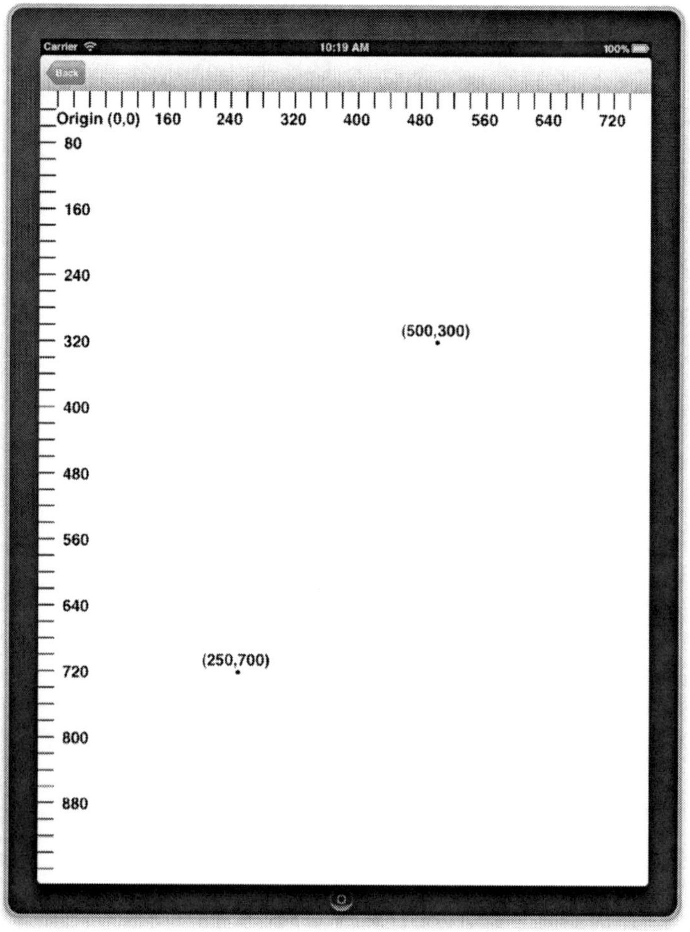

Figure 16–2. *View coordinate system*

Things get a little tricky when we're drawing in CoreGraphics, however. By default, when drawing directly onscreen in a view (via the CGContext), the coordinates follow the same, top-left origin coordinate space; but if you draw text, your text appears upside-down, as shown in Figure 16–3.

Figure 16–3. *By default, when drawing onscreen, your y-axis is upside-down.*

Pretty weird eh? That's because, by default, CoreGraphics actually uses a different coordinate space, where the origin is at the bottom-left, and the y-axis is inverted, as shown in Figure 16–4.

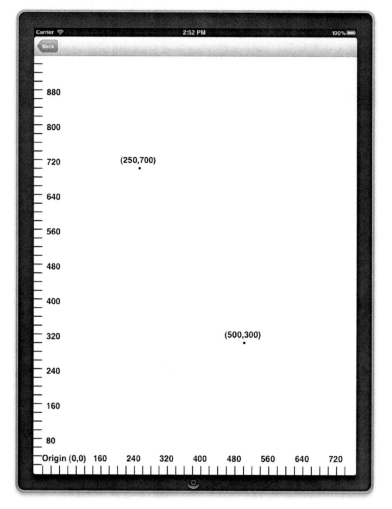

Figure 16–4. *CoreGraphics coordinate space*

So when it tries to draw text, it assumes that you're using the CoreGraphics bottom-left origin coordinate space. So, really, everything you draw is actually flipped upside-down. Not just text. For instance, if you draw an image in there, it will also appear flipped upside-down.

There are a couple ways to deal with this. The first and easiest is to draw off-screen, using a `CGBitmapContext`, and then draw your off-screen image to your view. This way, you never have to worry about flipping things upside-down.

Another important reason this is preferable is that most drawing systems in the computer world use a bottom-left coordinate space. So for instance, if you're converting scalable vector graphics (SVG) drawings, encapsulated post-script (EPS) files, portable document format (PDF) files, and so on, all the coordinates for their shapes are based on a bottom-left coordinate space. Even all the Apple CoreGraphics/Quartz samples assume a bottom-left origin.

For example, Figure 16–5 shows a screen from the companion `Example_Drawing` code, which includes a screen that has a MonoTouch port of the U.S. flag-drawing example pulled from the *Quartz 2D Programming Guide*.

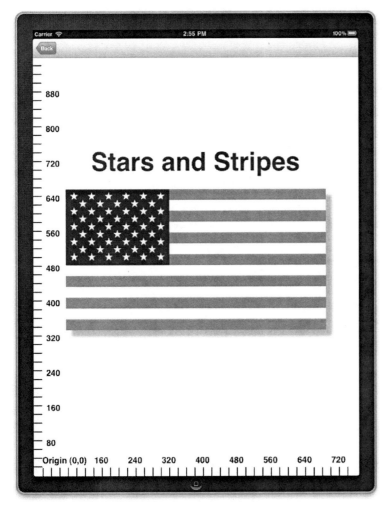

Figure 16–5. *When drawing off-screen, text is correctly rendered.*

For these reasons, it's generally much easier to draw off-screen, and then draw that onto your view. That way, you don't need to worry about any kind of translation.

With that said, however, drawing off-screen has the following disadvantages:

- **Performance:** Drawing off-screen causes a performance lag, because you have to allocate additional memory to store the off-screen context, and then spend processing cycles to push (blit) that image onto the screen.

- **Setup:** Drawing off-screen requires more setup, because the onscreen context already knows the parameters of the context, such as the color space, size, and so on.

If you don't want to draw off-screen, you have of the following options for dealing with the inverted coordinate space:

- Transform the context coordinate space.

- Transform the coordinates of individual drawing operations.

Transforming the Context Coordinate Space

We'll talk about transformations in more detail later, but for now, Listing 16–5 will change the coordinate space of your onscreen context to be the off-screen coordinate space.

Listing 16–5. *Flipping and moving the onscreen coordinate space*

```
using (CGContext context = UIGraphics.GetCurrentContext ())
{
        CGAffineTransform affineTransform = CGAffineTransform.MakeIdentity ();
        affineTransform.Scale (1, -1);
        affineTransform.Translate (0, this.Frame.Height);
        context.ConcatCTM (affineTransform);

        // do your drawing
}
```

This code flips the y-axis by performing a scale transform on it, and then moves the origin to the top left.

Transforming the Coordinates of Individual Drawing Operations

You can also transform the coordinates of individual drawing operations by calling SaveState on the context, doing the transform in Listing 16–5, and then calling RestoreState on the context. SaveState and RestoreState allow you to apply temporary changes to your context and then restore it back to how it was when you called SaveState.

MORE ON STATE: CoreGraphics uses a state stack to determine how to perform operations. This means that instead of passing things like fill color or line width to a method every time you want to draw something, you simply set the current fill color or line width on the state stack. When a method is called, CoreGraphics looks at the current state settings and uses those to perform its operations. Sometimes, however, you may want to set temporary settings and then unload them. To allow this, the graphics context exposes SaveState and RestoreState methods. SaveState allows you to set a save point that you can then revert back to via RestoreState.

Additionally, you can utilize the `ConvertPointToView` and `ConvertRectToView` calls to convert individual points and rectangles to the onscreen coordinate system.

Drawing Tools

Now that your brain is awash with coordinate spaces, onscreen and off-screen contexts, and color theory, let's look at how we can actually draw in CoreGraphics. When drawing, you have the following drawing tools at your disposal:

- Paths
- Primitives
- Text
- Images
- Patterns
- Shadows

Let's look at each one of these in detail.

Paths

Paths form the basis of nearly all drawing in CoreGraphics. A path is kind of like an invisible pen. You tell the pen to move to a certain spot on your drawing surface where you want to start your path, and then you tell the pen to extend the path to another point using a line or a curve. You keep moving it to subsequent locations, drawing lines or curves between each one, until you've finished your path.

Once you have a completed path, you can choose to either stroke the path (give it an outline) or fill it.

Stroking and Filling Paths

Listing 16–6 draws a rectangle, and then strokes the path.

Listing 16–6. *Drawing a rectangle using a path, and then stroking the path.*

```
using (CGContext context = UIGraphics.GetCurrentContext ())
{
        //---- draw a rectangle using a path
        UIColor.Blue.SetStroke ();
        context.BeginPath ();
        context.MoveTo (220, 10);
        context.AddLineToPoint (420, 10);
        context.AddLineToPoint (420, 110);
        context.AddLineToPoint (220, 110);
        context.ClosePath();
        context.DrawPath (CGPathDrawingMode.Stroke);
}
```

In the first line we set the stroke color. `UIColor` has shortcut methods that can set the color of the stroke or fill on the current context. However, there may not always be a default context available, which is the case when you're working with layers. In that instance, you can also set the stroke and fill color on the context directly by calling `SetRGBFillColor` and `SetRGBStrokeColor`.

Next, we start the path by calling the `BeginPath` method on the context. This tells our context that our subsequent path operations should be performed on this new path. We don't actually have to specify this if no paths exist yet; but if they do, then this makes sure that this path is not connected to the last one. If we didn't make this call in this case, then it would stroke any path stuff that we did before when we tell it to stroke the path.

Next, we move our path pen to a point and add lines. We then call `ClosePath` so that the last path line is automatically generated for us. Finally, we call `DrawPath` and tell it we want to stroke it. We could also tell it that we want to stroke and fill, just fill, or one of a couple other options. For example, if we added Listing 16–7, it would fill the rectangle with dark gray as well.

Listing 16–7. *Drawing a rectangle using a path created from a rectangle*

```
        UIColor.DarkGray.SetFill ();
        context.DrawPath (CGPathDrawingMode.FillStroke);
```

Primitives

As a shortcut, instead of creating individual lines to create a shape, you can actually add simple shapes, known as primitives, directly to the path. For example, Listing 16–8 creates the same rectangle as before, but instead of manually creating the lines, it uses the `AddRect` method to create a path from a `RectangleF`.

Listing 16–8. *Drawing a rectangle using a path created from a rectangle*

```
using (CGContext context = UIGraphics.GetCurrentContext ())
{
        //---- draw a rectangle using a path
        UIColor.Blue.SetStroke ();
        CGPath rectPath = new CGPath ();
        rectPath.AddRect (new RectangleF (new PointF (220, 10), new SizeF (200, 100)));
        context.AddPath (rectPath);
        context.DrawPath (CGPathDrawingMode.Stroke);
}
```

You can even use primitives without explicitly creating a path, because they create and manage them behind the scenes.

For example, Listing 16–9 draws a blue, 200x100 point rectangle at the point (10,10), using the StrokeRect method.

Listing 16–9. *Drawing a rectangle using the StrokeRect method*

```
using (CGContext context = UIGraphics.GetCurrentContext ())
{
        //---- draw a rectangle using fill rect
        UIColor.Blue.SetStroke ();
        context.StrokeRect (new RectangleF (10, 10, 200, 100));
}
```

One of the drawbacks of using primitives directly without a path like this is that if you need the path later (as we'll see in a bit when I talk about hit-testing), you don't have access to it without re-creating it.

Text

CocoaTouch includes a number of text related controls, including UILabel, UITextField, and UITextView, that provide rich features for managing the drawing of text. When you want to display text in your application, these controls should be your go-to resource.

With that said, sometimes you need to draw text yourself. This is especially true if you're creating images. In this case, CoreGraphics offers limited text drawing capabilities. Drawing text is fairly easy. Listing 16–10 draws the string "Hello World!" at a text height of 20 points, using Helvetica Bold, at the point (20,0).

Listing 16–10. *Drawing text*

```
using (CGContext context = UIGraphics.GetCurrentContext ())
{
        string text = "Hello World!";
        int textHeight = 20;
        context.SelectFont ("Helvetica-Bold", textHeight, CGTextEncoding.MacRoman);
        context.SetTextDrawingMode (CGTextDrawingMode.Fill);
        context.ShowTextAtPoint (20, 20, text, text.Length);
}
```

This is fine for left-aligned text, at a known size, but what if you want to change the alignment of the text, or fit text to an area? Well, this is where things get a little more complicated. If you need to do anything like that, you need to draw the text invisibly first, measure it, and then adjust accordingly. If you need to make it fit into a particular area, you may have to render it multiple times, resizing the text each time until it fits.

Listing 16–11 draws center-aligned text at a point by first rendering the text invisibly, measuring the size, and then drawing the text at a modified point.

Listing 16–11. *Pre-rendering text in order to center it*

```
public void DrawCenteredTextAtPoint (CGContext context, float centerX, float y
        , string text, int textHeight)
{
        context.SelectFont ("Helvetica-Bold", textHeight, CGTextEncoding.MacRoman);
        context.SetTextDrawingMode (CGTextDrawingMode.Invisible);
        context.ShowTextAtPoint (centerX, y, text, text.Length);
        context.SetTextDrawingMode (CGTextDrawingMode.Fill);
        context.ShowTextAtPoint (centerX - (context.TextPosition.X - centerX) / 2
                , y, text, text.Length);
}
```

The TextPosition property returns you to the last location at which text was drawn, so we can draw the visible text based directly on the invisible text's position.

After looking at that code, it's easy to see how much work the existing UIKit controls can save you, especially for complicated text operations.

Images

CoreGraphics also allows you to draw pre-existing images onto your drawing surface. All CGContext derived objects expose a method, DrawImage, that takes a RectangleF that describes the size and location of where to draw the image, and a CGImage of the image to draw. UIImage wraps CGImage, and exposes it as the CGImage property, so it's very easy to load an image from a file and draw it, as shown in Listing 16–12.

Listing 16–12. *Drawing a UIImage onto a context*

```
UIImage apressImage = UIImage.FromFile ("Images/Apress-512x512.png");
RectangleF imageRect = new RectangleF (0, 0, apressImage.CGImage.Width
        , apressImage.CGImage.Height);
context.DrawImage (imageRect, apressImage.CGImage);
```

In Listing 16–12, we created a UIImage by loading it from a file, created a rectangle at the (0,0) at the same size as the image, and then drew it onto the context.

You don't have to draw the image at the same size as the original; you're free to resize up or down, or even change the aspect ratio. Additionally, CoreGraphics provides extensive options for blending, as well as masking when drawing images. For more information, read the *Quarts 2D Programming Guide* that ships with the iPhone SDK.

Patterns

A pattern is a repeating drawing operation. You can use a pattern in CoreGraphics just like you would a color. This means that you can define a pattern and then use it when you fill or stroke a path, or draw primitives. Figure 16–6 shows is a pattern that has been used as a fill in a view.

Figure 16–6. *A pattern used as a fill*

In the previous example, the pattern is simply a circle that is filled in. When we fill the view, we tell the iPhoneOS that we want to use our circle pattern, which it then repeatedly draws.

Patterns are even faster than layers, but they're not quite as versatile.

There are two kinds of patterns in CoreGraphics:

- Color patterns
- Stencil patterns

Colored patterns have their color information built in to the pattern, so whenever you paint with that pattern, it uses whatever colors are built into it.

Stencil patterns are patterns that don't have any colors associated with them. They're like a stencil that you spray-paint – you can reuse a stencil over and over and assign a different fill color to it each time.

Creating a Color Pattern

To create a color pattern you need to create a delegate that CoreGraphics will call to draw the singular draw operation that will be repeated. Listing 16–13 is a simple example of this that draws the circle used in Figure 16–6.

Listing 16–13. *A simple pattern callback that draws a gray circle*

```
protected void DrawPolkaDotPattern (CGContext context)
{
        context.SetRGBFillColor (.3f, .3f, .3f, 1);
        context.FillEllipseInRect (new RectangleF (4, 4, 8, 8));
}
```

Next, when we want to use a pattern, we must do the following things:

1. Specify the pattern color space.

2. Instantiate and configure the pattern.

3. Set the pattern to be a fill or stroke.

Once we've done these things, we can use the pattern just as we would a color. Listing 16–14 configures and fills a view using the pattern callback.

Listing 16–14. *Using our pattern callback*

```
RectangleF patternRect = new RectangleF (0, 0, 16, 16);
context.SetFillColorSpace (CGColorSpace.CreatePattern (null));
CGPattern pattern = new CGPattern (patternRect
        , CGAffineTransform.MakeRotation (.3f), 16, 16, CGPatternTiling.NoDistortion
        , true, DrawPolkaDotPattern);
context.SetFillPattern (pattern, new float[] { 1 });
context.FillRect (this._imageView.Frame);
```

Let's look at the interesting parts of this code. The first important thing is to specify the color space of the pattern. When using color patterns, we want the pattern to take care of the color, so we create a pattern color space by calling CGColorSpace.CreatePattern and passing a null value. We then set our fill color space to that color space that we just created.

Next, we create a new CGPattern object and configure it. We tell it the size of the pattern as well as any transformations we want to do with it. I'll talk about transforms in just a bit, but in this case we're passing a MakeRotation transform so we can rotate the pattern. If we didn't want to transform it, we could just pass an identity transformation via CGAffineTransform.MakeIdentity. Next, we tell it the pattern size, then we specify how we want it tiled. There are a number of options for how it does tiling. In this case, we're telling it not to distort our pattern size ratio.

Next, we pass in true for the isColored parameter, which tells CoreGraphics that it's a color pattern. The final constructor parameter is our actual pattern draw delegate, so we pass our DrawPolkaDotPattern method that we created earlier.

Next, we set our pattern as a fill pattern, since we're going to fill with it. We also pass in an alpha component to tell CoreGraphics how transparent we want the pattern blending to be. In this case, we pass in a 1 to make it completely opaque.

Finally, we fill the area defined in our view.

As you can see, it's very easy to use a pattern, and they're very powerful.

Creating a Stencil Pattern

Creating a stencil pattern follows the exact same procedure as a color pattern, but with a couple of minor changes.

The first change is that in our pattern draw delegate, we don't specify any colors. See Listing 16–15.

Listing 16–15. *When creating a color stencil delegate, you don't specify any colors.*

```
protected void DrawPolkaDotPattern (CGContext context)
{
        context.FillEllipseInRect (new RectangleF (4, 4, 8, 8));
}
```

All we do is our drawing operations, with no fill or stroke colors defined.

Next, when we set our pattern color space, instead of passing a null value, we create it from an actual color space. RGB is the most common, but you could use CMYK, or other color spaces as well. Listing 16–16 creates an RGB space using the device color profile.

Listing 16–16. *Creating an actual color space for use with a stencil pattern*

```
context.SetFillColorSpace (CGColorSpace.CreatePattern (CGColorSpace.CreateDeviceRGB()));
```

Next, when we instantiate our CGPattern, we pass a false value for the isColor parameter. See Listing 16–17.

Listing 16–17. *Passing false to tell CoreGraphics that we're using a stencil pattern*

```
CGPattern pattern = new CGPattern (patternRect, CGAffineTransform.MakeRotation (.3f)
        , 16, 16, CGPatternTiling.NoDistortion, false, DrawPolkaDotPattern);
```

Finally, when we set our fill, or our stroke, this time we pass in a fill color specification. See Listing 16–18.

Listing 16–18. *Telling CoreGraphics to use red to color our stencil pattern*

```
context.SetFillPattern (pattern, new float[] { 1, 0, 0, 1 });
```

When we run our code now, we see a screen similar to Figure 16–7.

Figure 16–7. *A stencil pattern using red as the fill color*

That's it! Those are the only differences between using color patterns and stencil patterns.

Shadows

Shadows can add depth to your drawings in CoreGraphics, and they are incredibly simple to create. You can add either grayscale or color shadows to any draw operation, including shapes, lines, images, and text. See Figure 16–8.

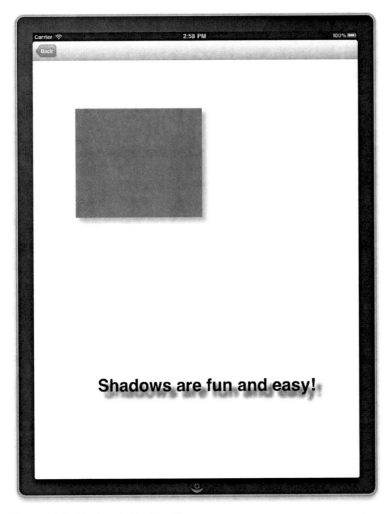

Figure 16–8. *Shadows in CoreGraphics*

Grayscale Shadows

To add a grayscale shadow, perform the following steps:

- Save the graphics state.
- Call SetShadow on your graphics context.
- Perform the drawing operations that you want shadowed.
- Restore the graphics state.

Listing 16–19 creates a grayscale shadow that is offset 10 points below and 10 points to the right of a rectangle, with a blur value of 15.

Listing 16–19. *Creating a grayscale shadow*

```
context.SaveState ();
context.SetShadow (new SizeF (10, -10), 15);
context.SetRGBFillColor (.3f, .3f, .9f, 1);
context.FillRect (new RectangleF (100, 600, 300, 250));
context.RestoreState ();
```

Color Shadows

Color shadows are exactly like grayscale shadows, except that instead of using SetShadow, you call SetShadowWithColor. Listing 16–20 specifies a blue shadow extending 15 points below and 15 points to the right, with a blur of 10

Listing 16–20. *Specifying color shadow options*

```
context.SetShadowWithColor(new SizeF (15, -15), 10, UIColor.Blue.CGColor);
```

Transformations

CoreGraphics includes a very powerful and easy to use system of tools for transforming your drawing and drawing operations. For example, with a single call, you can move, rotate, scale, or flip your drawing.

Under the hood, CoreGraphics uses matrix math to perform transformations, but for the most part, you don't need to know about any of that. That's because CoreGraphics provides you with shortcut methods to simply apply transformations directly to the context.

We saw earlier how we could use transformations to change the entire graphics context, so that all subsequent drawing is in a new coordinate space. However, transformations are more often used to change the coordinate space temporarily, so that we can transform a particular drawing operation, and then change it back, so we can draw other stuff.

In order to do this, you do the following:

1. **Call SaveState on your context:** This allows you to revert back to the original coordinate space.

2. **Apply your transformations:** Do any of your scaling, moving, rotating, and so on to the context.

3. **Perform your drawing:** Any drawing will occur in the transformed coordinate space.

4. **Call RestoreState on your context:** This resets the coordinate space on your context back to the save point.

Translation (Moving)

Translation makes it very easy utilize the origin (0,0) as your base point for drawing, because you can draw something at (0,0) and then move it to wherever you want. For example, Listing 16–21 draws a rectangle at the origin, but because of our translation, it actually is drawn at (50,50) in the view coordinate space.

Listing 16–21. *Using TranslateCTM to move your coordinate space*

```
context.SaveState ();
context.SetRGBFillColor (1, 0, 0, 1);
context.TranslateCTM (50, 50);
context.FillRect (new RectangleF 0, 0, 20, 20));
context.RestoreState ();
```

In Listing 16–21, we made a call `TranslateCTM` to perform our translation. CTM stands for current transformation matrix, and it references the matrix that stores the current transformations on the context. Even though we drew the rectangle at (0,0), it actually appears at (50,50) because of our temporary translation.

Scaling

Scaling is performed via the `ScaleCTM` call. Listing 16–22 makes our rectangle twice as big (40x40) as we've drawn it (20x20).

Listing 16–22. *Using ScaleCTM to scale your coordinate space*

```
context.SaveState ();
context.SetRGBFillColor (1, 0, 0, 1);
context.ScaleCTM (2, 2);
context.FillRect (new RectangleF 0, 0, 20, 20));
context.RestoreState ();
```

One of the interesting things about scaling is that you can actually use it to flip your coordinate space as well. For example, Listing 16–23 flips the y-axis so that your drawing gets flipped upside-down.

Listing 16–23. *Flipping the y-axis by passing a negative value for y in ScaleCTM*

```
context.SaveState ();
context.SetRGBFillColor (1, 0, 0, 1);
context.ScaleCTM (1, -1);
context.FillRect (new RectangleF 0, 0, 20, 20));
context.RestoreState ();
```

To flip the y-axis, we simply passed a -1 for the y parameter of `ScaleCTM`.

Rotation

It becomes apparent why drawing at the origin is useful when we look at rotation. Because rotation rotates the entire coordinate system around the origin, if you drew your object at (50, 50), when you rotated the coordinate space your rectangle would actually move in an arc, equidistant from the origin. However, by centering your drawing over the origin, rotating, and then translating, you can rotate without moving your object.

For instance, Listing 16–23 draws a rectangle at (50,50), and rotates it 45 degrees clockwise.

Listing 16–23. *Using RotateCTM to rotate your coordinate space*

```
context.SaveState ();
context.SetRGBFillColor (1, 0, 0, 1);
context.RotateCTM ((float)(Math.PI * 2 / 8));
context.TranslateCTM (60, 60);
context.FillRect (new RectangleF -10, -10, 20, 20));
context.RestoreState ();
```

Rotation is specified in radians (2 * pi = 360 degrees), so 45 degrees is 2 * pi / 8. Our rectangle is 20x20 points, so to draw it centered at the origin, we draw it a (-10,-10).

Notice that we perform our rotation before our translation. The order of operations is important in rotation. Getting the order wrong can cause the same problem as when we don't draw our stuff at the origin.

Custom Transforms

If you're familiar with matrix transformations, CoreGraphics includes a number of classes so that you can use them in all kinds of ways. For more information, see the *Quartz 2D Programming Guide*.

Hit Testing

So, all this custom drawing stuff is fun, but often you need to be able to tell if a user has touched within a certain area in your drawing surface. This is especially true if you're making custom button functionality.

Ordinarily, this would require doing complicated geometry to determine whether the location of a user's touch was within a given shape. Fortunately, Apple has given us a method that does the hard part for us.

CGPath exposes a method called `ContainsPoint` that will return true if a given location falls within the path. Additionally, the `UITouch` object (which we get when we're handling touch events) tells us the location of the touch. To determine whether a user's touch was within a given path, we can simply override the TouchesBegan event and call the ContainsPoint method, as shown in Listing 16–25.

Listing 16–25. *Determining if a user's touch was within a given path*

```
public override void TouchesBegan (NSSet touches, UIEvent evt)
{
        base.TouchesBegan (touches, evt);

        UITouch touch = touches.AnyObject as UITouch;
        if (touch != null)
        {
                if (this._myPath.ContainsPoint (touch.LocationInView (this), true))
                {
                        // code to handle the touch
```

```
        }
      }
}
```

```
myCGPath.ContainsPoint (myUITouch.LocationInView(myView), true)
```

So as long as you store your path, it's easy to determine if a touch fell within it. The caveat to this, however, is that usually we want the equivalent of the TouchUpInside event. That is, we want to know that when the user raises his finger off of the screen, that he also started within the area we're testing. This allows a user to cancel a button press by sliding his finger off the button and then raising it off the screen. This is also a recommendation in Apple's *Human Interface Guidelines* for the iPhone OS.

In order to do this, we must do the following things:

1. **Create a boolean flag:** We need to store whether the touch began within the area specified.

2. **Override the** TouchesBegan **event:** If the touch began within our specified path, we set our flag to true.

3. **Override the** TouchesEnded **event:** If our flag is equal to true, we know that the touch began in our path, so in the TouchesEnd event, we check to see if it also ended there.

4. **Override the TouchesCancelled event:** In the event that the touch was cancelled, we should clear our flag.

The following UIView class does exactly that. It draws a rectangle and stores the path as a class-level variable, and then it overrides our touch events, tracking whether the touch started and ended within our path. If it did, it shows an alert. See Listing 16–26.

Figure 16–26. *A sample UIView class*

```
public class View : UIView
{

        CGPath _myRectangleButtonPath;
        bool _touchStartedInPath;

        public View () : base()
        {
        }

        /// <summary>
        /// rect changes depending on if the whole view is being redrawn,
        /// or just a section
        /// </summary>
        public override void Draw (RectangleF rect)
        {
                Console.WriteLine ("Draw() Called");
                base.Draw (rect);

                using (CGContext context = UIGraphics.GetCurrentContext ())
                {
```

```
                            //---- draw a rectangle using a path
                            this._myRectangleButtonPath = new CGPath ();
                            this._myRectangleButtonPath.AddRect (new RectangleF (new PointF
                                    (100, 10), new SizeF (200, 400)));
                            context.AddPath (this._myRectangleButtonPath);
                            context.DrawPath (CGPathDrawingMode.Stroke);
                    }
            }


            /// <summary>
            /// Raised when a user begins a touch on the screen. We check to see if
            /// the touch
            /// was within our path. If it was, we set the _touchStartedInPath = true
            /// so that
            /// we can track to see if when the user raised their finger, it was also in
            /// the path
            /// </summary>
            public override void TouchesBegan (NSSet touches, UIEvent evt)
            {
                    base.TouchesBegan (touches, evt);
                    //---- get a reference to the touch
                    UITouch touch = touches.AnyObject as UITouch;
                    //---- make sure there was one
                    if (touch != null)
                    {
                            //---- check to see if the location of the touch was within our
                            // path
                            if (this._myRectangleButtonPath.ContainsPoint
                                    (touch.LocationInView (this)
                                    , true))
                            {
                                    this._touchStartedInPath = true;
                            }
                    }
            }


            /// <summary>
            /// Raised when a user raises their finger from the screen. Since we need
            /// to check to
            /// see if the user touch started and ended within the path, we have to track
            /// to see
            /// when the finger is raised, if it did.
            /// </summary>
            public override void TouchesEnded (NSSet touches, UIEvent evt)
            {
                    base.TouchesEnded (touches, evt);

                    //---- get a reference to any of the touches
                    UITouch touch = touches.AnyObject as UITouch;

                    //---- if there is a touch
                    if (touch != null)
                    {
                            //---- the point of touch
                            PointF pt = touch.LocationInView (this);

                            //---- if the touch ended in the path AND it started in the path
```

```
                    if (this._myRectangleButtonPath.ContainsPoint (pt, true)
                            && this._touchStartedInPath)
                    {

                            Console.WriteLine ("touched at location: " + pt
                                    .ToString ());
                            UIAlertView alert = new UIAlertView ("Hit!"
                                    , "You sunk my battleship!", null, "OK", null);
                            alert.Show ();
                    }
            }

            //---- reset
            this._touchStartedInPath = false;
    }

    /// <summary>
    /// if for some reason the touch was cancelled, we clear our _touchStartedInPath
    /// flag
    /// </summary>
    public override void TouchesCancelled (NSSet touches, UIEvent evt)
    {
            base.TouchesCancelled (touches, evt);
            this._touchStartedInPath = false;
    }

}
```

As you can see, we have to track our touch, but it's really not too bad – the heavy lifting is done in the CGPath.ContainsPoint method, which really saves us a lot of work.

Updating the Drawing Surface in Real-time

So far, everything we've done has been static drawing, e.g., drawing something and displaying it to the page. What if you want to draw in real-time, like in response to user touches?

The answer lies in two UIView methods: SetNeedsDisplay and SetNeedsDisplayInRect.

SetNeedsDisplay specifies that the entire view should be redrawn. SetNeedsDisplayInRect specifies that only a certain section (specified by a RectangleF) needs to be redrawn.

When you call either of these methods, the OS will then call your Draw method when it deems it appropriate. If your view isn't onscreen, it may not even get called.

The rendering pipeline is very tightly controlled in the iOS, so you can't call the Draw method yourself. By giving you those methods, the OS takes on the burden of calling Draw when appropriate.

Full View Update

Doing an update of the entire screen is fairly simple. Listing 16–27 is an excerpt taken from the Example_Drawing companion application. It overrides the TouchesBegan method, so that when a user touches the screen, it captures the location and creates a custom Spot object (defined elsewhere) at that location and then adds it to a list. It then calls SetNeedsDisplay so that the OS will call the Draw method.

Figure 16–27. *Calling SetNeedsDisplay to force a Draw call to update the entire view*

```
public override void TouchesBegan (NSSet touches, UIEvent evt)
{
        base.TouchesBegan (touches, evt);

        //---- get the touch
        UITouch touch = touches.AnyObject as UITouch;
        if (touch != null)
        {
                //---- create a random color spot at the point of touch, then add it
                // to the others
                Spot spot = Spot.CreateNewRandomColor (touch.LocationInView (this));
                this._touchSpots.Add (spot);
                //---- tell the OS to redraw
                this.SetNeedsDisplay ();

        }
}
```

Partial View Updates

You can do partial view updates via the SetNeedsDisplayInRect call. It takes RectangleF parameter that is passed to your Draw method and allows you to just draw a portion of the screen. The difficulty with this call, however, is that it invalidates that rectangle, so if you have anything already drawn in there, and you want to draw over it, it will erase it, even if you mask off (clip) just the area you want to draw.

Other Features of CoreGraphics

Wow, CoreGraphics is a huge, powerful library, this is a large chapter, and we've only scratched the surface. Every subject we've covered has more functionality than we've touched on. It's no wonder entire books have been devoted to the subject.

With that said, there are a number of other elements of CoreGraphics that I would like to just briefly mention, so that you know they exist and if you need them, you can go research them:

- **Frame rate synchronization:** There is a class called CADisplayLink that allows you to synchronize screen updates to coincide with the refresh rate of the display that you're using. For example, if you're building a video playback engine, you can determine which frame to display next, based on the timestamp of the last screen refresh and the refresh rate.

- **Dashed lines:** Lines don't need to be continuous. CoreGraphics has rich support for dashed lines, and you can specify the dash pattern, interval, and so on.

- **Fill modes:** I've shown only the simplest of fills, but CoreGraphics also supports filling with all kinds of gradients. It also supports advanced fill-modes that clip certain overlapping regions and multipath fills so you can do things like create donuts.

- **Blending:** Out of the box, CoreGraphics supports a number of sophisticated blending options for specifying how draw options are overlayed on top of each other, just like you see in high-end photo-editing suites such as Adobe Photoshop.

- **Transparency layers:** CoreGraphics has a feature called transparency layers that allows you to group drawing operations together as a single object, so that you can apply effects such as shadows to the entire set without them appearing as separate objects on top of each other.

- **Clipping masks:** Clipping masks lets you apply masks on top of drawing objects to control what gets drawn to the screen.

- **Image masks:** Image mask are like clipping masks, but you can also pull out parts of an image and draw them elsewhere, plus a whole lot of other neat functionality.

- **PDF creation:** CoreGraphics allows you to save your drawing surfaces directly out as PDF files, handling all the necessary serialization, file formatting, and so on, making PDF creation a cinch.

As I've mentioned before, Apple's documentation on CoreGraphics is quite extensive, and it's required reading if you want to dive deeper. Start with the *Quartz 2D Programming Guide* and you'll be well on your way.

Summary

Wow, that was a lot of information. This chapter should get you well on your way to understanding CoreGraphics. You should now understand all of the fundamentals of CoreGraphics, and then some. But remember, there is a lot more to it, so you should definitely check out the Apple docs on it.

Chapter 17

Core Animation

One of the iconic things about iOS is its cinematic user experience. GUI elements slide on and off screen, fade in, fade out, flip, curl, and bounce, the result of which is an interface that feels very smooth, dynamic, and organic.

Powering this cinematic experience is one of iOS' foundation technologies, Core Animation. The Core Animation API provides you with a number of `UIView`-based animation features that allow you to easily animate changes in your interface so that your applications can provide the same cinematic experience that users have come to expect from iOS applications. View-based animation includes two types of animations: transition animations and same view animations. Transition animations are animations that occur when you're changing between views. For instance, you might want to load another view and use a flip transition so that when it appears, the whole screen appears to flip with the new view on the side that rotates in. Same view animations are animations that occur on a single view, such as moving subviews around.

In addition to the view-based animation features, the core animation API exposes lower-level animation functions that operate on `CALayer` objects, rather than `UIView` objects, and provide a powerful 2D animation framework that you can use to create more complex animations, and even power games.

For most applications the view-based animation framework is the only part of Core Animation you'll ever use. They provide a powerful way to give your interface that cinematic feel without much work. In fact, if you've been reading this book front-to-back, you've already been exposed to it. In this chapter, we'll explore it a little deeper and take a look at how to work with it in more detail. Then, we're going to dig into the lower-level core animation API to see how advanced animation can be accomplished in the iOS.

As with Chapter 16, this chapter covers most of everything you'll ever need to use with animation; however, the Core Animation API is massive. If you're doing advanced animation, you should check out the *Core Animation Programming Guide* in the Xcode developer documentation after you've read this chapter.

You can find all the examples used in this chapter in the `Example_CoreAnimation` sample code and application.

View-Based Animation Framework

There are two different approaches when working with the view-based animation framework: the new way and the old way. The new way (available since the iOS v4.0 release) is the way recommended by Apple, but both ways have their advantages. Let's take a quick look at examples of both methods so that you have a clear understanding of them.

View Animations via the Animation Blocks

First, the old way is to call `BeginAnimations`, optionally configure the animation options, make your view changes, and then call `CommitAnimations`. See Listing 17–1.

Listing 17–1. *Animating changes on a UIView using the BeginAnimations and CommitAnimations methods*

```
UIView.BeginAnimations("ImageMove");
//code to make changes to the view (move controls, swap views, etc.)
UIView.CommitAnimations();
```

Using this method, iOS will automatically animate any changes that occur between the `BeginAnimations` and `CommitAnimations` calls.

Technically, Apple refers to this method of animation as Animation Blocks, but as we're about to see, that's really confusing, given that the new way is called Block-Based Animation. I'll just refer to it as "the old way" to avoid confusion.

View Animations via Block-Based Animation

The new way is to make a call to the `Animate` method, specify the duration of the animation, optionally specify any of the animation options, and then pass a method (or code as a lambda) that makes the changes that should be animated. See Listing 17–2.

Listing 17–2. *Animating changes on a UIView using an animation block method*

```
UIView.Animate(0.2, () => { /* code to animate */ });
```

In this case, to simplify things, I've used the C# lamdba syntax, but you could also pass an anonymous delegate, as shown in Listing 17–3.

Listing 17–3. *Using the delegate syntax instead of a Lambda expression*

```
UIView.Animate(0.2, delegate() { /* code to animate */ });
```

This approach is known as block-based animation. It's called such because in objective-c, the analog to code that's passed in to execute is called a `block`. If you take a look at the prototype for the `Animate` methods (there are several overrides), they all take `NSAction` objects for their blocks. MonoTouch automatically does the magic of converting an anonymous delegate into an `NSAction` for you, so it's a very clean and seamless integration with the underlying Objective-C runtime.

Comparison of the Two Approaches

While Apple recommends the new block-based animation approach, it's not exactly forthcoming in terms of why it's recommended. It's likely because it more closely ties into Apple's new paradigm of parallel tasking (see the Grand Central Dispatch article on Wikipedia.org for more information, at `http://en.wikipedia.org/wiki/Grand_Central _Dispatch`).

Regardless of why Apple recommends the new approach, it's arguably cleaner. Since the code that performs the view modifications is actually passed to the animation function, there's no method wrapping magic that has to happen.

However, block-based animation is missing the following two key features that are possible with the old way:

- **Fixed repetition count:** You cannot specify how many times the animation should repeat; you can only set it to not repeat, or to repeat indefinitely.

- **Automatic duration:** With the old way, the default duration (the time it takes for you animation to happen) of your animation is calculated by the iOS. With block-based animation, however, you must specify the animation duration.

Having to specify the duration isn't a huge deal, but not being able to specify a fixed repetition count is very difficult to work around, if you need that particular feature.

Hopefully, at some point, Apple will realize the oversight and add these features back in. Until then, if you need to specify a fixed repetition count, you should use the old approach.

In this chapter, we're going to examine both approaches to view-based animation.

What Is Animatable?

View-based animation is based on a view's property changes. There are a number of properties that, when changed within the context of a view-based animation (either a block based animation or animation blocks), will get automatically animated. Those properties are as follows:

- Frame
- Bounds
- Center
- Transform
- Alpha
- BackgroundColor
- ContentStretch

The upside to this is that, if your animations are based on changes to any of these properties, view-based animation is very easy. The downside is that if you want to animate other properties, you need to use Explicit Layer Animations (as we'll explore later in this chapter). Fortunately, however, these properties cover most animation needs.

Configuring Animation Behavior

There are a number of options that you can configure that affect the behavior of an animation, namely the following:

- **Duration:** The amount of time the animation takes to complete. You have to specify this when you use block-based animations, but it's an optional configuration when using the older style.

- **Delay:** The amount of time to wait before the animation should start.

- **Curve:** The acceleration and speed of the animation.

- **Repetition:** Whether the animation repeats.

- **Auto reverse:** Whether the animation automatically reverses.

Nested Animations

It's possible to nest animations by calling methods to generate an animation from within an already executing animation block. Nested animations run the same way non-nested animations do, but, by default, these nested animations inherit their duration and curve from the parent animation.

Specifying Behavior via Animate Method Overloads

If you're using the block-based animation approach, these options are specified via parameters in the various Animate method overloads. See Listing 17–4.

Listing 17–4. *Various Animate method overloads*

```
Animate(double duration, MonoTouch.Foundation.NSAction animation)
Animate(double duration, MonoTouch.Foundation.NSAction, MonoTouch.Foundation.NSAction
        animation)
Animate(double duration, double delay, UIViewAnimationOptions options,
        MonoTouch.Foundation.NSAction animation, MonoTouch.Foundation.NSAction
completion)
```

Let's take a look at the various parameters in these overloads.

- **Duration:** Just as it seems, the duration parameter specifies the amount of time, in seconds, that an animation should take to occur.

- **Animation:** The animation parameter takes an anonymous delegate of the code that actually gets animated. Any view changes that occur during this block of code will get animated.

- **Delay:** Again, self-explanatory the `delay` parameter specifies the time, in seconds before an animation should start.

- **Options:** We'll look at the options available in the very next section. The `options` parameter takes a set of flags from the `UIViewAnimationOptions` enumeration which contains a number of animation options you can specify.

- **Completion:** The `completion` parameter takes an anonymous delegate of code that gets called when the animation completes.

UIViewAnimationOptions Enumeration

Duration and delay get their own parameters, but all other options are specified via a `UIViewAnimationOptions` enumeration. The `UIViewAnimationOptions` is a bitmask enumeration, so you can set multiple options via the pipe ("|") operator, as shown in Listing 17–5.

Listing 17–5. *Configuring animation behaviors using block-based animation*

```
double duration = 1;
double delay = 2;
UIViewAnimationOptions animationOptions =
        UIViewAnimationOptions.CurveEaseIn | UIViewAnimationOptions.Repeat;
UIView.Animate(duration, delay, animationOptions, () => { /* animation code */ }, null);
```

The `UIViewAnimationOptions` have the following general animation enumeration values:

- **AllowUserInteraction:** By default, while an animation is running, user interaction is not enabled, that is, buttons can't be touched, and so on. If you specify this value, then user interation will be enabled during animation.

- **AutoReverse:** If this flag is set, the animation will automatically reverse and go backward. However, once the animation is done, the elements that have changed will "jump" back to their final location, so this flag is meant to be used in conjunction with the `Repeat` flag to create looping animations.

- **BeginFromCurrentState:** By default, if an animation is already in progress (also known as "in-flight"), other (non-nested) animations will be queued and run sequentially after the previous animation finishes. By specifying the `BeginFromCurrentState` flag, an animation will execute, even if other animations are running, allowing concurrent animations.

- **Curve*:** There are several curve settings such as `CurveEaseIn`, `CurveEaseOut`, and so on. They specify the acceleration speed of the animation. We'll explore them more in the upcoming "Animation Curves" section.

- **LayoutSubviews:** If LayoutSubviews is specifed, LayoutSubviews will be called on the view when the animation starts, and any changes will also be animated. This is a very powerful feature because it allows you to easily animate layout changes.

- **OverrideInheritedDuration:** Nested animations automatically inherit their duration from the parent animation, rather than using the duration specified when the nested animation was generated. Sometimes this isn't desirable, so you can use the OverrideInheritedDuration flag to make sure the nested animation uses it's specified duration, rather than the inherited duration.

- **OverrideInheritedCurve:** OverrideInheritedCurve is similar to OverrideInheritedDuration, except that it makes sure the nested animation uses it's specified curve rather than the inherited curve.

- **Repeat:** If specified, the animation will repeat indefinitely.

Animation Curves

Table 17–2 lists the animation curves available in CoreAnimation:

Table 17–1. *Animation Curves in CoreAnimation*

Type	Description	Graph
CurveEaseInEaseOut	Accelerates at the beginning of the animation and decelerates at the end of the animation. Provides the most natural feeling animation for most animation types and is the default animation curve.	
CurveEaseIn	Accelerates at the beginning of the animation. Good for animations that send things off-screen.	
CurveEaseOut	Decelerates at the end of the animation. Good for animations that bring things onscreen.	

Type	Description	Graph
CurveLinear	No acceleration curve at all, therefore the animation speed is constant from start to finish. Linear curves are useful for animations that don't require a natural acceleration/deceleration.	

View Transitions

In addition to using view animations to move things around on a view, you can also animate adding and removing views from a controller. This allows you to provide a cinematic way to transition between screens. For example, you could apply a flip transition that "spins" a new view onto the screen, or a "curl" animation that lifts the current view off the screen and displays another.

The UIViewAnimationOptions enumeration contains a number of values that apply only to transition animations:

- **ShowHideTransitionViews:** If you specify this value, then the view that you're transitioning to will be shown and the view your transitioning away from will be hidden. This is different than the default behavior, which actually adds the new view and removes the old view. If you do specify this option, the view that you're adding must already be in the parent view's list of subviews.

- **Transition*:** There are several transition types, including FlipFromleft, FlipFromRight, CurlUp, and CurlDown. To specify which one you'd like your transition to use, simply specify the transition type flag, such as TransitionFlipFromLeft, to get a flip transition that starts from the left side of the screen.

- **AllowAnimatedContent:** AllowAnimatedContent specifies whether the iOS renders the animation and caches the frames. If set to true, caching will occur; if set to false, no caching will occur. This is the equivalent of the Cache parameter when using the older method style animations. If set to true, performance may be better (setting it to false may noticeably affect frame rate, especially on older devices); however, you must not update the view manually during the transition or the rendering could be incorrect.

Specifying Behavior via Methods

If you're using the older animation methods, then behavior options are configured using various methods. See Listing 17–6.

Listing 17–6. *Configuring animation behaviors using method based animation*

```
UIView.BeginAnimations("MyAnimation");
UIView.SetAnimationDelay(2);
UIView.SetAnimationCurve(UIViewAnimationCurve.EaseIn);
UIView.SetAnimationDuration(1);
//… animation code goes here
UIView.CommitAnimations();
```

All the UIView animation methods are static, and the following are available to configure the animation properties if you're using the older animation methods. Most of these correspond 1:1 with either parameters in the Animate method or flags from the UIViewAnimationOptions enumeration:

- **SetAnimationDuration:** The equivalent of specifying the duration parameter of the UIView.Animate method.

- **SetAnimationDelay:** The equivalent of specifying the delay parameter of the UIView.Animate method.

- **SetAnimationStartDate:** Specifies a DateTime at which the animation will start. You can use this in conjunction with specifying a delay. The delay will begin counting down at the DateTime you specify for start date.

- **SetAnimationCurve:** Sets the animation curve. Values are available in the UIViewAnimationCurve enumeration and equivalent to the respectively named options in UIViewAnimationOptions.Curve* flags.

- **SetAnimationRepeatCount:** Allows you specify how many times the animation will repeat. This option is not available in the block-based animation technique.

- **SetAnimationRepeatAutoReverses:** The equivalent of the AutoReverse flag in the UIViewAnimationOptions enumeration.

- **SetAnimationBeginsFromCurrentState:** The equivalent of the BeginFromCurrentState flag in the UIViewAnimationOptions enumeration.

- **SetAnimationsEnabled:** Enables/disables animations.

- **SetAnimationDidStopSelector:** Specifies a selector method that will run when the animation finishes. Similar to of specifying a completion parameter via the UIView.Animate method.

- **SetAnimationWillStartSelector:** Specifies a selector method that will run with the animation starts.

If you're using the method-based animation technique, and you want to execute code after the animation finishes, you should call the `SetAnimationDidStopSelector` method, which takes a `Selector` that points to your method. See Listing 17–7.

Listing 17–7. *Configuring a method to be called when the animation completes*

```
UIView.SetAnimationDidStopSelector(new Selector("AnimationStopped"));
```

Since the method takes a `Selector`, you must also mark your method with the `ExportAttribute` so it's visible to the underlying Objective-C runtime. See Listing 17–8.

Listing 17–8. *Marking a method with Export so that it's visible to the Objective-C runtime*

```
[Export]
public void AnimationStopped()
{ Console.WriteLine("Animation completed"); }
```

Advanced Core Animation with Layers

View-based animation is great because it makes common animation tasks simple. However, sometimes you need more control than what it offers. For example, let's say you wanted to animate the moving of an object, but you want to specify a particular path that isn't just a straight line (see Figure 17–1).

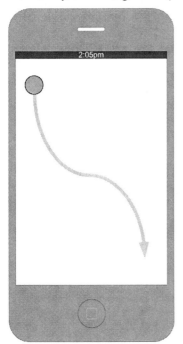

Figure 17–1. *Moving an object along this path is not all that easy using view-based animation.*

You could possibly accomplish this by making lots of calls to the Animate method and moving the object a little bit each time, but that would mean a lot of math, a lot of code, and a lot of headache.

There's another place that view-based animation falls short: games. In addition to the lack of control (such as not being able to specify a path when moving objects), view-based animation lacks the speed necessary for game development. Thirty frames per second (fps) or higher has become standard in the gaming world. It's roughly the same frame rate as video/television (film is generally 24fps), and is generally accepted as the lowest framerate that provides a smooth gaming experience. Accomplishing that frame rate with view-based animation can be very difficult, because it's not guaranteed to be hardware-accelerated.

There is an alternative, however, that provides both higher control and much more performance through hardware acceleration: layer-based animation.

Layer-Based Animation

As the name suggests, layer-based animation involves the use of layers (represented by the CALayer object). Don't confuse CALayers with CGLayers. They are similar in concept, but are fundamentally different under the hood and cannot be interchanged.

You can create CALayers one of two ways. The easiest way is to simply get the layer from an existing UIView. All UIView objects in iOS are known as layer-backed views. This means that each view has a layer-tree hierarchy that represents the items in a view, and you can access it via the Layer property on any UIView object. The other way to get a CALayer is to create one manually, which is a bit more involved. We'll take a look at how to do that in just a second.

Layers are interesting in that they're not directly responsible for drawing themselves. Instead, they are an object hierarchy that contains information that describes the state of a UIView. However, under the hood, there is another set of layer information that is used in the rendering loop. When you change a property on the layer, it will actually feed incremental changes to the rendering loop so that the change that you've applied is rendered incrementally over the animation duration.

This functionality is all encapsulated for you, so you don't have to perform the math associated with changes, the layer system does it for you.

Layer Animation Types

There are two types of layer-based animations:

- **Explicit:** You must create an Animation object and then apply that to the layer you want animated.

- **Implicit:** Changes to properties are automatically animated. Implicit animations are only possible if you use CALayer objects directly, rather than ones that are created from a UIView.

Superficially, implicit animations seem easier to use. However, they required that you manually create your layers, which can be complicated. Explicit animations require more code to actually do the animation, but because you can use them with layers that are created via a view, they are actually easier to implement.

We're going to look at explicit animations first, and then we're going to turn to implicit animations and cover how to create CALayer objects manually.

Explicit Animations

Explicit layer-based animations are a little different from the other animations that we've looked at so far. Instead of creating an animation block and executing it, you configure the animation parameters and then tell the animation what property to listen for changes to. When that property's value changes, the animation specified runs. For instance, to achieve the animation illustrated in Figure 17–1, we would do something like Listing 17–9.

Listing 17–9. *Implementing a keyframe animation that moves an object along a path*

```
this.btnAnimate.TouchUpInside += (s, e) => {
    //---- create a keyframe animation that listens for changes to the "position"
    // property
    CAKeyFrameAnimation keyFrameAnimation =
            (CAKeyFrameAnimation)CAKeyFrameAnimation.FromKeyPath("position");
    keyFrameAnimation.Path = this._animationPath;
    keyFrameAnimation.Duration = 3;
    //---- add the animation to the layer
    this.imgToAnimate.Layer.AddAnimation(keyFrameAnimation, "MoveImage");
    //---- kick the animation off by changing the position to the final position
    this.imgToAnimate.Layer.Position = new PointF(700, 900);
};
```

This would result in the animation shown in Figure 17–2.

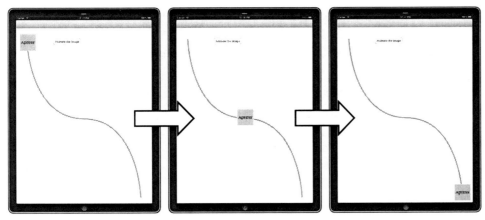

Figure 17–2. *An explicit layer animation that moves an object along a path*

You can see this animation at work in the Example_CoreAnimation companion code and application.

In Listing 17–9, we created instantiated a CAKeyFrameAnimation object and passed the constructor the name of the property we want to listen for. In this case, we want to listen for the Position property, but it expects the Objective-C visible property name (generally the same name but starting with a lowercase letter), in this case it would be "position." We'll talk about the different types of animations later, but for now, know that a keyframe animation will animate movement along a path.

Next, we configure our animation, this case, because it's a keyframe animation, we supply it a path defined in a CGPath object (check out Chapter 16 for more information about CGPaths).

After we've configured the animation, we add it to the layer and give it a name. We name it so that later on, if we want to stop the animation (by removing it), we can do something like Listing 17–10.

Listing 17–10. *Removing an animation. If you remove an animation while it's in flight, the animation is stopped.*

```
this.imgToAnimate.Layer.RemoveAnimation("MoveImage");
```

Finally, to kick off our animation, we set the property that we're listening for changes on to its final value. Once we've done that, the animation will begin.

Animation Types

In Listing 17–9 we created a CAKeyFrameAnimation that animates along a set of positional points, however, there are a number of animation classes available for use:

- **CATransition:** Used to provide transition animations, such as fading in/out, or pushing onto/off the view stack. You can extend the stock transition effects by creating your own custom Core Image filters.

- **CAPropertyAnimation:** CAPropertyAnimation is an abstract base class for providing animations for custom layer properties that can be reused.

- **CABasicAnimation:** Used for simple movement animations that go from from a start point to an end point.

- **CAKeyFrameAnimation:** Animates an object along a path, as seen in Figure 17–2.

Additionally, there is one additional class, CAAnimationGroup, which allows you to group a set of the previous animation classes together into an array and run them concurrently. For a more in-depth look at these classes, checkout the *Core Animation Programming Guide* as well as the *Animation Types and Timing Programming Guide* in the Xcode developer documentation.

Creating CALayers Manually

Now that you understand how to animate layers that are attached to a UIView, let's take a look at how to create layers manually. By creating layers manually, you have a choice of whether to use either the explicit, or the implicit animation technique.

There are the following three ways to manually create a CALayer object:

- **From an image:** One of the easiest ways to create a CALayer is to set its Contents property to a CGImage.

- **Specify a content delegate:** You can create a CALayerDelegate class and assign it to your CALayer object. You should override DrawLayer in your delegate class to draw your layer content.

- **Subclass CALayer:** You can create a custom class that derives from CALayer and override the DrawInContext method. This is effectively the same thing as creating a layer delegate.

If you choose to draw a layer manually, you can follow the techniques outlined in the last chapter.

All three of these methods are illustrated in Listing 17–11.

Listing 17–11. *The various ways to create a CALayer*

```
//==== Method 1: create a layer from an image
protected CALayer CreateLayerFromImage()
{
        CALayer layer = new CALayer();
        layer.Contents = UIImage.FromBundle("Images/Icons/Apress-114x114.png").CGImage;
        return layer;
}

//==== Method 2: create a layer and assign a custom delegate that performs the drawing
protected CALayer CreateLayerWithDelegate()
{
        CALayer layer = new CALayer();
        layer.Delegate = new LayerDelegate();
        return layer;
}

public class LayerDelegate : CALayerDelegate
{
        public override void DrawLayer (
                CALayer layer, MonoTouch.CoreGraphics.CGContext context)
        {
                //---- implement your drawing
        }
}

//===== Method 3: Create a custom CALayer and override the appropriate methods
public class MyCustomLayer : CALayer
{
        public override void DrawInContext (MonoTouch.CoreGraphics.CGContext ctx)
        {
                base.DrawInContext (ctx);
```

```
                            //---- implement your drawing
                }
    }
```

If you're interested in learning more about the details of layers, check out the *Core Animation Programming Guide* in the Xcode developer documentation.

Drawing Layers on a View

Once you've created the layer objects that you want to animate, you probably want to display them. The problem is, you can't add them directly to a UIView, as you would other view controls. Instead, you have to add them to a UIView's layer hierarchy via the AddSublayer method. For example, the UIViewController code in Listing 17–12 calls a method from Listing 17–11 to create a layer and then adds it to the controller's view layer tree.

Listing 17–12. *Adding a layer to a view's layer tree*

```
this._imgLayer = this.CreateLayerFromImage();
this._imgLayer.Frame = new RectangleF(200, 70, 114, 114);
this.View.Layer.AddSublayer(this._imgLayer);
```

Implicit Animations

Implicit animations are animations that are automatically invoked whenever you a change a property. This may seem like an awesome way to do layer animation, but there is one huge caveat: implicit animations are *not* available on layers that are created from a UIView. Instead you have to either use explicit layer animations, or view-based animations. This is because when you change the value of a property on a layer, it asks its delegate whether or not it should animate. If a layer is attached to a UIView, the view acts as the layer's animation delegate and says "no." This, presumably, is because most view changes don't require animation.

Listing 17–13 uses the layer we created and added to the layer hierarchy in Listing 17–12. When a user clicks on a button, the code changes the Frame and Opacity properties of the layer.

Listing 17–13. *Implicitly animating a change to a layer*

```
this.btnAnimate.TouchUpInside += (s, e) => {
        if(this._imgLayer.Frame.Y == 70)
        {
                this._imgLayer.Frame = new RectangleF(new PointF(200, 270)
                        , this._imgLayer.Frame.Size);
                this._imgLayer.Opacity = 0.2f;
        }
        else
        {
                this._imgLayer.Frame = new RectangleF(new PointF(200, 70)
                        , this._imgLayer.Frame.Size);
                this._imgLayer.Opacity = 1.0f;
        }
};
```

This results in a cinematic transition between the two states, as shown in Figure 17-3.

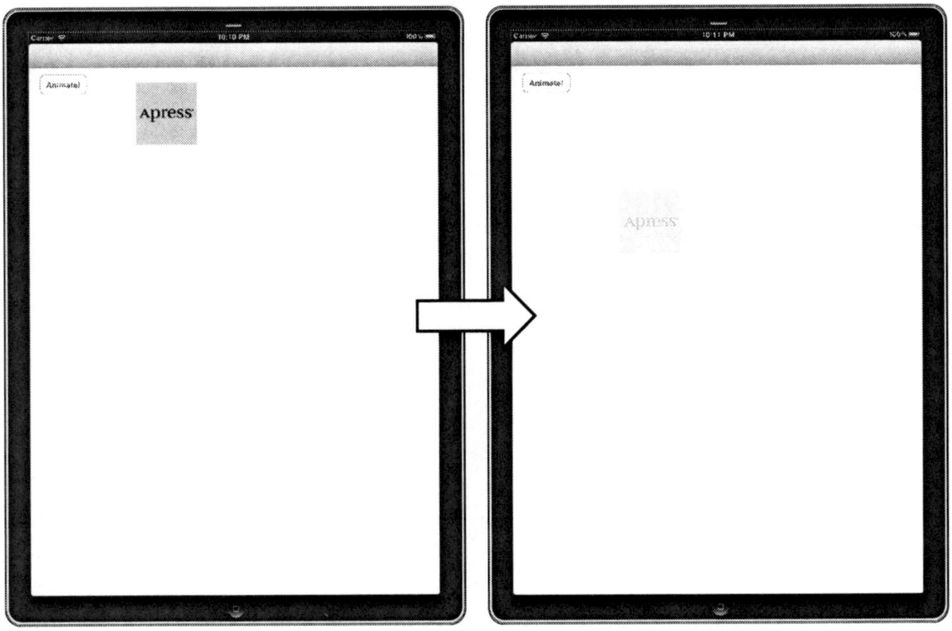

Figure 17-3. *Implicit layer animation between two layer states*

You can see this animation at work in the Example_CoreAnimation companion code and application.

Summary

In this chapter we covered the four ways to perform animation in iOS, the two options that are available via views, Animation Blocks and Method-Based Animation, as well as the two that are available via layers, Explicit and Implicit animations. You learned that layer-based animations offer far more control over the animation, and work much faster, however, they're more complicated to implement. I also covered how to work with layers, including creating and rendering.

This chapter is by no means an exhaustive look at animation in iOS. It should cover 95 percent of what you need to accomplish, but the core animation framework is very large and powerful and entire books are devoted to the subject. If you're interested in learning more, start with the *Core Animation Programming Guide* document in the Xcode developer documentation.

If you've been reading this book from front to back, you should now have an expert understanding of the presentation methods available in iOS. In the next chapter we're going to switch gears and talk about the various ways to work with data in iOS.

Chapter 18

Notifications

Notifications in iOS provide a way to notify the user when a particular application-specific event is happening when the application is not in the foreground. For example, if you're building an instant messaging application, you might want to let your users know that they've received a message, even though they might have another application open, or even have the phone in standby mode. If your application is in the background or not running at all, the user can be presented with an alert message, or you can badge the application icon. You can even play a sound in addition to the alert message. For example, when you get a new mail message, the Mail Application's icon badge number increases by 1 and a sound is played.

You can also use notifications to let the user know when certain events happen, even while the application is running. For instance, if you're building a calendar application, you can enable pop-up alerts when a notification fires, letting your user know of an event that is coming up.

There are two kinds of notifications: local and remote (also known as push notifications). Local notifications are scheduled with iOS to occur at a certain time (or immediately) and push notifications are registered and delivered via the Apple Push Notification service. However, whether they're local or remote, they're handled the same way.

In this chapter we're going to look at how notifications work, how to schedule notifications, how to handle notifications, and finally, we'll examine how to register and work with remote (push) notifications.

How Notifications Work

Notifications can occur regardless of the state the device and/or application is in. For example, Figure 18–1 shows a notification happening when the device is locked, when the device is unlocked but the application is not running in the foreground, and finally, when the device is running in the foreground.

Figure 18–1. *Notifications occurring in a variety of application states*

In the examples in Figure 18–1, the notifications are presented via alert views; however, this is not a requirement, and you can choose to simply modify the application icon badge. You can even play a sound (or vibrate, if the sound is off) when you modify the icon badge or display the alert. This is the default behavior for the Mail Application, for instance.

How the notification actually appears to the user when the application is not in the foreground is specified when you configure the notification. How the notification appears when the app is running in the foreground is specified by the handlers in your application that are called when the notification is received.

Let's take a look at how to schedule local notifications, to see how the first case is handled.

Scheduling Local Notifications

Local notifications are a welcome new feature in version 4.0 of the iOS. They're nice because they're extremely easy to schedule (configure), and unlike push notifications, they don't require any complicated interaction with any outside services. They're also quite powerful – not only can you schedule a notification event to occur once, but you can also schedule them to recur at specified intervals. The iOS handles all the plumbing and calendaring for you; you simply schedule the event and when it's time for it, it'll notify your application.

To schedule a local notification you create a UILocalNotification object, configure the FireDate, and then add it to iOS via the ScheduleLocalNotification method on the static SharedApplication property of the UIApplication class. For example, Listing 18–1 schedules a local notification that will occur one minute in the future.

Listing 18–1. *Scheduling a local notification*

```
UILocalNotification notification = new UILocalNotification();
notification.FireDate = DateTime.Now.AddMinutes(1);
UIApplication.SharedApplication.ScheduleLocalNotification(notification);
```

If you want to display an alert when the notification fires, you can set the title of the action bar (or slider, if the phone is locked) via the AlertAction property, and the message of the alert via the AlertBody property. See Listing 18–2.

Listing 18–2. *Configuring the alert behavior on a local notification*

```
notification.AlertAction = "View Alert";
notification.AlertBody = "Your one minute alert has fired!";
```

If you want the badge the icon with a number, you can set it via the ApplicationIconBadgeNumber property. See Listing 18–3.

Listing 18–3. *Configuring the badge on a local notification*

```
notification.ApplicationIconBadgeNumber = 1;
```

You can also play a sound when the alert appears. If you choose to play a sound, you should also either show an alert or badge the application icon, otherwise the user won't know what the alert is for. To play a custom sound, set the SoundName property to the path to your sound file. Your sound file should be less than 30 seconds long; otherwise the default sound will play. Additionally, if you just want to use the default sound, you can use the static DefaultSoundName property on the UILocalNotification class. See Listing 18–4.

Listing 18–4. *Configuring the sound for a local notification*

```
notification.SoundName = UILocalNotification.DefaultSoundName;
```

Now let's look at handling notifications when they occur.

Handling Notifications

Handling a notification is nearly the same whether it's a local or a push notification. If the application is running, the ReceivedLocalNotification or ReceivedRemoteNotification (for local and remote notifications, respectively) method on your app delegate class will be called by iOS, passing in the notification information.

How you handle the notification is up to you. For instance, if your notification were simply an event reminder, you might want to show an alert, reminding your users. Or, you might use a notification to modify something in your application's user interface to show a new message. For example, Listing 18–5 shows an alert with the alert title and message body information that was created on the notification.

Listing 18–5. *Handling a notification in your app delegate*

```
public override void ReceivedLocalNotification (UIApplication application
        , UILocalNotification notification)
{
        new UIAlertView(notification.AlertAction, notification.AlertBody
                , null, "OK", null).Show();
        UIApplication.SharedApplication.ApplicationIconBadgeNumber = 0;
}
```

If your application isn't running, iOS presents the notification via however you've defined it (alert, sound, icon badge). If the user clicks the action badge in the alert (or slides the action slider), your application is launched by iOS and the FinishedLaunching method on your app delegate is called, passing in the notification information via the options parameter.

If it's a local notification, you can access it from the options NSDictionary via the LaunchOptionsLocalNotificationKey key. If the resulting object isn't null, you know that the application was launched from a local notification. See Listing 18–6.

Listing 18–6. *Accessing a local notification in FinishedLaunching*

```
public override bool FinishedLaunching (UIApplication app, NSDictionary options)
{
        …

        UILocalNotification localNotification =
                options[UIApplication.LaunchOptionsLocalNotificationKey];
        if(localNotification != null)
        {
                new UIAlertView(localNotification.AlertAction
                        , localNotification.AlertBody, null, "OK", null).Show();
                //---- reset our badge
                UIApplication.SharedApplication.ApplicationIconBadgeNumber = 0;
        }

        …

}
```

If it's a remote notification, you still pull the object from the options NSDictionary; however, you use the LaunchOptionsRemoteNotificationKey key, and the resulting object is an NSDictionary object with the remote notification payload. You can extract the notification payload via the "alert," "badge," and "sound" keys. See Listing 18–7.

Listing 18–7. *Accessing a remote notification in FinishedLaunching*

```
NSDictionary remoteNotification =
options[UIApplication.LaunchOptionsRemoteNotificationKey];
if(remoteNotification != null)
{
        // code. To get the alert use remoteNotification["alert"], etc.
}
```

For more information on the remote notification payload, see "The Notification Payload" section of the *Local and Push Notification Programming Guide* in the iOS developer documentation.

Push Notifications

Push notifications are also known as remote notifications, and unlike local notifications, which are very easy to implement, they are very complex and require considerable development overhead. They require not only extra steps in development of the iOS application, but they also require a separate application (in the technology of your choosing) that is responsible for sending the notifications to Apple's Push Notification Gateway Server (APNS), which in turn, locates the intended device recipient and sends the notifications to your iOS application. See Figure 18–2.

Figure 18–2. *Push notification topology*

However, despite their complexity, they're the only reliable way to implement certain functionality in your application. For instance, let's say we're building an e-mail client. In order to make sure that our application always has the latest e-mails, we need to make it poll a server every so often and check for new e-mail. This works somewhat okay when the application is in the foreground, but it presents a real problem when the application is in the background. Since our application isn't one of the four types of applications that we can register to be allowed to perform continuous background tasks (see Chapter 11 for more information), there is no way for the application to check for new e-mail when it's in the background. Additionally, even when the application is in the foreground, it would have to poll the server fairly often to ensure that e-mail delivery is timely. This means a lot of network calls and battery drain.

Push notifications are designed specifically for this type of scenario. Instead of having our application continuously poll a server for data, we can push a small message to the application that tells it that it needs to do something.

In this section of the chapter, we're going to take a look at how to set up the required iOS infrastructure to enable remote notifications, and we're going to look briefly at an open-source .NET library that will allow us to communicate with APNS.

However, before we delve into the specifics of how to get push notifications working, let's first take a look at some restrictions and limitations we should bear in mind when designing an architecture that uses them.

Restrictions and Limitations

While push notifications are a powerful solution to a difficult problem, they the following very import limitations that necessitate certain design decisions:

- **256kB message limit:** The entire message size of the notification, including its header and other attributes, cannot exceed 256kB.

- **No confirmation of receipt:** APNS does not give you a confirmation that the notification made it to the intended recipient. In fact, if the device is unreachable and multiple notifications are sent from one source, only the last notification that was sent will be delivered to the device when it becomes reachable again.

- **Secure certificates are specific to each application:** In order to communicate with APNS, you need to authenticate over SSL and the certificate required to do this is unique to each application. This means that if you have two applications that receive push notifications, your application that send the notifications must use a different certificate depending on what application it's notifying.

Because of the size limit of notifications, as well as the fact that your sending application doesn't give you receipt confirmation, the notification messages themselves should only contain the necessary information to notify your iOS application that it needs to make a call to your server application to pull down new data.

For instance, in our e-mail example, when a new e-mail came in, we would only notify iOS application that a new e-mail has arrived, so that it can retrieve it from the server. We wouldn't send the e-mail in the notification itself.

The Sandbox and Production Environments

Apple maintains two environments for APNS: a Sandbox and a Production environment. The Sandbox environment is meant for testing during the development phase and can be found at gateway.sandbox.push.apple.com, outbound TCP port 2195. The Production environment is meant to be used in applications that have been deployed and can be found at gateway.push.apple.com, outbound TCP port 2195.

For each environment, a separate certificate is needed, which I'll cover in just a bit.

APNS-Sharp

The protocols for interacting with APNS are very low-level binary calls over HTTPS, rather than easily accessible XML or JSON web services. You can read more about them in the *Local and Push Notification Programming Guide*, which can be found in the iOS developer documentation. With that said however, the APNS services have been wrapped many times over, using many different technologies, so there's no need to implement the plumbing yourself.

In this chapter, we're going to explore calling APNS using APNS-Sharp, an open-source C# library written by Jon Dick that does all the hard work for us. You can find the APNS-Sharp project at http://code.google.com/p/apns-sharp. Both the pre-compiled DLL binaries and the source code can be found there. There is also an example MonoTouch client application, as well as server examples, showing how to use the library.

Identifying Devices

When your server application sends a remote notification, it needs to specify the device that should receive it. In order to accomplish this, each iOS device has a unique device token that identifies it from other devices. When you send a notification via APNS, it expects a device token, which it then uses to route the notification to the correct device.

It's the responsibility of your server application to store the device token of each iOS device that it sends notifications to. Typically, the pattern is as follows:

- **Application registration:** An iOS application registers itself with your server application (typically via an http web service call), and passes its device token, as well as any other relevant information.

- **Notification sending:** Your server application calls APNS with the appropriate application certification and passes the device token of the intended recipient device, as well as the notification message that will be sent.

At that point, APNS will try and contact the device identified by the token via its last known IP address.

Registering for Remote Notifications and Getting a Device Token

Getting a device token requires the following two steps:

1. Register with iOS for remote notifications.

2. Listen for successful or failed registration.

Let's take a look at how to do each of these.

Registering to Receive Remote Notifications in iOS

In your FinishedLaunching method of your application delegate class, you need to call RegisterForRemoteNotificationTypes on the current UIApplication object. This calls the APNS in the background, which generates a device token and pushes it back to the device.

When you register your application to receive remote notifications, you must tell iOS what kind of notification accouterments you'd like to use (found in the

UIRemoteNotificationType enumeration). For example, the following code specifies that a remote notification for your application should cause an alert, and badge your application icon (the badge number that will be applied is sent in the notification itself). See Listing 18–8.

Listing 18–8. *Registering with iOS to receive remote notifications*

```
UIRemoteNotificationType notificationTypes =
        UIRemoteNotificationType.Alert | UIRemoteNotificationType.Badge;
UIApplication.SharedApplication.RegisterForRemoteNotificationTypes(notificationTypes);
```

Receiving the Token

Once the device receives a reply from APNS with a device token, it calls the RegisteredForRemoteNotifications method in your application delegate class and passes the registered device token. You should override this method and in it, call your server application to register the device token. The device token can change every time the device is registered with APNS, however, in practice it doesn't change very often, so you can optimize this method to cache the last token and only re-register it with your server application if the token has change.

The token is passed as an NSData object that you can call ToString on, in order to use it. See Listing 18–9.

Listing 18–9. *Retrieving the device token*

```
public override void RegisteredForRemoteNotifications (UIApplication application
        , NSData deviceToken)
{
        this._deviceToken = deviceToken.ToString();
        // code to register with your server application goes here
}
```

Listening for Registration Failure

If the device isn't connected to the Internet, registration will fail, in which case FailedToRegisterForRemoteNotifications will be called. If you have any logic that relies on remote notifications, you may want to set a timer and retry calling RegisterForRemoteNotificationTypes. Additionally, you can choose to show the error to the user, for example, Listing 18–10 shows an alert view if registration fails.

Listing 18–10. *Showing an error when remote notification registration fails*

```
public override void FailedToRegisterForRemoteNotifications (UIApplication application
        , NSError error)
{
        new UIAlertView("Error registering push notifications"
                , error.LocalizedDescription, null, "OK", null).Show();
}
```

Retrieving Expired Tokens with the Feedback Service

Device tokens change and expire. As such, you don't necessarily want to keep a bunch of expired tokens stored in your server application. When your application sends a push notification to a device that has an expired token, APNS tracks that and saves it. It then provides a mechanism to query that data and find out what tokens have expired.

This is known as the Feedback Service, and is exposed as an HTTPS endpoint that authenticates via the same certificate used to send push notifications. Once you connect to the endpoint, it responses back a binary stream of data that contains a list of the tokens that have expired. For more information on the details of this service, see the *Local and Push Notification Programming Guide* in the iOS developer documentation.

To retrieve expired tokens using APNS-Sharp, you instantiate a new `FeedbackService` object, wire up the `OnFeedback` event and call Run on the object. See Listing 18–11.

Listing 18–11. *Retrieving expired tokens using APNS-Sharp*

```
FeedbackService service = new FeedbackService(sandbox, p12Filename, p12FilePassword);
service.Feedback += new FeedbackService.OnFeedback(service_Feedback);
service.Run();
```

The FeedbackService class needs a Personal Information Exchange (PKCS12) certificate that you've registered with Apple for your application, which I'll cover in the very next section.

The `OnFeedback` event handler is called for each expired device token and is passed a Feedback object. The token itself is available via the `DeviceToken` property of the Feedback object.

For more information, and to see this code in action, check out the `JdSoft.Apple.Apns.Feedback.Test` project, which is part of the APNS-Sharp source download.

Creating a Push Notification Certificate

In order to use APNS, you need to first create a push notification certificate for your application. Ultimately, you will need to create a certificate for both the Sandbox and the Production environment, but during development, you only need the Sandbox certification.

Push notification certificates are created at developer.apple.com, by doing the following:

1. Log in at developer.apple.com and navigate to the iOS Provisioning Portal, shown in Figure 18–3.

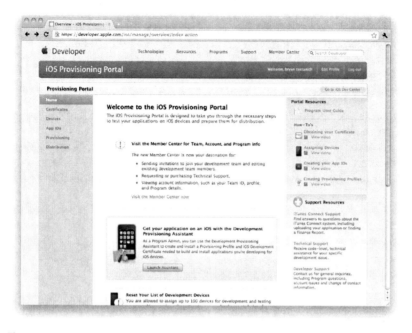

Figure 18–3. *iOS Provisioning portal*

2. Next, navigate to the App IDs section and create a new App ID. The
    resulting app ID will look something like Figure 18–4.

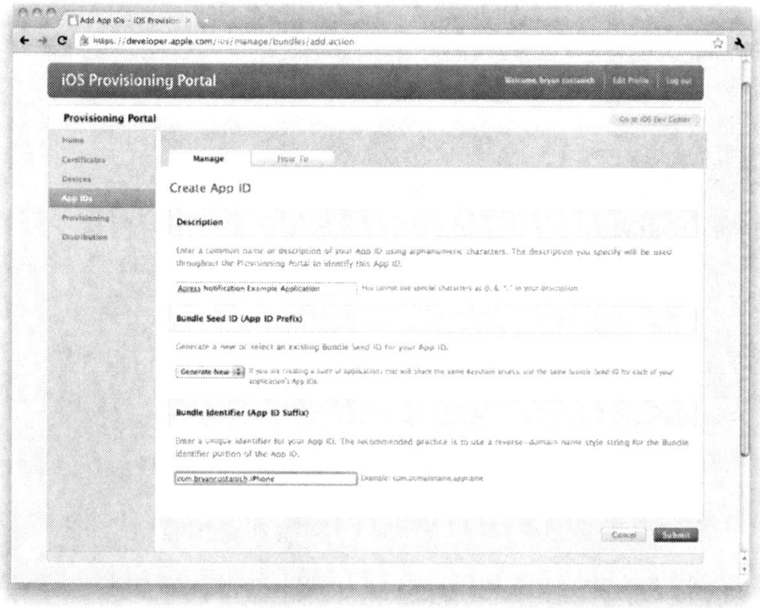

Figure 18–4. *Creating a new App ID*

> **CAUTION:** Make sure that when you create the Bundle Identifier you don't create a wildcard (an identifier that ends with * and is good for multiple applications), because push notification certificates are application specific.

3. Next, you need to create the certificate for that app ID. Check the **Enable for Apple Push Notification Service** for the environment you want, (development or production). See Figure 18–5.

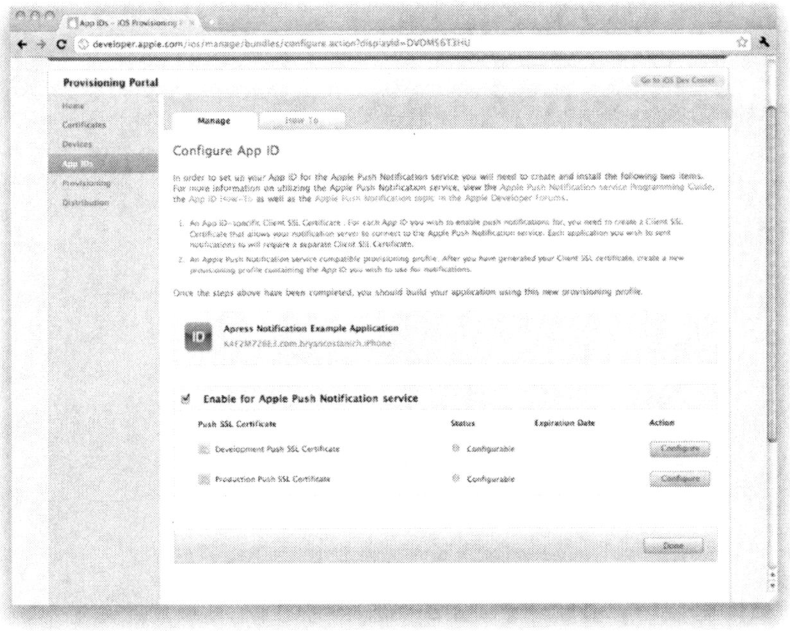

Figure 18–5. *Configuring the newly created App ID*

This will launch a wizard that will take you through the process of creating a Certificate Signing Request using the Keychain Access Application and then uploading it to the Apple Developer Portal so that a certificate can be created.

You should make sure to use Safari or Firefox, because this process fails miserably in Google Chrome.

Creating and Installing a Provisioning Profile

After you've created the certificate, you need to create an install a provisioning profile that uses it. Once you have created and installed the provisioning profile, you build your application with that provisioning profile, which will sign your application with the certificate that is registered with apple for push notifications.

Provisioning profiles are created in the iOS Provisioning Portal, similarly to creating app IDs.

To create a provisioning profile, perform the following steps:

1. Sign in at developer.apple.com and navigate to the iOS Provisioning Portal.

2. Select the Provisioning tab and create a new provisioning profile with the correct application selected, and any devices you want to enable it for. See Figure 18–6.

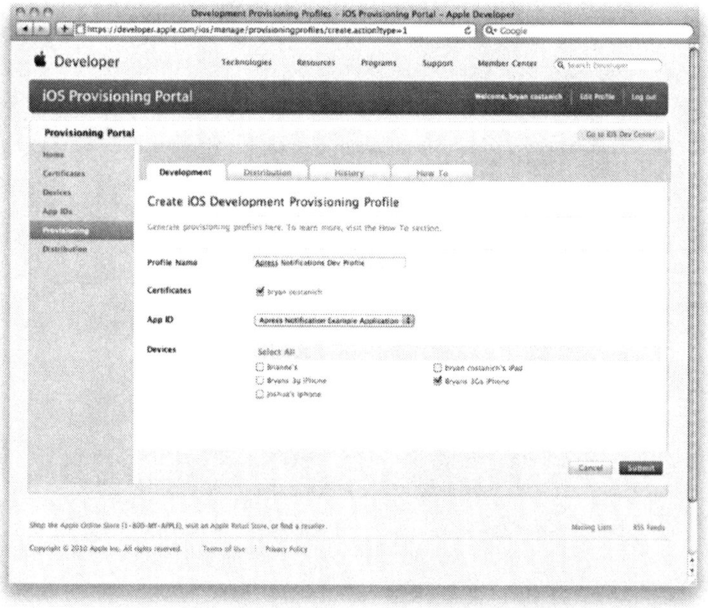

Figure 18–6. *Creating a new provisioning profile*

3. Once you've created the provisioning profile, open your Xcode Organizer and refresh it. It should now show up as in Figure 18–7.

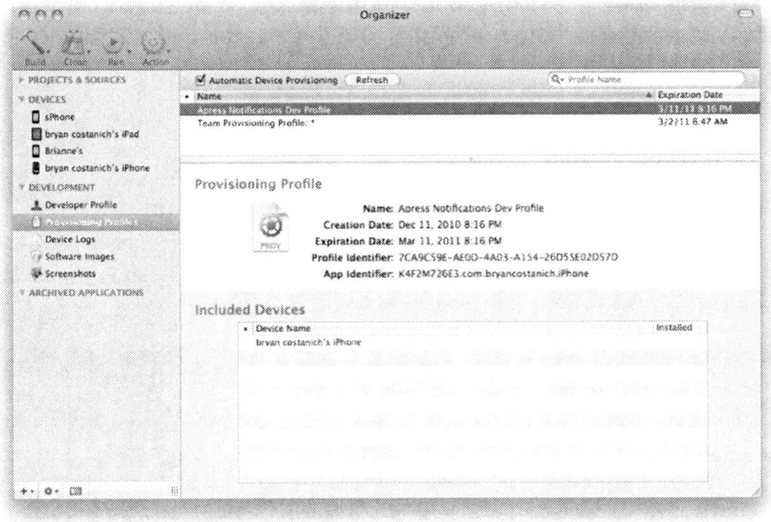

Figure 18–7. *Creating a new provisioning profile*

Sometimes the new profile doesn't show up right away. If that happens, you can download it from the iOS Provisioning Portal and manually import it into the Xcode Organizer.

Once you have your provisioning profile installed in the Xcode Organizer, you need to configure your project in MonoDevelop to use it. Right-click on your project and choose **Options**, then choose **iPhone Bundle Signing** and select the new provisioning profile that was created for notifications. See Figure 18–8.

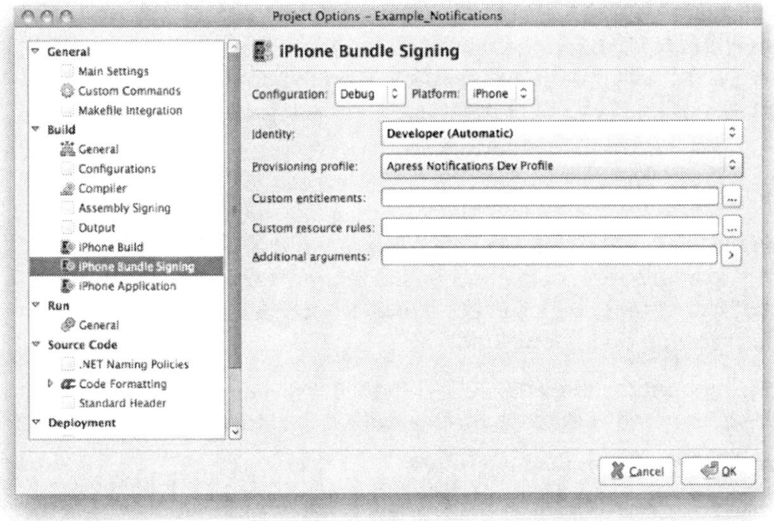

Figure 18–8. *Configuring the provisioning profile to be used in MonoDevelop*

Now your application is configured to utilize your push notification provisioning profile. We already covered how to handle remote notifications in the Handling Notifications section, so let's take a look at how to send some.

Sending Push Notifications

The body of the notification itself is just a JSON formatted string, however, communicating with APNS can be quite tedious if you're implementing your own library. If you are, the protocol and format is well documented in the *Local and Push Notification Programming Guide* in the iOS developer documentation.

This section assumes you're writing a .NET server application using APNS-Sharp, which saves you from writing all the plumbing necessary to communicate with APNS.

Converting the Certificate

The push notification certificate created via the iOS Provisioning Portal is in DER format, however, APNS-Sharp needs it in Personal Information Exchange (PKCS12) format. The easiest way to convert is to do the following:

- **Download the certificate file:** Login to the iOS Provisioning Portal, choose the Certificates tab, select the certificate associated with the correct provisioning profile and choose Download.

- **Open Keychain Access:** You can find key it under Applications/Utilities.

- **Import the certificate:** If the certificate isn't already installed, click the "+" button, navigate to the certificate, and select it.

- **Export the certificate:** Expand the certificate so the associated private key is visible, select both and right-click on the selection, and choose Export. It'll prompt you to name it and then ask for a password.

Sending a Notification

After you've exported the .p12 certificate, you can now use APNS-Sharp to send a notification. For the full example of how to send notifications, check out the JdSoft.Apple.Apns.Notifications.Test sample console application project (which is part of the APNS-Sharp source code download).

To use the application, open up the Main.cs file and modify the values in following lines to match your settings, and copy the certificate into the output directory. See Listing 18–12.

Listing 18–12. *Configuring the APNS-Sharp notification test code*

```
string testDeviceToken =
"fe58fc8f527c363d1b775dca133e04bff24dc5032d08836992395cc56bfa62ef";
string p12File = "apn_developer_identity.p12";
string p12FilePassword = "yourpassword";
```

Then, run the application, and a notification will be sent to your iOS application via APNS.

Summary

In this chapter we covered both local and push (remote) notifications. We saw that handling both types of notifications is nearly identical, however local notifications are much easier to code. Local notifications provide a mechanism in which applications running in the background can prompt users to bring the application to the foreground and push notifications provide a way for your application to be updated via server applications.

In the next chapter, we're going to finish up the section on core iOS features and examine how to work with local SQLite database in iOS.

Chapter **19**

Working with Data

When building applications of any complexity, it's quite common to need to persist and retrieve data locally. There are a few different options at your disposal within MonoTouch. First, you can use the XML features in .NET to read and write to XML files and access data that way. Second, you can use the built-in SQLite database and access it via various technologies. Finally, you can use Apple's CoreData framework as a data persistence and access technology.

We won't cover either XML or CoreData, for a couple reasons. First, reading and writing XML in MonoTouch is just like reading and writing XML in .NET, so if you're interested in that, I would recommend the .NET documentation. Second, as compared to even the most basic ADO.NET and XML serialization technology in .NET, CoreData is fairly antiquated, and since we've got the .NET base class library (BCL) at our disposal, there's no need to use with CoreData.

Instead, we're going to focus on SQLite (which is built into iOS), and cover the following data access technologies that we can use to communicate with it:

- **ADO.NET**

- **SQLite-Net**

- **Vici Cool Storage**

- **NHibernate**

By the end of this chapter, you'll have a solid understanding of SQLite and how to work with it. You'll also have a good understanding of several data access technologies that work with it, and be able to make an informed decision on which technology to use, depending on your needs.

Let's get started by first examining SQLite.

SQLite

SQLite (http://sqlite.org) is an open-source, cross-platform, embedded database technology created by D. Richard Hipp and initially released in 2000.

SQLite is what's known as an embedded database, because, unlike server or desktop databases, SQLite does not run in its own process and listen for connections. Instead, it's a referenced library that runs within the same process of the application that uses it. Furthermore, iOS has the SQLite library included by default, and you don't have to explicitly reference it in your application in order to use it (MonoTouch actually handles this for you under the hood).

SQLite is also incredibly fast and lightweight, though it lacks a number of features that you would find in full-blown databases, such as Microsoft SQL Server or Oracle. We'll take a look at some of these limitations in just a bit.

All in all, SQLite is a very solid database technology that is optimized for mobile and embedded applications. However, let's take a look at some of its limitations first, before we dig into working with it.

Limitations of SQLite

Because SQLite is a lightweight, embedded database, it doesn't have some of the features that you'd expect to find in an enterprise relational database management system (RDBMS), such as:

- **No stored procedure support:** SQLite doesn't have a concept of store procedures, or stored queries that are saved to the database and then later executed by name.

- **Read-only views:** Views in SQLite are read-only; they cannot be edited.

- **Partial trigger support:** Trigger support in SQLite is very basic.

- **Limited alter table support:** The Alter Table SQL statement doesn't allow column deletion or modification.

- **Limited database and object sizes:** There are a number of limits on the size of the database, the length of columns, data sizes, and so on. For a full list see www.sqlite.org/limits.html.

■ **No concurrency support:** To keep SQLite technologically uncomplicated, it implements Reader/Writer locks, so that whenever a process is reading or writing to any part of the database, all other processes are blocked until the action is finished. In most mobile application situations, this doesn't really matter, because the locks only persist for a few milliseconds, and it's nearly impossible to spin up enough threads and eek out enough processing power on an iOS device to make this have any real impact.

There are also a number of other limitations not mentioned here. For more information, check out the SQLite documentation at www.sqlite.org/docs.html.

Because of the nature of mobile applications, however, most of the limitations of SQLite are inconsequential.

Version Matrix

Although not terribly important, as features have changed little between versions that are deployed with iOS devices, Table 19–1 is a version matrix of what version of SQLite is installed in what iOS version.

Table 19–1. *Version Matrix*

iOS Version	SQLite Version
3.1.3	3.6.12
4.0.2	3.6.22
4.1.0	3.6.23.2
4.2.0	3.6.23.2

If you run into any strange issues across different iOS versions, you may want to reference this matrix to determine if there was a bug in the particular version of SQLite that was deployed with that particular version of iOS.

Creating a Database

There are two ways to create a SQLite database: either with a tool, or programmatically at runtime. Because of the simple nature of most mobile application database needs, it's typically far more common to create the database at runtime, and I cover how to do this later on when we examine the various SQLite data access technologies available in MonoTouch.

However, if you prefer to create your database beforehand, there are a number of tools available. Some of the more popular ones are as follows:

▪ **SQLite Manager:** SQLite Manager (https://addons.mozilla.org/en-US/firefox/addon/5817/) is a free plugin for Mozilla Firefox that provides a comprehensive GUI for designing, creating, and querying SQLite database files.

▪ **SQLite Studio:** SQLite Studio (http://sqlitestudio.one.pl) is a free, standalone, cross-platform GUI that does essentially the same thing as SQLite Manager.

▪ **Navicat for SQLite:** Navicat for SQLite (www.navicat.com/en/products/navicat_sqlite/sqlite_overview.html) is a commercial product based on the Navicat application, which is available for a number of different database technologies. The GUI is a little more polished than the previous two applications I mentioned, but it doesn't really have much more to offer in terms of features, primarily because SQLite is such a simple database product.

▪ **Visual Studio:** Visual Studio has a built-in database designer that can be used with SQLite by installing the ADO.NET SQLite provider. For a tutorial of how to use it with SQLite, see Peter Bromberg's excellent post at www.eggheadcafe.com/tutorials/aspnet/20f7912e-6fa7-40eb-b31b-b6f46d4f2c6a/get-started-with-sqlite-a.aspx.

With the aforementioned products in mind, I recommend reading through the SQLite data access technologies section before creating a SQLite database with one of these tools. You may find, especially in the case of the SQLite-Net ORM tool, it can be far easier to simply create the database programmatically, as part of your application logic.

Backups and Data Update Strategy

One of the more challenging things when building iOS applications is how to handle application upgrades, and peripherally, backup and restores.

Backups

Handling application backup and restores in the iOS is fairly easy. If you want your application to retain its data in the event that the application is being restored from a backup in iTunes, you should make sure to store the database file in one of the folders that gets backed up such as the Documents or Library folder. If you're application allows file-sharing in iTunes, any files that are in the Documents folder are editable, so if you want to hide your database from users, you should put it in the Library folder.

Both of these folders are also preserved during application updates.

For more information on application folders, see Chapter 13.

Application Updates

If you want your database to persist when the application is updated (e.g., you upload a new version to the App Store), you should store your database in either the Documents or the Library folder. When iTunes installs a new version of the application, the items in the Documents and Library folder are copied over to the new application directory, and the old application directory is deleted.

This is fine if your application update doesn't require any schema changes. However, if it does, this is where things get tricky. If you create a new version of your application that has a change to the database schema, but you want it to retain the data from the old application install, you need to write logic to migrate the data. Generally, the process I recommend is as follows:

- **Version your database:** By giving either your database file a versioned name, such as MyAppData_v1.db or MyAppData_v1_2.db, when your application gets upgraded, you can check to see what existing database version is present, and it knows what upgrade path to take.

- **Check for old databases when first run:** If you version your application and data schema, the application should check to see if an existing database exists with an older schema. If it does, then you should go to the next step.

- **Migrate old data:** If an older database is present, your application should run code to create a new database, and import data from the old database. While this is occurring, you should let the user know that the application is being configured for first use by showing an alert or a screen with a message and a busy activity indicator.

- **Delete the old database:** Once the old data has been migrated, your code should delete the old database so any future application launches won't see it and try to import stale data.

Additionally, because an end user can skip application updates, you'll want to write migration paths for different versions of your database schemas. For example, say you have application and database schema versions 1, 2, and 3. In version 3 of your application, you should have migration code for not only version 2 to version 3, but also version 1 to version 3. However, in order to save on code and testing, you may also simply want to call successive upgrade paths. For instance, version 3 of your application could include both a version 1 to version 2 upgrade path, as well as a version 2 to version 3 upgrade path. Then, if the user upgraded to version 3 from version 1, your application would first migrate the data to the version 2 schema, and then, the version 3 schema.

Data Access Technologies

Like any other popular database technology, SQLite has considerable driver support, and as such there are a number of data access technologies that you can use to communicate with it.

I'm going to cover a few of these that are popular and/or readily available for use in MonoTouch.

To keep the sample code simple and easy to understand, I'm going to do the following tasks with each technology:

1. **Create a database:** The database will be a blank SQLite database with no schema or data in it.

2. **Create a simple schema:** I'll create a single table, called People, that has FirstName and LastName columns, as well as an auto-incrementing primary key column called ID.

3. **Add data:** Next, I'm going to add several records to it.

4. **Retrieve data:** Finally, I'm going to retrieve the rows that I added and display it in a table.

You can see each of these examples in the Example_Data companion application and code.

Additionally, in the source code, I've included some rough performance checking code that measures the time taken by each of these technologies to perform these tasks.

Okay, onto the data access technologies. Let's take a look at tried and true ADO.NET.

ADO.NET

ADO.NET (System.Data) was introduced in 2001, and aside from LINQ to SQL and Entity Framework (both of which are built on top of it, and neither of which are available in Mono on the iPhone), it hasn't changed much since then.

As such, it's pretty outdated from an architectural perspective; however, it's still a reliable and well-known way to access data. It's architecturally outdated, because it requires you to do everything manually – there is no built-in mapping to entities or any other data access sugar. Instead it's all queries, record sets, and the like.

The heavy lifting in MonoTouch's SQLite ADO.NET implementation is actually in the Mono.Data.Sqlite assembly (which can be referenced in your project by right-clicking on the References folder and selecting Edit References), which largely mirrors the System.Data implementation for SQL Server databases and the like. This is where you'll find the SqliteConnection class, which is responsible for most of the work.

Creating a Database

To create a new, blank SQLite database, you simply call the static `CreateFile` method on the `SqliteConnection` class and pass a path to where the file should be created. So for instance, if we wanted to create a database file named db_adonet.db3 in your application's documents folder, you would do the following (see Listing 19–1).

Listing 19–1. *Creating a new, blank SQLite database on disk*

```
string dbName = "db_adonet.db3";
var documents = Environment.GetFolderPath (Environment.SpecialFolder.Personal);
string db = Path.Combine (documents, dbName);
SqliteConnection.CreateFile (db);
```

Creating a Schema and Adding Data

When working with SQLite via ADO.NET, you simply send it queries described in SQL statements. For a full list of what statements that SQLite understands, see http://sqlite.org/lang.html.

For example, to create a table in SQLite, you can build a CREATE TABLE SQL statement and then call ExecuteNonQuery on the SqliteCommand object that you create from a SqliteConnection object. Likewise, for inserting data, you build an INSERT statement and execute it the same way (see Listing 19–2).

Listing 19–2. *Executing queries that create a table and then insert data into it*

```
//---- create a an array of commands
var commands = new[]
{
        "CREATE TABLE People (PersonID INTEGER PRIMARY KEY AUTOINCREMENT
                , FirstName ntext, LastName ntext)",
        "INSERT INTO People (FirstName, LastName) VALUES ('Peter', 'Gabriel')",
        "INSERT INTO People (FirstName, LastName) VALUES ('Thom', 'Yorke')",
        "INSERT INTO People (FirstName, LastName) VALUES ('J', 'Spaceman')",
        "INSERT INTO People (FirstName, LastName) VALUES ('Benjamin', 'Gibbard')"
};

//---- execute each command, using standard ADO.NET calls
foreach (var cmd in commands)
{
        using (var c = connection.CreateCommand())
        {
                c.CommandText = cmd;
                c.CommandType = CommandType.Text;
                connection.Open ();
                c.ExecuteNonQuery ();
                connection.Close ();
        }
}
```

Selecting Data

As with creating database objects and inserting data, to select data you construct queries and then execute them as commands. If you want to get a record set back, you can call ExecuteReader on the command. If your query returns a single value, you can call ExecuteScalar.

For example, Listing 19–3 selects all rows from the People table, loops through each row, and adds the data to a List of string objects so we can display it on the page.

Listing 19–3. *Executing a query that brings back a record set*

```
//---- create a command
using (var cmd = connection.CreateCommand ())
{
        //---- open the connection
        connection.Open ();
        //---- create a select statement
        cmd.CommandText = "SELECT * FROM People";
        using (var reader = cmd.ExecuteReader ())
        {
                //---- loop through each record and add the name to our collection
                while (reader.Read ())
                        { this._people.Add(reader[1] + " " + reader[2]); }
        }
        //---- close the connection
        connection.Close ();
}
```

As you can see, using ADO.NET with SQLite is fairly straightforward, although it requires manual creation of all your queries.

SQLite-Net

One of the most popular technologies for data access in MonoTouch is SQLite-Net. SQLite-Net is an open-source (http://code.google.com/p/sqlite-net), lightweight object-relational mapping (ORM) framework created by Frank Krueger (an active member of the MonoTouch community and the author of iCircuit, one of my top-10 favorite iOS applications).

SQLite-Net is incredibly fast, up to five times faster than ADO.NET in my crude testing, and also greatly simplifies data access.

Like all ORMs, SQLite-Net provides a mapping between your business objects and your database, which allows you to persist and retrieve data from your database without having to write queries or convert records into objects. Instead, ORMs do that work for you.

Because of its simplicity and lightweight design, however, SQLite-Net is not a full-featured ORM that handles complex mappings, such as NHibernate. However, for 99% of the data requirements of a mobile application, it's more than sufficient, and its speed is unbeatable.

SQLite-Net is available as a single C# file (sqlite.cs) that is intended to be integrated directly into your project. There is no binary to reference, you simply copy the file into your project and reference the classes within it.

Database Creation

To create a new, blank SQLite database, you simply instantiate a new SQLite.SQLiteConnection and pass it the path to the database. If the database doesn't exist, it will create it and return a connection to the database. For example, Listing 19–4 creates a database (if one doesn't already exist).

Listing 19–4. *Creating a database with SQLite-Net*

```
string dbName = "db_sqlite-net.db3";
var documents = Environment.GetFolderPath (Environment.SpecialFolder.Personal);
string dbPath = Path.Combine (documents, dbName);
SQLiteConnection db = new SQLiteConnection(dbPath);
```

If the database already exists, it will simply create a connection object specific to that database that we can then use to persist and retrieve data.

Object Mapping

To understand how SQLite-Net works, we need to first understand object mappings. In the ADO.NET examples, we added data via queries, and retrieved data via a DataReader that was created from a query. With ORMs, you don't typically use queries in that manner. Instead, you define an object model that maps to your database. For example, consider the following class in Listing 19–5, which maps 1:1 with our People table.

Listing 19–5. *A Person object, which maps to the People table*

```
[Table("People")]
public class Person
{
        public Person () { }
        [PrimaryKey, AutoIncrement]
        public int ID { get; set; }
        public string FirstName { get; set; }
        public string LastName { get; set; }
}
```

We can use this class to automatically create our table schema, and persist data to the database with it.

Table Creation and Data Import

To create a table in SQLite-Net, you call the CreateTable<T> method on the instantiated SQLiteConnection object and pass in the object that defines the table for T. CreateTable<T> is a safe call (like instantiating a new SQLiteConnection object), in that it will only create the table if the table doesn't already exist.

You can then add data to the database directly via instantiated objects that map to that table. For example, given the Person class illustrated in Listing 19–5, Listing 19–6 creates a connection to a database (who's path is defined in dbPath), creates the People table (via CreateTable<Person>), and then adds a collection of Person objects to that table via the InsertAll method.

Listing 19–6. *Creating a table and inserting data using object mappings rather than SQL queries in SQLite-Net*

```
using(SQLiteConnection db = new SQLiteConnection(dbPath))
{
        //---- create the tables
        db.CreateTable<Person>();

        //---- declare vars
        List<Person> people = new List<Person>();
        Person person;

        //---- create a list of people that we're going to insert
        person = new Person() { FirstName = "Peter", LastName = "Gabriel" };
        people.Add(person);
        person = new Person() { FirstName = "Thom", LastName = "Yorke" };
        people.Add(person);
        person = new Person() { FirstName = "J", LastName = "Spaceman" };
        people.Add(person);
        person = new Person() { FirstName = "Benjamin", LastName = "Gibbard" };
        people.Add(person);

        //---- insert our people
        db.InsertAll(people);

        //---- close the connection
        db.Close();
}
```

Additionally, we could have inserted a single object via the Insert method.

Interestingly enough, even though SQLite-Net uses reflection to determine the nature of the data and perform the mapping to the database, if you run this example side-by-side with the ADO.NET example, which does the same thing, you'll find that this runs anywhere from four to ten times as fast.

It also provides an architecture that is much easier to work with, because you can work with objects directly, rather than complicated SQL queries and lots of manual code to turn data that comes back from them into objects.

Selecting Data

As with table creation and data insertion, selecting data is also very easy, and you get populated business objects back, rather than record sets. For example, to get a collection of all the Person objects in the People table, you would simply do the following (see Listing 19–7).

Listing 19–7. *Selecting data from the People table*

```
var people = from p in db.Table<Person>() select p;
```

Because the Person object maps to that table, all the hard work is done for us.

There are many more ways to query data. For example, Listing 19–8 returns a Person by its ID.

Listing 19–8. *Selecting a single record from a table*

```
public Person GetPerson (int id)
{
        return (from i in Table<Person> () where i.ID == id select i).FirstOrDefault();
}
```

You can also do advanced filtering and sorting as well. For more information, check out the wiki documents up on the project home page at http://code.google.com/p/sqlite-net/w/list.

Vici CoolStorage

Another ORM that is available for MonoTouch is Vici CoolStorage (http://viciproject.com/wiki/Projects/CoolStorage/MonoTouch).

Vici CoolStorage is somewhere between SQLite-Net and NHibernate in terms of features. It's not as simple as SQLite-Net to use, but has some more features when it comes to mapping. However, it's not as powerful as NHibernate, but is slightly faster.

I personally do not care for Vici CoolStorage. It requires quite a bit of mangling and modification to your business classes, and it's architecturally awkward. It requires the use of its specialized list classes and subclasses your business objects, and those subclasses are then what you use for in your application. This in turn tightly couples your application to your data access layer, a huge architectural no-no, because it prevents you from easily switching out data access technologies.

It's also, in my crude performance testing, twice as slow as SQLite-Net. However, it does have more advanced mapping features than SQLite-Net (including relationship maps, which don't exist in SQLite-Net).

Let's first take a look at the object mapping in Vici CoolStorage.

Object Mapping

Setting up your object maps in Vici CoolStorage is a little strange. Like many ORMs, you can attribute your classes to describe the mapping. However, Vici CoolStorage takes it even further. Your class has to inherit from the CSObject class, which can throw a wrench in your design, since C# only has single inheritance. Additionally, because of a quirk in how it was designed (and a limitation in MonoTouch that Reflection.Emit is unavailable), your properties have to be wrappers on underlying getters and setters provided by the CSObject class.

For example, the Person class in Listing 19–9 provides the same mapping as we saw in Listing 19–4, but is mapped per Vici CoolStorage's requirements.

Listing 19–9. *Object mapping in Vici CoolStorage*

```
[MapTo("People")]
public class Person : CSObject<Person, int>
{
        public Person () { }
        public int ID { get { return (int)GetField("PersonID"); } }
        public string FirstName { get { return (string)GetField("FirstName"); }
                set { SetField("FirstName",value); } }
        public string LastName { get { return (string)GetField("LastName"); }
                set { SetField("LastName",value); } }
}
```

Creating a Database

Creating a database is similar to creating a connection in SQLite-Net. You call the static SetDB method on the CSConfig object, pass it the path to the database, provide an option to create the database if it doesn't exist, and finally, a delegate to execute after the database is created and the connection is made.

One of the major flaws in this architecture, however, is that unlike SQLite-Net, or even ADO.NET, once you've set your database context via SetDB, you can only connect to that one database. Whereas in SQLite-Net or ADO.NET, the database is connection object specific, so you can work with multiple databases at once. See Listing 19–10.

Listing 19–10. Creating and connecting to a SQLite database with Vici CoolStorage

```
CSConfig.SetDB(dbPath, SqliteOption.CreateIfNotExists, null);
```

Table Creation and Data Import

Creating tables and other objects in Vici CoolStorage is also kind of a drag, since it requires you to write SQL statements, and you don't get any of the ORM sugar you get with SQLite-Net. Inserting data, however, works mostly the same. You can add object data directly to the database (as long as the objects are mapped). There is one important difference, though: data persistence and retrieval is built into the objects themselves, and so instead of calling insertion or query methods on the database connection, you call them directly on the objects.

For example, Listing 19–11 expands on the previous example, and instead of just creating a database, it also creates our People table, and then inserts data into the table.

Listing 19–11. *Creating a table and inserting data*

```
//---- determine whether or not the database exists
bool dbExists = File.Exists(GetDBPath(dbName));

//---- configure the current database, create if it doesn't exist, and then run the
// anonymous delegate method after it's created
CSConfig.SetDB(GetDBPath(dbName), SqliteOption.CreateIfNotExists, () => {
        CSDatabase.ExecuteNonQuery("CREATE TABLE People
                (PersonID INTEGER PRIMARY KEY AUTOINCREMENT, FirstName text
                , LastName text)");
```

```
//---- if the database had to be created, let's populate with initial data
if(!dbExists)
{
        //---- declare vars
        CSList<Person> people = new CSList<Person>();
        Person person;

        //---- create a list of people that we're going to insert
        person = new Person() { FirstName = "Peter", LastName = "Gabriel" };
        people.Add(person);
        person = new Person() { FirstName = "Thom", LastName = "Yorke" };
        people.Add(person);
        person = new Person() { FirstName = "J", LastName = "Spaceman" };
        people.Add(person);
        person = new Person() { FirstName = "Benjamin", LastName = "Gibbard" };
        people.Add(person);

        //---- save the people collection to the database
        people.Save();
}
});
```

Notice that instead of List<Person>, we had to use CSList<Person>. Additionally, to persist the data to the database, we call the Save method on the Person object itself. This architecture prevents a coupling problem, in that now your application code is reliant on specialized classes that are used throughout the different layers of your application, which tightly bind it to the Vici CoolStorage library.

Query Data

As with persisting data, retrieving data is also performed on the object itself. See Listing 19–12.

Listing 19–12. *Retrieving all rows in a table*

```
CSList<Person> people = Person.List();
```

As with SQLite-Net, there are of course a number of ways to select single items, filter, sort, and the like. For more information, see the documentation at http://viciproject.com/wiki/Projects/CoolStorage/Doc/Walkthrough.

NHibernate

NHibernate (http://nhforge.org) is one of the, if not *the*, most popular ORM technologies available for the .NET platform. It started life as a port of Hibernate, which is essentially the same thing, for the Java platform. However, NHibernate has grown into a product in its own right, with a number of plugins and frameworks that are only available in .NET. NHibernate (and Hibernate for that matter) are open-source frameworks with lots of active community developers behind it, as well as a number of commercial tools for working with it.

NHibernate is more complicated to setup than SQLite-Net or Vici CoolStorage, but it is one of the most extensible and powerful ORMs in the market, while still being very fast.

For 99.99% of all mobile apps, NHibernate is overkill, so I'm only not going to spend much time on it. However, for the .01% of apps out there that have extremely complex schemas and complex mapping, NHibernate is a great product.

One of the biggest problems of using NHibernate with MonoTouch is that you cannot use the binaries directly, as they're compiled against the full desktop profile of .NET (rather than the client profile that MonoTouch uses). The code also references a couple features that are only in the full .NET profile, such as System.Configuration. However, it is possible to use NHibernate is MonoTouch (and MonoDroid for that matter), with a few tweaks.

If you're looking to build NHibernate for MonoTouch, I suggest first picking out which pieces and frameworks you want to use, as there are many to choose from, then building them into a console app to get it working. Once you've got the requisite pieces together, you can then move the source into MonoTouch projects and make the tweaks necessary to get it compiling and working under MonoTouch.

I have successfully gotten NHibernate + Fluent to compile and work under MonoTouch, but it did take some tweaking, and, as I mentioned, it's really only appropriate for certain situations. I recommend, instead, using SQLite-Net.

Summary

After reading this chapter, you should have a thorough understanding of how to work with SQLite, the built-in database technology in iOS. We covered what SQLite is, what its limitations are, some of the tools available for managing it. We also covered how to handle application upgrades and backups, and a number of data access technologies that are available on MonoTouch for accessing SQLite at runtime.

In terms of data access strategies, I recommend SQLite-Net for 99% of all MonoTouch/iOS applications. It's fast, lightweight, simple, and well architected. For the 0.9% of the time in which you need ADO.NET, it's also available, and for the 0.1% of all mobile applications that have extremely complex data needs, there is NHibernate.

This concludes the third part of this book. If you've been following along from front to back, and you've made it this far, pat yourself on the back. You're now a MonoTouch expert. In the next section we'll cover a few advanced/peripheral topics such as third-party libraries, integrating with Objective-C code, and submission to the App Store.

Chapter 20

Publishing to the App Store

So you've plowed through this book, and you've built an awesome application, and you're ready now to get it into Apple's App Store – the crowning achievement of iOS app developers. Well, let's cover a few things out of the way first, so that your submission to the App Store is as smooth as can be.

Submitting to the App Store can be a frustrating process, or it can be a quick, painless step along the way to making a profitable app. The goal of this chapter is to provide some guidance for your application so that your experience is closer to the latter of the two.

In this chapter we're going to cover the following path through App Store submission:

- Review Guideline Conformity
- Build the Application for Distribution
- Submit to App Store

This chapter assumes that you're already a member of Apple's developer program. If you're not, you'll need to sign up at `developer.apple.com` in order to be able to distribute applications in the App Store.

Review Guideline Conformity

The first thing you need to do when you're ready to publish to the App Store is to review Apple's guidelines and make sure that your application conforms to them. You can find the guidelines on the Apple Developer Site at:
`https://developer.apple.com/appstore/resources/approval/guidelines.html`.

NOTE: It's important to understand that these guidelines are just that, guidelines. They are not strict rules. While adherence to these will definitely improve your chance of getting your application approved for distribution via the App Store, Apple can be unpredictable. There have been many publicized instances of good applications not being approved. This, is, unfortunately Apple's playground, and it rules it absolutely.

The guidelines are subject to non-disclosure agreement, and Apple reserves the right to change the document. Therefore, I cannot reproduce them here, but the following are big no-nos when creating applications for the App Store:

- **No explicit content:** Steve Jobs has been extremely vocal about his aversion to allowing pornography in the iOS application ecosystem. As such, if your app has any explicit content that's not in an educational context, it will get rejected. This is a particularly sensitive sticking point with Apple, so I would urge you to err on the side of caution.

- **No private API calls:** There are many methods that you can call in the underlying iOS that are undocumented, and, therefore, are not public APIs. If you stick to the MonoTouch APIs, this isn't a problem, as they've only wrapped the public APIs. However, if you're manually calling undocumented Objective-C selectors, and your application reviewer(s) find out, your app stands a high chance of being rejected, as Apple has automated scanners that look for these calls in your binary.

- **No major bugs:** According to Apple, bugs (more specifically, crashing bugs) are the most common cause for rejection into the App Store. Before submitting, you should thoroughly test and stabilize your application. Some reviewers seem to be more thorough than others, but generally you should make sure that your application doesn't have any major bugs or crashes during normal usage.

- **Missing/incorrect functionality:** Aside from crashing bugs, the other thing that Apple notes as a common reason for getting rejected is missing functionality or functionality that doesn't match the description. You should make sure that your application works as advertised; if you say that your app has some particular functionality, make sure it has it.

Those are some of the biggest sticking points in the App Store submission review process, but there are many other things that are covered in the guidelines. Be sure to review them and make sure that your application conforms to them.

Apple Blog

In addition to the published guidelines, Apple maintains a public blog that is constantly being updated with tips on getting accepted to the app store, as well as a heads-up on changes and some common missteps. Be sure to check it out at `http://developer.apple.com/news/ios/appstoretips`.

Building for Distribution

After you've reviewed the guidelines and you've made sure that your application is stable and doesn't break the App Store rules, it's time to build it for submission.

Building for submission isn't much different than building for development, except that you have to sign it with a distribution identity that Apple recognizes. The general process is as follows:

1. Create a Distribution Provisioning Profile with Apple.

2. Install the Distribution Provisioning Profile.

3. Create a Distribution Build Configuration in MonoDevelop.

4. Configure Bundle Signing.

5. Build and zip the project in MonoDevelop.

Let's examine each of these steps.

Creating and Installing a Distribution Provisioning Profile

The first thing you need to do in order to build your application for distribution in the App Store is to create a provisioning profile for distribution and install it. Provisioning profiles are created and managed in the iOS Provisioning Portal, which can be found at developer.apple.com. Log in, navigate to the portal, and do the following:

1. **Create an App ID:** If you haven't already created an App ID for your application(s), create one. In the portal, click on **App IDs** on the left-hand navigation and follow the instructions to create a new App ID. If you want to share keychain information across multiple applications, you can use a single App ID for the entire application suite.

2. **Create a Distribution Provisioning Profile:** In the portal, click on **Provisioning** and then choose the **Distribution** tab. Click on the **New Profile** button and follow the instructions for creating a new profile. Make sure to choose the App ID that you just created.

3. **Install the Distribution Provisioning Profile:** Launch Xcode and open the Organizer from the **Window** menu. Click on **Provisioning Profiles** on the left-hand nav and then click **Refresh** in the main info pane. It will prompt you for your Apple developer login and download and install your newly created Distribution Provisioning Profile.

Once you have your new Distribution Provisioning Profile created and installed, you need to create a build configuration in MonoDevelop to use it.

Adding a Distribution Build Configuration

MonoDevelop automatically finds and uses your developer distribution profile/identity when building. However, if you want to distribute for the App Store, you must use your distribution identity, which will sign the application with the key recognized by Apple for distribution.

To create a distribution build configuration, right-click on your solution in MonoDevelop and choose **Options**. Then, under **Build ➤ Configuration**, add a new configuration named **Distribution** or some such, and select **iPhone** for the platform. See Figure 20–1.

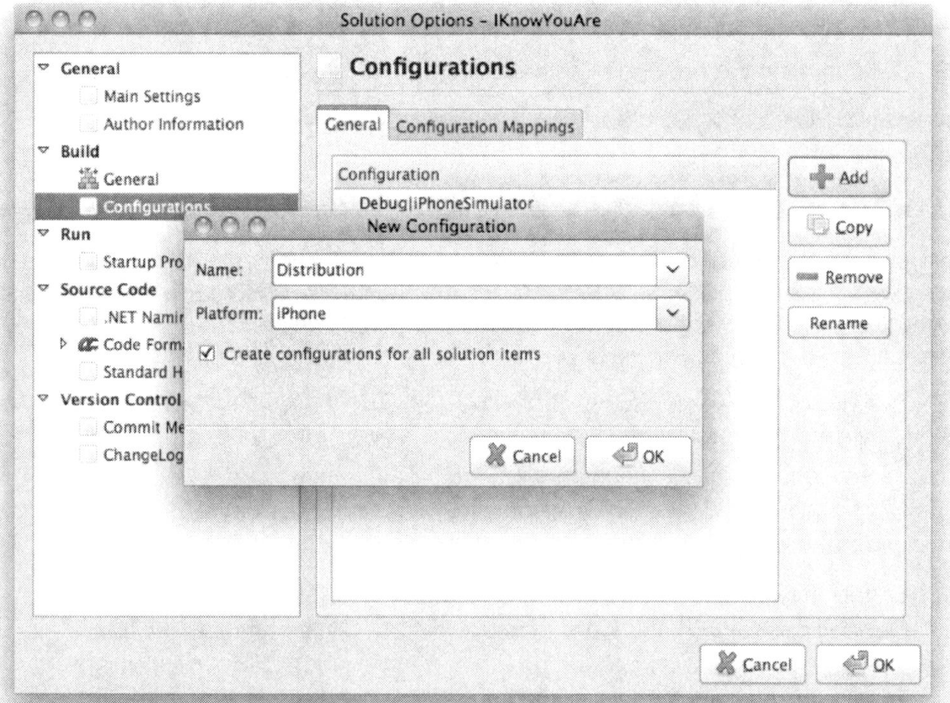

Figure 20–1. *Creating a distribution configuration in MonoDevelop*

NOTE: We've chosen iPhone as the platform, but all that really means is that we're not using the simulator, we're using the device. Really, the choices should be either iOS Simulator or iOS Device, and hopefully the MonoTouch team will update MonoDevelop in the future to reflect this and avoid confusion.

After we've created our distribution build configuration, we need to configure it to use the distribution provisioning profile that we created earlier.

Configure Distribution Bundle Signing

To configure the new distribution build configuration to use the distribution provisioning profile, right-click on the application project in MonoDevelop, choose **Options**, then choose **iPhone Bundle Signing** on the left. Next, change the configuration to be the distribution configuration (the one we created in the previous step), and then select your distribution identity for Identity and your newly installed distribution provisioning profile (see Figure 20–2).

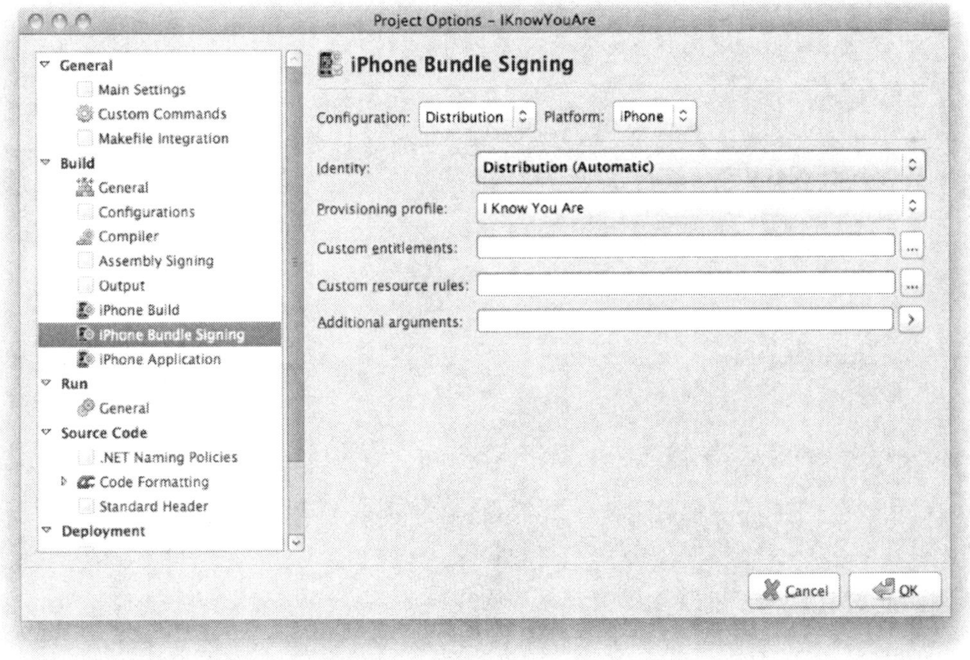

Figure 20–2. *Configuring distribution bundle signing*

Now you're ready to build your application.

Building

Our application is now ready to be built, but since we added a new build configuration, we need to make sure that all of our configuration options are set up for the new configuration. This is also a good opportunity to make sure that we're building with the latest iOS SDK. Apple will only accept applications built with the latest RTM (non-beta) SDK.

To configure your build, open the project options for you application and select **iPhone Build**. Change the configuration to **Distribution** and verify your build configuration (see Figure 20–3).

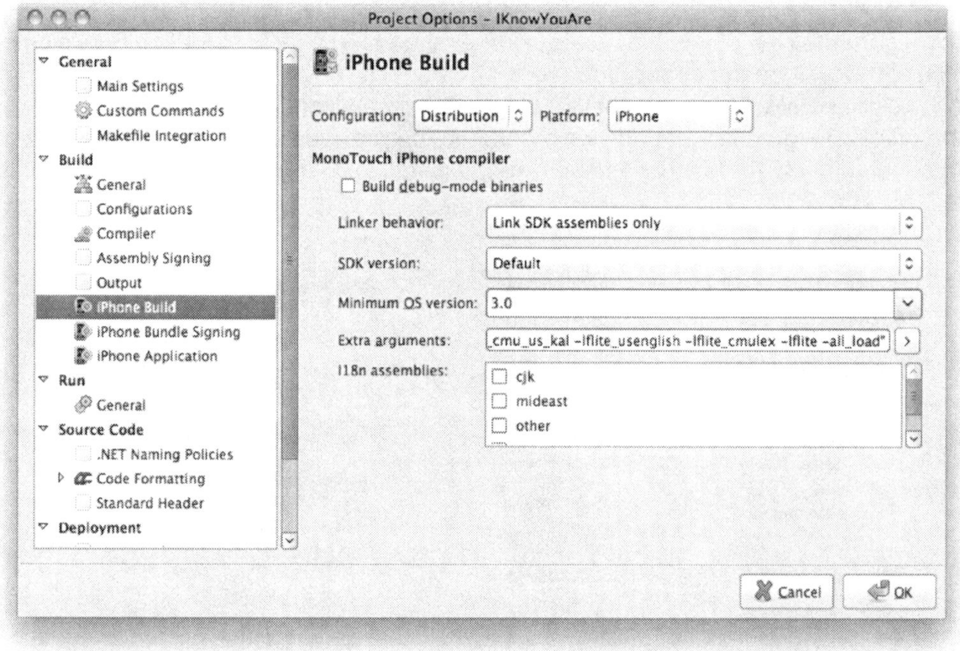

Figure 20–3. *Configuring distribution build*

Make sure that if you need any extra arguments for your build that they're in this configuration. When you're finished, click **OK**.

After your distribution build settings are configured, you can now build and zip the application bundle. You have two choices here: you can either do it manually or have MonoDevelop do it for you. I'll cover both methods, so that you know the easy way (having MonoDevelop do it for you), and also have an understanding of what's actually happening, by doing it yourself.

In either scenario, you first need to choose **Distribution|iPhone** from the active configuration drop down in the MonoDevelop toolbar (see Figure 20–4).

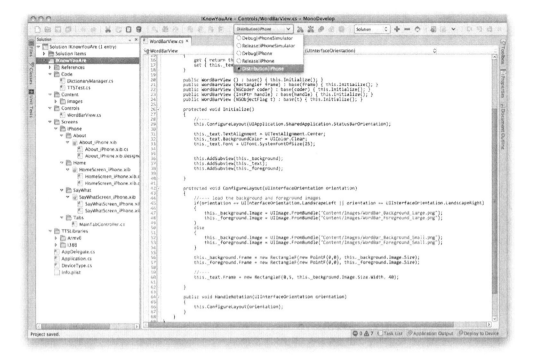

Figure 20–4. *Selecting the distribution build target*

This ensures that when your application is built, it uses the distribution profile you configured earlier.

Having MonoDevelop Build and Zip for You

To have MonoDevelop create the zipped bundle choose **Project ➤ Zip App Bundle** from the menu, and then choose the location to save the zip file (see Figure 20–5).

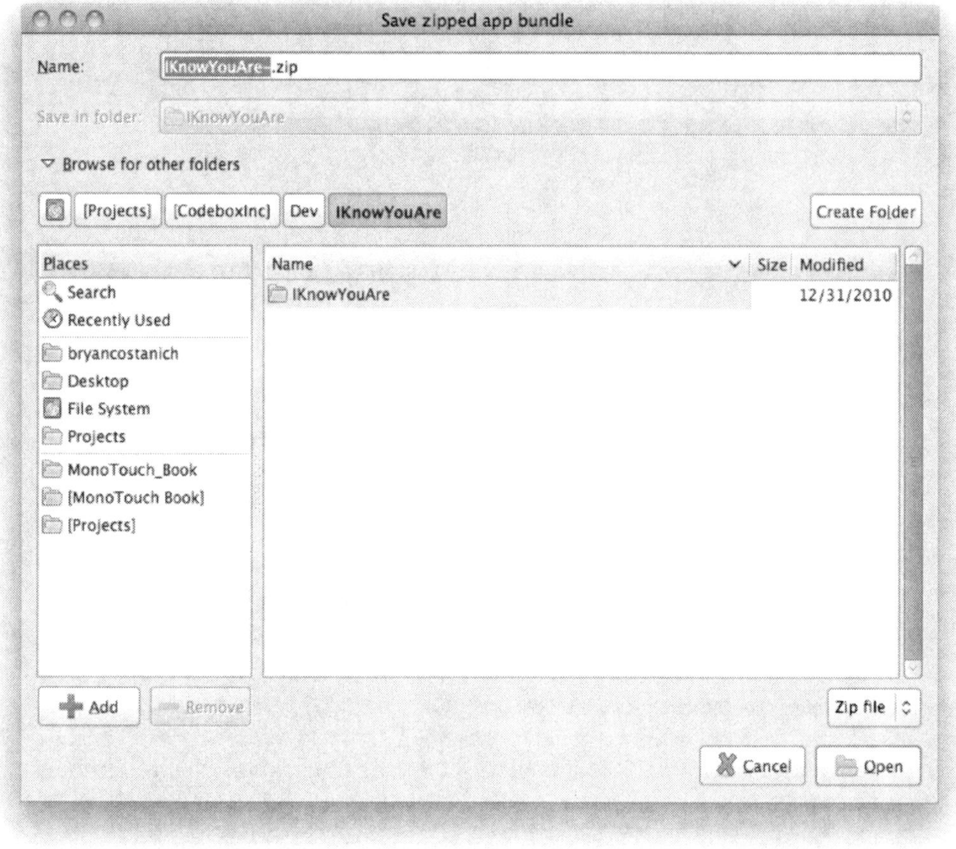

Figure 20–5. *Selecting the location to save your zipped application bundle*

This will build your application and then zip it up.

Manually Building and Zipping

If you don't want to use the tool in MonoDevelop, you can simply build as you normally do. Then, after your application is built, you need to go get the resulting .APK file that you'll upload to Apple. Right-click on your project and select **Open Containing Folder**. Then navigate to the iPhone/Distribution folder and find the application file for your application (see Figure 20–6).

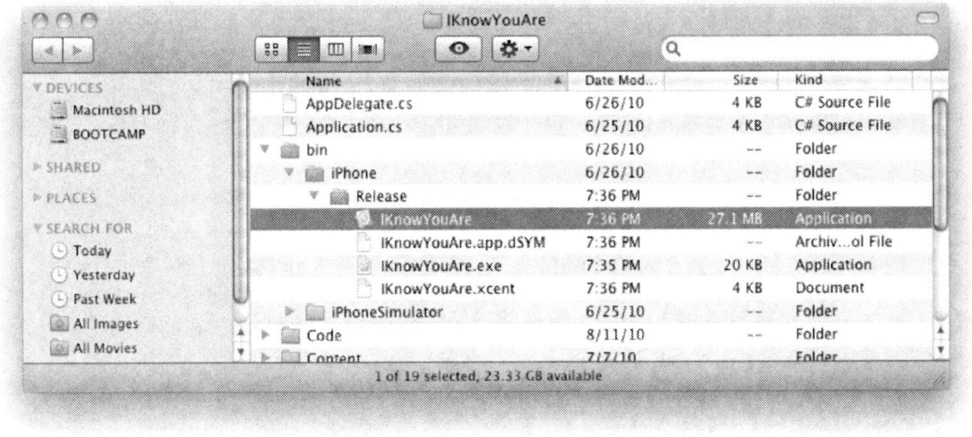

Figure 20–6. *Application file for submission*

Right-click on the application and choose **Compress...** from the context menu. That will create a zip file that you can upload.

> **NOTE:** This would be a good time to copy your .dSYM file to a place of safe-keeping so that you can symbolicate crash reports from Apple.

Now that you have a zip file of your application bundle (using either method), it's time to submit your application!

Submitting Your App via iTunes Connect

Application submission is done through iTunes Connect, which you can find at http://itunesconnect.Apple.com. iTunes Connect is the management portal for all things App Store related. It's also where you'll find sales reports, manage users, and the like.

In order to submit your application, you need to first do the following:

- **Configure users (Optional):** When you first signed up to be a developer in the iOS program, you provided information about yourself. That information is used to create the admin user that has full control to manage things in iTunes Connect. If you'd like to add other people to your iTunes Connect membership, you can. You can even configure specific permissions to different people so that only certain people have certain abilities. For example, you could set up a person that can manage financial things such as viewing reports, setting app prices, and so on, and another person that is allowed to submit apps. To configure users, choose **Manage Users** from the iTunes Connect home screen.

- **Accept contract (for pay apps only):** If you're planning to sell your applications in the App Store (as opposed to giving them away for free), you need to request a contract and accept it. From the iTunes Connect home screen, select **Contracts, Tax, and Banking** and then follow the steps provided to request and accept a contract for the services you plan to utilize.

- **Set up bank, tax, and contact info (for pay apps only):** After you've accepted the contract, you need to setup your contact, bank, and tax information so that Apple knows where to deposit your application earnings, verify your legal standing (and report taxes), and finally, contact you if they need to. You can configure these things in the same place that you requested a contract (they will be options available after the contract is accepted).

- **Ready your application in iTunes Connect:** To submit your application, choose **Manage Your Applications** from the iTunes Connect home page, then **Add New App**, and follow the instructions.

After that stuff is complete, you're ready to submit. To submit your application, you need to run the Application Loader application. To launch this, open Spotlight and type "Application Loader" and launch the application (see Figure 20–7).

Figure 20–7. *Application Loader*

If you've set up the application in iTunes Connect, when you click Next, you should see a screen similar to Figure 20–8.

Figure 20–8. *Selecting the application to submit in the Application Loader*

Click **Next** after you've selected the application you want to submit and follow the instructions. It'll have you upload the zip file you created earlier and let you know when it has successfully been submitted.

That's it! Now you just have to wait for the application to be approved (and if you've followed the advice in here, it should be).

Application Rejection Dispute Resolution

So you've worked really hard on an awesome application, you submitted it, and it got rejected. Well, don't fret. Most rejections are because of easy-to-fix reasons.

If your application is rejected, you will be notified of why it was rejected. The most common rejections are caused by major bugs or missing or incomplete functionality. If this is the case, simply fix the issue and resubmit a new version of the application.

However, if you feel that your rejection was unwarranted, Apple now has an App Review Board that allows you to submit an appeal, explaining why you feel that the rejection was unwarranted. You can find a link to the appeal form on the Apple developer at http://developer.apple.com/appstore/guidelines.html.

Finally, if you've used the appeal process, and Apple still won't approve your application, you may consider going public with your rejection. Be warned though: Apple hates having a stink made about itself in the press (even if it's warranted), and its rejection letters are subject to the NDA that you signed when you signed up for the developer program. With that said, however, there have been many cases in which the public criticism of an app rejection has caused Apple to reverse their decision (or more often, quietly approve the submission).

Summary

In this chapter we covered the process of readying your app for submission, including creating a distribution provisioning profile, signing the bundle, and building for distribution. You then learned about iTunes Connect, Apple's managed portal for all things App Store related. Finally, we covered the process of submitting the app, and what to do if it gets rejected.

In the next chapter, we're going to take a look at calling web services from your iOS application.

Chapter 21

Third-Party Libraries

One of the most powerful features of MonoTouch is its ability to utilize third-party libraries from C# source code, Objective-C libraries, and even C/C++ libraries.

As such, there has been a lot of work in the community to build third-party MonoTouch libraries, and also wrap existing Objective-C libraries.

In this chapter, we're going to take a quick look at some of the largest and most popular libraries, which will give you an idea of some of the libraries available for use.

There are a couple good resources for finding MonoTouch libraries, including the following:

- **MonoTouch Wiki:** There is a community-maintained wiki that has a number of libraries at http://wiki.monotouch.net/. While being a good starting point, however, it is not always up to date, and there are a number of libraries not mentioned there.

- **MonoTouch Bindings on Github:** Available at https://github.com/mono/monotouch-bindings, several prominent community members (and a couple MonoTouch team members) maintain bindings to popular Objective-C libraries.

There are a lot of libraries available for the iOS and MonoTouch. This chapter is meant to give you an idea of what is out there, but is by no means exhaustive. We're going to take a look at the following third-party libraries:

- **MonoTouch.Dialog:** A powerful toolkit built by Mono's founder, Miguel de Icaza, that helps simplify building screens in MonoTouch.

- **MonoTouch-Facebook:** A MonoTouch library that wraps the Facebook iOS SDK written in Objective-C.

- **Three20:** Comprehensive UI Toolkit based on the Facebook application's control set. Written in Objective-C and bound for use with MonoTouch.

- **Tapku:** A lightweight UI Toolkit that includes a number of useful controls including a graph control.

- **MonoTouch-Controls:** A small set of useful controls that includes some C# ports of controls from the Tapku library built by Eduardo Scoz.

Additionally, in Chapter 22, we're going to take a look at how to bind Objective-C libraries yourself.

MonoTouch.Dialog

By far one of the most powerful and popular third-party toolkits available for MonoTouch, MonoTouch.Dialog was created by Miguel de Icaza and has an active community of developers extending it. For brevity, MonoTouch.Dialog is often referred to as MT.D, and I will follow that precedent for that very reason here. I highly recommend using MT.D in your projects where applicable; it will significantly reduce the amount of code you have to write and reduce the potential for application bugs.

MT.D is based on the idea that most of what you do with tables in MonoTouch is repetitive, and can be abstracted in such a way that you can describe your layout with objects, and then have a framework that automatically builds the UI and binds the input to your objects.

For instance, see Figure 21–1 was created using MT.D.

Figure 21–1. *A screen built entirely using MonoTouch.Dialog*

The only code needed to create that is shown in Listing 21–1.

Listing 21–1. *Creating a screen from an object that is bound to a DialogViewController*

```
public class AccountInfo
{
        [Section]
        public bool AirplaneMode;

        [Section ("Data Entry", "Your credentials")]

        [Entry ("Enter your login name")]
        public string Login;

        [Caption ("Password"), Password ("Enter your password")]
        public string passwd;
}
...
this._accountInfo = new AccountInfo();
BindingContext bc = new BindingContext(this, this._accountInfo, "Account Information");
this.NavigationController.PushViewController(new DialogViewController(bc.Root), true);
```

As you can see, MT.D is extremely powerful, yet Miguel has done an excellent job in making it super simple. In fact, once you start developing with MT.D, it's hard to develop without it.

> **NOTE:** This section will give you a good understanding of MT.D, but it is by no means comprehensive. For more information and clarity on anything presented in here, check out the documentation at https://github.com/migueldeicaza/MonoTouch.Dialog. If you scroll down past the file listing, there is documentation, further explaining MT.D.

Let's take a look at the constituent parts of MT.D, so we can get an understanding of how to use it.

DialogViewController

The main class in MT.D that handles UI is `DialogViewController`. DialogViewController subclasses `UITableViewController`, and is responsible for actually creating the interface. You use a DialogViewController just as you would any custom `UITableViewController`, but the difference is, instead of having to go through the hassle of implementing a data source and a delegate, you simply instantiate it with a `RootElement` object that contains your UI information (which we'll examine in a moment). You can then push it onto a navigation controller, assign it to a tab in a tab bar controller, or as the master view in a split view controller, and so on.

For example, assuming that you've created a `RootElement` called myRoot, you can push DialogViewController onto the navigation stack as shown in Listing 21–2.

Listing 21–2. *Pushing a DialogViewController onto a navigation controller*

```
this.NavigationController.PushViewController(new DialogViewController(myRoot), true);
```

MT.D allows provides a mechanism for nested screens as well. For instance, you can have items on the DialogViewController that, when clicked on, open new screens and push them onto the stack as well.

In addition to using the stock DialogViewController, you can subclass it to customize its appearance and behavior. For more information, see the MT.D documentation.

RootElement, Sections, and Child Elements

The DialogViewController is populated via a hierarchal set of items, beginning with `Section` objects, which contain `Element` objects that represent the items on the interface. At the root of this tree is a class called `RootElement`. When you create a new DialogViewController, you pass the constructor an instantiated `RootElement` object.

Sections

Sections represent a section in a table view. They can have header and footer text, or can even be created from a view and they themselves can contain `Element` (including `RootElement`, for nested screens) objects. Creating a new section is very easy, and there are a number of constructor overloads that allow you to specify the header and footer text, or even custom views for the header and footer. For example, Listing 21–3 creates a new section with some header and footer text.

Listing 21–3. *Creating a new Section item and specifying the footer and header text*

```
Section mySection = new Section ("My Header Text", "My Footer Text");
```

As I mentioned, you can create header and footers from views. For example, Listing 21–4 specifies an image to be used for the section header.

Listing 21–4. *Creating a new Section from with an image view as the header*

```
UIImageView myHeaderImage = new UIImageView (Image.FromBundle ("Images/sample.png"));
Section mySection = new Section (myHeaderImage);
```

Elements

Element objects are created as children of a Section, and MT.D ships with a number of standard elements, and if those don't quite do what you need, you can also create custom elements. Elements that are used for form information/user data expose a `Value` property that gets updated when the user enters information.

The standard elements are as follows:

- **BooleanElement:** Creates an item that has a `UISwitchView` in it.

- **CheckboxElement:** Creates an item that has a checkbox in it.

- **FloatElement:** Creates an item with a UISliderView and UIImageView views to the left and right of the slider.

- **HtmlElement:** Creates an item that, when clicked on, loads a new screen that contains a `UIWebView` that loads the specified URL.

- **ImageElement:** Creates an item that, when clicked on, loads an image picker.

- **StringElement:** Creates an item that displays a string value. You can pass a delegate to this for more advanced functionality.

- **StyledStringElement:** Similar to `StringElement`, but allows you to specify the styling of `Font`, `TextColor`, and `BackgroundColor` to be set.

- **MultilineElement:** A subclass of `StringElement`, `MultiLineElement` allows multiple lines of text.

- **RadioElement:** Creates an element that serves as a radio-button item. Multiple `RadioElement` objects can be grouped together.

- **EntryElement:** Creates an item that has a `UITextView` and allows users to enter text. You can also specify that the entry is a password, and then it masks the input.

- **DateTimeElement:** Creates an item that, when clicked on, opens a new screen with a date-time spinner control that allows the user to enter a date and time.

- **DateElement:** Similar to `DateTimeElement`, but only allows date entry.

- **TimeElement:** Similar to `DateTimeElement`, but only allows time entry.

- **BadgeElement:** Creates an item that shows an image and text.

- **UIViewElement:** Creates an item from the specified view.

- **ActivityElement:** Creates an item that shows a `UIActivityView`.

- **LoadMoreElement:** Creates an item that allows users to click on it to load more items. You pass an `NSAction` that gets called when the user clicks the item that contains your custom code to load more items.

- **OwnerDrawnElement:** An abstract base class that can be overridden to create an item in which you override the `Draw` (and other methods) to render the item.

Each one of these elements has a high level of customization available out of the box. For more information, make sure to check out the documentation over at the project page in Github.

Using MT.D

There are two distinctly different ways to create the element tree/hierarchy to define screen content in MT.D:

- **Creating the hierarchy manually:** When creating the hierarchy manually, you create a RootElement, and then add Sections and Elements to it as needed.

- **Using automatic binding:** When using the binding method, you define specially attributed classes , and then MT.D will build out the hierarchy (and bind the data from the screens to the objects) for you.

The binding method is a high-level usage pattern that relies on a BindingContext object to do all the work for you. You simply create your object (or object hierarchy), pass it to a new `BindingContext`, and then use the `Root` property of the `BindingContext` object, which returns the `RootElement` (and subsequent tree) based on your object.

The binding pattern can save you a lot of work; however, it relies on reflection to build the hierarchy, and is therefore slightly slower than creating the hierarchy yourself.

Additionally, creating the hierarchy yourself gives you more flexibility, because you have direct control.

We're going to take a look at creating the hierarchy manually first, so that we have a good idea of how MT.D works, and then we're going to look at how to simplify things using the binding pattern.

Creating the Element (Content) Tree Manually

Creating the element tree/hierarchy manually sounds tedious, but in fact, with the use of C# 3.0 initializers, it can be quite easy. For example, Listing 21–5 creates a rather complex tree, but users very little code.

Listing 21–5. *Creating an element tree using the C# 3.0 initializer syntax*

```
RootElement myElementTree = new RootElement ("Demos")
{
        new Section ("Element API", "optional footer text")
        {
                new BooleanElement ("Airplane Mode", false),
                new StringElement("Foo", "A test!")
        },
        new Section ("Another Section!")
        {
                new ImageElement(UIImage.FromBundle("Images/Icons/Apress-50x50.png")),
                new EntryElement("Login", "please enter e-mail", ""),
                new EntryElement("Pass", "", "", true),
                new FloatElement(UIImage.FromBundle("Images/Icons/Apress-50x50.png"),
                        UIImage.FromBundle("Images/Icons/Apress-50x50.png"), 40),
                new BadgeElement(UIImage.FromBundle("Images/Icons/Apress-50x50.png")
                        , "badge element!")
        }
};
```

In addition to the standard elements, you can also create custom elements by subclassing any existing element, or the `Element` class itself.

Using the Object Binding Pattern

The object binding pattern provides a powerful mechanism in which to build a UI from view model objects. Using the binding pattern, MT.D items are built out by looking at the public fields in your class, and they are added in the order that items are declared. Additionally, you can decorate your class with attributes to specify how the element tree gets created.

For example, back in Listing 21–1, I created an `AccountInfo` object that had a number of fields that were automatically displayed, and the attributes affected where the sections were and how the items were displayed.

Object binding is extremely powerful and very configurable. I strongly recommend digging into the MT.D documentation at the project home page on Github for more information on it.

LINQ Support

The classes that make up the element trees in MT.D also support LINQ. For example, through the clever usage of LINQ and C#'s initialization syntax, you can use LINQ to create your trees, as shown in Listing 21–6.

Listing 21–6. *Creating an element tree from LINQ*

```
this._linqBuiltElementTree = new RootElement ("LINQ root") {
        from x in new string [] { "one", "two", "three" }
                select new Section (x) {
                        from y in "Hello:World".Split (':')
                                select (Element) new StringElement (y)
                }
};
```

You could combine this with data from a database or an XML file, and you can see how easy it is to create MT.D element trees. For instance, you could write a simply LINQ query and define a good portion of your application's screens with XML!

MonoTouch-Facebook

MonoTouch-Facebook was created (and maintained) by Kevin McMahan. It's a MonoTouch wrapper on the official Facebook iOS SDK (published by Facebook) and was created using btouch (covered in Chapter 22).

You can find the latest build of it at the online open-source repository, Github.com, at https://github.com/kevinmcmahon/monotouch-facebook.

In order to use it, you must first get an application ID from Facebook, which can be obtained at www.facebook.com/developers/createapp.php.

MonoTouch-Facebook includes a sample application called FacebookSDKExamples, which is a direct port of the official Facebook SDK Examples application. You can grab FacebookSDKExamples from the Github site. In order to run the example application, you need to add your application ID to places:

- **info.plist**

- **main.cs**

The info.plist file already has a place for the application id under URL Types : Item 0 : URL Schemas : Item 0. The application id should be prefixed with an "fb," so a correctly configured info.plist will look something like the Figure 21–2.

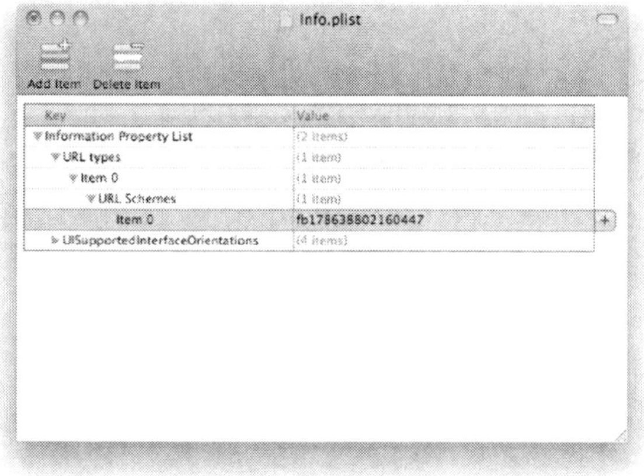

Figure 21–2. *Adding your Facebook Application ID to the info.plist file*

After you've edited the info.plist file, you should also edit the main.cs file and add set your application id to the kAppId variable (line 29 as of writing):

```
const string kAppId = "112345678960447";
```

If you've configured your application ID correctly, when you run the example application, you should get a screen like that shown in Figure 21–3.

Figure 21–3. *Opening screen of the Facebook SDK Example application*

When you click on Login button, it will open up Safari and present you with the Facebook site, which will require you to log in and ask you to authorize the application to access your data. After you've logged into Facebook and authorized your application, it requests a specifically formatted URL, which the MonoTouch-Facebook library has subscribed to. The iOS will then switch back to your application, and you'll see a screen similar to Figure 21–4.

Figure 21–4. *Facebook SDK Example application after you've logged into Facebook*

This means the application has successfully authenticated with Facebook and gives your application the ability to access your profile data, post updates, photos, and the like.

For more information on using the SDK, see the official Facebook iOS SDK homepage (also on Github) at https://github.com/facebook/facebook-ios-sdk.

Three20

Three20 is a heavy-duty open source Objective-C library that consists of a collection of sub-projects that are all derived from the Facebook iOS application. You can find the project and source code at https://github.com/facebook/three20. It includes a number of things that are actually already available in .NET, such as a JSON parser, and so on; however, it does have a very powerful UI library that contain many of the controls found in the Facebook application (see Figure 21–5).

Figure 21–5. *Three20 UI library*

Because it's written in Objective-C, it needs to be bound for use in MonoTouch. However, there has been some community effort involved in binding it. You can find the btouch project at http://code.google.com/p/btouch-library/, as well as the latest wrapper DLL. As of writing this book, the binding is still fairly rough, but some controls are useable.

I cover using btouch in Chapter 22 if you're interested in using Three20.

Tapku

Tapku is a lightweight and fast, open-source, Objective-C UI library created by Devin Ross. You can find the Tapku library on Github at https://github.com/devinross/tapkulibrary. It contains a number of extremely useful (and non-trivial to replicate) controls, including a very nice graph, a cover flow control, a calendar, and a number of nice alert controls (called HUD, or heads-up-display, controls in this library), some of which are shown in Figure 21–6.

Figure 21–6. *Tapku controls library*

Like Three20, Tapku has seem some community effort to bind for MonoTouch, and again, the source of such efforts can be found at https://github.com/mono/monotouch-bindings. Additionally, in the next chapter when I cover btouch, I'm going to walk through binding the Tapku coverflow (TKCoverflowView) control using btouch.

MonoTouch-Controls

The MonoTouch-Controls library is an open-source C# library of UI controls created by Eduardo Scoz. It can be found on Github at https://github.com/escoz/monotouch-controls. It is partially based on the Tapku library, and as such has C# ports of the monthly calendar view and some of the HUD controls. Additionally, it has a web image view control that displays images directly from a URL, and has a nifty text field that formats numbers with commas and decimals as the number is entered. There are also a few other controls. Some of the controls are shown in Figure 21–7.

Figure 21–7. *ESCOZ's MonoTouch-Controls library*

At the time of writing, the library hasn't been updated in a while, and some of the controls need a little bit of work. Generally, though, it's a solid library, and if nothing else, it can serve as a basis if you're looking to create controls that expand on its functionality.

XNATouch

XNATouch is an open-source project that allows you to port games written for Windows and Windows Mobile 7 to iOS with minimal effort. You can find XNATouch at http://monogame.codeplex.com.

As of writing, it doesn't yet support XNA 4.0, only 3.1, but 4.0 support is said to be on its way soon by the developer.

To use XNATouch, add all of your source code files to your project, add a reference to the XNATouch dll, and then launch your game loop in your application delegate's FinishedLaunching method (see Listing 21–7).

Figure 21–7. *Launching an XNA game in MonoTouch*

```
using MonoTouch.Foundation;
using MonoTouch.UIKit;
using XnaTouch;
using XnaTouch.Samples;
using XnaTouch.Samples.Storage;

namespace XnaTouch.Samples.Storage
{
        [Register ("AppDelegate")]
        class Program : UIApplicationDelegate
        {
                private Game1 game;

                public override void FinishedLaunching (UIApplication app)
                {
                        // Fun begins..
```

```
                        game = new Game1();
                        game.Run();
                }

                static void Main (string [] args)
                {
                        UIApplication.Main (args,null,"AppDelegate");
                }
        }
}
```

Summary

In this chapter you learned about a few major third-party libraries available for MonoTouch, including MonoTouch.Dialog, which may be the single most useful library available and can greatly increase your productivity. We also learned where to locate third-party libraries for MonoTouch.

In the next chapter, we're going to take a look at binding Objective-C libraries for use in MonoTouch.

Chapter 22

Using Objective-C Libraries and Code

In addition to third-party libraries that are written in C# and C/C++, MonoTouch can utilize libraries and code written in Objective-C. This makes MonoTouch extremely powerful, because you can draw functionality from a plethora of sources.

In this chapter, we're going to take a look at how to bind Objective-C libraries for use in MonoTouch using btouch, a tool that simplifies the binding process. In the process, your're going to get some real-world experience by walking through the process of binding the open source Tapku library.

The general process of binding Objective-C code for use in MonoTouch applications involves creating MonoTouch DLLs that "bind" the native code. This means creating C# classes to represent the Objective-C classes that invoke the underlying Objective-C selectors, wrap properties, and so on via the `MonoTouch.Foundation` classes and attribute syntax.

There are two ways to accomplish this. The first is the hard way, which involves writing all the binding classes and code by hand. You can find documentation on how to do this here http://monotouch.net/Documentation/Binding_New_Objective-C_Types/Binding_Details.

I'm not going to cover that in this book, though, because there's a much easier way to bind Objective-C libraries: using btouch.

btouch

The easiest way to use Objective-C libraries is to use a utility tool created by the MonoTouch team called btouch. It works by automatically generating a MonoTouch DLL that wraps the library for you based on an API Definition File that you create to describe the binding. You can also provide to it C# source files of any additional helper classes, enums, and the like that you write to expand the binding and make it easier to use.

Once you have generated your wrapped DLL, you can then reference it in your project, along with the original .a file that contains the Objective-C library, and use it as you would any other .NET library. See Figure 22–1.

Figure 22–1. *Using btouch to bind an Objective-C library to create a MonoTouch DLL*

You can find really good documentation on creating API Definition Files and using btouch at http://monotouch.net/Documentation/Binding_New_Objective-C_Types.

Instead of duplicating the coverage that the team gives there on btouch, this chapter instead serves as a practical companion to understanding the process of using the rules described in the documentation.

btouch Process

The workflow of this process generally involves the following steps:

1. **Compile library in Xcode:** If the library isn't already built, you need to open it in Xcode and build it. The resulting assembly is a static library (.a) file.

2. **Create API definition:** Create the API definition file as well as any helper classes, enums, and so on that will make up the MonoTouch usable DLL.

3. **Run btouch:** btouch will create a DLL from the source files and API definition that you give it.

4. **Add the Objective-C library to your project:** Copy the .a file(s) into the project.

5. **Reference the DLL:** Add the btouch-generated DLL as a reference in your project.

6. **Configure build:** Add special compiler flags to the build that load the Objective-C library as a source.

Let's examine this process step by step by actually binding a library. In this case, we're going to use btouch to create a MonoTouch usable library of Tapku.

A Quick Objective-C Primer

Before we get too far along in this process, it's important to get a basic Objective-C overview. It's a very different language than C# (or even C/C++ for that matter), and binding it is a lot easier if you know a little bit about it.

The intent of this primer is to give you enough of a background in Objective-C to be able to bind it, but it is by no means exhaustive. For a complete Objective-C primer, check out *Learning Objective-C: A Primer* in the development documentation, or at http://developer.apple.com/library/mac/#referencelibrary/GettingStarted/Learning_Objective-C_A_Primer/_index.html.

Additionally, Wikipedia has a great article on Objective-C that compares its syntax to C and C++. You can find it at http://en.wikipedia.org/wiki/Objective-c.

Files

There are three types of files in Objective-C (and by extension, Xcode iOS projects). They are defined in Table 22–1.

Table 22–1. *Objective-C File Types*

Extension	Type
.h	Header files that contain the definitions (prototypes) for the corresponding source code files and include things like class, function, and constant declarations.
.m	Source code files that contain the actual implementation of what's been defined in the header files. You may see both Objective-C and C code in .m files.
.mm	Source code files that contain Objective-C++ and C++ source.

I mention C and C++ because sometimes in iOS projects you'll those languages in addition to Objective-C.

Typically, you'll see a 1:1 relation between .h and .m files, because the .h files define what's in the .m files. This separation between definition and implementation is a legacy feature of the C language.

Classes

Objective-C has a class construct, just like C#, though it looks pretty different. As I mentioned earlier, classes are defined in header files.

Class definitions in Objective-C are preceded with an @interface declaration and are concluded with an @end declaration. There is typically then a code block delineated with brackets ("{" and "}"), which contain member variables. After the member variables, methods are declared, outside of the bracketed code block. Consider the class definition in Figure 22–2.

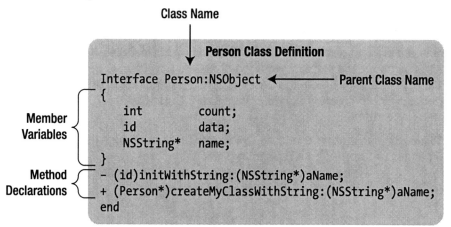

Figure 22–2. *A typical Objective-C class definition*

Objective-C looks a little strange if you're used to C, C++, or C#, but underneath it all it's not all that different.

Objective-C has both strong-typing (definitive/known types) of variables, and weak-typing. In Figure 22–2, the data variable is weakly-typed, which is signified by the id type. Just like in C#, there are both value types and reference types. Reference types are passed via pointer, which is what the asterisk ("*") after the NSString means. Weakly-typed variables are also passed via pointer reference, with the id type implying a pointer reference.

You very rarely need to look at the actual implementation when binding Objective-C methods, because really what you're interested in is the definition of classes, and the like.

Let's take a look at the method declarations next.

Methods/Messages

Methods are where the syntax of Objective-C really starts to diverge from traditional C-based languages. This is due to its legacy from NeXTSTEP OS (which Apple bought), which, in turn, owes a lot of its syntax from Smalltalk.

Instead of always calling methods on objects, most of the time in Objective-C, you pass messages to objects. This, while strange to those coming from C-based backgrounds, actually adds a tremendous amount of power to Objective-C, because it allows it to be more dynamic.

Consider the Objective-C method declaration in Figure 22–3.

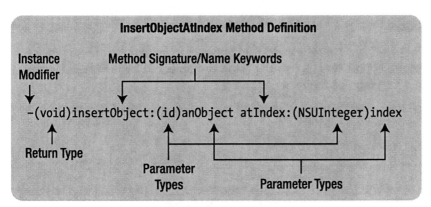

Figure 22–3. *An Objective-C method declaration*

As you can see, rather than grouping things together, Objective-C splits everything apart. To build the selector name for this method, we need to concatenate all of the method name keywords together, including the colons. So, for the previous method, the selector name would be what you see in Listing 22–1.

Listing 22–1. *Conversion from method declaration to selector name*

```
insertObject:atIndex:
```

Figuring out the selector name is very important, because, as we'll see in moment, when exposing methods to C#, we must know the selector name of the Objective-C method.

When exposing this method as a C# method, it would literally translate to Listing 22–2.

Listing 22–2. *A literal translation of 22–4 into C#*

```
public void InsertObjectAtIndex(NSObject anObject, uint index);
```

However, we would likely clean it up (following the .NET framework guidelines) and expose it as Listing 22–3.

Listing 22–3. *A sensible translation of 22–4 into C# following the .NET framework guidelines*

```
public void Insert(NSObject item, int index);
```

I'm going to delve into this deeper in just a bit, but the important thing to grasp here is that when wrapping Objective-C, you need to know how to derive the selector name from the method declaration, and then you'll want to expose that via a sensible name in C# that fits to the .NET guidelines.

Instance vs. Static

Instance methods are preceded with a dash ("-") and static methods are preceded with a plus ("+").

Invoking Methods

Remember, in Objective-C, you message objects rather than invoke their methods. Messages are wrapped in brackets ("[" and "]") and the object to be messaged is on the left side, and the message package is on the right.

For example, to call the previous method on an object called `myArray`, you would do the following (see Listing 22–4).

Listing 22–4. *Invoking an Objective-C method via a message*

```
[myArray insertObject:someObject atIndex:0];
```

Objective-C also allows you to chain messages together to pass the result of messages in as parameters of other messages, as in Listing 22–5.

Listing 22–5. *Using the result of a message as a parameter in another message*

```
[[myAppObject theArray] insertObject:[myAppObject objectToInsert] atIndex:0];
```

Properties

Unlike C#, Objective-C doesn't have true properties. Instead, it has `getter` and `setter` methods that can be auto generated by the compiler. For example, if you wanted a count property, you (or the compiler) would implement a count method for retrieval (`getter`), and a `setCount` method for persistence (`setter`). These pseudo-properties are declared, like any other method, in the header file, and are in the form "`@property (optional attributes) Type name`," as in Listing 22–6.

Listing 22–6. *Property declarations in Objective-C*

```
@property BOOL flag;
@property (copy) NSString *nameObject;  // Copy the object during assignment.
@property (readonly) UIView *rootView;  // Declare only a getter method.
```

Properties can be given attributes that describe their behavior. Attributes fall into the following three categories:

- Access level
- Memory management
- Thread-safety

There are two access-level properties, `readwrite` and `readonly`, which specify whether the property is readable and writeable (has both a `getter` and `setter`), or if it's only readable.

There are also three memory management attributes – `assign`, `retain`, and `copy` – that specify the semantics of how the memory is handled when the property is set.

Finally, the last attribute is `NonAtomic`, which specifies that the property does not do any thread-safe locking.

Later on, when we bind the Tapku library, we'll look at how these attributes are important; for now, we just need to be aware of them.

Property retrieval is performed with dot-notation, as in Listing 22–7.

Listing 22–7. *Retrieving a property value in Objective-C*

```
count = myObject.count;
```

However, setting a property can be performed either via a setter method (in the form of a message) that takes the form of setPropertyName, or dot-notation, as in Listing 22–8.

Listing 22–8. *Setting a property in Objective-C using a message and a dot-notation, respectively*

```
[myObject setCount:5];
myObject.count = 5;
```

The compiler can generate the property getter and setter methods for you. To do this, you use the @synthesize keyword in your class implementation, as shown in Listing 22–9.

Listing 22–9. *Using the @synthesize keyword to make the compiler implement property methods*

```
@synthesize flag;
@synthesize nameObject;
@synthesize rootView;
```

Protocols

We covered protocols in the first section of this book, but as a quick review, protocols are similar to Interfaces in C#, with the following differences:

- Protocols do not define instance variables.

- Method declarations in protocols can be optional.

Protocols that a class conforms to (implements) are specified after the class name declaration in angle brackets < and >. For example, the class in Listing 22–10 implements the UIApplicationDelegate and AnotherProtocol protocols.

Listing 22–10. *Specifying that a class implements certain protocols*

```
@interface MyClass : NSObject <UIApplicationDelegate, AnotherProtocol> {
}
@end
```

Declaring Protocols

Protocols are declared via the @protocol keyword. For example, Listing 22–11 defines a protocol for XML serialization.

Listing 22–11. *Declaring a protocol*

```
@protocol MyXMLSupport
- initFromXMLRepresentation:(NSXMLElement *)XMLElement;
- (NSXMLElement *)XMLRepresentation;
@end
```

By default, any methods declared in a protocol are required, but you can also specify that a method be optional with the @optional keyword, as in Listing 22–12.

Listing 22–12. *Required and optional methods in a protocol*

```
@protocol MyProtocol
- (void)requiredMethod;
@optional
- (void)anOptionalMethod;
- (void)anotherOptionalMethod;
@required
- (void)anotherRequiredMethod;
@end
```

Protocols are one of the most extensive features in Objective-C, and you may find while binding an Objective-C library that a protocol is more complicated than the rules presented here. In that case, I recommend reviewing the section on protocols in Apple's Objective-C programming language documentation at http://developer.apple.com/library/mac/#documentation/Cocoa/Conceptual/ObjectiveC/Chapters/ocProtocols.html.

Now that we're seasoned Objective-C experts (sarcasm), let's look at actually compiling an Objective-C library so that we can use it in MonoTouch.

Compiling the Objective-C Library

The first step in the process of binding an Objective-C library to use in MonoTouch is to actually build the library. Objective-C libraries that you use in the iOS have their roots in Unix, and compile down to Static Object Code Library files. These files have an "a" file extension.

When doing iOS development, you actually need three .a files. One file should be built for the i386 architecture (instruction set). This file will be used by the iOS Simulator. The other files should be built for the ARMv6 and ARMv7 architecture, which will be used by the actual devices (older devices only run v6, whereas the new devices run v6 and v7).

ARCHITECTURE? WHAT? Different CPUs have different sets of instructions that they understand. Each common set of instructions is called an architecture. Most computers these days use the i386 instruction set, which has remained unchanged since the Intel 386 CPU. However, mobile devices typically use a smaller, optimized set of instructions that allow the chips to be smaller and draw less power. iDevices are no different in this respect; for example, the iPhone 3G and earlier only understand the ARMv6 instruction set, whereas the iPhone 4 and iPad and iPad 2 can run both ARMv6 and ARMv7 code. However, Apple throws a bit of a monkey wrench into the situation even more by requiring ARMv7 code be run on newer devices, even though they support ARMv6.

If you just have some Objective-C code, and don't have an Xcode library project, then you'll need to create one. You can find instructions on how to create Xcode library

projects in the Xcode developer documentation at
http://developer.apple.com/library/ios/#documentation/ToolsLanguages/Conceptual/
Xcode4UserGuide/Introduction/Introduction.html.

Building the Tapku Library

We are going to use the Tapku library, which can be download from Github at
https://github.com/devinross/tapkulibrary. Click the Downloads button to have Github
assemble and zip the source code into an archive.

When you download and unzip the file, you should see two folders: **src** and **universaldemo**.
The src folder contains the library project that we'll compile, and the universaldemo
folder contains a sample iOS application that demos the library.

Open the TapkuLibrary.xcodeproj file in the src folder. Xcode should open up and you
should see something like Figure 22–4.

Figure 22–4. *Xcode project window showing the Tapku library project*

In the upper left, you can set your current build target. If you click on it and don't have the options you see in Figure 22–5, you probably need to change the SDK target to be the iOS SDK.

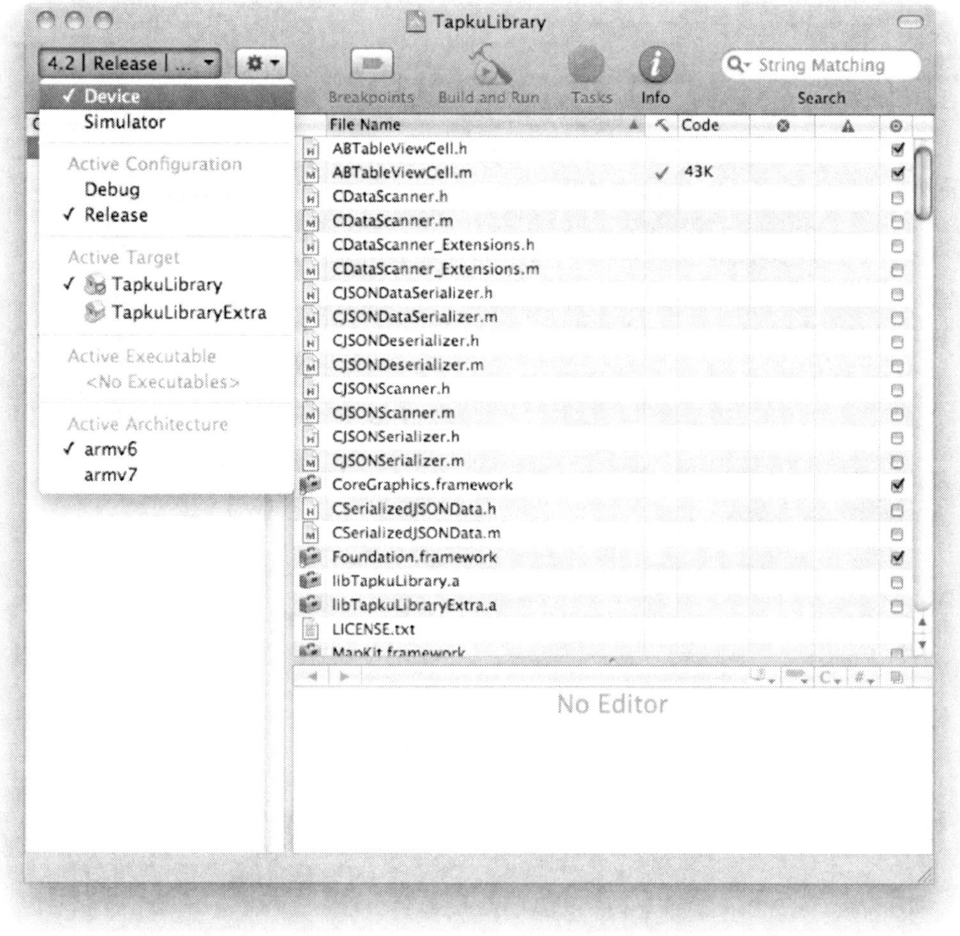

Figure 22–5. *Build configuration in Xcode*

Specifying the iOS SDK

To change the base SDK target, click on the **Project** menu and then choose **Edit Project Settings**. Then, in the **Base SDK** setting, choose **Latest iOS…**, as shown in Figure 22–6.

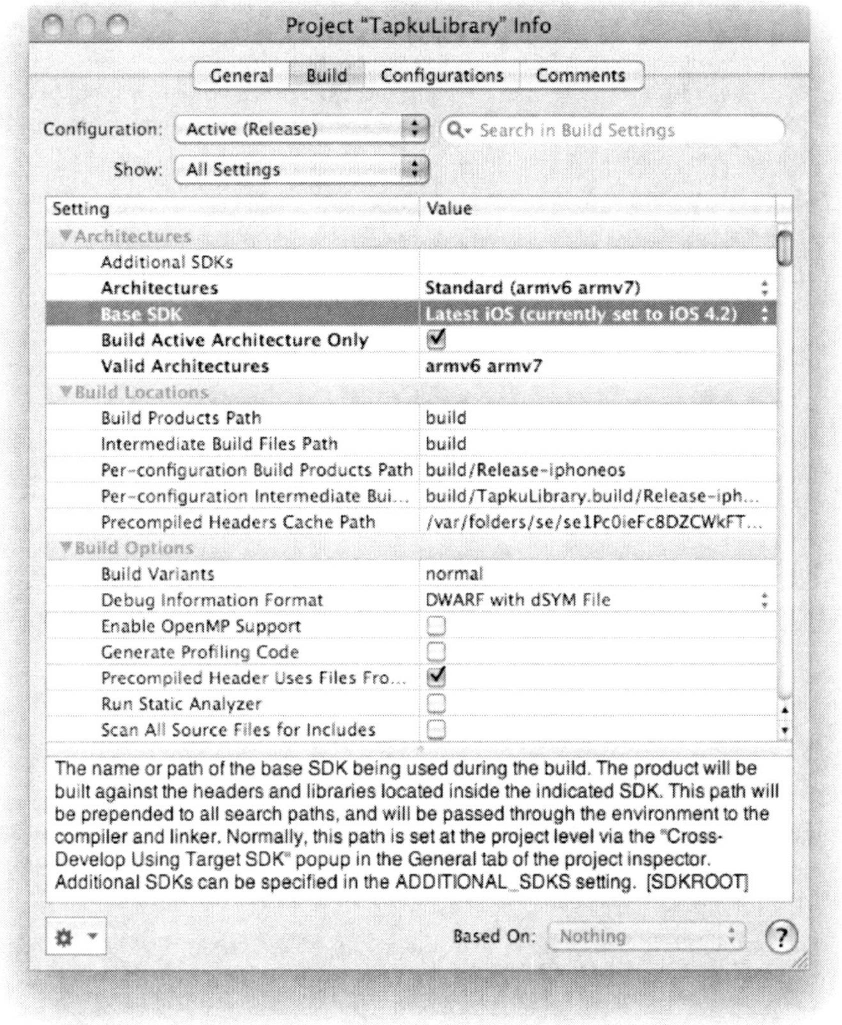

Figure 22–6. *Setting the Base SDK to be the latest iOS SDK in the Xcode project settings*

This will set the library to build against the iOS SDK (as opposed to the Mac OSX SDK, which is usually the default). Due to a bug in Xcode, you may have to close the project and re-open it, for the SDK changes to go into effect.

Compiling

Once the SDK is set, we need to build the library. First we need to set our build options (via the dropdown shown in Figure 22–7).

We'll want to change the **Active Configuration** to **Release**, since it's smaller and faster (and, at this point, the Objective-C code should already be tested and stabilized).

In the case of the Tapku library, we also need to change the **Active Target** to the TapkuLibrary. There is a second target called TapkuLibraryExtra, which will build another library with extra features in addition to the base library. For the purposes of this example, we only need the main library.

Finally, make sure that **armv6** is selected, and then choose **Device**. Your build options should now look like Figure 22–7.

Figure 22–7. *Proper build settings to compile a release build for the device*

We're now ready to build. You can either select the **Build** menu, then **Build**, or you can just press **Command(⌘) + B**. Xcode will give you the build status in the bottom left of the window. Yours should say, "build succeeded." If it doesn't, make sure your Base SDK is set, then close and reopen the project.

When the build is complete, there should be a new folder called "build" in the src folder. In it will be the build outputs arranged into folders named per the configuration. You should see a folder called "Release-iphoneos," and in it, a file called libTapkuLibrary.a.

We want to also build for armv7, but unfortunately it'll put the .a file into the same output directory as the armv6 build, so rename this directory Release-iphoneos armv6 and copy it to a folder somewhere, then change your build version to armv7, and repeat the build steps. Then, rename the output directory Release-iphoneos armv7 and copy that folder to the same place you put the armv6 folder. Now you have both device architectures built.

Now that we have the library built for the device architectures, we also want to build one for the simulator, so change the build option to **Simulator** and rebuild. You should now see a **Release-iphonesimulator** folder in the build folder, along with the new library.

> **NOTE:** MonoTouch 3 does not include Thumb support, so if you compile your library with Thumb architecture support, it will crash when you try to run it. MonoTouch 4 does not have this limitation, however.

Combining Build Architectures with LIPO

Now that we have our library built for all of our architectures, we need to stitch them all together into one single .a file. Mac OSX ships with a command utility called LIPO that allows you to combine multiple architectures of a library into a single "fat" assembly.

LIPO can be executed via a terminal window. To use LIPO to combine builds, use the –create argument and pass an –arch [archtype] [sourcefilename] argument for each architecture you want to include, and specify an –output [filename] argument to specify the output file. For example, the following command will combine an i386, ARMv6, and ARMv7 build into one library, as in Listing 22–13.

Listing 22–13. *Using LIPO to combine different architecture builds of a library into one*

```
lipo -create -arch i386 "../Release-iphonesimulator/libTapkuLibrary.a"
        -arch armv6 "../Release-iphoneos armv6/libTapkuLibrary.a"
        -arch armv7 "../Release-iphoneos armv7/libTapkuLibrary.a"
        -output ./libTapkuLibrary.a
```

For more information on LIPO, check out the documentation at http://developer.apple.com/library/mac/#documentation/Darwin/Reference/ManPages/man1/lipo.1.html.

Creating API Definition File and Helper Code

An API definition file is just a C# file that contains a set of interfaces that define the contracts that the btouch tool will use to create your wrapper DLL that calls the underlying Objective-C library.

API Definition File

For example, the API definition file in Listing 22–14 is pulled from the btouch how-to on the MonoTouch.net site and provides a contract for the Cocos2D.Camera object.

Listing 22–14. *A sample API definition file to build a wrapper for the Cocos2D Camera class*

```
using MonoTouch.Foundation;
namespace Cocos2D
{
        //---- Camera class contract
        [BaseType (typeof (NSObject))]
        interface Camera
        {
                //---- Property Definitions
                [Static, Export ("getZEye")] float ZEye { get; }
```

```
//----- Method Contracts
[Export ("restore")] void Restore ();
[Export ("locate")] void Locate ();
[Export ("setEyeX:eyeY:eyeZ:")] void SetEyeXYZ (float x, float y
        , float z);
[Export ("setMode:")] void SetMode (CameraMode mode);
    }
}
```

When you run btouch, it will look at this API definition file and create a Camera class in the Cocos2D namespace and implement a read-only property called ZEye, and a number of methods. The property and methods will automatically call or invoke the appropriate items in the Objective-C library based on the attribution defined in the Interface.

As I mentioned before, the MonoTouch team has written a very good reference on how to write API Definition Files, which you can find at http://monotouch.net/Documentation/Binding_New_Objective-C_Types. Instead of rehashing their excellent work, I'm going to stick to a high-level look at the process and cover the practicalities of how to do this in practice. I recommend having that page open and, as we go through the exercise of binding the Tapku library, read the appropriate section for the type of item we are binding. That will serve as a reference for the discussion that will follow.

Additional Code

There's one thing missing in the previous example. Notice that the SetMode method takes a CameraMode type. I mentioned earlier that, in addition to the API definition file, you might want to write some extra code to help create a more useful binding to use. In this case, we would want to create a CameraMode enumeration that describes the camera mode that we pass to SetMode. So for instance, we might create an enums.cs file and place the Listing 22–15 in it.

Listing 22–15. *Creating an enumeration to use in addition to the API definition file*

```
public enum CameraMode
{
        FlyOver,
        Back,
        Follow
}
```

We could create a CameraMode.cs file rather than an enums.cs file, but we'd have to pass all our extra files btouch via command-line arguments when we execute it, so it's easier to just create one file for all enumerations.

In addition to enumerations, you might also need to define any other types, structs, and so on.

Additionally, you often need to add functionality to the classes that are generated via the API definition file. However, since the API definition file can only contain interfaces, not implementation, you can add functionality by creating a partial class definition. For instance, if we wanted to add a `ToString` method to the `Cocos2D.Camera` class, we could create write the following, and put it in a classes.cs file, as in Listing 22–16.

Listing 22–16. *Creating a partial class definition to expand on the classes automatically generated*

```
namespace Cocos2D
{
        public partial class Camera
        {
                //---- Provide a ToString method
                public override string ToString ()
                {
                        return String.Format ("ZEye: {0}", ZEye);
                }
        }
}
```

As with the enums.cs file, we would pass our classes.cs file as an argument when we run btouch, and it would get compiled into our assembly.

> **TIP:** Partial classes are also a good place to put triple-slash documentation, since btouch will ignore any documentation you put in the API definition file.

Now that we have a good understanding of how the pieces fit together, let's look at the practical exercise of actually creating the API definition file and associated code.

Wrapping Tapku

Wrapping an Objective-C library can be a big undertaking, especially if the library is large. For this reason, it's best to undertake it in stages. I recommend starting with just the pieces that you need. Let's start with Tapku's Coverflow control (TKCoverflowView).

In order to create an API definition file, you have to figure out what you're wrapping. In fact, this is the trickiest part of binding to Objective-C libraries. Even with good documentation, you almost always have to look at the source. We'll see an example of this in just a bit. Let's start with the documentation. You can find the Tapku documentation at https://github.com/devinross/tapkulibrary/wiki/. If you click on "Coverflow" under the "Classes Overview" section, it gives you a rundown of what constitutes the `TKCoverflowView` class.

Compared to most, this is actually pretty good documentation.

The first thing we want to do is create an interface for the `TKCoverFlowView` class; however, in looking at the documentation, it doesn't say what it derives from. Off to the code we go. If you open up the TKCoverflowView.h file in Xcode, you'll see that it has the declaration shown in Listing 22–17.

Listing 22–17. *The `TKCoverflowView` declaration in the `TKCoverflowView` header file*

```
@interface TKCoverflowView : UIScrollView <UIScrollViewDelegate>
```

From this, we see that TKCoverflowView derives form UIScrollView, and implements the UIScrollViewDelegate protocol. So we can start our Tapku.cs API definition file as shown in Listing 22–18.

Listing 22–18. *The beginnings of a Tapku API definition file*

```
using System;
using MonoTouch.Foundation;
using MonoTouch.CoreFoundation;
namespace Tapku
{
        [BaseType(typeof(UIScrollView))]
        interface TKCoverFlow
        {

        }
}
```

By the way, if you haven't taken a look at the documents on creating an API definition file at http://monotouch.net/Documentation/Binding_New_Objective-C_Types, now is a good time to do so.

As you bind a class, you'll find that you often have to bind other things first. Tapku's cover flow control is no different. If we go back to the TKCoverflowView documentation, it looks like there are the following several other classes that we'll need to create before we finish the TKCoverflowView binding:

- TKCoverflowViewDelegate
- TKCoverflowViewDataSource
- TKCoverView

TKCoverView is pretty straightforward; it just has a couple of properties. However, the delegate and data source are a bit different. We want to be sophisticated, so we want to expose the delegate's methods as events on the TKCoverflowView class. Additionally, the data source is a protocol, so that's a little different as well.

TKCoverflowCoverView

Let's start with TKCoverView. We need to figure out what it derives from, which isn't in the docs. If we pop back over to Xcode and try to find a TKCoverView.h file, there isn't one. It turns out the docs are wrong, and there is in fact a TKCoverflowCoverView class, rather than TKCoverView, and it derives from UIView (which makes sense). As you can see, while docs are good at giving you an idea of how to bind (or even use) a library, you really have to look at the source for an authoritative, accurate, answer.

Furthermore, if we look at the TKCoverflowCoverView.h file, we see the property declarations shown in Listing 22–19.

Listing 22–19. *TKCoverflowCoverView property declarations*

```
@property (retain,nonatomic) UIImage *image;
@property (assign,nonatomic) float baseline;
```

I mentioned earlier in the Objective-C primer that properties can be decorated with attributes that describe their behavior, and that there were three categories of property attributes; access level, memory management, and thread-safety. When binding, we only care about the first two.

Access level attributes describe whether the property is read- only. By default, unless a property is attributed with the read-only attribute, it's both readable and writeable, so we should declare both a get; and a set; for it. If it's read-only, we should only declare a get;.

The memory-management attributes specify how the memory is managed when the property is set. When wrapping Objective-C properties, we should use the ArgumentSemanticAttribute to describe how to wrap the properties. The ArgumentSemanticAttribute has three values that map to the Objective-C attributes: Assign, Retain, and Copy.

In the case of Listing 22–19 the properties have the retain and assign keywords, respectively. Those aren't in the docs, but as I just mentioned, they're important for binding. This is another example of why we need to look at the source to do a proper binding.

According to the API definition file documentation, this class should translate to what you see in Listing 22–20.

Listing 22–20. *(Mostly) complete* TKCoverflowCoverView *API definition*

```
// @interface TKCoverflowCoverView : UIView
[BaseType(typeof(UIView))]
interface TKCoverflowCoverView
{
        // @property (retain,nonatomic) UIImage *image;
        [Export("image", ArgumentSemantic.Retain)]
        UIImage Image { get; set; }

        // @property (assign,nonatomic) float baseline;
        [Export("baseline", ArgumentSemantic.Assign)]
        float Baseline { get; set; }
}
```

I've put in the original Objective-C definitions to show what has been bound where.

This class looks finished, but there is one thing that's missing here. When you run btouch on an interface it creates a class, and in that class it creates the following standard constructors for you:

- Foo ()
- Foo (NSCoder coder)
- Foo (IntPtr handle)
- Foo (NSEmptyFlag t)

This is great, but classes that derive from UIView should also generally implement a constructor that takes a RectangleF frame parameter so you can set the frame when you initialize the view.

For this reason, we need to also add Listing 22–21 to our TKCoverflowCoverView interface.

Listing 22–21. *UIViews generally should get an* initWithFrame *constructor*

```
[Export("initWithFrame:")]
IntPtr Constructor(RectangleF frame);
```

Our completed TKCoverflowCoverView API Definition should now look something like Listing 22–22.

Listing 22–22. *Complete TKCoverflowCoverView API definition*

```
// @interface TKCoverflowCoverView : UIView
[BaseType(typeof(UIView))]
interface TKCoverflowCoverView
{
        [Export("initWithFrame:")]
        IntPtr Constructor(RectangleF frame);

        // @property (retain,nonatomic) UIImage *image;
        [Export("image", ArgumentSemantic.Retain)]
        UIImage Image { get; set; }

        // @property (assign,nonatomic) float baseline;
        [Export("baseline", ArgumentSemantic.Assign)]
        float Baseline { get; set; }
}
```

Now that we've got the TKCoverflowCoverView bound, let's bind the TKCoverflowDataSource.

TKCoverflowDataSource

TKCoverflowDataSource is a fairly straightforward class to bind. It has only one method, coverAtIndex, which passes a reference to the coverflow control that is calling it, and an index parameter (as in integer) and expects a coverflowView in return. Once again, I've included the original Objective-C definitions as comments in the API definition for clarity (see Listing 22–23).

Listing 22–23. *Complete TKCoverflowDataSource API definition*

```
// @protocol TKCoverflowViewDataSource <NSObject>
[BaseType (typeof (NSObject))]
[Model]
interface TKCoverflowViewDataSource
{
        // @required
        // - (TKCoverflowCoverView*) coverflowView:(TKCoverflowView*)coverflowView
        //         coverAtIndex:(int)index;
        [Export("coverflowView:coverAtIndex:"), Abstract]
        TKCoverflowCoverView GetCover(TKCoverflowView coverflowView, int index);

}
```

Remember from our Objective-C primer, earlier in the this chapter, that the selector name is actually the combination of the method keywords. For instance, we need to derive the selector from Listing 22–24.

Listing 22–24. *Sample Objective-C method signature*

```
- (TKCoverflowCoverView*) coverflowView:(TKCoverflowView*)coverflowView
coverAtIndex:(int)index
```

Therefore, the full name of the selector would be what you see in Listing 22–25.

Listing 22–25. *Objective-C method signature translated to a selector name*

```
coverflowView:coverAtIndex:
```

As you can see, even though the selector that we're wrapping is `coverflowView:coverAtIndex:`, we've exposed it as `GetCover` in order to be consistent with the .NET framework design guidelines. As a by-product, we're also more consistent with the MonoTouch framework; for example, `UITableViewDataSource` is a similar class and has a get `GetCell` method.

There's also one other thing that's interesting in there. I've provided an `Abstract` attribute. Because the method in the prototype is marked as `@Required`, we need btouch to actually create an implementation for the method. The `Abstract` attribute tells btouch to mark the method as abstract, which will force the user of the wrapper DLL to actually implement a method body.

Let's take a look at the delegate next.

TKCoverflowViewDelegate

`TKCoverflowViewDelegate` is a little more complicated. It has two methods: `coverAtIndexWasBroughtToFront:` and `coverAtIndexWasDoubleTapped:` We want to rename these methods to get rid of the redundancy of `AtIndex`, and we also want to expose them as events on the `TKCoverflowView` class.

Renaming is easy enough – we can name them whatever we want as long as the `ExportAttribute` is correct. However, exposing them as events is a two-part process. When we finish binding `TKCoverflowView`, we're going to add some special attribution to tell it to look to the delegate interface to see what to expose as events. This means that, on our delegate interface, we need to specify what kind of event args the methods will use when they're turned into events.

By specifying the `EventArgsAttribute`, we do just that. For example, by adding `EventArgs("Foo")`, btouch will create a `FooEventArgs` class. For a more in-depth discussion, see the btouch documentation at http://monotouch.net/Documentation/Binding_New_Objective-C_Types.

Following our binding rules, our `TKCoverflowViewDelegate` API definition should then look something like Listing 22–26.

Listing 22–26. *Complete TKCoverflowViewDelegate API definition*

```
// @protocol TKCoverflowViewDelegate <NSObject>
[BaseType (typeof (NSObject))]
[Model]
interface TKCoverflowViewDelegate
{
        // @required
        // - (void) coverflowView:(TKCoverflowView*)coverflowView
                coverAtIndexWasBroughtToFront:(int)index;
        [Export("coverflowView:coverAtIndexWasBroughtToFront:"), EventArgs ("Coverflow")
        , Abstract]
        void CoverWasBroughtToFront(TKCoverflowView coverflowView, int index);

        // @optional
        // - (void) coverflowView:(TKCoverflowView*)coverflowView
                coverAtIndexWasDoubleTapped:(int)index;
        [Export("coverflowView:coverAtIndexWasDoubleTapped:"), EventArgs ("Coverflow")]
        void CoverWasDoubleTapped(TKCoverflowView coverflowView, int index);

}
```

Notice that only the required method gets the `Abstract` attribute.

Also, by specifying the "Coverflow" as the value to the `EventArgs` attribute, btouch will automatically declare those events as you see in Listing 22–27.

Listing 22–27. *Event declarations generated by btouch*

```
public event EventHandler<CoverflowEventArgs> CoverWasBroughtToFront;
public event EventHandler<CoverflowEventArgs> CoverWasDoubleTapped;
```

The `CoverflowEventArgs` are automatically generated based on the parameters in the method declaration. So in this case, they'll get generated as you see in Listing 22–28.

Listing 22–28. *Custom EventArgs generated by btouch*

```
public class CoverflowEventArgs : EventArgs
{
        public CoverflowEventArgs (int index);
        public int Index { get; set; }
}
```

As you can see, btouch is extremely powerful and saves you lots of work from hand-binding APIs.

Okay, now that we have the peripheral classes bound, we can finish our `TKCoverflowView` binding.

Finishing the TKCoverflowView Binding

I mentioned before that exposing delegate methods as events is a two-part process. We've already seen the first part, which actually defines the events and custom EventArgs; now we're going to look at the second part: telling btouch to which class those events should actually be attached to.

To do this, we attribute a class with an `Events` attribute that expects an array of `Type` objects of what classes to look for the event methods in. It then adds the events that it finds to whatever class that `Events` attribute is on. For instance, we want to expose the methods in `TKCoverflowViewDelegate` on our `TKCoverflowView` class, we would add the attribute in Listing 22–29 to the `TKCoverflowView` interface.

Listing 22–29. *Specifying what classes to look into to create events from their methods*

```
Events = new Type [] { typeof (TKCoverflowViewDelegate) }
```

With that in mind, and what we've learned with the other classes, we can now bind our `TKCoverflowView` class. See Listing 22–30.

Listing 22–30. *Complete TKCoverflowView API definition*

```
// @interface TKCoverflowView : UIScrollView <UIScrollViewDelegate>
[BaseType(typeof(UIScrollView), Delegates=new string [] { "Delegate" }
        , Events=new Type [] { typeof (TKCoverflowViewDelegate)})]
interface TKCoverflowView
{
        //==== constructors
        [Export("initWithFrame:")]
        IntPtr Constructor(RectangleF frame);


        //==== Properties

        // @property (nonatomic, assign) CGSize coverSize; // default 224 x 224
        [Export("coverSize", ArgumentSemantic.Assign)]
        SizeF CoverSize { get; set; }

        // @property (nonatomic, assign) int numberOfCovers;
        [Export("numberOfCovers", ArgumentSemantic.Assign)]
        int NumberOfCovers { get; set; }

        // @property (nonatomic, assign) float coverSpacing;
        [Export("coverSpacing", ArgumentSemantic.Assign)]
        float CoverSpacing { get; set; }

        // @property (nonatomic, assign) float coverAngle;
        [Export("coverAngle", ArgumentSemantic.Assign)]
        float CoverAngle { get; set; }


        //==== Methods

        // - (TKCoverflowCoverView*) dequeueReusableCoverView;
        [Export("dequeueReusableCoverView")]
        TKCoverflowCoverView DequeueReusableCoverView();

        // - (TKCoverflowCoverView*) coverAtIndex:(int)index;
        [Export("coverAtIndex:")]
        TKCoverflowCoverView GetCover(int index);

        // - (int) indexOfFrontCoverView;
        // bind this as a read-only property
        [Export("indexOfFrontCoverView")]
```

```
int FrontCoverIndex { get; }

// - (void) bringCoverAtIndexToFront:(int)index animated:(BOOL)animated;
[Export("bringCoverAtIndexToFront:animated:")]
void BringCoverToFront(int index, bool animated);


//==== Prototype properties

// @property (nonatomic, assign) id <TKCoverflowViewDelegate> delegate;
// hides the underlying delegate property, so we need to add the new attribute
[Export("delegate", ArgumentSemantic.Assign), New]
TKCoverflowViewDelegate Delegate { get; set; }

// @property (nonatomic, assign) id <TKCoverflowViewDataSource> dataSource;
[Export("dataSource", ArgumentSemantic.Assign)]
TKCoverflowViewDataSource DataSource { get; set; }

}
```

Most of this is pretty straightforward; there are really only two new things here. The first is shown in Listing 22–31.

Listing 22–31. *Exposing a method as a read-only property*

```
[Export("indexOfFrontCoverView")]
int FrontCoverIndex { get; }
```

indexOfFrontCoverView is a method, but we expose it as a read-only property, since it has no parameters and really seems like a property more than a method. I liken this to SelectedItem in a dropdown or something like that.

The second thing we did differently here is to use a New attribute on the Delegate property, as in Listing 22–32.

Listing 22–32. *Using a New attribute to mark an implementation with the new keyword*

```
[Export("delegate", ArgumentSemantic.Assign), New]
TKCoverflowViewDelegate Delegate { get; set; }
```

UIView already has a Delegate property, so the New attribute tells btouch to mark the property with the new keyword when it generates it.

Weak Delegate Pattern

This is as far as you need to take the binding to get it to work. However, if you want maximum flexibility in how to wire up the delegate methods in MonoTouch, you should follow the weak-delegate pattern. I cover the pattern extensively in Chapter 6, but briefly, it allows the consumers of the library to either assign a strongly-typed-delegate on the object, or use any class that has the appropriate methods.

Following the weak-delegate pattern is very easy; we just have to do the following tweaks:

■ Create a WeakDelegate property of type NSObject, and add a NullAllowed attribute.

- Change the Delegate property to have a Wrap attribute that specifies the WeakDelegate property.

For example, our delegate property declarations following the weak-delegate pattern would look like Listing 22–33.

Listing 22–33. *Implementing the weak-delegate pattern*

```
[Export ("delegate", ArgumentSemantic.Assign) , New][NullAllowed]
NSObject WeakDelegate { get; set; }

[Wrap ("WeakDelegate"), New]
TKCoverflowViewDelegate Delegate { get; set; }
```

Very simple!

Complete Tapku Coverflow Binding

That seemed like a lot, because I narrated the process fairly thoroughly, but the entire binding necessary for a complete Tapku Coverflow usage is now done. I've included it here to show the entire thing altogether. I've stripped out the comments for brevity (see Listing 22–34).

Listing 22–34. *The complete binding necessary to use the Tapku Coverflow control*

```
using System;
using System.Drawing;
using MonoTouch.UIKit;
using MonoTouch.ObjCRuntime;
using MonoTouch.Foundation;
using MonoTouch.CoreFoundation;

namespace Tapku
{
        [BaseType(typeof(UIScrollView), Delegates=new string [] { "Delegate" }
                    , Events=new Type [] { typeof (TKCoverflowViewDelegate)})]
        interface TKCoverflowView
        {
                [Export("initWithFrame:")]
                IntPtr Constructor(RectangleF frame);

                [Export("coverSize", ArgumentSemantic.Assign)]
                SizeF CoverSize { get; set; }

                [Export("numberOfCovers", ArgumentSemantic.Assign)]
                int NumberOfCovers { get; set; }

                [Export("coverSpacing", ArgumentSemantic.Assign)]
                float CoverSpacing { get; set; }

                [Export("coverAngle", ArgumentSemantic.Assign)]
                float CoverAngle { get; set; }

                [Export("dequeueReusableCoverView")]
                TKCoverflowCoverView DequeueReusableCoverView();
```

```
        [Export("coverAtIndex:")]
        TKCoverflowCoverView GetCover(int index);

        [Export("indexOfFrontCoverView")]
        int FrontCoverIndex { get; }

        [Export("bringCoverAtIndexToFront:animated:")]
        void BringCoverToFront(int index, bool animated);

        [Export ("delegate", ArgumentSemantic.Assign), New][NullAllowed]
        NSObject WeakDelegate { get; set; }

        [Wrap ("WeakDelegate"), New]
        TKCoverflowViewDelegate Delegate { get; set; }
        [Export("dataSource", ArgumentSemantic.Assign)]
        TKCoverflowViewDataSource DataSource { get; set; }

    }

    [BaseType(typeof(UIView))]
    interface TKCoverflowCoverView
    {
        [Export("initWithFrame:")]
        IntPtr Constructor(RectangleF frame);

        [Export("image", ArgumentSemantic.Retain)]
        UIImage Image { get; set; }

        [Export("baseline", ArgumentSemantic.Assign)]
        float Baseline { get; set; }
    }

    [BaseType (typeof (NSObject))]
    [Model]
    interface TKCoverflowViewDataSource
    {
        [Export("coverflowView:coverAtIndex:"), Abstract]
        TKCoverflowCoverView GetCover(TKCoverflowView coverflowView, int index);

    }

    [BaseType (typeof (NSObject))]
    [Model]
    interface TKCoverflowViewDelegate
    {
        [Export("coverflowView:coverAtIndexWasBroughtToFront:")
                , EventArgs ("Coverflow"), Abstract]
        void CoverWasBroughtToFront(TKCoverflowView coverflowView, int index);

        [Export("coverflowView:coverAtIndexWasDoubleTapped:")
                , EventArgs ("Coverflow")]
        void CoverWasDoubleTapped(TKCoverflowView coverflowView, int index);

    }
}
```

Now that we have a completed binding, lets run btouch to generate our DLL.

Running btouch

Actually running btouch is very easy. It's a command-line executable that can be found in the /Developer/MonoTouch/usr/bin/ directory. To run it, open a terminal window (open Spotlight and type **Terminal**, or find it in the Applications directory), change directories to where your API Definition File is, and execute the following:

```
/Developer/MonoTouch/usr/bin/btouch [API Definition File Name]
        -s:[any other source file names]
```

For instance, if you've named the API Definition File for Tapku, tapku.cs, your command line instruction would look like Listing 22–35.

Listing 22–35. *Calling btouch from the command line*

```
/Developer/MonoTouch/usr/bin/btouch Tapku.cs
```

If btouch doesn't have any errors, it will exit silently, as shown in Figure 22–8.:

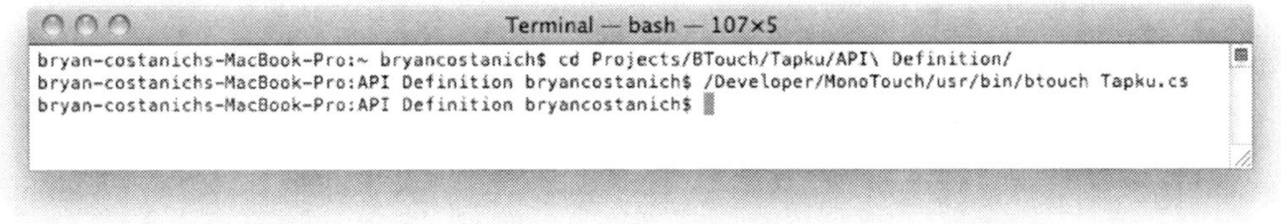

```
Terminal — bash — 107×5
bryan-costanichs-MacBook-Pro:~ bryancostanich$ cd Projects/BTouch/Tapku/API\ Definition/
bryan-costanichs-MacBook-Pro:API Definition bryancostanich$ /Developer/MonoTouch/usr/bin/btouch Tapku.cs
bryan-costanichs-MacBook-Pro:API Definition bryancostanich$ 
```

Figure 22–8. *Running btouch in the terminal*

The dll will be output to the current directory, and will have the same name as the API definition file, except with a ".dll" extension. For btouch command help, you can run btouch -h.

Once you've built the library and the wrapper DLL, you need to add them to your project. Let's look at adding the library first.

Adding the Compiled Objective-C Library

Earlier, we built three versions of the Tapku Library: two for the device and one for the simulator, and then used LIPO to stick them all into a single .a file. In order to use it, we need to add it to our project. See Figure 22–9.

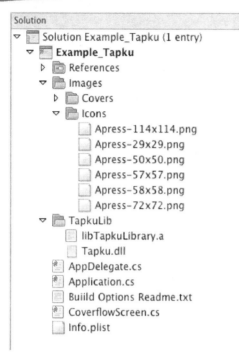

Figure 22–9. *Adding the Tapku .a library and wrapper dll to the project*

As you can see, I've created a **TapkuLib** folder and in it I have added both the library and the wrapper dll. I've added the wrapper dll to the project just to keep track of it.

Next, we need to reference the DLL we generated with btouch.

Referencing the Wrapper DLL

You can reference the btouch-generated wrapper DLL as you would any other MonoTouch library. Just follow these steps:

1. Right-click on the **References** folder and choose **Edit References**.

2. In the dialog, choose the **.NET Assembly** tab and browse to the Tapku.dll file that we copied to the TapkuLib folder.

3. Double-click on the DLL, and it should show up in the **Selected** references pane shown in Figure 22–10.

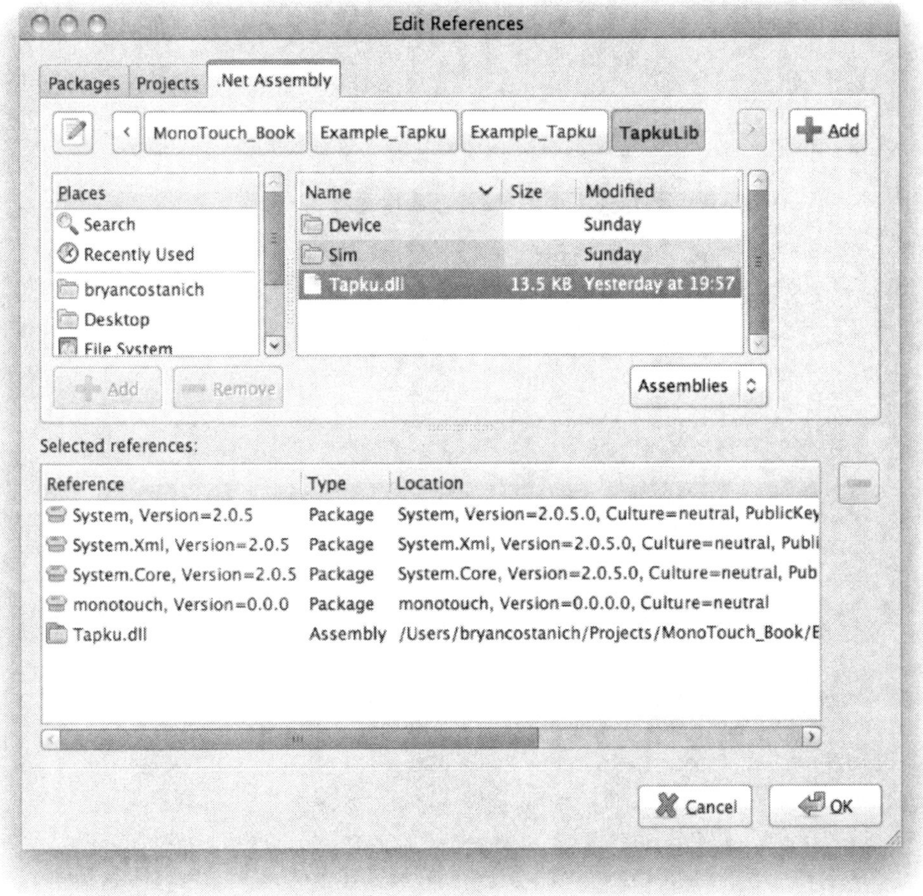

Figure 22–10. *Referencing the wrapped DLL is like referencing any other MonoTouch library.*

Once you've referenced the DLL, you're almost ready to use it. There is one final step.

Configuring the Build

Even though you've added the Objective-C library to the project, it won't actually get compiled unless you tell the MonoTouch compiler to look for it and load it.

To do this, you need to edit the **iPhone Build** options in the **Project Options** dialog (right-click on the project and choose options).

We're going to add some information to the **Extra Arguments** field to let the MonoTouch compiler know that we'd like it to load our Objective-C library, and where to find it.

We need to specify the extra arguments for each build configuration and platform. See Figure 22–11.

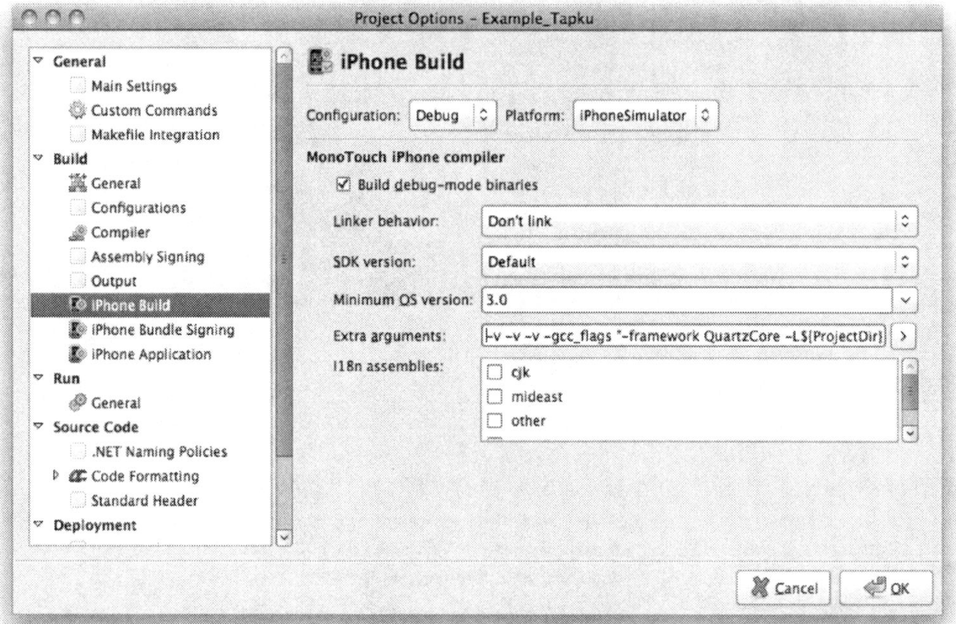

Figure 22–11. *Adding extra arguments to load our library in the Project Options dialog.*

We're going to use the arguments in Listing 22–36.

Listing 22–36. *Arguments to load the simulator version of the Tapku library*

```
-v -v -v -gcc_flags "-framework QuartzCore -L${ProjectDir}/TapkuLib -lTapkuLibrary
      -force_load ${ProjectDir}/TapkuLib/libTapkuLibrary.a"
```

Note that ${ProjectDir} is a macro that that evaluates to the project directory on disk.

Let's break down the arguments:

- **-v -v –v:** This isn't strictly needed; it turns on extra verbose mode in the build process, which will give you helpful errors in the build output if something were to go wrong.

- **-gcc_flags:** This tells the compiler that what follows are special flags that determine how the compiler should behave.

- **-framework QuartzCore:** Tapku needs the QuartzCore iOS feature in order to work properly; however, MonoTouch doesn't have any knowledge of the library that we're including (and therefore its need for QuartzCore), so we have to add this ourselves.

- **-L${ProjectDir}/TapkuLib –lTapkuLibrary:** This tells MonoTouch to link against the library called TapkuLibrary ("lib" turns into "l"), and specifies where to find it.

- **-force_load ${ProjectDir}/TapkuLib/libTapkuLibrary.a:** This tells the compiler to load that particular library without removing any code that isn't used.

Now that we have all that out of the way, we can finally use our library.

Using the Library

Once we have our library wrapped, it's time to use it. Using our library is like using any other MonoTouch library. The TKCoverflowView is a lot like a UITableView; we need to create a data source class (see Listing 22–37).

Listing 22–37. *An example of a TKCoverflowViewDataSource implementation*

```
/// <summary>
/// Our data source for the cover flow. It works pretty much just like a UITableView's
data source
/// </summary>
public class CoverFlowDataSource : TKCoverflowViewDataSource
{
        /// <summary>
        /// A List of images we'll show
        /// </summary>
        protected List<UIImage> _coverImages = null;


        public CoverFlowDataSource(List<UIImage> images) : base()
        {
                this._coverImages = images;
        }

        /// <summary>
        /// GetCover is just like GetCell on a UITableView DataSource.
        /// </summary>
        public override TKCoverflowCoverView GetCover (TKCoverflowView coverflowView
                , int index)
        {
                //---- try to dequeue a reusable cover
                TKCoverflowCoverView view = coverflowView.DequeueReusableCoverView();
                //---- if we didn't get one, create a new one
                if(view == null)
                {
                        view = new TKCoverflowCoverView(new RectangleF(0, 0, 244, 244));
                        view.Baseline = 224;
                }

                //---- set the image
                view.Image = this._coverImages[index];

                //---- return the cover view
                return view;
        }

}
```

Creating and then assigning the data source is also as one would expect (see Listing 22–38).

Listing 22–38. *Populating and assigning a data source*

```
List<UIImage> images = new List<UIImage>();
images.Add(UIImage.FromBundle(
        "Images/Covers/Cover_DeathCabForCutie_PhotoAlbum_Resized.jpg"));
...
images.Add(UIImage.FromBundle(
        "Images/Covers/Cover_Stars_SetYourselfOnFire_Resized.jpg"));
this._coverflowDataSource = new CoverFlowDataSource(images);

//---- assign the datasource to the cover flow
this._coverflow.DataSource = this._coverflowDataSource;
```

We can also consume our events that we've exposed (see Listing 22–39).

Listing 22–39. *Handling events*

```
//---- wire up a handler for when a cover is brought to the front
this._coverflow.CoverWasBroughtToFront += (object s, CoverflowEventArgs e) => {
        Console.WriteLine("Cover [" + e.Index.ToString() + "], brought to front");

};
//---- wire up a double tap handler
this._coverflow.CoverWasDoubleTapped += (object s, CoverflowEventArgs e) => {
        new UIAlertView("Coverflow", "Cover [" + e.Index.ToString() + "] tapped."
                , null, "OK", null).Show();
};
```

To see the entire code (and the coverflow in action), check out the Example_Tapku companion code and application.

Summary

In this chapter we discussed how to incorporate Objective-C code and libraries into our project for use in MonoTouch. We covered how we need to create an intermediary C# layer that wraps the Objective library and exposes the underlying Objective-C library to our MonoTouch project. We also looked a bit at Objective-C and how to build Objective-C libraries. Then we discussed btouch, the MonoTouch tool that can generate these bindings for us, and we walked through using it with the Tapku library.

The knowledge of how to use btouch opens up a huge world of possibilities by enabling you to use any number of the Objective-C libraries for the iOS available out there.

Index

▨F

◼T

■W

CPSIA information can be obtained at www.ICGtesting.com
Printed in the USA
LVOW050843110412

277098LV00005BA/5/P